121

The Big Book of TV Lists, TV Lore, and TV Bests

TV Land
to go

Tom Hill
Foreword by Adam West
A FIRESIDE BOOK

Published by Simon & Schuster

New York London Toronto Sydney Singapore

FIRESIDE
Rockefeller Center
1230 Avenue of the Americas
New York, NY 10020

For information about special discounts for bulk purchases, please
contact Simon & Schuster Special Sales: 1-800-456-6798 or
business@simonandschuster.com

Designed by Bonni Leon-Berman

Manufactured in the United States of America

10   9   8   7   6   5   4   3   2   1

Library of Congress Cataloging-in-Publication Data
Hill, Tom.
    TV Land to go: the big book of TV lists, TV lore, and TV bests / Tom Hill.
        p.   cm.
    Includes index.
    1. Television programs—United States—Miscellanea.   I. Title: Big book
of TV lists, TV lore, and TV bests.   II. TV Land (Television network)
III. Title.
PN1992.3.U5 H54   2001
791.45'75—dc21   2001040227

ISBN 0-684-85615-8

acknowledgments

AND APPRECIATIONS

Above all, a deep bow of appreciation to the many writers, actors, and TV creators whose work we honor in this book. Second, my thanks to the researchers and TV writers who came before me, whose work helped inform and inspire this one.

My sincere appreciation goes to everyone at TV Land, who work every day to make sure "There's Always Something On!" That starts with Larry Jones and the strategy team: Kim Rosenblum, Laura Hunter, Rob Pellizzi, Paul Ward, Michael Gaylord, Jaci Rann, Christine Heye, Seth Levin, Maria Caulfield, Sal Maniaci, and Sarah Kirshbaum. Thanks also to our glorious leaders Herb Scannell and Jeff Dunn, programming whiz Diane Robina, master of Celebrity Connections Barry Greenberg, plus faithful TV Landers Jocelyn Jones, Gennifer Birnbach, Steve Wishnoff, Robin Silverman, Margaret Milnes, and Gary Engel. (Steve, Gennifer, Gary—you get extra points for helping catch mistakes in early drafts!) And a very special nod of appreciation to Fred Seibert, TV visionary, whose name also belonged on the Nick at Nite book among the founding fathers.

Let me also express my appreciation for the inspiration, vitality, and passion of the whole darned TV Land Brand Creative Group: Melissa Abad, Mike Bernstein, Tracey Bobb, Joe Boyd, Josh Braunstein, Jason Cohen, Gina Cole, Laura DeMaria, Katie Dominguez, Kevin Hartman, Dave Herman, Lia Jenkins de Salcedo, Kenna Kay, Nancy Kirwan, Penny Mailander, Nicole Margagliotta, Georgina Martinez, Christopher McDonald, Tiffany Mitchell, Ann Marie Morris, Shakira Peterson, Gwen Powell, Eric Rosner, Vicky Stewart, Tim Tierney,

Alissa Tomson, Dominique Vitali, and Debbie Whyte. Thanks to Jeff Berg for all his work in designing the cover, and a fine tip o' the hat to my fellow scribes Laura Belgray and Bruce Bernstein. Thanks also to Laura for her contributions to the TV Land Haiku canon herein. Thanks to Candice Gordon for ever-cheerful support, and to Sheldon Yeager for the same, plus research and editing help.

Thanks also to my other TV compatriots and collaborators over the years: Rick Groel, Dennis Shinners, Agi Fodor, David Rieth, Nancy Burrows, Mark Sullivan, and Rich Williams. A deep bow to Will McRobb with whom this book was conceived and begun back in 1989. His groundbreaking research was instrumental in developing the "Big TV Satisfaction" formula. Thanks to Kurt Bumbulis for help with rights and clearances, to Jim Ward for corralling some key tapes, and to David Bushman at the Museum of Television and Radio for wise advice along with access to the inestimable collection. Thanks also to Elizabeth Bogner who helped shape this work in its early stages; and to my editor, Marcela Landres, who brought the monster to life.

Thanks also, along with hugs and love, to Deke and Fred, America's youngest proofreaders, fact checkers, and classic TV experts, who allowed our "video movie night" to become "more of Dad's old shows" night.

And finally, my utmost thanks and love to my steadfast, insightful, beautiful, and ever-loving wife Michelle Piccolo Hill, the very best thing TV Land ever brought me.

Dedicated to the memory of Tom Pomposello,

a founding father of TV Land whose music and inspiration live on

foreword

I did not grow up with television. I had cowboys and outlaws at the local movie house. That doesn't mean I'm old. It just indicates a certain ignorance of TV history and program anatomy. No longer! Reading Tom Hill's amazing book, *TV Land to Go,* was an education. The backstage details and stories were delightful, even to a veteran of the entertainment industry, and the analysis of story and joke structures is truly original, and often very funny. You hold in your hands an astute, witty, and clever romp through TV Land.

And, of course, I was flattered to have my work ranked so highly in the "Top 100 Episodes" section, along with a detailed appreciation of what made Batman tick. Thanks, Tom. Your good taste and laser-beam perception are widely acclaimed.

Adam West

preface

Television is great, but there are times when it just isn't practical to watch. Airplane flights, picnics, while you are trapped on elevators, these are all times when this book will have to serve as the next best thing to a great show. This book, the first from TV Land, is an affectionate celebration of everything that makes television so wonderful. We may poke fun now and then, but always with a sincere spirit of appreciation. After all, we really do love TV.

TV Land is a twenty-four-hour cable network devoted to classic reruns, everything from *Gunsmoke* to *Charlie's Angels, The Andy Griffith Show* to *My Favorite Martian*. We have the widest, most varied collection of television in the known universe, and we work hard to bring our viewers all those shows with that magic quality we call "rewatchability." It could be classic sitcoms, beloved dramas, even shows so bad they're good, or otherwise forgettable shows that feature big stars in their early roles. We're delighted to be curating the incredible pop cultural blender of shows and retromercials from the fifties through the nineties that comprise our daily lineup. Do you sometimes find that there is nothing on TV? You must not have TV Land, because with our time-tested reliable shows, there's always something on. Something good!

TV Land was founded in 1996, born of the success of sister network Nick at Nite, the evening portion of Nickelodeon that first gave credibility to the idea of making reruns into a way of life. For so many other networks, second-run television is used as filler, but for Nick at Nite and now TV Land, classic television is all we do. It's our passion and our expertise. We like to think no one presents it quite the way we do.

TV Land to Go is also a series on on-air vignettes seen on the network in which the author, yours truly, is featured dispensing television stories and arcane trivia from a handsome drive-through booth in a mall. Our hope is that those who haven't been able to make use of our drive-up service will find all the information they need in this volume.

TV Land to Go was written and organized to allow you to read it straight through, or explore at random whatever strikes your fancy. There are various lists that explore all the realms of television, from Endora's favorite names for Darrin to the lessons sitcoms teach us. There are some features based specifically on features of the TV Land channel: the innovators vignettes and 60-Second Sitcoms are here for fans to enjoy. There are TV Land haiku, a glimpse at the future of television, and a time line of its history stretching back to the dawn of mankind.

The major feature of the book is the Top 100 Episodes of All Time, an effort to bring the very latest scientific research to bear on deciding which individual episodes are the very best. A detailed introduction to this feature begins on page 128, and the hundred honorees are covered in great detail, with credits, special notes, and much more.

An early reader of this book said, "Reading this book really made me want to watch television," then realized that perhaps that statement could be taken the wrong way. But frankly, there could be no higher praise. We hope you enjoy the book, get a few laughs, and find yourself ready to go back to the television with a more profound sense of satisfaction at all that the medium can be. We hope the book makes you, too, want to watch television! Enjoy!

Tom Hill
VP/Creative Director, TV Land

more than 2001 years of television

A COMPLETE HISTORY

Let's begin at the beginning. People think television is a mere fifty years old, seventy-five tops, and in a literal sense, this is true. But why just look at the tip of the iceberg? In a larger sense, television is a splendid cultural flowering whose roots lie in the distant past. The histories of all modern and ancient civilization can be seen—and should be seen!—as precursors to the glory that is television today.

Our calendar, the one that tells us the new millennium has come, begins with the birth of Christ. Christ's birth, of course, has been celebrated by Christians for two thousand years. Today, thanks to television, Christmas is celebrated by people of all religious backgrounds. Just think, if it weren't for Christmas, there would be no Grinch, no Burl Ives as Frosty, and no reruns of *It's a Wonderful Life*. Charlie Brown's tree would never have brightened our TV sets. Most Christmas specials have almost no religious aspects at all, as Hollywood writers searched for some way of expressing the "true meaning" of the holiday without making anyone feel left out.

Christmas's contribution to television cannot be understated, but the roots of television run still deeper into the past. Let us now turn further back, beyond the calendar and to the ancient past.

Five billion B.C. (Before Cable)

The Earth is formed.

Three billion B.C.

The first signs of primeval life in the ooze. Bacteria and blue-green algae emerge as a slime. *Super Sloppy Double Dare* becomes a possibility.

Genesis 1

God creates woman from Adam's rib. The spin-off is born.

500,000 B.C.

Man forms crude tools. Man falling down gets first laugh. From this mere accident came the long history of falling down. Today, on television, falling down is an art form, taken to its dramatic height by practitioners like Chevy Chase as Gerald Ford, Dick Van Dyke on the ottoman, and, of course, the ski jump guy from *ABC's Wide World of Sports.*

70,000 B.C.

Neanderthal man. Use of fire and more advanced tools. Discovery: If I use a stick, I can poke fire without burning my hands.

50,000 B.C.

Discovery: If I use a longer stick, I can poke the fire without getting up. The underlying principle of the remote control is formed.

40,000 B.C.

The invention of the wheel is a major breakthrough; however, primitive automobiles must still be powered "courtesy of the driver's two feet." Other advances include the bird-phonograph and the dino-crane construction machine.

10,000 B.C.

The first evidence of planned agriculture. Some scientists believe that this is when *Hee Haw* began its original run in syndication, but this is based on carbon-dating of the jokes found in recent shows, so it remains an estimate.

3000 B.C.

Evidence of early mathematics among the ancient Sumerians. Strangely enough, these earliest numbering systems began with the number 2 and only went as high as 13.

1000 B.C.

Moses leads the Israelites out of slavery and into the promised land. He also delivers the Ten Commandments. Though it paves the way for many Top Ten lists to come, it is not as funny as any of David Letterman's, except for the part about coveting thy neighbor's ass.

776 B.C.

First recorded Olympic games. Ratings were strong among key demographics, but the concepts of branding and local marketing were still in a fledgling stage. Men wrestled nude, and prudish event programmers kept female viewership to a minimum.

350 B.C.

Aristotle's *Poetics* sets forth the basic principles of dramatic excellence. Strangely, there is no mention of the "double take" or "spit take."

A.D. 30

The first "look-alike" episode. In baby name books you'll find that the name Thomas means "the twin." This comes from the fact that Christ's disciple Thomas bore a striking resemblance to him. That is why Judas was paid to identify Christ by kissing him—the guards didn't want to confuse him with Thomas. Essentially, this was the first "look-alike" episode—leading to many individual episodes and the entire *Patty Duke Show*.

54

Emperor Claudius's reign ends when he is poisoned by Nero. There must have been plenty of half-naked slave girls around, otherwise PBS would not be able to defend, on the basis of historical authenticity, all the topless slave girls on the series *I, Claudius*.

ca. 1000

The Chinese invent gunpowder. *Gunsmoke* becomes a possibility.

1455

The advent of movable type. Johannes Gutenberg. The printer's ability to alter printed text with relative ease would eventually lead to the creation of *TV Guide*. Importantly, it would also lead to modern man's ability to scroll winter storm warnings over shows without interrupting the dramatic flow.

1492

Columbus discovers America. Thankfully, or we'd all be stuck watching nothing but *Benny Hill* and *Yes, Minister*.

1509

Michelangelo paints the ceiling of the Sistine Chapel. It's lovely, but, more important, he discovers that great art can be enjoyed from a reclining position.

1543

Copernicus states his belief that the Earth is spinning while revolving around the Sun. He advances the notion that today is basically of rerun of yesterday.

1564

Playwright William Shakespeare is born. He is perhaps best known for *Hamlet*, the play upon which the famous *Gilligan's Island* musical episode "The Producer" is based. (See page 315.)

1596

Invention of the indoor flush toilet by John Harrington in England. But the sound of a flush will not be used for comic purposes until Archie Bunker yelled downstairs in October 1971.

1644

The end of the Ming dynasty in China. Later, the Ming vase will become well known in television as an extremely valuable item that almost every wealthy person owns, and that is also constantly in danger of being smashed to smithereens.

1752

Ben Franklin's famous kite experiment establishes the principles of electricity, which will one day power our sets. Furthermore, his image will also inspire the opening montage of *That Girl*.

1773

The Boston Tea Party. The Boston News Four Action Team is there on the scene, and publishes a snappy leaflet at eleven.

1791

The Bill of Rights establishes First Amendment rights of free speech, as our founding fathers are unable to imagine the possibility of Morton Downey Jr.

1803

The Louisiana Purchase is made. The United States now owns most of what will become the Central Time Zone, where prime time happens an hour early.

1822

The birth of Milton Berle.

1840

Lower and Upper Canada united. No one notices. The underdog and outsider status of its people will one day make Canada the world's leading exporter of improvisational comedians: from Dan Aykroyd to John Candy, Mike Myers to Dave Foley.

1851

Herman Melville's *Moby Dick* is published. For literally millions of teenage students to come, it will be the final straw, a book so thick that it convinces them to give up on reading and stick to television.

1871

In the Southwest, the Native American Hekawi tribe signs a secret treaty with O'Rourke and Agarn.

ca. 1900

The earliest recliner chairs are introduced. Scientists begin feverishly working to create something to look at while reclining.

1917

Dr. Sigmund Freud publishes *Introduction to Psychoanalysis*. His colleagues Bob Hartley and Frasier Crane will later modify and popularize his groundbreaking work.

1918

The Germans nearly win World War I, but luckily Doug and Tony from *The Time Tunnel* were able to intervene and change the course of history, once again!

1929

General Electric begins experimental television broadcasts in Schenectady, New York.

1939

NBC inaugurates regular broadcasts at the World's Fair.

1939–44

World War II interrupts the continued development of broadcast television, among other things.

1946

Networks begin regular broadcasts.

And so begins the glorious era of modern television, the zenith of modern culture and the greatest achievement of mankind.* So far.

* With the possible exception of indoor plumbing.

the seven lessons sitcoms teach us

OR, EVERYTHING I NEEDED TO KNOW I LEARNED FROM SITCOMS

1. If you have an especially beloved pet (especially a fish, turtle, or bird) do not under any circumstances leave it with a trusted friend while you are out of town. Unless, of course, you want it replaced with a similar looking fish, turtle, or bird. This rule does not apply to dogs and cats.*

2. Planning on a nice quiet evening at home almost assures that total chaos, unwanted relatives, or the local police will be involved before the night is through.

3. It is surprisingly common to meet someone who looks exactly like you; but be careful, many such people are, unlike you, very bad. (One sure sign is that, unlike you, they sport a pencil-thin mustache.)

4. It is incredibly easy to walk into a hotel and borrow a bellhop's uniform in order to sneak into someone's room.

5. If your child is considering running away from home, you should encourage him.

6. Major singing stars will appear at your local event, if only you ask them.

7. Surprise parties really are a bad idea.

* Maude actually did kill Blanche's dog, but more often than not, larger animals are safe.

everything
else I
needed
to know

I LEARNED FROM DRAMAS

1. A fairly minor blow to the back of the neck will render anyone unconscious.

2. When you give in and tell the bad guy where you hid the money, he won't say "Thank you, you may go now."

3. The police will never believe your story.

4. Almost anyone can knock a door down by running into it shoulder-first.

5. Opening a lock with a bobby pin, hot-wiring a car, and breaking into the CIA's computers are all very easy, but no one can tie you up using a decent knot.

6. Before the mid-seventies, there were many different phone numbers, but after that all American phone numbers were changed to begin with the 555 exchange.

7. The entire country—Connecticut, Ohio, Vermont, Texas, Florida—looks a lot like Los Angeles, and that is why palm trees can be spotted in the background of car chases throughout the continental United States.

the ten
best
genres OF EPISODES

1. Amnesia episodes

2. Evil twin episodes

3. Episodes with guest stars

4. Series-ending episodes

5. Two-part sitcom episodes

6. Character-claims-to-know-a-celebrity episodes

7. Role-reversal episodes

8. Episodes with rock 'n' roll guest stars

9. Character is "discovered by Hollywood" episodes

10. Unwanted-relatives-visiting-on-sitcom episodes

the 29 most important

COMIC FORMULAE IN SITCOMS

Observers have often drawn parallels between comedy and music. Both depend upon timing, structure, expectations, emotions. Many great comedians have also had music in their background, from the Marx Brothers and Jack Benny to Woody Allen and Christopher Guest. Both comedy and music are more art than science. But like music, comedy is a deeply formulaic and systematic art form. Without the underlying mathematics, there could be no comedy. Thus, the tools of science and mathematics can help us understand comedy better. Below, you will find twenty-nine of the most important principles that underlie all situation comedy.

1. The Take

The most basic and important piece of comic acting: finding just the right external expression to capture the moment of internal transmission. In comic strips, a floating exclamation point, flying sweat beads, or a lightbulb approximate different variations on the take.

2. The Triple

This is the most important principle in joke structure. Basically, the concept is that the magic number is three, because it takes two examples to establish a pattern or expectation, and one more to disturb that pattern with the comic event. More than three can work, but three is the pithiest and, therefore, almost always the most effective. In the BTVS Top 100 Episodes list, we have highlighted examples of the vast variety that the triple can encompass. There are simple soliloquy triples, triples executed by three characters, and even triples that encompass the entire story structure like the episode in which Patty and Cathy Lane are faced with a third look-alike cousin.

3. The Conclusion Leap

Fairly self-explanatory, this is the plot device that often serves as the backbone for entire episodes. Examples: Lucy thinks Desi is trying to murder her; Dobie thinks everyone has forgotten his birthday, etc.

4. The Reverse

In its most basic execution, this is when a character is in midstream when suddenly he must deal with new information and change direction. An example: "I'm not leaving. Why should we? We have every right. . . . [nasty and territorial hillbilly takes out a bowie knife]. . . . to find another place for our picnic, c'mon gang!"

5. Grand-to-Petty

A comic principle that is often combined with others, it is in essence an abrupt shift in tone. It could be from philosophical to mundane ("Why is there evil in the world? And is there any chance I could borrow your car?") or from the complex to the simple ("We could reconfigure the duplicative cyclotron processors, or just toss it.")

6. Absurd Non Sequitur

Comedy at its simplest, mathematically speaking. Simple, but not easy. *Seinfeld* is replete with masterful examples, as each character moved through his or her disconnected story arcs. The conclusion of the "Bubble Boy" episode is a fine example, as George watches his fiancée's beloved summer cottage go up in flames, and suddenly remembers that she didn't chip in for the tolls on the drive up.

7. The Catchphrase

These are generally very minor jokes that acquire resonance only through repetition. The first time you heard Homer say "D'oh" it was just a well-observed verbal nuance. Then, with time, it became both that as well as a reminder of Homer's endless string of metaphorical rugs pulled from under his thought patterns.

8. The Double Take

This is when characters accept information once without understanding the full implication; then after a brief delay, they demonstrate that the full meaning has hit home. Example: "Oh look, Betty, Pebbles is in the boxing ring. . . . Pebbles is in the boxing ring!! Pebbles!" The double can also be extended to triples, quadruples, and even more. In these cases, the person looks, goes back to what he was doing, looks again, still doesn't react and returns to what he was doing, for as many times as desired.

These multiple takes can be very effective, especially as the period of time between takes is varied. Short, short, long is a personal favorite. The unspoken subtext, what goes through the "taking" subject's mind, is something like this: That can't be an elephant. (Short) Is that really an elephant? (Short) Okay, I'm in a Manhattan shoe store so I'm going to look over there one more time, because I know that I can't possibly be seeing an elephant. (Long!) In the otherwise forgettable film *Which Way to the Front?* (1970), Jerry Lewis executes the rarely attempted septuple take. He is reacting to an inane comment that hardly deserves such an extravagant reaction, but it works beautifully as the takes indicate a series of steps in his refusal to believe that his comrade could really have said something so stupid and his inability to formulate any kind of a verbal response.

9. The Inane Comment

The "stupid" or "disconnected" character who misses the obvious is a component of even the most highbrow situation comedy. Gracie Allen, Lisa Douglas, Rev. Jim, Kramer, Ted Baxter, Woody: they all brought grace to their role. Of course, there are also flat-out dumb characters, but we won't mention any of them. (Not even Squiggy.)

10. The Deadpan

This is the obverse of the take. It communicates the same thing, the moment of internal realization, but through nonaction or nonchange. Bob Newhart is the acknowledged modern master, but Jack Benny was television's original deadpan artist.

11. The Delay Take

Some consider this to be simply a variation on the double take, but it can encompass a wider range of possible reactions. The greatest delay take in television history took place in an episode of *Car 54, Where Are You?* entitled "Muldoon's Star." In this episode, written by Harold Flender, Francis Muldoon is pouring himself a glass of milk when he is told that his idol, a gorgeous Hollywood starlet, will be coming to stay in his mother's boardinghouse. He freezes, and the milk fills the glass, then overflows until the carton is empty. The rest of that day, his partner, Toody, is busily arranging things; eight hours pass until it is nighttime. Finally, Toody and some others return home and turn on the kitchen light. There they find Muldoon, still absolutely frozen with the milk carton and full glass. Now that's a delay!

12. Parallel Conversation

The simple, but often elegant, effect when both parties think that the other knows what they are talking about. For a pithy example, we will provide an Icelandic joke.* By way of a linguistic preface, note that in Icelandic, the words for father and puppy both sound a lot like "poppy." In one family, there was a beloved young pooch who unfortunately was run over by a truck. When the children came home from school their mother gathered them around and said, "You must be brave, but I have some sad news. Poppy was run over and killed today." To her surprise, they are solemn, but stoic. In a good example of parallel conversation, they talk about missing him, but doing their best to get by. They leave, only to find the dead dog in the backyard, and return to their mother wailing and disconsolate: "We thought you said 'Pappy'!"

13. Dissembling Non Sequitur

As opposed to the absurd non sequitur, number 6, above. This is a non sequitur by which a character is consciously making a change in direction, or one that is directly related to the events before us. Often in sitcoms this is used to show that a character is avoiding the situation, or simply to defy viewers' expectations. Example: boy holding a dog who followed him home, looking up at his parents, "Hi, is that a new shirt, Dad?"

* Yes, there are such things.

14. The Slow Burn

Another species of the delay take, but one with enough specific attributes to deserve distinct mention. This is also known in some circles as a "Mr. Mooney," after one of its greatest practitioners. It is simply the behavior of one who, for whatever reason, cannot or will not react in an outward and aggressive manner, and so reacts only with a growing tension that is manifested by pursed lips, a glare, or an eye twitch.

15. Slapstick

Schadenfreude is the word the Germans have for pleasure taken in another's pain. There have been many theories about the underlying psychological appeal of seeing someone fall down and hurt himself, or step on a tack, or be squeezed into a closing door. One compelling theory is that these violent events incite our own "fear" instinct, causing biochemical adrenaline reactions that are immediately relieved by the "comic-fictional" context of the events, causing the adrenaline to be experienced as heightened awareness-pleasure and not as a "flight" order. Of course, that particular theorist had his government grant rescinded when he was found to have littered sidewalks with banana peels, so take it for what it's worth.

16. Whee Wohn

The "whee wohn" is a name for the use of film editing to create comic transitions. The most classic example is when a character denies something, then is immediately faced by its reality. A man says, "I refuse to wear a dress," and then there is a cut, sometimes with a sound effect, to the same man in a dress saying, "Am I wearing too much blush?" Or a character says, "Unless Mr. Johnson shows up, we're home free," and cut to "Good evening, Mr. Johnson, what a delight to see you!" The name "whee wohn" is an onomatopoeia derived from the sound effect that often accompanies the visual transition.

17. Digging the Hole Deeper

Blunders and faux pas are certainly funny enough in real life, but no sitcom blunder would be complete without some "digging the hole deeper." Let's say that our lead male has just been caught saying that his girlfriend's sister is "hot." "What did you just say!?" yelps his girlfriend,

15

and under pressure, he digs that hole deeper: "I said she's hot . . . aren't you hot? I was just saying if she's hot she shouldn't wear a sweater . . . I mean she shouldn't *not* wear a sweater, she just shouldn't wear clothes . . ." for as long as the actor and writers care to milk it.

18. The Oblivious Restatement

To some degree this is another form of "grand-to-petty." Here's how it works. Some effete or just intelligent character uses an unusual vocabulary word, or complex language; the simpler character pretends to understand but reveals his ignorance by restating what was just said in simpler terms. Professor: "A two-dollar donation? What a penurious miser!" Student: "Yeah, and cheap, too!"

19. The Spit Take

Close kin to the double take, this is when surprising or infuriating information is delivered right at the moment when a character is drinking. In the grand old tradition, this involves a big spritz, but sitcoms of more recent vintage often choose the gagging-on-the-drink take, perhaps because it's easier to clean up.

20. Fish Out of Water

This well-known and self-explanatory comic structure has often served as the underlying premise of an entire series—*Fresh Prince of Bel Air, The Beverly Hillbillies, Third Rock from the Sun, The Nanny, Perfect Strangers*—but it is also used in individual scenes and episodes. The mathematical purity of it is eloquent. There are essentially two separate interpretations to every event or comment; therefore, throughout the story, the actors and writers can leap back and forth with impunity.

21. Stating the Obvious

Again, fairly self-explanatory. The suds overflow the room and someone suggests dryly, "That might have been too much soap."

22. Here We Go Again

Hackneyed, but delightfully so. Example: A character gets a swollen head because his rock band might get a record deal. The episode finally brings the character back down to earth—his big show was a comical disaster. At the very end of the show, he learns that a big Hollywood agent was at the show and thought the "comedy" was so good, maybe our character could be an actor.

23. Just the Wrong Thing

A variation on the "here-we-go again" episode capper is the "just the wrong thing" ending. (Also known as the "Gift of the Magi" ending.) For example, Lucy and Ethel return from their travails at the candy factory, where Fred and Ricky are willing to admit defeat and switch roles. In fact, to say they're sorry, the boys bought them each a big box of chocolates!

24. The Missing Link

This familiar piece of dialogue structure can be executed in many ways, but the most common is simply that a character is unaware of some key detail, like that he is talking not to a random stranger, but to his new girlfriend's father.

25. Dissonant Tone

The is the generic formula for when a character defies clichéd expectations. Common examples are these: little kids who know all about sex, old ladies who are still interested in sex or who use salty language, and a motorcycle hoodlum who likes to press wildflowers.

26. The Unnatural Conclusion

This is a sort of combination of "inane comment" and the "jumping to conclusions." One character suggests that he needs to raise money, and the other makes an "unnatural conclusion" that "I'm too young to die!" Naturally, he is asked to explain, and he provides some elaborate chain of illogic that leads from his buddy's get-rich-quick schemes to his early demise, perhaps involving the sale of his internal organs.

27. Keppler's Specificity Theorem

It is one of the great mysteries of comedy science, and, like the four-color map theorem, there is no proof that it is true; however, Keppler's specificity theorem is almost universally accepted. It states simply that, in general, the more specific the detail, the funnier. Here's an example of Keppler's theorem at work: Imagine an insensitive male sitcom character considering a date: "Martha? Are you kidding? I'd rather date a dog." This line, for what it's worth, can be improved by being more specific: "Martha? Are you kidding? I'd rather date a Rottweiler!" You will find many examples of this principle at work wherever better sitcoms are shown. Another example: No one named Keppler had anything to do with formulating or propagating the theorem, but isn't it just a little bit funnier to call it "Keppler's specificity theorem" rather than just the "specificity theorem"? Yet another example: Isn't a list of "29 Important Formulae" just a little bit more absurd than "30 Important Formulae"?

28. The Principle of Delayed Gratification

This is a subtle underlying structure, but it is a fascinating one to study as you observe sitcoms and, in fact, any comic performance or writing. The principle states that in any joke or comic line, the funniest word should be as close as possible to the end. Here's a simple example of a TV Land promo line, in three different versions: "You won't have to see any frogs smoking cigars when you turn to the dependable television of TV Land."

Okay, a non sequitur that echoes other advertising by sounding like the assurances many products offer, while also making a simple point about TV Land. But to make it funnier to the listener, we need first to establish the normality of the line, then interrupt it: "When you turn to the dependable television of TV Land, you won't have to see any frogs smoking cigars."

That's better, but we can apply the principle one more time. In this particular context, of things you won't have to be bothered by, "smoking" is more expected than "frogs." Therefore, the best possible structure for this line is: "When you turn to the dependable television of TV Land, you won't have to see any cigar-smoking frogs."

When you watch sitcoms, it's instructive to notice how this classic principle works. Learn it well, and it can come in handy the next time you need to write a snappy toast or an amusing note on someone's get-well card.

29. The Redefined Echo

We the viewers are aware that two characters have said the same exact line, but with a different meaning and context. Example: Jed had a conversation in which he manages to utterly confuse someone because of his backwoods ways. The woman on the other line apparently loses her temper. Jed hangs up, saying with a southern drawl, "She's got the nastiest temper!" Later, Drysdale calls the same woman, and even though what he says makes sense, she loses her temper being reminded of the earlier call. Drysdale covers the phone and says to Miss Jane, with precise enunciation, "She's got the nastiest temper!"

the 10 best inventions

AND TECHNOLOGIES

1. Remote control
2. Cable TV
3. VCR
4. Mute button
5. TiVo
6. Last channel button
7. Instant replay
8. Picture in picture
9. Satellite dishes
10. Three-camera system of shooting sitcoms

don't
forget the
amnesia!

In the Cheers and Jeers section of *TV Guide*, the editors once jeered a contemporary sitcom for "resorting" to an amnesia-themed episode. Naturally, we took pen to paper and fired off a pointed reply from TV Land: "We were saddened to see you 'jeer' what we consider to be an important part of our television heritage, and a vital rite of passage for *any* show: the amnesia episode. Superman, Mister Ed, even Flipper have suffered from amnesia. The only thing that might be jeer-worthy is that contemporary television shows sometimes fail to utilize the time-honored second-bump-on-the-head cure."

While in real life amnesia is an extreme rarity except in cases of shock or trauma, in TV Land it happens every time someone accidentally gets hit in the head. (Go ahead, name a time someone got hit in the head and didn't get amnesia!)* And like any great sitcom concept, it has been presented in many variations, including fake, induced, and partial amnesia. In one classic *Amos 'n' Andy* episode, Kingfish actually convinces Andy that he must have had amnesia, despite his logical question: "If I had amnesia all week, how come I ain't got it now?"

If you've forgotten who has suffered from TV Land's most common neurological disorder,

* Gary "The Professor" Engel has accepted this challenge and provided two examples. Gilligan got hit in the head and his mouth became a radio; he was also hit in the head and got double vision. Of course, there are also numerous cases of people being hit in the head and simply being knocked out (see, for example, every episode of *Mannix*), and there are many cases when people simply said "Ow!" and suffered no memory loss at all.

perhaps this chart will refresh your memory. However, the list is incomplete, because we can't for the life of us recall how Mannix got it, or got better. We just remember him walking around in a daze.

SHOW	VICTIM	CAUSE	CURE
F Troop	Agarn	Hits head; a fall off a horse	Hits head; a fall off a horse
The Munsters	Herman	Hits head; falling safe	Hits head
Green Acres	Lisa Douglas	Hits head; falling hammer	Hits head; fall from balcony
Mister Ed	Ed	Hits head; falling bucket	Hits head; falling bucket
The Addams Family	Gomez	Hits his head, and is then struck on the head purposely by one well-meaning Addams after another*	A dizzying series of purposeful blows
The Adventures of Superman	Superman	Hits head; meteor	Hits head; meteor
Flipper	Flipper	Hits head; underwater explosion	Hits head; collision with shark
The Lucy Show	Lucy	Hits head; falling box	Hits head; planter
Alfred Hitchcock Presents	Man	Hits head; falling board	Passage of time
Get Smart	Max	Pills	Passage of time (one hour)
The Dick Van Dyke Show	Rob	Hits head; violin	Passage of time

* This astonishing series, which takes the amnesia episode into a daring new realm, is no doubt why you can find this episode in the 100 Best Episodes list. See page 248.

the
BRADY
BUNCH
open

The opening and theme song of *The Brady Bunch* are among the most resonant ever created. The classic back-story song and the nine squares are etched indelibly on the American consciousness. Naturally, the open has been the subject of much analysis and discussion among the TV experts of TV Land.

While many conclusions can be drawn, one fact is inescapable. Part of the power of the piece comes from the choreography. I believe that you could watch the open without music or lyrics and completely understand the story, based only on who is looking at whom, and in what order (aided, of course, by the hair color). Here, for your further edification and study, is a chart of the "opening looks." First the lyrics, then, broken out by character, where they are looking. For example, Carol begins looking straight ahead (to camera), then looks to Marcia, Jan, and finally Cindy. During the final stanza, Bobby looks at the camera, Peter, Jan, Cindy, and finally Mike. This charting was made from the second-season version of the open, but each season follows a similar pattern.

"Here's the story of a lovely lady,

who was bringing up three very lovely girls,

all of them had hair of gold,

like their mother, the youngest one in curls."

Carol: Camera, Marcia, Jan, Cindy

Marcia: Camera, Carol, Camera

Jan: Camera, Carol, Camera

Cindy: Camera, Carol

"It's the story of a man named Brady,

who was busy raising three boys of his own.

They were four men, living all together,

but they were all alone."

Mike: Camera, Greg, Peter, Bobby

Greg: Camera, Mike, Camera

Peter: Camera, Mike

Bobby: Camera, Mike

"Till but one day when this lady met this fellow,"

Carol: Camera, Mike

Mike: Camera, Carol

"and they knew that it was much more than a hunch,

that this group must somehow form a family,

that's the way we all became the Brady Bunch."

Carol: Camera, Marcia

Mike: Carol, Camera, Marcia

Marcia: Greg (across Carol), Camera

Jan: Greg, Camera

Cindy: Peter

Greg: Camera

Peter: Jan, Camera

Bobby: Jan, Camera

"The Brady Bunch, the Brady Bunch,

that's the way we became the Brady Bunch."

Carol: Marcia, Jan, Cindy, Greg, Peter

Mike: Cindy, Bobby, Peter, Greg, Camera

Marcia: Jan, Carol, Peter, Jan, Carol

Jan: Cindy, Marcia, Peter, Greg, Camera

Cindy: Peter, Marcia and/or Jan, Bobby, Mike, Camera

Greg: Carol, Peter, Camera, Jan

Peter: Jan, Mike, Carol, Peter, Alice

Bobby: Camera, Peter, Jan, Cindy, Mike

Alice: Camera

Again, the most important reading we can take from the choreography is the way that it pithily recapitulates the story. There is Mother: she acknowledges each of her three daughters. There is Father: he, in turn, acknowledges his three sons. They look at each other, hunch-free, then acknowledge each of their new children. Finally, the blended family acknowledge one another.

This reading is indisputable, but further study and analysis remain to be done. There are questions the text still poses. Why does Alice acknowledge no one? Why is it only Peter who glances in her direction? Perhaps he was actually trying to look across at Jan? And what about the slight variations that exist from season to season? And, ultimately, the most frightening question of all: What would have happened to this carefully constructed and elegantly choreographed open if Oliver had caught on and the series had continued for more seasons?

tv anagrams

When you rearrange the letters of a show title or a person's name, sometimes shocking semantic truths reveal themselves. Other times, the result is just nonsense. Take a look and decide (decode?) for yourself. If you like playing word games, cover the left column and try to figure out on your own what the original show or person was!

12 SHOWS

The A-Team	Tame hate
I Dream of Jeannie	A feminine jar ode
The Munsters	These nuts, Mr.
The Addams Family	Madam Death is fly
Laverne and Shirley	Leaden hens rivalry
The Donna Reed Show	Honed a tender show
The Honeymooners	No money? He, she rot.
Sonny and Cher	Her canny nods
The Brady Bunch	Nerd hubby chat (or) Thy cherub band
The Andy Griffith Show	Adrift? Why then, go fish!
The Mary Tyler Moore show	Smooth my ethereal worry
Gilligan's Island	Idling snails lag

12 CHARACTERS

Barney Fife	Fine by fear
Maude Findlay	Media fun lady
Gomer Pyle	"Mr. Gee" ploy
Laura Petrie	Reptile aura
Rob Petrie	Rob EE Trip
George Costanza	Eggs on to a craze
Lucy Ricardo	Curly or acid?
Archie Bunker	Rub keen chair (or) Birch? Nuke ERA!
Jethro Bodine	Hobo in red jet
Louie De Palma	I loud male ape!
Alice Kramden	Lack remained
Mork	Mr. OK!

12 ACTORS AND PERSONALITIES

Ed McMahon	He command
Walter Cronkite	Talk now, reciter
David Letterman	Mr. Validated Ten
Conan O'Brien	NBC air no one
Tracey Ullman	Am nearly cult
Milton Berle	Mr. "Libel Tone"
Barbara Walters	A rare brat bawls
Norman Lear	Mr. "Ran Alone"
Lorne Michaels	Heroic SNL Male
Howard Cosell	All words echo
Liberace	Be a relic
Ed Sullivan	Unveil lads

the 18 best tv books ever

1. *TV Land to Go*

You're holding it! The best book ever about television. But if you hunger for more prose studies of the video medium, we recommend these other fine works.

2. *Unsold Television Pilots: 1955 Through 1988,* Lee Goldberg (Jefferson, N.C.: McFarland & Company, 1989).

Think what you see on TV is pretty odd? Wait until you see what *didn't* make it. Brief descriptions of hundreds of the pilot shows that "coulda, woulda, shoulda" been contenders for your viewing pleasure. Some are simply bland, but, more often, they are wonderfully strange, and every one is a springboard for the imagination. The book is a fine work of research; more than that, though, it's an endlessly browsable delight, a fascinating study that reveals the way Hollywood thinks.

3. *Television Character and Story Facts: Over 110,000 Details from 1,008 Shows, 1945–1992,* Vincent Terrace (Jefferson, N.C.: McFarland & Company, 1993).

This is a strange and wonderful book. To some, it may seem to be a mere compendium of facts. The author has collected as many details as humanly possible about almost every popular TV show ever made: names, addresses, phone numbers, license plates, favorite colors, favorite foods, nicknames, pet names, relatives, employment history, and on and on. That's all well and good, but when you read it, strung together as prose . . . ? The collection takes on new meaning, especially when you're reading about shows you've never heard of. To some, television character and story facts may be a research tool. To others, it's a fascinating semiological experiment in fiction. In either case, this is an astonishing book, obviously another labor of love.

4. *Cult TV: A Viewer's Guide to the Shows America Can't Live Without,* John Javna (New York: St. Martin's Press, 1985).

A spirited, eclectic, and thoroughly clever survey of the television shows that have inspired passionate fandom. Peppered with information, anecdotes, and trivia presented in little nuggets that are perfect for the short attention spans of TV fans.

5. *TV Sets: Fantasy Blueprints of Classic TV Homes,* Mark Bennett (New York: TV Books, 1996).

The author is a Beverly Hills postal worker who began making architectural drawings of what he imagined, based on the portions we saw, would be the actual homes in television land. The drawings are fascinating and full of arcana relating to the shows. If you've ever wanted to know where Granny's still was in relationship to the "cement pond" or how exactly the Brady house was laid out, this is the volume for you.

6. *The Complete Directory to Prime Time Network and Cable TV Shows, 1946–Present,* Tim Brooks and Earle Marsh (New York: Ballantine Books, 1999).

A vast and detailed encyclopedia of shows, it includes casts, broadcast history, and much more in its almost 1,400 pages.

7. *The Great TV Sitcom Book,* Rick Mitz (New York: Perigee, 1988).

With detailed essays about every important sitcom since the dawn of television, this is clearly another work of passion. But this one is informed by a fine critical appreciation of the genre, and a sense of what makes sitcoms tick, and stick!

8. *The Honeymooners' Companion,* Donna McCrohan (New York: Workman Publishing, 1978).

This paean to the classic original thirty-nine episodes was an original in and of itself. It was the first great retrospective fan's book.

9. *The Emmys: The Ultimate, Unofficial Guide to the Battle of TV's Best Shows and Greatest Stars,* Thomas O'Neil (New York: Perigee, 1998).

An incredibly detailed work that provides not only all the winners, but all the nominees, all the backstage gossip, and all the information a TV fan could ask for. Plus, O'Neil provides it all with verve and an evident affection for the medium.

10. *Written Out of Television: A TV Lover's Guide to Cast Changes 1945–1994,* Steven Lance (Lanham, Md.: Madison Books, 1996).

One of the most insanely detailed books about any subject, this book is about much more than cast changes. Lance offers a detailed discussion of even the most minor cast change, with the backstage reasons, specifics on how the scripts reflected the changes, and on and on. An incredibly informed study of the medium.

11. *Experimental Television, Test Films, Pilots and Trial Series, 1925 through 1995: Seven Decades of Small Screen Almosts,* Vincent Terrace (Jefferson, N.C.: McFarland & Company, 1997).

Almost as good as Goldberg's *Unsold Television Pilots,* with many additional details.

12. *Growing Up Brady: I Was a Teenage Greg,* Barry Williams with Chris Kreski (New York: HarperPerennial, 1992).

Very few TV celebrity autobiographies are readable, much less interesting, but this well-crafted story blends scandal, wisecracks, and wry observation in laying bare the behind-the-scenes life of that most saccharine of TV families.

13. *The Unofficial Gilligan's Island Handbook,* Joey Green (New York: Warner Books, 1988).

A zesty, well-written tribute and episode guide. Green has since brought his deft touch, sense of humor, and devotion to dissecting pop culture to such books as *Hi Bob: A Self-Help Guide to The Bob Newhart Show, The Get Smart Handbook,* and others.

14. *Total Television: The Comprehensive Guide to Programming from 1948 to the Present,* Alex McNeil (New York: Penguin Books, 1996).

Not quite as detailed as Brooks and Marsh, but this massive tome does include non–prime time shows: cartoons, game shows, syndicated fare, etc. It's also just a touch more opinionated, which can be fun.

15. *Why We Watch: Killing the Gilligan Within,* Dr. Will Miller (New York: Fireside/Simon & Schuster, 1996).

Nick at Nite's teletherapist delves deeply into our national psyche as he shows us the true psychological meanings of the shows to which we are so innocently drawn. The sexual metaphor that is Mister Ed. Furthermore, the book is a parody of self-help books, offering to turn our television sets into tools of psychological healing.

16. *The Beverly Hillbillies,* Stephen Cox (New York: HarperPerennial, 1993).

Almost every show under the sun has been the subject of a trade paperback of some ilk, but few have the grace to mix sincere appreciation with well-researched, behind-the-scenes stories and a sense of humor about the whole. Stephen Cox has authored a number of well-written books that have just that grace. This was his first.

17. *Mayberry 101: Behind the Scenes of a TV Classic,* Neal Brower (Winston-Salem, N.C.: John F. Blair, Publisher, 1998).

What started as a column in the fan club newsletter became a life's work. Rev. Brower has interviewed the writers and creators of the series at length, and he lovingly annotates seventy-nine classic episodes. The charm, warmth, and intelligence of the interviewees comes through as Brower paints a fascinating picture of how northeastern city–bred writers living in Hollywood managed to bring a small North Carolina town to life.

18. *Nick at Nite's Classic TV Companion,* Tom Hill (New York: Fireside/Simon & Schuster, 1996).

A brilliant, effervescent, and thoroughly enjoyable collection of episode guides for the shows then airing on TV Land's sister network: *Taxi; The Munsters; Welcome Back, Kotter,* and more.

tv's 10 best miniseries

OR LIMITED SERIES

1. *Roots*
2. *The Civil War*
3. *I, Claudius*
4. *An American Family*
5. *Eyes on the Prize*
6. *Rich Man, Poor Man*
7. *Lonesome Dove*
8. *The Ascent of Man*
9. *Shogun*
10. *The Adams Chronicles*

some things you didn't know

Tired of old-fashioned TV trivia? Think you know it all? Well, here are some things you definitely didn't know until now.

Did you know . . .

. . . that architect Mike Brady is a distant cousin of TV's Alan Brady?

. . . that the show *Lassie* popularized the idea of keeping dogs as pets? Before the show, almost no one in America did; but within only a few years after it hit the airwaves, dogs replaced antelopes as America's most popular pets.

. . . there were actually two actors who played the role of Superman? The second was necessary because George Reeves didn't have the ability to fly.

. . . the character Sylvester J. Cat was originally created by playwright Tennessee Williams for a one-act play set in the West Virginia sponge mines?

. . . that *Addams Family*'s Lurch was played by former child actress Shirley Temple Black?

. . . the role of Flipper was played by former Mousketeer Carl "Cubby" O'Brien? It took him almost two hours each day to get into his makeup.

. . . that eggplant is actually neither an egg nor a plant? It's an amphibian.

. . . that last fact really wasn't about television at all? Sorry, the rest of the list will be all about television, I promise.

. . . that Mike Brady and Wilbur Post went to the same architecture school?

. . . the first day of filming on the set of *Bewitched* was almost a disaster because witches don't show up on film? Luckily, they were able to get special witch-sensitive film shipped in overnight from Japan.

. . . Ralph Kramden only used sixty-three distinct vocabulary words in the entire run of *The Honeymooners*?

. . . *Love, American Style* won a number of prestigious awards for its educational content?

the 8 least memorable tv shows

OF ALL TIME

Some shows seem like they will last forever, like *I Love Lucy*. Some shows have short runs but live on as cult classics, like *Police Squad*. Others gain eternal fame for the magnitude of their failure—*Turn On!* Or for the extremity of their concept—*My Mother the Car*. Many others fall somewhere in between, in the realm of rerun or at least the "oh yeah, what ever happened to that show."

But those are for other lists. These are the forgotten ones. The real shows that draw only blank stares or "really?" These are the eight shows that, despite having good reasons to have made some impact, have been forgotten by the American public. It is TV Land's sworn duty to bring as many of these shows as possible back to the small screen. In the meantime, we can only describe them.

1. *Domestic Life*

Produced by Steve Martin and starring Martin Mull, this 1984 sitcom was a sort of *Home Improvement* as Mull played Martin Crane, a commentator who provided a regular humorous report entitled "Domestic Life" on a local Seattle TV station. Those two gentleman have a pretty good track record, but this isn't part of it.

2. Dusty's Trail

Everyone knows *Gilligan's Island* and *F Troop*, too, but the world has forgotten the strange combination of the two that aired in 1973. It was the exact same plot as *Gilligan*, except that Bob Denver was now leading a lost wagon train in circles around the Old West. Forrest "Sarge" Tucker took on the Skipper's role, and there was a pair of wealthy aristocrats along with some pretty women and one more guy to round things out. There was never, needless to say, a made-for-TV reunion movie for this show.

3. Duck Factory

Back in 1984, Jim Carrey was Skip Tarkenton, a fresh-faced rookie cartoonist in a Hollywood animation studio. The show also featured Jack Gilford, perhaps best known for his sad-faced roles in the long-running series of Cracker Jack advertisements.

4. Circus Boy

A kid show featuring future Monkee Micky Dolenz as an orphan traveling with the circus.

5. Rags to Riches

Not seen in syndication, apparently because the underlying music rights make it either very complicated or very expensive to show. Joe Bologna starred in this *Bachelor Father* meets *Cop Rock*. He was the wealthy playboy who got stuck adopting a houseful of orphan girls. Here's the kicker: they would burst into song, generally sixties pop rock or R&B with new lyrics that related to the episode's story line.

6. The Hathaways

Jack Weston and Peggy Cass taking care of a family of performing chimpanzees! As far as shows with monkeys go, this one was among the very best, definitely better than Ted Bessell's *Me and the Chimp*, and rivaling *Lancelot Link*.

7. The Mothers-in-Law

Lucy-and-Ethel-esque situation comedy with Eve Arden and Kaye Ballard, along with their hubbies and the occasional appearances of executive producer Desi Arnaz as bullfighter Raphael del Gado.

8. *Saturday Night Live*

No, not NBC's *Saturday Night Live*, *Saturday Night Live with Howard Cosell*. This was the fall 1975 premiere that attempted to bring the verve and spontaneity of live television back to the American viewing public with comedy, music, and variety. This was the one that didn't work. (Even though Bill Murray was actually a featured player on this *Saturday Night Live*, he didn't join the other one until later.)

tv's 10 best moments

1. The Moonwalk: Neil Armstrong first steps on the Moon
2. The Beatles on *The Ed Sullivan Show*
3. The Moonwalk as performed by Michael Jackson in the *Motown 25* special
4. Keith Hernandez spit reenactment
5. "Oh my nose!" as Marcia is hit by the errant forward pass
6. Sammy Davis Jr. kissing Archie
7. John-John's salute
8. Nixon's cameo on *Laugh-In*
9. Soupy Sales asking kids to send money
10. The Krystle and Alexis catfight

the greatest "premiums" in Nick at Nite

AND TV LAND HISTORY

What's a "premium"? It's an item created exclusively to be given away as a promotional item to our clients. TV networks have a large and varied group of people to please, including advertisers, cable affiliates, program distributors, and various other television industry folks.

The items we create—since they aren't being sold to make a profit—have a wide-open canvas. Many are practical: bags, shirts, jackets, pens. But a few break the mold. Sometimes we go too far. We had planned on making Vermont maple sugar candies of Bob Newhart's likeness when we launched *Newhart*, but Mr. Newhart objected. (Actually, he laughed amiably when it was suggested, so we went ahead and had the candy molds made; when it came time for him to approve the artwork, he said, however, "I assumed you were joking!")

But we did manage to make a few good ones. Here are some of our favorites.

1. Mr. T Chia Pet

A bust of B. A. Baracus from *The A-Team*, made by the real Chia Pet people so that you could grow him a Chia mohawk.

2. Frank Sinatra martini glass

When TV Land aired the never-before-broadcast Rat Pack concert, we needed a high-class item, and martini glasses with the Chairman of the Board's likeness etched on them was just the ticket. No better way to enjoy some olive soup.

3. Fonzie votive candle

Remember how the Fonz was supposed to be a hood, but he quickly became a voice of virtue and moral righteousness that would rival Joe Friday or Mother Teresa? We decided it was time for the Fonz to be sainted and used to decorate a tall votive candle. Sacrilege? Not to *Happy Days* fans!

4. Mister Ed glue

A little sick, sure, but a simple, hard-to-resist concept.

5. *Taxi* air freshener

Just like the ones that dangle in real taxis!

6. Twip coffee mugs

Remember Twip? It was a series of ad parodies made for TV Land—sort of our own Retro-mercials—and we made handsome coffee mugs for sipping the all-purpose Twip as a beverage.

7. Superman commemorative plate

You know those "special," "mint," "collectible" ceramic plates? We had one designed for Superman.

8. Time Warp Jiffy Pop

Real Jiffy Pop, with our own packaging design to promote a special night in TV Land when we created a 1972 time warp and brought together that classic ABC Friday night lineup: *Brady Bunch, Partridge Family, Room 222, The Odd Couple* and *Love, American Style.*

the 9 best production slates

In order to state their role and ownership of television shows, production companies are generally granted a brief two-to-three second "production slate" that is attached to the shows and airs with it. For the first few decades, these were simply the stodgy self-glorifying corporate creations you'd expect from Paramount and 20th Century Fox Television, but beginning in the sixties, show creators formed their own production companies and claimed their own slates.

1. **Jack Webb's Mark VII hammer.** Memorable and groundbreaking. This was one of the first slates that truly "branded" a group of television shows.

2. **MTM's meowing cat.** A good idea on its own—spoofing MGM—but it was also altered, on occasion, a little lagniappe to the attentive viewer. The meow would be provided by Bob Newhart, or the cat would be wearing a Santa Claus hat, etc.

3. **The "Mutant Enemy" animation** monster at the end of *Buffy the Vampire Slayer.*

4. **The *X-Files's*** "I made this."

5. ***Taxi*'s "Good night, Mr. Walters."**

6. **"This has been a Filmways Presentation, Darling,"** as read by Eva Gabor for *Green Acres*. A playful moment for an otherwise stodgy corporate slate.

7. **The classic 20th Century Fox** architectural block letters.

8. **Sit, Ubu, sit.** Gary David Goldberg's UBU Productions' slate.

9. **Viacom.** We know where our bread is buttered.

world's toughest tv trivia test

So you've read this far and maybe you're still not impressed. You already knew lots of these fun facts and heard of all the so-called "obscure" shows we have discussed. Well then, you're definitely ready for this. It's an open book test. Prepare your Number 2 pencil. You may begin now.

1. Can you rearrange the letters of the popular sitcom *Taxi* and come up with one of its stars?

2. When *Car 54, Where Are You?* ceased production, there were three script ideas in development that producer Nat Hiken was high on. Name two of them.

3. Name three successful spin-offs of *CHiPs*.

4. Can Samantha Stevens use her magic to create a rock so heavy that she herself cannot lift it?

5. *Punky Brewster* is based on which Ibsen play?

6. When the author was dubbing shows to take home and screen, he accidentally cut off the last ten minutes of which Bob Newhart episode?

7. When Superman uses his "superbreath" to freeze a pond, what prevents his lips from getting frozen, too?

8. The cast of *Just the Ten of Us* are in a boat rowing upstream at six miles per hour, but the

water is traveling at three miles per hour. The cast of *Family* is rowing downstream at ten miles per hour. The cast of *Fish*, with the exception of Abe Vigoda, are throwing rocks at both boats. Why isn't Abe throwing rocks?

9. You probably know that *ALF* stands for "Alien Life Form," but you probably didn't know that *Malcolm in the Middle* is also an acronym. What does it stand for?

10. Why did they keep making *Welcome Back, Kotter* after all the jokes had been used up by the second episode?

Answers:

1. No, you can't.

2. Nat Hiken was never high on anything but scotch. Being "high on an idea" was a Hollywood concept that didn't exist until the mid-1970s.

3. *After CHiPs, Me and the CHiPs, Good-bye, Mr. CHiPs.* Since they never existed, you could name them anything you want.

4. A keen example of the logical flaw known as contradictory premises. If there is an immovable force, there can be no irresistible object. That also includes Endora.

5. A trick question: *Punky Brewster* was not based on an Ibsen play at all, but on Shakespeare's *Troilus and Cressida.*

6. Episode 99, "Caged Fury." But I got another copy.

7. They freeze, but only very briefly, as his supercirculation brings them back to normal.

8. He has strained his shoulder earlier in the day throwing rocks at the four members of *The Banana Splits* during their rock-and-roll costume characters raft race.

9. It is not an acronym. We meant anachronism. And it's not that either.

10. No one could stand to tell Horshack that the show should be canceled.

Give yourself one point for each correct answer. Then give yourself a small present as a way of saying, "Thanks for playing, better luck next time."

the 10 best made-for-tv dramas

1. *Brian's Song*
2. *The Boy in the Plastic Bubble*
3. *Helter Skelter*
4. *Requiem for a Heavyweight*
5. *The Autobiography of Miss Jane Pittman*
6. *Steambath*
7. *The Day After*
8. *First You Cry*
9. *The Jericho Mile*
10. *The Burning Bed*

the best tv websites

There are more and more websites about television every day—with all the links you need to get lost for days and even weeks—but here are a few well-crafted spots at which to start.

1. tvland.com

What do you expect? Modesty? There is loads of information about our shows and the latest on what's happening on the channel.

2. imdb.com

It stands for Internet Movie Database, and the focus is on movies; nonetheless, it is simply the greatest entertainment research facility around. The searchable bank of acting, writing, and directing credits is peerless.

3. tvparty.com

How exactly they have secured the legal rights and clearances to provide all the fabulous video clips of vintage television shows, commercials, promos, etc., is a mystery, but while it's there, enjoy! They've got a real trove.

4. jumptheshark.com

A fabulous high-concept ongoing debate forum. The idea is to establish the moment in a TV series after which it is all downhill; that is, the moment that they "jump the shark." (The name of the site is derived from the episode of *Happy Days* when Fonzie did just that.) A wide range of opinions is available, and it's hard to resist getting caught up in the arguments.

5. meldrum.co.uk/mhp/testcard/history.html

Okay, this one is a little more obscure, but all the more brilliant in its way. Contained herein is a detailed and illustrated history of what the British call "test cards" and we generally call "test patterns." It is a UK-based site, but it includes a fair sampling of North American test patterns. Moreover, it is an enlightening study of early television technology.

Chuck Woolery's 6 careers

1. Country songwriter

He started in Nashville and enjoyed some success, having his songs recorded by such luminaries as Tammy Wynette.

2. Country singer

Gave it a shot on his own and made his TV debut on *The Jimmy Dean Show*.

3. Hippie rock star

His psychedelic rock group, Avant Garde, scored a minor hit with the song "Naturally Stoned," which cracked the Top 40 in 1968.

4. Children's TV star

He was part of *The New Zoo Revue*, helping create the character Mr. Dingle.

5. Movie star

He appeared in a 1974 B-movie entitled *Treasure of Jamaica Reef*, in which future Charlie's Angel Cheryl Ladd also starred.

6. Game show host

He started on *Wheel of Fortune* but made his name ("Back in two and two") on *The Love Connection*.

the 13 greatest Bosleyisms

What is a Bosleyism? It's when two actors are so similar in looks, mannerisms, general effect, or the roles they play that they are often mistaken for each other by the viewing public. It is named, naturally, after the character that David Doyle played on *Charlie's Angels*.

1. Tom Bosley and David Doyle

Put side by side, the two are not really that similar in looks, but something about their voice and manner makes them indistinguishable to many. To complicate matters further, there is a growing contingent of observers who believe that Dick Van Patten forms the third element of a mysterious confused-actors triangle.

2. Paul Lynde and Alan Sues

Lynde is a legend, and if he hadn't snapped up all the "Paul Lynde" roles, you'd probably know Alan Sues's name better. Sues was a regular on *Laugh-In*, playing the sportscaster "Big Al," among other roles.

3. Arte Johnson and Henry Gibson

Speaking of *Laugh-In*, go ahead tell me quickly which one was "Very interesting" and which one recited the poems. They were both diminutive and dry-witted, and with all the fast-cutting and shared stock phrases on that show, it's a wonder we ever kept them apart. Jo Anne Worley and Ruth Buzzi were a lot easier to differentiate.

4. Bob Barker and Monty Hall.

A case of similar emcee roles. Barker was *Truth or Consequences*; Hall was *Let's Make a Deal*.

5. George Peppard and George Kennedy

Which one was Banacek? Which was the Blue Knight? You tell me, but I know one of them led the A Team.

6. Robert Vaughn and Robert Culp

The same name often accentuates naturally occurring Bosleyisms. Some have suggested you could easily throw Robert Conrad and Robert Wagner into the same mix of tough, masculine cowboy/detective/spies that are often confused. Robert Hegyes, who was Epstein among Kotter's sweathogs, is for some reason not confused with any of the others. You could include Richard Crenna in this group, and he's not even a "Robert."

7. Maurice Gosfield and Buddy Hackett.

And quite a pair of beauties, too.

8. Richard Chamberlain and James Franciscus

Tall, fair-haired, high-cheekbones . . . either is a fine choice for your next miniseries.

9. Cheryl Ladd and Cheryl Tiegs

The former was the Angel; the latter was the reigning queen of *Sports Illustrated* swimsuit issues during the mid-1970s.

10. Art Carney and Barnard Hughes

Barnard Hughes said he was often mistaken for Carney by fans.

11. Bob Hope and E. G. Marshall

Sure, it's unlikely anyone ever really confused them, but they do sort of look alike.

12. Simon Oakland and Claude Akins

Twin burly men.

13. Mary Kate Olsen and Ashley Olsen

It's eerie, don't you think?

the most popular shows

When people in TV land watch television, what do they watch? Some people watch the same shows that you do. Kevin Arnold and his family can be seen watching *Mister Ed*, *The Flintstones*, *Sonny and Cher* and many more. But many of the people in TV land watch series that don't show up in our *TV Guide*s. Here are some of them.

1. *The $99,000 Answer*

One of many popular game shows in TV land. Ralph Kramden appeared on this one.

2. *The Alan Brady Show*

Songs, dances, and plenty of comedy from a great, if rather small, writing staff.

3. *FYI*

The weekly newsmagazine.

4. *Rhoda Barrett from Hollywood, Monster Chiller Horror Theater* with Count Floyd, *Farm Film Report, Marcel Cousteau's Underwater Mime, Great White North Report,* and everything else on the SCTV channel.

5. *Krusty the Klown Show*

Springfield's beloved children's entertainer. Includes the "Itchy and Scratchy" cartoon series.

53

6. *Tool Time*

Handy advice from Tim Taylor, with Al Borland to help, and, of course, Lisa the "tool girl" (Pamela Anderson) was nice too.

7. *The WJM News*

With the Twin Cities' least regarded anchorman, Ted Baxter.

8. *Vermont Today*

Morning talk hosted by local bed-and-breakfast proprietor Dick Loudon.

9. *The Larry Sanders Show*

The favorite late-night talk-fest.

10. *Undercover Woman*

Police drama starring Joyce Whitman (*The Betty White Show*).

British invasion!

THE 21 MOST SUCCESSFUL BRITS ON AMERICAN TV

1. Angela Lansbury

Murder, She Wrote, plus plenty of made-for-TV movies.

2. Richard Dawson

Survey says . . . the number two answer.

3. Frank Oz

Don't know the name? He's the man behind, in, or under Bert, Cookie Monster, Grover, Fozzie Bear, Animal, and Miss Piggy.

4. Alfred Hitchcock

He had his own shows, and had a fair amount of success with his movies, too.

5. Joan Collins

Alexis, yes, but also the definitive vixen in many series and TV movies.

6. Alan Napier

Alfred, sir.

7. John Cleese

Python's most active alum, guesting on *Third Rock from the Sun* and making other appearances on this side of the big pond.

8. Sebastian Cabot

Yes, French was English.

9. Jane Seymour

First all those made-for-TV movies, then Dr. Quinn!

10. Diana Rigg

Yes, *The Avengers* was an import, but the impact was made.

11. Eric Idle

Python, and many memorable *SNL* bits, too.

12. Boris Karloff

Hosted his own suspense anthology *Thriller*, and was the voice of the Grinch.

13. Patrick Macnee

The other Avenger.

14. Lucy Lawless

Xena!

15. Davy Jones

The cutest Monkee, and Marcia's prom date!

16. Judy Carne

Laugh-In's daffy import.

17. Benny Hill

Another British-made star, but he was big here, too.

18. Alistair Cooke

Masterpiece Theatre.

19. Olivia d'Abo

Managing to land a role in the oh-so-American *Wonder Years*.

20. Robin Leach

Lifestyles.

21. J. Pat O'Malley

Frequently seen character actor, he was Rob Petrie's father, among other things.

For the record, Bob Hope was born in England, but he was an American and raised in Cleveland, Ohio. Likewise, Henny Youngman was born in Liverpool, but he was raised in New York City.

the 10 best movies with stars

WHO FIRST MADE THEIR MARK IN TELEVISION

To be eligible for this list, the actor in question must be primarily a television personality. Judy Garland's TV show doesn't make *The Wizard of Oz* eligible; nor does *You Bet Your Life* qualify Groucho's film work. Both were originally, and primarily, film stars. And if people know Agnes Moorehead as Endora above all, well, we're saying that her work on *Citizen Kane* as well as other films and stage plays was first and foremost.

1. *Forrest Gump*—Tom Hanks

Bosom Buddies ran for two full seasons and had a life in syndication, so we're gonna claim Hanks had "made his mark" for TV Land.

2. *Pulp Fiction*—John Travolta

Who? What? Where? Indeed.

3. *Spinal Tap*—Michael McKean

And director Rob Reiner, of course.

4. *Ordinary People*—Mary Tyler Moore

And Judd Hirsch, too.

5. *Dirty Harry*—Clint Eastwood

Clint was TV's Rowdy Yates for seven top-rated years.

6. *Groundhog Day*—Bill Murray

Some might say *Caddyshack* belongs, too.

7. *American Graffiti*—Ron Howard

And Cindy Williams and Suzanne Somers, too.

8. *Back to the Future*—Michael J. Fox

And Christopher Lloyd!

9. *Animal House*—John Belushi

Yes, it spawned a thousand bad imitations, but it was an original.

10. *A Funny Thing Happened on the Way to the Forum*— Phil Silvers

Good play, too.

the top 30 tv land Oscars

Though they may have won their Academy Award before, after, or during their TV career, all of these Oscar-winning actors (and a few stray writers and directors) owe some debt to the small screen for their fame and fortune. That's why these are our favorite Oscar winners.

RANK	ACTOR	AWARD	BEST-KNOWN TV ROLE OR SHOW; OTHER NOTES
1	Art Carney	Best Actor 1974, *Harry and Tonto*	Ed Norton
2	Donna Reed	Best Supporting Actress 1953, *From Here to Eternity*	Donna Stone
3	Shirley Jones	Best Supporting Actress 1960, *Elmer Gantry*	Shirley Partridge
4	Ernest Borgnine	Best Actor 1955, *Marty*	Lieutenant Commander Quinton McHale
5	Sally Field	Best Actress 1979, *Norma Rae* Best Actress 1984, *Places in the Heart*	Gidget and Sister Bertrille

RANK	ACTOR	AWARD	BEST-KNOWN TV ROLE OR SHOW; OTHER NOTES
6	Shirley Booth	Best Actress 1952, *Come Back, Little Sheba*	Plus an Emmy for *Hazel*, and a Tony for the stage
7	Cloris Leachman	Best Supporting Actress 1971, *The Last Picture Show*	*Phyllis*
8	Patty Duke	Best Supporting Actress 1962, *The Miracle Worker*	Patty and Cathy Lane
9	James L. Brooks	Best Director and Best Screenplay 1983, *Terms of Endearment*	Writer and producer: *The Mary Tyler Moore Show*, *Taxi*, *The Simpsons*, etc.
10	Walter Brennan	Best Supporting Actor 1936, *Come and Get It* Best Supporting Actor 1938, *Kentucky* Best Supporting Actor 1940, *The Westerner*	*The Real McCoys* (despite Brennan's unhappiness with doing it) was a hit that ran for six years, from 1957–63
11	Red Buttons	Best Supporting Actor 1957, *Sayonara*	*The Red Buttons Show*
12	George Burns	Best Supporting Actor 1975, *The Sunshine Boys*	*The George Burns and Gracie Allen Show*
13	Paddy Chayefsky	Best Screenplay 1955, *Marty* Best Screenplay 1971, *The Hospital* Best Screenplay 1976, *Network*	Chayefsky wrote numerous dramas for television's Golden Age
14	Jack Lemmon	Best Supporting Actor 1955, *Mister Roberts* Best Actor 1972, *Save the Tiger*	Got his start in early TV, a 1949–50 sitcom called *That Wonderful Guy*, and various comedy shows
15	Rita Moreno	Best Supporting Actress 1961, *West Side Story*	She's a four-trophy winner: a Tony for *The Ritz*, a Grammy for *Electric Company* music, and Emmys for guest appearances on *The Muppet Show* and *The Rockford Files*

RANK	ACTOR	AWARD	BEST-KNOWN TV ROLE OR SHOW; OTHER NOTES
16	Jack Albertson	Best Supporting Actor 1968, *The Subject Was Roses*	The Man (with Chico)
17	Cher	Best Actress 1987, *Moonstruck*	Sonny's wife
18	Helen Hunt	Best Actress 1997, *As Good as It Gets*	Jamie Buchman
19	Robin Williams	Best Supporting Actor 1997, *Good Will Hunting*	Mork
20	Burl Ives	Best Supporting Actor 1958, *The Big Country*	*Frosty the Snowman* (narrator)
21	Clint Eastwood	Best Director 1992, *Unforgiven*	Rowdy Yates
22	Jodie Foster	Best Actress 1988, *The Accused* Best Actress 1991, *The Silence of the Lambs*	None of her regular roles made it big, but she was a frequently seen child actor on TV
23	Karl Malden	Best Supporting Actor 1951, *A Streetcar Named Desire*	*The Streets of San Francisco*
24	George Chakiris	Best Supporting Actor 1961, *West Side Story*	Buz Murdock, *Route 66*
25	Tom Hanks	Best Actor 1993, *Philadelphia* Best Actor 1994, *Forrest Gump*	Kip "Buffy" Wilson
26	Goldie Hawn	Best Supporting Actress 1969, *Cactus Flower*	*Laugh-In*
27	Broderick Crawford	Best Actor 1949, *All the King's Men*	*Highway Patrol*
28	Yul Brynner	Best Actor 1956, *The King and I*	*Kojak* (just kidding)
29	Michael Douglas	Best Actor 1987, *Wall Street*	*The Streets of San Francisco*
30	Geena Davis	Best Supporting Actress 1988, *The Accidental Tourist*	Okay, they were short-lived, but she starred in two sitcoms: *Buffalo Bill* (1983–84) and then *Sara* (1985)

15 tv actors who have

GONE ON TO DIRECT

What they really wanted to do was direct, and they have, with more or less success, depending.

RANK	ACTOR/ DIRECTOR	BEST-KNOWN TV ROLE(S)	DIRECTING CREDITS
1	Rob Reiner	Meathead	*Spinal Tap, When Harry Met Sally*
2	Ron Howard	Opie and Richie	*Cocoon, Splash, Apollo 13*
3	Penny Marshall	Laverne	*Big, A League of Their Own, Riding in Cars with Boys*
4	Albert Brooks	Player in *SNL* films	*Real Life, Lost in America*
5	Carl Reiner	Player in *Your Show of Shows*, Alan Brady	*Fatal Instinct, The Jerk, Where's Poppa?*
6	Betty Thomas	Officer Lucy Bates (*Hill Street Blues*)	*The Brady Bunch Movie, Howard Stern's Private Parts*
7	Jerry Paris	Jerry Helper, the Petries' neighbor on *The Dick Van Dyke Show*	*Police Academy 3: Back in Training;* episodes of *The Odd Couple, Mary Tyler Moore, Happy Days*
8	Peter Bonerz	Jerry Robinson, the orthodontist in *The Bob Newhart Show*	Episodes of *The Hughleys, Friends, ALF, News Radio*

RANK	ACTOR/ DIRECTOR	BEST-KNOWN TV ROLE(S)	DIRECTING CREDITS
9	Bill Bixby	Eddie's father (Tom Corbett) and many others	Many episodes of *Blossom*
10	Dwayne Hickman	Dobie Gillis	Episodes of *Designing Women; Get a Life; Sister, Sister*
11	Dick Martin	Host of *Laugh-In*	Episodes of *Newhart*
12	Ivan Dixon	Kinchloe, running Hogan's ham radio	Episodes of *Quantum Leap, The A-Team, Bionic Woman*
13	Anson Williams	Potsie	Episodes of *Sabrina, the Teenage Witch; Diagnosis Murder; Melrose Place*
14	Michael Lembeck	Max on *One Day at a Time*	Episodes of *Friends*
15	Tim Matheson	Voice of Jonny Quest	*Buried Alive 2* (made for TV)

10 noteworthy films featuring

TV LAND STARS

1. *The Brass Bottle* (1964)

Barbara Eden in a movie about a magic genie in a bottle, but in this movie—made well before *I Dream of Jeannie*—she plays a mortal human opposite Burl Ives's genie. Incidentally, to further confuse things, it's Tony Randall who plays the role of the befuddled master who must explain the dancing harem girls to his girlfriend, Eden. This movie was an acknowledged inspiration for *I Dream of Jeannie*'s creator, Sidney Sheldon.

2. *Alligator II: The Mutation* (1991)

Bill Daily, our beloved Roger Healey/Howard Borden, plays the role of Mayor Anderson, who is corrupted by greedy developers but really didn't intend that anyone should get hurt. Sadly, he kills himself when he sees the havoc he has allowed to occur.

3. *The Feminist and the Fuzz* (1971, made for TV)

Directed by Jerry Paris, a prolific television director, and written by James Henerson, a frequent writer of *I Dream of Jeannie* episodes. It has a cast of TV Land all-stars, including Barbara Eden, David Hartman, Jo Anne Worley, Herb Edelman, Julie Newmar, John McGiver, Farrah Fawcett, Harry Morgan, and Sheila James Kuehl.

4. *Yours, Mine and Ours* (1968)

Lucille Ball stars as the widowed mother of eight who marries a widower (Henry Fonda) with ten of his own. The Brady brood had nothing on this household. Tom Bosley plays the family doctor, and a young Tim Matheson is one of the many, many kids. The story was written by longtime *Lucy* writer Bob Carroll Jr.

5. *Cold Turkey* (1971)

It's not only Dick Van Dyke in the starring role, but a movie conceived and directed by Norman Lear! A whole town decides to quit smoking at the same time. Tom Poston, Bob Newhart, and Jean Stapleton add to the TV star quotient. Not to mention Edward Everett Horton, the voice of "Fractured Fairy Tales."

6. *Three Little Pigskins* (1934)

Lucille Ball again, this time with a small role in a—yes, it's true—Three Stooges movie. She plays a gun moll, and does not get a saw raked across the top of her head.

7. *The Brothers Karamazov* (1958)

A critically acclaimed film starring Yul Brynner but, most important for our purposes, also starring William Shatner as the devout Karamazov brother.

8. *The Fish That Saved Pittsburgh* (1979)

It's Flip Wilson who drew our attention to this movie, but he's not the only TV star of note to join in the antics of this film, which is about a basketball team that turns to astrology to save its season. Sometimes all you need to know is who makes up the cast: Kareem Abdul-Jabbar and Marv Albert play themselves. Stockard Channing is Mona Mondieu. Meadowlark Lemon is Rev. Grady Jackson. Harry Shearer is the television news reporter. Flip Wilson is Coach "Jock" Delaney. And Jonathan Winters plays Harvey Tilson. One dynamite combination.

9. *On the Waterfront* (1954)

Who is that tall young gangster? That's right, it's Fred Gwynne, right after college and before he was typecast! Gwynne had a small, uncredited role in this classic film. It was many years later—after the whole *Munster* thing died down—that he could again take part in real movies like *The Cotton Club* (1984), in which he gave a memorable performance as Frenchy De-mange.

10. *Superdad* (1974)

Bob Crane took on a rare post-Hogan role as the overprotective dad in this incredibly lame comedy. He tries to keep his collegiate daughter away from such bad influences as boyfriend Kurt Russell. Sadly, Crane's character has no superpowers, which would have helped the film immensely.

the 10 best tv shows

BASED ON MOVIES

1. *M*A*S*H*

The classic.

2. *The Odd Couple*

Both descended from the stage.

3. *Alice* (from *Alice Doesn't Live Here Anymore*)

"Kiss mah grits" did not appear in the film.

4. *Buffy the Vampire Slayer*

The underlying comic formula is really the same as *The Munsters:* the contrast of horror's conventions and quotidian high school angst.

5. *The Courtship of Eddie's Father*

Often forgotten, the 1963 film featured little Ron Howard (then known as Ronny) trying to find a match for his dad Glenn Ford.

6. *Fame*

A kitsch classic.

7. *Lassie*

And the movie came from a book.

8. Zorro

Often remade tale.

9. Dr. Kildare

The original 1937 film was entitled *Internes Can't Take Money*, which led to the series of forties films featuring Lew Ayres as Dr. Kildare.

10. Alien Nation

Zesty sci-fi drama.

the 10 worst shows

BASED ON MOVIES

1. *Logan's Run*

Don't trust anyone over thirty!

2. *RoboCop: The Series*

Both movie and show were, of course, based on Shakespeare's *Troilus and Cressida*.

3. *Harry and the Hendersons*

Syndicated hit that ran three entire seasons, to the astonishment of anyone in his or her right mind.

4. *Weird Science*

Remaking mediocre movies is always a chancy proposition.

5. *Ferris Bueller* (from *Ferris Bueller's Day Off*)

Featuring an early series role for Jennifer Aniston.

6. *Private Benjamin*

This show actually ranked fifth in the ratings among all shows in the 1980–81 season.

7. *9 to 5*

Rachel Dennison, who took on the role Dolly Parton played in the movie, was actually Dolly Parton's sister.

8. *Fast Times* (from *Fast Times at Ridgemont High*)

An early TV role for Courtney Thorne-Smith.

9. *Mr. Roberts*

Forgettable 1965 sitcom based on the great 1955 film *Mister Roberts,* which starred Henry Fonda and earned Jack Lemmon an Oscar for his supporting role.

10. *Freddy's Nightmares*

And ours.

the 8 best movies

BASED ON TV SHOWS

Frankly, we were planning to cover ten of each; but eight on the plus side and twelve on the debit side seemed more like it (generous even).

1. *The Untouchables*

Brian De Palma at the helm, with Robert De Niro, Kevin Costner, and Sean Connery. A great flick.

2. *Mission: Impossible*

Incomprehensible, but another Tom Cruise box office smash.

3. *The Addams Family*

Barry Sonnenfeld's updating of the classic worked the first time, with Anjelica Huston and Raul Julia plus the young Christina Ricci.

4. *Star Trek* movies

Pick one.

5. *The Fugitive*

Harrison Ford.

6. *The Brady Bunch Movie*

Irreverent embrace of the kitsch factor.

7. *Twilight Zone: The Movie*

Original stories by Joe Dante, John Landis, George Miller, Steven Spielberg, and Rod Serling.

8. *George of the Jungle*

Don't laugh. Brendan Fraser actually saves the picture with his sincere effort to make his ridiculous character live.

the 12 worst movies

BASED ON TV SHOWS

1. *Dennis the Menace*

Not a total disaster, with Walter Matthau's Mr. Wilson, but John Hughes was lost in his *Home Alone*–induced haze of violent comedy.

2. *Dragnet*

A worthy effort, but loving a show isn't always enough.

3. *The Avengers*

Uma Thurman did look nice.

4. *Car 54, Where Are You?*

A tragic dismantling of a great show.

5. *Sgt. Bilko*

Even Steve Martin makes mistakes.

6. *Lost in Space*

Lost us.

7. *The Beverly Hillbillies*

Jim Varney's second-best leading role after *Ernest Goes to Camp*.

8. *The Wild, Wild West*

Barry Sonnenfeld went back to the well once too often. Should have been good.

9. *The Nude Bomb (Get Smart)*

Without 99, Max was lost.

10. *Flipper*

Why!

11. *My Favorite Martian*

What a sad waste of Christopher Lloyd. We'd rather have seen *My Favorite Reverend Jim*.

12. *Leave It to Beaver*

Should have left it alone.

top 3 places to hide

ON SITCOMS

1. In the closet
2. Under the bed
3. Back in the closet!

those darn Canadians! the 30 most successful Canadians

ON AMERICAN TV

We are slowly being taken over by an insidious foreign culture! They are the Canadians: threat from the North. Already, they have made their way into our television shows, playing beloved heroes like Perry Mason, Wilbur Post, and Tonto. They have taken over our mission to explore new worlds as Captain Kirk and Chief Engineer Scotty. They bring us our news, talk shows, game shows, sitcoms. Even our New Year's Eve legend Guy Lombardo was nothing less than an invader from the hinterlands.

Most frightening of all: Many of "our" finest impressionists are from Canada. Imagine it! Rich Little *and* the SCTV crew. Between them they could imitate every known performer in Hollywood, and soon, our once-hallowed entertainment capital would be a ghost town! A chilling specter indeed.

1. Raymond Burr
2. Michael J. Fox
3. William Shatner
4. Paul Shaffer
5. Alan Young
6. Lorne Greene
7. Dan Aykroyd
8. Peter Jennings

9. John Candy
10. Mike Myers
11. Eugene Levy
12. Jim Carrey
13. Alan Thicke
14. Conrad Bain
15. Dave Foley
16. Phil Hartman
17. Rich Little
18. Martin Short
19. Leslie Nielsen

20. Jay Silverheels
21. Dave Thomas
22. Alex Trebek
23. Howie Mandel
24. Rick Moranis
25. Catherine O'Hara
26. Scott Thompson
27. Morley Safer
28. Yvonne De Carlo
29. James Doohan
30. Monty Hall

10 wacky stunts that may have

GONE TOO FAR

TV Land—and Nick at Nite before it—have a rich tradition of special stunts, events and spots that demonstrated our wacky and irreverent sensibility. What were the strangest? The wildest? The ones that may have pushed the envelope right to the edge and then fallen off?

1. Pretty Picture Frame Nite

What could be better than watching classic reruns? Why, watching classic reruns inside a pretty picture frame! In this 1991 event, a series of lovely frames were placed over the night's programming from midnight to 5:00 A.M.—and due to technical limitations, they simply covered the outer portion of the show, causing everything to look, well, oddly framed. Among the shows was *The Best of SNL* and series creator Lorne Michaels was one of the few late-night viewers to catch the event. The next morning he called to ask, in so many words, what the heck was going on.

2. We're Watching *Seinfeld*

In the spring of 1998, while all of America gathered over at NBC to watch the series finale of this landmark sitcom, TV Land hung up a "gone fishin' " sign that boldly declared that WE'RE TV FANS; WE'RE WATCHING *SEINFELD*, which stayed up for the entire hour. Our ratings were about what you'd expect. So were theirs.

3. Daylight Savings No More!

Every spring you lose an hour of precious television! TV Land decided to do something about it, and at 2:00 A.M. EST on April 2, 2000, we ran two episodes of *Emergency!* at the same time. We shrank both images so that they would fit comfortably on the screen, and one episode's audio played while the other had captioning. That way our viewers would still get a full forty-eight hours of programming over the weekend. Sure, it made no sense, really, but to us, it mattered.

4. The String-a-thon

Way back in 1987, Nick at Nite hosted a weeklong event that parodied public television's fundraising marathons. The event gathered such talent as Burt Ward and weatherman Lloyd Lindsey Young. They explained that without string, it would be impossible for Nick at Nite to continue airing our shows, and they asked viewers to call and "pledge" string to add to our growing ball. Retro-kitsch meets theater of the absurd!

5. Cinco de Mayo

To celebrate Mexico's national holiday in 1994 we presented four classic TV shows as they were seen south of the border—dubbed into Spanish! To ease the transition, English subtitles were provided so that viewers could still enjoy every word of Sergeant Joe Friday, Mork, and Lucy and Desi. The highlight came when Ricky and Fred Mertz talked about what they would make for dinner. Ricky suggests "arroz con pollo." Fred is confused until Ricky explains that it means "chicken with rice." That's all well and good, but when the scene was translated, Ricky breaks from his Spanish to suggest "chicken with rice" and Spanish-speaking Fred is confused until Ricky explains that it means "arroz con pollo." Mind-bending. Among the responses from viewers, an anonymous caller from Florida who suggested, "This is America, speak American."

6. Off the Clock!

In 1998, fresh off the "going dark for *Seinfeld*" event, TV Land decided that the best way to take on the new network shows would be to give up. We ceded them ten minutes at the top of the hour, figuring that every TV fan is tempted to try the new shows, but betting that after ten minutes, they'd be ready to return to the tried-and-true television favorites of TV Land. Did it work? Well, can you remember any new shows from that year? Or from last fall?

7. The Wearing of the Green

To celebrate St. Patrick's Day in 1995, Nick at Nite tinted an evening of classic black-and-white programming a sickly shade of green. Cute, but ultimately hard to watch.

8. Abe Lincoln in the Chocolate Factory

As part of the 1994 Classic TV Countdown, which featured unusual reenactments of classic TV scenes, we paid tribute to American history by having two Honest Abes facing the ever-accelerating chocolate factory assembly line. Among the other "highlights" were puppets reenacting the first episode of *Mary Tyler Moore* and the "Blue Boy" episode of *Dragnet*, along with a Shakespearean version of the "Chuckles Bites the Dust" episode.

9. The Odd Couple on Ice

It began as a hit Broadway play, then became a classic film, then a classic TV show. Until Nick at Nite came along, however, Neil Simon's work had never been translated to an ice-skating spectacular. In 1996, two giant heads were created, and "Oscar" and "Felix" took center rink for the first time as the "hosts" of our weeklong marathon. Bizarre and eye-catching, the promos confused some viewers. Luckily, the presence of Tony Randall and Jack Klugman, acting as sports commentators, gave the marathon a dose of reality. Perhaps the low point came during the filming of the ice-skating sequence, when the "Felix" skater, who had been under the weather, couldn't breathe well in the mask. He was exhausted by repeated takes, skated off to the side of the rink, pulled off the head, and lost his lunch.

10. The Dead Giveaway

Alfred Hitchcock Presents is a classic of the genre, dark tales with ironic twist endings, but it didn't always fit in among the *The Donna Reed Show* and *Mister Ed* reruns. Our Dead Giveaway was a contest that asked viewers to watch our weeklong marathon of the show and guess how many characters died. As host Wink Martindale explained in his upbeat, jolly way: "It's like guessing the jelly beans in a jar—but instead of jelly beans, it's cadavers!" Despite the obvious humorous intention, high-level executives suffered last-minute pangs of doubt about the appropriateness of the concept for family viewing. Most of the spots were pulled from the air, or aired only after 10:00 P.M.

characters, tv shows, and tv stars

NOT RECOGNIZED BY SPELL CHECK

Here's are some interactive lists! If you'd like to play along, cover the right-hand column. We've taken the names and titles of some popular actors, characters and series, run them through spell check and accepted the suggestions of this popular computer tool. Can you figure out who's who and what's what?

CHARACTERS

Some of these suggestions create a sort of Joycean subtext for understanding the character better; others are just non sequiturs.

Eddy Hassle	Eddie Haskell
Leonine and Squeegee	Lenny and Squiggy
Carry, Darkly, and Darkly	Larry, Darryl, and Darryl
Stove Oracle	Steve Urkel
Mr. Maggot	Mr. Magoo
Fox Murder	Fox Mulder
Horseback	Horshack
Balder	Beldar
Toupee Gig	Topo Gigio

Milieu Helper	Millie Helper
Falafel, Bingo, Dropper, and Snore	Fleagle, Bingo, Drooper, and Snork
Elder Food	Elmer Fudd
Father Guide Sardonic	Father Guido Sarducci
Deadly Drought	Dudley Doright

TV SHOWS

Boy, the mysterious workings of Spell Check leave us with quite a schedule. Poor abandoned children getting all liquored up in the afternoon, the Marines gone wild, and what about the wild goings-on at *Peyote Place?*

The Id Sultan Show	*The Ed Sullivan Show*
Michelle's Navy	*McHale's Navy*
The Jettisons	*The Jetsons*
Cagey & Lackey	*Cagney & Lacey*
Kodak	*Kojak*
Sangfroid and Son	*Sanford and Son*
Peyote Place	*Peyton Place*
It's Garb Changeling's Show	*It's Gary Shandling's Show*
Gomorrah Pyre, U.S.M.C.	*Gomer Pyle, U.S.M.C.*
The Orphan Winery Show	*The Oprah Winfrey Show*

TV STARS

Reed Fox	Redd Foxx
Tom Position	Tom Poston
Willing Farewell	William Frawley
Imagine Cocoa	Imogene Coca
Lucite Ball	Lucille Ball
Glider Radar	Gilda Radner
Freebie Prize	Freddie Prinze
Ermine Civics	Ernie Kovacs
Doom Deluges	Dom DeLuise

OTHER TV PERSONALITIES

Normal Learn	Norman Lear
Morally Safer	Morley Safer
Sickle and Exert	Siskel and Ebert
Agonies Nikon	Agnes Nixon
Alligator Cooker	Alistair Cooke
Liberate	Liberace
Jayvee P. Organ	Jaye P. Morgan
Emerald Ledgers	Emeril Legasse

worst possible men's softball team

COMPOSED OF CLASSIC TV STARS

C: Paul Lynde

SS: Howard McNear (Floyd the Barber)

RF: Werner Klemperer (Colonel Klink)

2B: David Hyde Pierce

LF: Jack Paar

CF: Hayden Roarke (Dr. Bellows)

3B: Jonathan Harris (Dr. Zachary Smith)

1B: Tony Randall

P: Jack Benny

best possible men's softball team

COMPOSED OF CLASSIC TV STARS

C: Bob Uecker—former major leaguer, even if he stank there

SS: Chuck Connors—former major leaguer

RF: Jack Klugman—to taunt Randall

2B: David Letterman—loves the game

LF: George Lindsey (Goober Pyle)—star college football player

CF: Burt Reynolds—same as Lindsey

3B: Tom Selleck—had aspirations of playing ball professionally

1B: Ted Danson—maybe playing an ex-pitcher rubbed off?

P: Art Carney—reports say he had a nice curveball back in high school.

Bench: Tony Danza (supposed to be an ex-major leaguer in *Who's the Boss*)

tv's 10 most popular cross-dressers

1. Flip Wilson as Geraldine

2. Uncle Miltie's burlesque outfits

3. Peter Scolari and Tom Hanks in *Bosom Buddies*

4. The series of male dogs who played the role of Lassie

5. Billy Crystal as *Soap*'s Jodie, who is planning on a sex change operation

6. Klinger on *M*A*S*H*

7. Max Baer as Jethrene Bodine

8. Joe Namath, doing that panty hose ad

9. Robert Blake, whenever Baretta needed to be an old lady

10. Peter Kastner, in the blessedly short-lived sitcom *The Ugliest Girl in Town*

Endora's 10 favorite misnomers for Darrin

Darrin Stevens's mother-in-law, Endora, made it a point never to refer to him by his proper first name. Throughout the series, regardless of whether it was Dick York or Dick Sargent, she called him anything but Darrin. When Samantha's father joined in, he picked up right where she left off.

1. Dobbin
2. Durwood
3. Delmore
4. Darryl
5. Daniel
6. Darwin
7. Dirndle
8. Delwood
9. David
10. Dingbat

the complete 60 second sitcoms

TV Land knows that our viewers lead busy lives, they don't always have time to watch a whole half hour. That's why we created 60 Second Sitcoms! Finally, everything you expect from a great sitcom—theme song, opening credits, problem, solution, comedy, closing credits, and out—all packed into the handy minute size!

Don't just take our word for it: *The Guinness Book of World Records* has recognized TV Land's 60 Second Sitcoms as the shortest television shows ever made.

There were three series made, each reflecting a different era in television, Here is a complete rundown of each series, with theme song and a synopsis of each episode.

ALL'S WELL (1952–58)

Finally, a sitcom that delivers the high-larious resolution without all that tedious buildup! Yes, you get the very ending of a great comic situation, hear a few words of wisdom that show that a lesson has been learned, and then get your end credits.

Theme song:

All's Well is just the happy ending
All's Well so concise, so nice
It's all swell, when it ends well, with *All's Well!*

Episode 1. "Amish Amiss"

Sponsor: Butler Pocket Combs: Sleek, efficient, and practically unbreakable!

Chipper and Dawn pushed the Amish too far, and the "yoke" is on them!

Episode 2. "Circus Daze"

Sponsor: Sugar Twip Crunch, the breakfast cereal with plenty of sugar, for energy!

Chipper learns how important it is not to distract a lion tamer.

Episode 3. "Yacht . . . Not"

Sponsor: Brickley's Dog Food: Almost too good to feed to your dog!

Chipper has to give back the yacht, but Mom baked pie!

Episode 4. "Chipper's Big Day"

Sponsor: Aunt Edie's Lard: Finally, lard in a can!

Did everyone forget Chipper's birthday. . . . no way. Bring on the pies.

Episode 5. "False Alarm"

Sponsor: America's Yeast Manufacturers: Yeast is the living fungus that helps you bake better!

By jumping to conclusions, Dad and Chipper alert the local militia.

Episode 6. "What a Relief"

Sponsor: Flexner's Ear Polish: Because people notice.

Turns out they won't have to sell the house, or finish off all the pies!

THE GAVELTONS (1961–67)

An ordinary suburban family with one little difference: they're incredibly litigious! No matter what hijinks they get into, you can bet the solution will be a lawsuit. (All in black and white except the 1966–67 season, and the 1965 Christmas special.)

Theme Song:

Whatever the situation,

Their solution is litigation,

Because the Gaveltons (rap, rap) are taking the stand!

Their first resort,

Is a trip to court,

It's the Gaveltons (rap, rap) the plaintiffs America loves!

Episode 1. "Baseball Fever"

Wendell's been cut from the baseball team, until Dad realizes that "restraint of trade" might apply to individuals as well as corporate entities!

Episode 2. "Double Date"

Wendell goofed up and has two dates for the same night . . . but it's no goof-up when Mom realizes that both girls made a binding nonstipulated agreement!

Episode 3. "Christmas with the Gaveltons" (in color)

Spike is a little disappointed, because Santa at the department store promised him a bicycle. Luckily, Santa's nonprofit status does not exempt him from federal trade regulations!

Episode 4. "Girls Are Trouble"

A girl at school is giving Spike a pain, following him all over . . . luckily, Mom and Dad are well aware of the courts' increasingly broad interpretation of stalking crimes.

Episode 5. "Sue's a Star"

Sue is glowing after her school play, but then Wendy of the school newspaper pans her performance . . . with malicious intent. Dad smells a big settlement!

SPIN AND CUTTER (1972–74)

A buddy sitcom that moves at the speed of sound. To move plots as quickly as they do, you'll need plenty of spin-cut "whee wohn" transitions, and that's exactly what these guys deliver!

Theme Song:

When you've got to move along . . . just cut!

When you've got to shift the plot . . . just spin!

Thing's really move along on the *Spin and Cutter* show.

Episode 1. "Spin and Cutter Do Hard Time"

Spin's "big plan" goes awry, and they end up in jail . . . playing cell-block hide-and-seek!

Episode 2. "Spin and Cutter in de Skies"

Their disguises having failed, the boys have to sneak back into the office to get back an important report, and end up falling off a ledge . . . on the fourteenth floor!

Episode 3. "Spin and Cutter on Broadway"

They've just got to see that show, even if it means Cutter has to . . . wear a dress!

the most popular tv shows

IN THE TWENTY-SIXTH CENTURY

It's the year 2525. Man is still alive, and not only that, but TV Land is the number-one rated network in the entire known universe, providing classic TV for over five hundred years! In fact, TV Land is now available on four distinct channels, as well as in the Pay-per-Think IntraPsychic System that broadcasts directly into your brain.

Why has TV Land survived and thrived when most other twentieth-century television networks have long since gone the way of the automobile? First of all, shows with believable characters, great stories, and funny writing really are timeless, and, of course, the ImagiTron helps, too.

The ImagiTron, first perfected in the early twenty-first century, takes digitally encoded television images and allows them to be recombined and rerealized in infinite variations. In other words, it can make *new* episodes of *The Donna Reed Show!* That's right, simply by analyzing the entire known digital library of Donna, Alex, Mary, and Jeff, as well as their home in Hilldale, the ImagiTron has all the necessary audio and visual data to work from to "shoot" new scripts and create new shows.

Episodes created by the ImagiTron allow TV Land to bring viewers all the warmth and lovability of its classic lineup, but with more "contemporary" twenty-sixth-century subject matter. And the original episodes are just as popular as ever! Don't believe it? Well, just take a look at a page from the TV schedule, from Monday, June 28, 2525. (It's definitely a Monday.)

	9:30	10:00
AMC		**Movie.** (Drama, 2:15) *Beverly Hills Cop XVIII,* starring Eddie Murphy III, Tito Puente, and Billy Barty. The same old story, some nice special effects, and Barty's posthumous Oscar for Posthumous Acting in a Supporting Role.
ANIMA		**Jetsons.** Cartoon.
ESPN	**Basketball.** New York Knicks vs. South Venus Vapors at Venus Coliseum. Tip-off, 9:35.	Telekinetic Ping-Pong Championships.
HIST		**Biography.** Documentary recounts the rise and triumphant accomplishments of America's forty-seventh president, Regis Philbin.
NBC/ ABC	**Entertainment Tonight.** Movies, TV, and the latest home virtual reality adventures	**Tomorrow's News.**
PBS	**This Old Biosphere.** Host Bob Vila helps renovate a beautiful twenty-third-century four-person mobile biosphere.	**The Collectibles Show.** Antique "clothes": various materials that were sewn together and used to cover the body in pre-twenty-third-century Earth.
PSY Psychic Network	No listing necessary	
TVL1	**The Bob Newhart Show.** A xenotropic lingual rhododendron comes to Bob seeking advice, but the tables are turned and Bob ends up taking part in a workshop where he learns to photosynthesize.	**The Dick Van Dyke Show.** Alan Brady wants to be the first show to go live from the center of a black hole, but it turns out Buddy's allergic to negative ions!

	9:30	10:00
TVL2	**I Love Lucy.** Lucy and Ethel plan a surprise party to welcome Fred back from his cryogenic deep freeze, but in a series of hijinks, they unfreeze the wrong man: guest star Walt Disney!	**TV Land Blenders Hour.** Ricky Ricardo doesn't know what to make of his newest singing guest at the Club Babaloo, Latka Gravas (Andy Kaufman), but Lucy does! Yup, this is the classic worm-hole episode.
TVL3	**Bewitched.** Darrin is stumped when the new client wants a whole new campaign for the Incandescent Proto Nubial Internet Translators. Then a visit from Aunt Clara inspires him, but also turns his client into a Xentronian—a very grumpy Xentronian!	**I Dream of Jeannie.** While on time-share, time-travel vacation in ancient Greece, Jeannie and Major Nelson run into Dr. Bellows. Bellows's attempts to spy on them enrages Zeus, who banishes him to take over for Sisyphus, until Jeannie intervenes.
TVL4	**The Honeymooners.** Ralph's new biotransport route takes him through the worst part of Alpha Centauri, so he and Ed take self-defense classes.	**Welcome Back, Kotter.** It looks as if the delinquents are finally going to graduate, until Epstein's mother arrives and says she never wrote those excuses. Guest star: Orson Welles.
VIA		**The Cuisine of Modern Pluto.** Cooking show (in odorvision where available).
WPIX	**The Three Stooges.** (R)	
ZPX	**Zxytron!** Discussion. Host Zxytron welcomes interdimensional couples and sees how they make their relationships work when they don't even exist in the same space-time continuum.	

old sitcom stars never die.

THEY SOLVE CRIMES!

Buddy Ebsen goes from affluent hillbilly to private investigator. Andy Griffith from small-town sheriff to small-town lawyer. Jack Klugman from slovenly sportswriter to crusading coroner. Dick Van Dyke from comedy writer to medical sleuth. Eddie Albert from befuddled farm hopeful, to con-game-busting ex-bunco man. Carroll O'Connor from bigoted dockworker to—well, barkeep first, but then—righteous southern sheriff.

Obviously, the television path to success and longevity leads from sitcom to crime drama (with the exception of Judd Hirsch, who was fighting crime as Delvecchio, then driving a taxi, and was last seen hanging out with Bob Newhart). Given this rule, we would like to suggest that the television machine begin work on the following ten shows.

1. *You Want I Should Solve the Crime Already?*

Move over Rhoda. Now Valerie Harper is Amy Friedman, a New York Jew running from her past and, more specifically, her mother. She takes up residence in the heart of Texas working as a police dispatcher whose irrepressible curiosity and knack for solving crimes often take her far from her switchboard.

2. *Feel the Burn*

If you thought *Three's Company* was steamy, just wait. Suzanne Somers plays Terry, a Tulsa aerobics instructor whose fine physical conditioning is often called upon by the local authorities, whether a speedy purse snatcher is on the loose, miscreants are fleeing up office stairs, or the key to unraveling the mystery lies in understanding a fine point of "jazzercise."

3. *That's the Man!*

If Oscar can do it, why not Felix? Tony Randall plays Neville Warwick, a classically trained artist who has fallen on hard times and taken up work as a police sketch artist. Neville's refined sensibility and distaste for mingling with riffraff can't overcome his burning desire to see justice done, no matter how many times he has to erase the nose and try again!

4. *We, Spy*

Tina Louise and Dawn Wells are off the island, and on a mission! Hired as CIA operatives, Ginger maintains her front as "movie star" while Mary Ann establishes a cover as her wardrobe assistant. The two travel the world of international espionage, taking on assignments from an unseen contact known only as Sherwood (voice of Jack Carter), and regularly make contact with "The Professor," who provides them with ingenious spy gadgets and weaponry.

5. *Law and Order III: Twin Justice*

Patty Duke has made enough made-for-TV movies; it's time for a triumphant return to series television. They're cousins, identical cousins, as Duke reprises her original dual role; now Patty Lane is the committed and idealistic public defender while Cathy Lane is the no-nonsense district attorney. Whether a matter of constitutional rights, or simple common sense, the two lock horns in the quest for justice. To ensure continuity with the original series, Cathy does still adore crêpes suzette, and a hot dog can still make Patty lose control.

6. *Carpaccio*

Robin Williams managed to escape being typecast as Mork, so why not ALF? Still an alien, still a puppet with an attitude, now he's Lieutenant Ralph Carpaccio, a Detroit police detective who's just about out of chances. Street-wise, insubordinate, he's one cop who plays by his own rules. Until they rip the badge off his fur, Carpaccio will do everything within his power to clean up the filth of the Motor City.

7. Bentley of the Yard

George Jefferson's effete upstairs neighbor is back in his native Britannia, and now he's taken up residence at Scotland Yard. Whether solving a crime, taking a spot of tea, or having his able assistant Sidney walk on his bad back, Bentley is unmistakably Bentley.

8. One Crime at a Time

Bonnie Franklin is back! Though *One Day at Time* started as a sitcom, it became the most maudlin, self-conscious, dreary show ever foisted upon the American viewing public. Now, it's a crime drama, and every bit as maudlin, self-conscious, and dreary, but that's okay, because now it's not supposed to be funny! Pat Harrington is back as Schneider, a Methodist minister who is confined to a wheelchair. Together, they search for wrongdoers and, more important, for a better understanding of themselves and their tortured emotional lives.

9. Small Thunders!

Gary Coleman, Soleil Moon Frye, and Emmanuel Lewis team up as a special internal security force at a major theme park. Undersized and undercover, this sexy trio claims no job is too big for them. Based in part on Coleman's real-life experience as a two-fisted security guard who plays by his own rules.

10. Meter Maid

Though Lucille Ball herself has passed away, the continuing love affair with the comedienne and the American public was too strong to resist. The star of this series is a life-size puppet version of the daffy redhead, with a voice provided by sampling and re-creating lines from her previous series. To explain the slightly technical quality of her voice, this Meter Maid is a newly invented robot. But sure enough, they gave her a little too much personality and "Lucy 1138" is never content with just handing out parking tickets, not when there are more serious crimes in which she could meddle!

tv's 15 greatest grumps

When things go wrong, when someone's crazy scheme unravels, when it's just ridiculous . . . that's when they go to work. The ornery, the cantankerous, the disbelieving. Pass the Prozac! Who are TV's quintessential grumps?

1. Perry "Don't Call Me Chief!" White

The world's toughest boss, you'd have to be Superman to please him.

2. Quincy

Always on a rampage. Must have been pent-up frustration from all those years of living with Felix.

3. Louie De Palma

Caged fury.

4. Archie Bunker

The last decent upstanding American left.

5. Captain Binghamton

The flip side of Bilko in a way; a sneering, fast-talking, bespectacled officer, but on the side of rules and regulations.

6. Mr. Mooney

Lucy had to keep topping every previous disaster she had created in ten years on TV. It's a wonder Mooney survived. (Gale Gordon makes the list twice, since he took a turn at Mr. Wilson, too.)

7. Oliver Douglas

A man who spent a lifetime as a lawyer, studying rhetoric, logic, and philosophy, only to land in a Kafkaesque world where truth was very flexible and logic had no meaning.

8. Ed Brown

The Man of *Chico and the Man,* although once you've seen Jack Albertson floating around Willy Wonka's chocolate factory, it's hard to take him too seriously.

9. Mr. Roper

He always wakes up on the wrong side of the bed . . . the side next to Mrs. Roper.

10. Uncle Charley

King Sourpuss. (Made Bub seem like a pussycat by comparison.)

11. Carla Tortelli

Deeply bitter and the only woman to make the "grump" list.

12. Mr. Wilson of *Dennis the Menace*

Joseph Kearns (the first one) was best, always in such torment, but Gale Gordon suffered, too.

13. Andy Rooney

How did this grumpy whiner get onto *60 Minutes* anyway? Just tickled Mike Wallace's funny bone or something?

14. Herbert T. Gillis

He didn't hold back his feelings about Dobie. His catchphrase? "I gotta kill that boy."

15. Dr. David Banner

Don't make him angry; you won't like him when he's angry . . . and he's gone through so many shirts already!

the punctuation awards

Perhaps it was *The Electric Company* that said it best: "Punc, punc, punc, punctuation! They are those little marks that use their influence . . . to help a sentence make more sense." Though underrated, and often overlooked, punctuation marks have played an integral part in our television heritage. Here are the most important uses of punctuation in the history of the medium.

Best Use of Abbreviation
St. Elsewhere

There have been lots of Mr.s and Dr.s and U.S.s, some P.I.s, and even one M.E. (*Quincy, M.E.*) but not many Saints (Besides *The Saint,* and Simon Templar spelled it out)

Best Use of a Comma
Welcome Back, Kotter

Only a schoolteacher would have insisted that it would be proper to include the partial stop in welcoming Mr. Kotter back to his roots. It seems to us that the show *Have Gun Will Travel* needed it more. Runners up include *Murder, She Wrote* and *Love, American Style.*

Best Use of an Exclamation Mark

E!

Would it have been a network, if not for the exclamation point? The mark declared this cable channel to be important, even urgent, as a source for self-promoting interviews and self-reflexive reports on "entertainment news" an oxymoron if ever there was one. They narrowly edge out *Emergency!*

Best Use of two Exclamation Marks

What's Happening!!

It's not just a show, it's an exclamation! And one exclamation point might be enough for *That's Incredible!* or *Sugar Time!* but for Raj, Dwayne, Rerun, and the rest, it took two to express how truly excited they were. And when it came time for *What's Happening, Now!!,* well, the excitement didn't come down one notch.

Best Use of Quotation Marks

The Nat "King" Cole Show

After all, we wouldn't want people to accidentally think he was really the King!

Best Use of Asterisks

*M*A*S*H*

Why no asterisk after the *H?* Army protocol, we suppose.

Best Use of A Colon

Wanted: Dead or Alive

Steve McQueen's TV Western.

Best Use of the Accent Ague

Exposé

This was the title used for syndication of the show *Target: The Corruptors*. I guess they thought they would have a better shot at a Punctuation Award if they got out of the colon category.

Best Use of a Slash

20/20

There was also *East Side/West Side*, a gritty 1964 drama starring George C. Scott, and, of course, *E/R*, the sitcom that preceded *ER*.

Best Use of the Ampersand

The Adventures of Ozzie & Harriet

The Nelsons were television pioneers in many ways, none more important than in paving the way for *Simon & Simon*, *Cagney & Lacey*, *Mork & Mindy*, *Laverne & Shirley*, *Kate & Allie* and many, many more.

Best Use of the Buck Sign

Vega$

In comparison to this innovative usage, such shows as *The $64,000 Question* seem positively bland. *Arli$$* is simply a cheap attempt to up the ante.

Best Use of an Apostrophe in a Contraction

Diff'rent Strokes

While the early television hit *Amon 'n' Andy* did actually have two apostrophes, the daring insertion of the apostrophe in the middle of a word gave the nod to Gary Coleman's first hit show. (Well, you never know, he might make another.) Claude Akins's drama about truckers, *Movin' On*, gets an honorable mention.

Best Use of an Apostrophe in a Possessive

Rowan & Martin's Laugh-in

Yes, there was also *Ryan's Hope* among many others.

Best Use of a Hyphen

Hawaii 5-0

And also best use of surfing footage, but that's irrelevant right now.

Best Absence of Hyphen

F Troop

Doesn't it just cry out for something? And yet that's the beauty of it.

Best Use of an Em-Dash

I'm Dickens—He's Fenster

Marty Ingels and John Astin were the leads in this unjustly forgotten sitcom.

Best Use of a Question Mark

Who's the Boss? (1954)

Who's the Boss? (1984–92)

What else could it be but a tie. The first was a game show in which we met the secretaries of famous personalities. The second, of course, was Tony Danza's situation comedy.

Best Combination of Two Punctuation Marks in one Title

Car 54, Where Are You?

Still one of the best show titles ever.

Best Use of Periods in an Acronym
The Man from U.N.C.L.E.

The United Network Command for Law and Enforcement. What else? The short-lived 1980 show *B.A.D. Cats,* which was about the L.A.P.D.'s "burglary and auto detail," finished a distant second, despite featuring an early TV role for Michelle Pfeiffer. Not to forget *T.H.E. Cat,* the 1966–67 half-hour action series featuring the young Robert Loggia as a cat burglar turned crime fighter. In that case, the letters were actually the initials of his name: "Thomas Hewitt Edward Cat."

Best Use of Irregular Capitalization
CHiPs

And the best use of Erik Estrada so far, although we are all waiting for his next vehicle.

Best and Only Use of a Decimal Point
Colt .45

It may surprise you, but this Western is apparently the only TV show ever to employ a decimal point in its title.

tv
land
haiku

The haiku is an ancient Japanese verse form. It is composed of a strict seventeen-syllable cadence, arranged in three lines of five, seven, and five syllables. In general it's a highly imagistic and allusive form, requiring poets to get at the essence of their subject with absolute economy of words and images. Thus, naturally, it is a wonderful form for expressing the essential truth in some of our favorite TV shows and characters.

"Family Affair"
Mom and Dad are gone,
But Uncle Bill is rich, yay!
Who wants pony rides?

"Three's Company"
Chrissie to Cindy.
Terri, too. Then: a butterfly!
Roper to Furley.

"Ralph Kramden Ink"
Oh, one of these days,
Yeah, Alice, one of these days
Bang Zoom, to the Moon.

"Deputy Festus Hagen"
Grizzled but righteous,
Gnarly Festus, rawhide tough,
Don't he never bathe?

"Green Acres"

Absurdity rains

On Hooterville's soil and it's

Eva not Zsa Zsa.

"Tripper Entendre"

A would-be Fairy

And the Beagle is Regal

Whose kisses are his?

"B.A. Baracus"

Who pities the fool?

Mr. T (B.A.) P.O.ed?

I pity the fool.

"Dragnet"

Stern morality

Blue squares bust far-out hippies.

The names have been changed.

"Petticoat Junction"

Movin' kinda slow

Rural maidens dance to spring

The dog has no name.

"Julia"

Her starched white linen

Why does Corey always yell?

Prejudice is bad.

"Kojak"

No sure things, baby.

Want a guarantee? Buy a

Refrigerator.

"Herman Munster"

Needy as a child

But eight feet tall with neck bolts

Don't run from Herman!

"The Douglas House"

Bub became Charley.

Out with Mike! Adopt Ernie!

Do you think Steve drank?

"Sanford and Son"

Junkyard of the soul.

Cast-off, forgotten. Say what?

Metaphor, dummy.

The Honeymooners

No one gets rich quick

Open your big mouth and laugh

You see, Ralph is fat.

"Gunsmoke"

Here in Dodge City

Ornery coots ain't done right

Stop! Bang. Good guys win.

"The Lone Ranger"

Hi ho masked lawman

Silver horse, silver bullets

Oh and Tonto, too.

"Hogan's Heroes"

Underground allies

What Tunnels? I know nothing.

Silly Old Germans!

"Lt. Theo Kojak"

Gritty crime-rid streets

His baldness and badness wreak

Lollipop justice.

"Jeannie"

Pink smoke hissing free

She hides her belly button

Or does she have one?

"My Three Sons"

Cartoon feet tap truths.

Problem? Solved! Lessons are learned.

What happened to Bub?

10
entertainment
careers

EACH BUILT ON A SINGLE IDEA

Not everybody needs to be Thomas Edison; sometimes all you need is that one inspiration.

RANK	PERSON	THE IDEA	THE RESULT
1.	Casey Kasem	Play the songs in reverse order of sales leading up to number one.	Top 40 Countdowns, with little stories to keep you tuned through the break.
2.	Allen Funt	Play practical jokes on people and tape it.	*Candid Camera* (and before that, a radio show called *Candid Microphone*).
3.	Vincent Price	The Creepy Thing.	A legend.
4.	Ross Bagdasarian	Use audio manipulations to create high-pitched versions of songs.	The Chipmunks and their "music."
5.	Robin Leach	Envy	A luxurious and fabulous lifestyle . . . for Leach.
6.	Foster Brooks	Drunk is funny.	A comedy hangover.
7.	Phyllis Diller	What if a woman in show business claimed to be unattractive?	A million variety shows, but never a series . . .
8.	Irwin Allen	Big effects on a limited budget.	His movies were disasters.

RANK	PERSON	THE IDEA	THE RESULT
9.	Clayton Moore	I *am* the Lone Ranger. (Anyway, it's my Lone Ranger mask, and I'm wearing it.)	A lawsuit.
10.	Ray J. Johnson	One bit, where he would explain, "You can call me Ray, or you can call me Jay . . ."	Well . . . we didn't guarantee that these were *big* careers.

the 11 greatest hair crises

IN TV HISTORY

1. Mary's hair "bump"
2. Ted Danson
3. Greg's hair dyed orange by Bobby
4. Monica's haircut
5. Jan's wig
6. The bizarre bottled red of *The Lucy Show* years
7. Laura blabbing that Alan Brady is bald
8. Bub's hair-growing tonic
9. Dobie going slowly brunette
10. David Letterman 1991–93
11. Jerry Seinfeld shaving his chest hair

the innovators
OF TV LAND

They were the originators, the founders, the legends of a golden age . . . they were "The Innovators of TV Land." Beginning with the 1996 launch, TV Land aired a vignette series—approximately one-minute-long spots—of contemporary interviews with the "forgotten" legends of the Golden Age of Television.

Each spot allowed the now-aging innovators to tell their story, in their own words. Primarily a series of close-ups on the weathered faces of these characters as they speak, the spots also featured occasional cutaways to mementos, photos, clips, and other documentary evidence of their work.

Were they real? No. The truth is that we created the characters and wrote their scripts. No doubt there is someone somewhere who invented the "blank" or first wrote the words "and now a word from our sponsor." But finding them seemed beyond us, so we were left with our imaginings. Although, after writing the parody about "Bowling for Bucks" we discovered that Robert Claster of Claster Productions was the man responsible for the real syndicated hit "Bowling for Dollars," as well as for "Romper Room" and many other fine productions. Perhaps, with more research, we can find the real innovators responsible for the very first "spit take" and all the others. Until then, what follows are the scripts for the complete series.

BUTCH "LAREDO" CLYDESDALE: THE BLANK

"Dangerous? Wull, hell yeah it were dangerous. But back in them days we was young and fool-hardy. And fearless. And stupid, too, in retrospect. That helped a lot.

"For movie folk, Westerns weren't so hard. But for television, see, you had to make the show every week—and what with all the gunfire, you'd constantly be losing extras, horses, even regular actors. And you could never do more than one take. It warn't hardly practical, d'y'see?

"So one time I'm laid up for a week—I took a couple of slugs in the shoulder—and I get to thinkin' and fiddlin' around with some casings, and I made the first blank. You could let 'er rip all day, and no one would get hurt!

"Funny story about that, the director of that picture swings by the hospital to visit us all, so I figure on a little practical joke. He walks in and I says, 'Johnson, I been plugged making one of your damn Westerns for the last time,' and I pull out a big old Colt and shoot one of the blanks at him.

"The fool keeled over and died right there. Heart attack they say. The very next week, we started filming the first-ever TV Western—shot 109 episodes without a single fatality. Gunshot fatality, anyhow."

CARL KLIPPINGER: VERTICAL HOLD

"My neck was getting tired—constantly watching the TV image pass by. [Mr. Klippinger moves his head as though following an image going up repeatedly.] Up and up and up.

"The first thing we tried was a sort of large spinning gyroscope. Then there was a rotisserie system—in which a series of televisions rotated, thereby keeping the actual image in a singular, if you will, place. But you could not change the channel without banging the living daylights out of your hand. Also, it scared the cat.

"Finally, rather than manipulating the external set, we began to tinker with the internal electronics—exploring the reinversion of existing technology not established for the express purposes of the holding of the . . . uh, vertical pattern. Essentially, we took the horizontal hold . . . and uh, we simply rotated it, 180 degrees.

"We added the button to control it later. Very clean, simple. Did not scare the cat. The cat could stay and watch the television."

MARY WESTON: THE TEST PATTERN

"Oh yes, yes, yes. I was a painter then. Painted all the time. Just paint, paint, paint morning till night. Oh Lord. Painting like a painting fool.

"Did I offer you fudge? What? Oh yeah. They just needed a little something to put on the air so people wouldn't think that their set was on the fritz. I painted firemen, and farms, but they wanted the outside to be lines that you could focus on, and the channel name and all that was left was a little tiny circle. And I just . . . painted an Indian Chief.

"It didn't have to be in color but I like color, so I painted it in color. I like colors. Do you like colors? Everyone likes colors. I bet even that stern old Indian chief likes the bright colors I made his headdress. Don't you, Mr. Chief?"

GOODMAN CARTER: COPYWRITER

"In those days, you see, it was all new. Television was new. We didn't know what we were doing, and we didn't care. There were no rules. We wrote, and it went on the air. It was in that context that I was able to create the phrase.

"Some of the funny boys had tried being cute with the throws to the commercials, you know, 'It's time to pay the bills'—but I knew there had to be a better way, simpler—who wants to pay the bills? Not me!

"I was working on the scripts when somebody says, real polite, 'Goodman, can I have a word with you?' Bingo! A word, what's a word? Nothing! A word from the sponsor—who could object to that?

" 'Sponsors?' Oh yeah. Today on the PBS . . . it makes me laugh they call them 'underwriters.' We used that—1951! And now a word from the underwriters. But people thought they were undertakers, see? [He laughs.]

" 'Stay tuned,' that was one of mine—and 'We'll be right back'—what can I say? It was a time of great creative opportunity.

"I also wrote 'Don't touch that dial'—very evocative if I do say so myself, but, of course, the residuals are drying up on that one. I'm probably the one guy in America who resents the remote control."

MARVIN DALRYMPLE: COMPOSER

"I have personally written over fourteen hundred songs, and nearly three hundred of what we in the music business call the musical stings. But I suppose I will always be remembered most of all for this little ditty. [Mr. Dalrymple plays a familiar cascading tune on his trombone: "wha wha wha whaaaah."]

"I was fast, very fast. Many of the top producers turned to me because I could score an episode in an hour. A theme song took me two, maybe three hours.

"So they're looking for a piece of music for this particular moment. He says to me, 'Marvin, it has to be funny, but Marvin, it has to have pathos, and Marvin, I need it tonight.' I say sure, and it also has to catch mice and stand on its hands—but I work on it anyway. And I got it. 'Wha wha wha whaaaah.'

"I also did 'whee wohn'—the sound for those kinda crazy cuts. You know, you know. Guy says, 'Oh no, *I'm* not wearing a dress,' then you cut, with a 'whee wohn,' and he's in the dress saying, 'How do I look?'

"Later, I became something of a specialist in creating the tunes of tuneless humming—you know, a guy's trying to be nonchalant, 'Yah dee dee, yah dee dah.' I *wrote* that! I love this business!"

MORTY SCHLICTER: THE SPIT TAKE

"People say to me, 'Morty Schlicter, you are a genius.' I say, 'I don't know, maybe I am.'

"[Mr. Schlicter brings visitors to a stained shirt that he has had framed and hung in his study.] This is the very shirt I was wearing. See? A lot landed on me. [At this, Schlicter grows contemplative.] I'm sorry—I'm a sentimental fool, but those coffee stains . . . they always get me.

"I'll say this. It was not an accident, it was not luck, it was not easy—it was something that came out of literally thousands of performances. Now drooling had been part of the act from way back, and we had toyed around with spitting toast—but it didn't fly right.

"That particular night, Bud was a mess—Bud Wohlers—he was something of a sauce artist, I think I can say that now. Anyway, he's stumbling his way through the script, and the idea occurred to me, 'boom' like that. Genius? I don't know. So I take a nice swig of the coffee—terrible coffee. Bud finally gets to his line—and I give him the spit take, the first spit take.

"Oh, it was a beauty, the explosion, the spritz, the froth—it was all there the very first time. Naturally, we kept it in—became a regular part of the show. Later, other people—some very big names, names you would know—came to me for coaching, to learn the spit take.

"A genius? Maybe. That's for others to say."

MARJORY WHITESIDE: BOWLING FOR BUCKS

"I had noticed three things. Four things. No, five things. Well, really only three things. I had noticed three things. Three things people like to do.

"[Mrs. Whiteside's memories are now somewhat scattered, and she is nervous before our cameras.] So they said, Marjory, fill a half hour, here's a camera. And it was not one of these shoulder-camera things—it was big and immobile. You had to park it. So I thought of the three things.

"This is my bowling ball. [She accidentally picks up a vase. Noticing the mistake, she puts it down and finds her bowling ball.] Oh yes, yes, *this* is my bowling ball. This isn't *my* bowling ball.

"The three things? Well, honestly I can't remember the other two, but one of them was watching local, honest homegrown talent try to win very small amounts of money by bowling.

"I think . . . you say I invented that?"

tv's 10 best specials

1. *A Charlie Brown Christmas*
2. Elvis Presley's 1968 comeback special
3. *The Grinch Who Stole Christmas*
4. *The Undersea World of Jacques Cousteau*
5. National Geographic specials
6. *Free to Be . . . You and Me*
7. Jackie Kennedy's White House Tour
8. Rankin/Bass Christmas specials
9. *A Very Brady Christmas*
10. Bob Hope Christmas shows

the 7 great works of literature

THAT LED TO THE SITCOM

While few contemporary critics will argue that sitcoms are actually *better* than the literary works that make up the "canon" of Western civilization, it is widely agreed that it is easier to place advertisements in TV shows than in epic poems. This is the sort of logic that allows us to propose that the works listed below—though certainly fine artistic works on their own—are, ultimately, best considered as precursors to the modern situation comedy.

1. *Don Quixote*

In fact, this sprawling sixteenth-century Spanish "novel" more closely resembles the contemporary sitcom than any other dramatic or literary form. It is a series of comic misadventures that return the key characters right back to where they started, and on the road to the next situation. The vain, misguided Quixote and his self-deprecating but more competent sidekick Sancho Panza are a familiar pair to sitcom fans. Think of Maxwell Smart and 99, Ralph Kramden and Ed Norton, even Lucy and Ethel.

2. *The Canterbury Tales*

It's really *Seinfeld*. (If only professors of Middle English could convince their students of that!) It's a poem about "nothing" in which the central plot is really just an excuse to tell stories that keenly satirize the strange realities of the contemporary scene. And "The Miller's Tale" is just as outrageous as "The Contest."

3. Six Characters in Search of an Author

Friends, by Luigi Pirandello?

4. A Midsummer Night's Dream

It's the great bard, sure, but it's often been argued that if he lived today, given his predilection for playing to the groundlings, he'd be writing sitcoms. And bawdy ones, no doubt. This play shows that he could have scripted some swell episodes of *Ally McBeal* or *The Larry Sanders Show*—if he could have quit with the iambic pentameter gimmick. Why this particular play among all his comedies? Sexual dalliances, strange pranks, and—like every great sitcom—it includes a famous two-part wedding episode.

5. Romeo and Juliet

Bridget Loves Bernie?

6. Waiting for Godot

Like *The Abbott and Costello Show* or Uncle Miltie's *Texaco Star Theater,* Beckett's great play is rooted in the vaudeville stage. It dramatizes the existential dilemma of the sitcom character—to whom nothing can really happen, because no matter what outlandish events seem to be occurring, we all know that nothing will really change, because they have to be back in the same basic situation for next week's episode.

7. The Castle

Again, the defining quality of the sitcomic structure is a lack of closure, the willingness to endlessly explore the same essential territory, with new lines each week. Franz Kafka's satirical novel could easily be broken up into episodes. If you cast Eddie Albert, Eva Gabor, and Arnold Ziffel, you wouldn't even have to change the lines that much. Can't you imagine the TV version of Kafka's protagonist sputtering, "But that's impossible! No one . . . but who? How the . . ." And Oliver Douglas could give an impassioned performance of the central character. "Because it was a message from the Castle, Mr. Douglas felt that it must have some meaning, but he could find none."

Jan
Brady's
13

GREATEST FAILINGS

13. Her irrepressible practical joking can get pretty annoying.

12. Her desire to be an only child almost cost her a trip to the "hoe down."

11. She lost those blueprints in Cincinnati.

10. Her secret admirer turned out to be Alice.

9. She thought the engraving for the platter cost 56 cents, not 56 cents per letter!

8. She never once convinced a rock star or professional athlete to visit.

7. Even though she did briefly hold the crown of Miss Popularity, the winner of the Honor Society award was *not* Jan Brady.

6. She wears glasses.

5. She makes up phony boyfriends.

4. She's not good at anything.

3. She has drab hair.

2. She has freckles.

1. She's not Marcia.

8 great knockoffs

IN TV HISTORY

So you're thinking of a career in television? That's terrific. You're reading the right book, because there's no better place to find the TV Hits of Tomorrow than in the TV Hits of Yesterday. Ever since TV got its birth by taking everything it could from radio, there has been a long and storied tradition of "stealing" or at least "reinventing" ideas. Just remember, there are no new ideas, just new executive producers.

1. *America's Funniest Home Videos*

An idea that could be dreamed up only in a world where the technology exists for people to make their own hilarious videos, right? Wrong. In 1963, George Fenneman (Groucho's sidekick on *You Bet Your Life*) hosted *Your Funny, Funny Films*, a collection of intentional and unintentional comedy created on home movies.

2. *The X-Files*

Cutting-edge drama that meshed gritty realism with fantastic creatures like vampires and werewolves and aliens, with a seeker of the truth who constantly battled to prove himself to skeptical colleagues. In 1974–75, it was Darren McGavin who starred as *Kolchak: The Night Stalker.*

3. *Who Wants to Be a Millionaire?*

Really just inflation's effect on *The $64,000 Question.*

4. Law and Order

The first half is a police procedural, the drama of the crime, investigation, and arrest. The second half moves to the courtroom, where prosecutors and the D.A. decide the fate of the accused. The show starred Ben Gazzara as the detective; Chuck Connors as the attorney. It was called *Arrest and Trial,* and it aired on ABC in 1963–64.

5. Murphy Brown

Mary goes network.

6. ER

You know what George Clooney would be good in? When I look at that big gorgeous hunk of man, those eyes that pierce your very soul, that understanding smile that makes everything okay, I'm thinking doctor! And to give us lots of stories and action, let's put the show in an emergency room. We'll set it in Chicago, and we'll call it *E/R*. And here's the kicker: It's a sitcom! That's right. George Clooney was in a 1985 sitcom called *E/R*—with a slash.

7. Face the Nation

Sure, now you think of it as a legendary long-running staple of television news, but when it launched in 1954, it was CBS's blatant knockoff of NBC's *Meet the Press,* which has been on the air since 1947.

8. Morton Downey

Let's put a guy named Morton Downey on TV to host his own show. In 1988, it was caustic son hosting *The Morton Downey, Jr. Show,* inciting controlled riots with his abusive liberal-baiting. Back in 1949, his father was a singer and host of a regular NBC live musical half hour *The Morton Downey Show* (also known as *The Mohawk Showroom*). Okay, maybe it doesn't exactly count as a knockoff, but Jerry Springer probably got inspired to air genuine mayhem from Junior (although Jerry's real inspiration may have been *The Richard Bey Show,* an equally tasteless melange of man's inhumanity to man, seen on UPN).

tv's 20 best actors

1. Art Carney
2. Mary Tyler Moore
3. Dick Van Dyke
4. Lucille Ball
5. Andy Griffith
6. Bill Cosby
7. Jackie Gleason
8. Bob Newhart
9. Carol Burnett
10. Carroll O'Connor
11. Buddy Ebsen
12. Don Knotts
13. Jack Benny
14. Patty Duke
15. Sid Caesar
16. Steve Allen
17. Alan Alda
18. Ed Asner
19. Fred Gwynne
20. Phil Silvers

the 7 worst things

TELEVISION CREATED

Television is a great and glorious achievement, but every advance of our civilization has some inevitable costs. Here are some of television's less fortunate legacies.

1. Low Reading Scores

Someday reading may be completely obsolete, but then how will anyone be able to read the *TV Guide?*

2. Professional Wrestling

Though some professional wrestling—staged "exhibitions" that purported to be competition—had existed before, it was television that created the tacky, ridiculous, and violent spectacles that we know today.

3. Short Attention Spans

Though some may point fingers at MTV, the decreasing attention span of the American public is a result of the very nature of television itself. Unlike reading, conversation, or contemplation, the tempo of entire experience is controlled, and any diminished interest could result in lower ratings. Thus, every kind of television, from comedy to music to the nightly network news, has become more manic than ever.

4. Local News Promotion

The promise of "Details at eleven!" has justified more misinformation, shock tactics, and shoddy journalism than three hundred years of newspaper headline battles put together. Yes, we all have morbid curiosity about train wrecks, sexual deviance, and celebrity scandals, and maybe the news even has a responsibility to cover them, but today you can't get through an evening of TV with the family without being interrupted by "Your water may be poison, and the serial rapist remains at large. Details at eleven." It's no wonder the American public is paranoid.

5. Public Access Pornography

Not only is it an ever-present threat to our children, but the quality is very poor.

6. Commercials

Yes, they can be entertaining, even enlightening, but we must point out the nefarious way that more and more commercial messages are jammed into our burgeoning minds. And on the niche channels, there just aren't enough sponsors to go around, so we end up seeing the same commercials with such deadening frequency that any sway they once may have had is lost to the bitter resentment that we come to feel toward the product.

7. Jerry Springer

Let's hope God isn't watching it, because if it's any representation of humankind at all, you can just wave in the next flood and start again.

the top 100 sitcom episodes

What are the best TV shows ever made? Not such a difficult question, really. A simple matter of finding the series that were hits, that proved their popularity the first time around and keep on proving it in syndication and cable. But which are the greatest individual *episodes*? That is a challenge.

How can one hope to sort out the apples and oranges the question places before us? How can we hope to compare Lucy's inimitable performance in "Vitameatavegamin" with the stunning final twist of *Newhart*? How to measure Ralph and Norton's unforgettable "$99,000 Answer" with *Leave it to Beaver*'s charming "Captain Jack"?

It would be too easy to engage in a subjective appraisal of each episode's merits. We each have personal favorites, moments that stand out, performances that helped define the sitcom genre. How can we eliminate subjective opinions and arrive at a scientific, objective, and therefore infallible system for measuring each episode?

The answer is the Big TV Satisfaction Formula.

THE BIG TV SATISFACTION FORMULA

We watch television for many reasons, but it all comes down to the pleasure we take in the show. How much are we involved with the characters' travails? Which episodes stay with us, as sturdy guideposts to living our own lives? How much do we laugh? So, in fact, it all comes down to a series of easily quantifiable variables, a collection of measurements that can isolate each possible factor that can increase our "viewing satisfaction."

With years of experience, the TV experts of TV Land were uniquely prepared to take on this challenge, to bring hard science to bear on this difficult series of questions. It was up to us to create the Big TV Satisfaction Formula.

For the casual reader the following details may be more technical than necessary. If you prefer, you can skip right to the list of great episodes along with all the other features of this volume. However, for the dedicated student of television, a close scrutiny of the formula itself will be amply rewarded. Furthermore, a thorough understanding of our system will dispel any doubts that our list of the Top 100 Episodes of All Time is not just another haphazard collection of opinions and hearsay, but is, in fact, the definitive and scientifically verifiable list.

The following is our best effort to explain, in laymen's terms, the patented formula that allows us to combine all the factors that contribute to Big TV Satisfaction into a single number for any episode ever made, or to be made.

THE FORMULA

This is the actual scientific formula (patent pending).

The Big TV Satisfaction Ratio =

$$\left\{ \frac{4\,(B + C)}{} + \frac{[(D + E) \times F] + 2A}{2} + \frac{G \times \sqrt{[H + I + (H - I)^2]}}{4} + \right.$$

$$\left. (1.9\,J + 1.9\,K + 0.4\,L + 1.2\,M + 0.6\,N) \right\} \times \frac{1}{3}$$

where

A = SyndicoDurability™

B = Comic Valence

C = Emotional Resonance

Writing is represented by (D + E)

D = Story

E = Characters

F = Acting

G = Quintessence

Total originality factor is $\sqrt{[H + I + (H - I)^2]}$

H = Series Originality

I = Episodic Originality

The Sitcom Factor is $(1.9\,J + 1.9\,K + 0.4\,L + 1.2\,M + 0.6\,N)$

J = Historical Significance

K = Celebrity

L = Gimmickry

M = Theme Song and Open

N = Kitsch

THE ANNOTATED BTVS FORMULA

Again, this section is probably too technical in nature for the general reader, but a careful study of our methodology can be very enlightening. For those seeking more information or background reading, we recommend basic algebra texts, the writing of baseball SABRmetrician Bill James, or just looking over old copies of *Entertainment Weekly*. For those seeking unrelated works of extremely dense and difficult writing, we recommend the essays of Max Weber or anything in the field of psycholinguistics.

THE VARIABLES

SyndicoDurability™

SyndicoDurability™ is the estimated number of times a given episode has been rerun per year since its initial run ended; plus or minus the video-availability factor. This is a very important factor to consider. Obviously, the impact of a given show on the American consciousness is limited by the number of times it has actually been seen.

The effects of this factor are many. One is that it practically eliminates shows of recent vintage. Even the finest current episode has little chance of achieving a high BTVS ratio until it has entered second run either on cable or local syndication. This explains why the overall list seems skewed toward older classics. Also, shows like *The Honeymooners*—with the original thirty-nine episodes in constant rotation—and *I Love Lucy* have extremely high SyndicoDurability™ quotients, while otherwise fine shows like *Car 54, Where Are You?* and *The Mothers-in-Law* score quite low in the category.

Comic Valence

This is a figure representing both the estimated laughter emission and the nonvocalized amusement levels in the standard demographically balanced ideal viewer. In simplest terms, this measures how funny the episode is.

Emotional Resonance

To measure raw comedy without the more subtle humor that engages the emotions is unfair and limiting. Many other kinds of responses legitimately increase our viewing satisfaction. How much pathos? Is there true wisdom? Is it a tear jerker?

Story and Characters

These two independent measures collectively judge the writing of the episode. Among the considerations are a cohesive logical story, well-drawn characters, and, of course, joke writing.

Acting

The overall performance of the cast, with special consideration toward sitcom acting icons: double takes, spit takes, etc.

Quintessence

This is an important measure. How much does the individual episode represent the essential qualities of the show, and of the genre itself? Credit is given for the appropriate use of catch-phrases, classic situations, and archetypal plots.

Originality

An important component of what makes specific episodes stand out among the many that have been created over the years. The formula balances series originality (*Mister Ed* ranks high; *The Donna Reed Show* ranks low) with episodic originality (blind date ranks low; a date from another planet ranks high). It also gives a less original series more credit for an original episode than an original series. In general, we did not hold shows accountable for having originated outside of television. In other words, the fact that *Mister Ed* was based on the Francis the Talking Mule movies, or that Lucy had done similar plots on radio, did not count against those shows. A small deduction was taken for shows that originated as TV shows in England. *All in the Family, Three's Company,* and *Sanford and Son* all had roots on the other side of the big pond.

The Sitcom Factor

A large part of our satisfaction in watching TV comes from what the literary critic Edmund Wilson called "the shock of recognition." This is the ineffable experience of seeing ourselves, our own experiences, in the show. As Homer Simpson once stated succinctly, "It's funny because it's real." As we measure it, it also reflects our recognition of the classic elements that go into every great sitcom. It is composed of five measurable elements, each of which are multiplied by an individual factor that reflects the ideal balance.

Historical Significance

These are key developments: introduction of new characters, first and last shows, marriages, births, and other changes. It also gives credit for groundbreaking firsts: breaking racial stereotypes, employing innovative plots and guests stars, showing couples sleeping in a double bed, etc. It also gives credit for important moments of self-referential television history: for example, when *Green Acres* did an episode in which the cast performs a stage play of *The Beverly Hillbillies.*

Celebrity

This is a measurement of the overall celebrity, which begins with the regular stars, but is helped immensely by the inclusion of special guest stars, cameos, and featured players who went on to greater glory. There is always a special sense of dislocation and delight when familiar faces appear in unfamiliar roles.

Gimmickry

While similar to episodic originality, this is a distinct measurement that focuses less on the plot's uniqueness and more on the use of unusual and entertaining devices. Dream sequences, flash-back or flash-forward sequences, experiments with point of view (the *Rashomon* story line), and strange props, sets, costumes, etc.

Theme Song and Opening Sequence

Sometimes overlooked, a memorable theme song sets the tone for a great sitcom. They take us away, remind us of the central ideas of the show, and echo in our minds, providing a powerful nostalgic experience. We include the opening sequence in general because there are shows with average music, but excellent visual montages. *The Odd Couple,* for example.

Kitsch

Situation comedies are pop culture. Our satisfaction in them often reflects our recognition of the silliness, the predictability and campiness of the form. We love them almost as much for how they fail (implausible stories and character developments) as for how they succeed. This is a small but important factor in judging shows with widely disparate aesthetic goals.

Frequently Asked Question about the Big TV Satisfaction Formula

"What about dramatic television shows? Where are *St. Elsewhere* and *Gunsmoke*, *Twilight Zone* and *The Outer Limits*?"

After years of careful research and testing, we've found that these shows, though fine and entertaining in many ways, providing their own unique sort of TV Satisfaction, are just not as consistently funny as sitcoms. No matter how we run the numbers, very few of them can compete with even the lamest sitcom. For example, the classic episode of *The Twilight Zone* where Burgess Meredith steps on his glasses? Well, "Time Enough at Last" was ranked with the same BTVS score as the episode of *Punky Brewster* in which Punky resists the temptation to join the "Chick-lets." Sad, but true. Sorry, Mr. Serling, by our measure, your shows just don't compare.

Perhaps there should be a separate formula that would better measure how dramatic shows compare to each other; perhaps, someday, with enough basic research and some breakthroughs in television theory, we will be able to create a general theory of relativity that allows us to scientifically compare dramas to sitcoms. Until then, we will have to leave such argument to the realm of the speculative.

"What about nonnarrative comedy? *SCTV, Monty Python's Flying Circus* or *Saturday Night Live*? Surely these shows deserve a place among your so-called 'Top 100.' "

Again, someday we may need a formula that better accounts for the differences in situation comedies and other forms of television comedy. For now, our formula demands story and characters. When shows like *SCTV* are measured by our formula, they inevitably rank lower than most subjective observers would place them. The same problem discriminates against parody-based shows like *Fernwood 2-Nite;* although, as you will see in the list, shows like *Mary Hartman, Mary Hartman, Get Smart*, and *Police Squad* have successfully created the characters and stories that allow them to rank among TV's finest half hours.

"What doesn't make sense to me is how an episode of, say, *Family Affair* could possible rank higher than any episode in the entire series of *The Honeymooners*."

This conundrum was first discussed by Professor Will McRobb in an article in *The Journal of Popular Culture*. He has suggested that the "episodic originality" quotient ends up causing what he dubbed "The McRobb Bias." This is a tendency of the BTVS formula to include many series. He pointed out that when episode originality is measured, you are comparing that single episode to all the others in that same series. The fact that an episode of "I Love Lucy" is not as good and original as others in the series mitigates the total BTVS. Any episode that is significantly better than the other episodes in its own series gets an abnormally high BTVS score. This may be an imperfection in the formula itself, but it does reflect the viewing experience that the formula is created to measure. Aren't you more impressed by a particularly good hamburger than by an ordinary filet mignon? Isn't a stand-out episode of *My Three Sons* more impressive than an ordinary *I Love Lucy*?

"Hold on. Isn't this really just a gag? I mean, you can break it down into individual categories all you want, but isn't each individual category still essentially a subjective call, an opinion? How can you really claim this is scientific?"

You've entirely missed the point of the Big TV Satisfaction Formula! By *eliminating* judgments and opinions, we've been able to make an *objective* measurement. Would we have put all this work into the formula and created all these long lists, charts, and mathematical formulas if it was just a "gag"? Would we have been able to work on the project thanks to a federal grant jointly given to us by the FCC and the Bureau of Weights and Measures?* I don't think so. Anyway, our system makes at least as much sense as the *U.S. News & World Report* formula for rating colleges, and everybody takes them seriously.

---

* We didn't really get a grant, but only because the application was really hard to figure out. We certainly deserved one.

"Is this Big TV Satisfaction Formula the system that TV Land really uses to select which shows it airs?"

While many of the same elements that make up the BTVS make up the rationale for our programming decisions—an appreciation of shows with great characters, stories, writing, and acting—there are a host of other considerations. For one thing, we air many genres besides comedy on TV Land: dramas, Westerns, variety shows. None of these can accurately be assessed by our current BTVS formula. For another thing, we like to provide a variety of different series, exploring the full breadth of the library of television shows to which we have access. In other words, we might air a less-popular series that hasn't been seen frequently in syndication. We like to find shows that will feel fresh.

Finally, and perhaps most important, there are financial and business considerations that are not always well understood by our viewers. Basically, we sell advertising and collect fees from cable affiliates. That's our income. Our costs are our programming—plus a little marketing, promotion, overhead, stuff like that. Now, TV Land, and networks like TV Land, don't own the shows that are aired, so even if we once aired *The Addams Family*, it doesn't mean we can air it again whenever we want. Every single time we play a show, we pay for that play. So every year we have a budget to pay for programming. That means that we can't just decide which twenty series we think are the all-time best and air them. Shows that garner high ratings command high prices. It's a complex balancing act that involves negotiations with the companies that "rent" us our shows, working out which shows are available and when, and a host of other technical issues that are too tedious to worry about. We have a significant staff devoted to this task.

What does it mean to you, the viewer? It means that some of your favorite shows may not make it to TV Land because they have a history of getting low ratings. Many of the shows from the fifties and early sixties are no longer able to command enough of a rating to make it on our schedule on a regular basis. Other shows may be too popular. Shows can make more money in first-run syndication—collecting fees from scores of local channels rather than one cable entity.

Our competitors on the cable dial may beat us to the punch and lock up shows that we might ideally want. Sci-Fi might grab *Batman;* and Fox will have *The Simpsons* forever. It's a competitive world.

At the end of the day, we work hard to bring our viewers a great channel of the shows we collectively love the most. For years, before the dawn of Nick at Nite, rerun television had only existed as "filler" that local stations would use in between their national affiliate broadcasts and their own news shows. With Nick at Nite, it became clear that there was a place in prime time for classic programming. TV Land is the ultimate celebration of the television we know and love, a twenty-four-hour channel devoted to keeping on the air those shows that are alive in our hearts and minds.

notes on the entries

TRIPLE

As a point of interest, we have isolated examples of this important comic formula from many episodes. The triple (see page 11) is a common joke structure. In its most basic form, it is where two examples form a pattern, and the third interrupts it.

WHEE WOHN

Again, as a point of interest, we have cataloged "whee wohn" usages where they occur. See page 15 for a full explanation of this and some other important comic formulae. It is basically the use of editing to create a compression of time and a comic effect.

TITLES

Nowadays, TV producers title their episodes with an awareness that those titles will be used in the future. In the early days, episode titles were often thought of as a mere production convenience and were created without a thought to cleverness or relevance. *The Dick Van Dyke Show* was one of the first to make episode titles an actual part of the on-air presentation.

CREDITS

The credits are represented in order and style as closely as possible to the way they are presented on the actual episodes. Where credits were read in voice-over only, we show them in quotation marks. Sometimes actors are credited at both the beginning and end of the show, with character names only at the end. In those cases, we present only the second set. Not all the credits seen on the episodes are represented here, and we apologize to the makeup, wardrobe, lighting, sound, and numerous others whose contributions no doubt helped make these legendary episodes possible. Space prohibits such detailed attributions. In a few cases, we have provided the names of uncredited performers when that information was available from other sources.

TV, unlike film, is a writers' medium. They run the shows. We have tried to represent those responsible for contributing to the writing of each episode. The use of titles has evolved over the years. Today, most "producers," "story editors," and "executive producers" function as writers. It is a collaborative effort more than ever.

One further note. An ampersand between two names generally signifies a team, while the word *and* means both were involved, either together or in turn.

EPISODE NUMBER

Television series episodes are numbered at least twice. An original production number, which represents the season and other production details, is assigned. When the series is prepared for syndication, episodes are generally given simpler numbers, beginning with 1, usually in the order the episodes originally aired. However, there are numerous exceptions. Some series are renumbered by later syndicators. Basically, all we're saying here is that you shouldn't be surprised if some other source lists a different "episode number" than we do. It's probably not a mistake, just a difference of opinion. Also, there are a few episodes for which we were not able to ascertain an episode number.

EDITING

Most of the episodes discussed were screened and judged based on the version that is currently seen in syndication, as opposed to the original air version. In general, episodes are edited down by two or three minutes after their initial network run because the economics of television syndication require that more ad time be sold. Some episodes were screened in their full-length version, on original master tapes, home video, etc. Altogether, the result is that some scenes or dialogue you remember may no longer be a part of the episode and may not have been considered in the BTVS. Sad but true.

Over the years, editing has become less and less of a problem, because the network's standard length has grown shorter, so the syndication version has less missing. Most sitcoms come in at around twenty-four to twenty-six minutes; many syndicated versions are twenty-three or even twenty-two minutes total. Although for a show like *The Simpsons*, for example, the scripts are so tightly constructed, it is quite apparent when material is edited out. Some early sitcoms like *I Love Lucy* varied in length, and some of the original versions were as long as twenty-nine and thirty minutes. In those early days, they would simply shift the schedule slightly to accommodate the commercials. Times change, and so, alas, in some cases, does great television.

100

"Casanova Klink"
hogan's heroes

Episode 68
Original air date: October 14, 1967
Original series run: 1965–1971
Series total: 168 episodes

THE BIG TV SATISFACTION FORMULA

SyndicoDurability	8.2
Comic Valence	8.3
Emotional Resonance	7.1
Writing, Story	8.6
Writing, Characters	8.7
Acting	8.8
Quintessence	9.5
Series Originality	7.9
Episode Originality	7.9
Historical Significance	7.2
Celebrity	7.8
Gimmickry	8.1
Theme Song	8.8
Kitsch	8.4
BTVS Ratio	**76.93**

Credits

Open: Starring Bob Crane. Co-starring Werner Klemperer and John Banner. With Robert Clary, Richard Dawson, Ivan Dixon, Larry Hovis. End: Written by Bill Davenport. Produced and Directed by Edward H. Feldman. Leon Askin as General Burkhalter. Kathleen Freeman as Gertrude Linkmeyer. Woodrow Parfrey as Hugo Hindeman. Created by Bernard Fein and Albert Ruddy.

Episode Review

Sgt. Schultz bursts in on a poker game. He is at his obsequious best because of the arrival of a Gestapo agent. Burkhalter's sister Gertrude Linkmeyer is coming to be Klink's secretary, and Klink is afraid that Burkhalter is matchmaking. Klink and romance are sure-fire comedy.

Hogan uses the situation as a distraction from their latest effort to unmask an infiltrator in the underground. He encourages Klink to romance her—"She'll be putty in your hands." To which Klink responds, "I don't want her to be putty in my hands!"

Then the boys get to business, with various hijinks based on listening in on conversations. At one moment, to cover himself, Carter picks up the phone and says, "No matter who you're calling, you have the wrong number. I don't even have a phone." And hangs up. (And they never got caught!) They eventually figure out which underground agent is the infiltrator, saving the day for the Allies once again.

Hogan can now safely dismantle the distraction. He gets Klink away from Frau Linkmeyer by portraying him as a wild Casanova in front of her; she decides there must be other fish in the sea.

Notes

- Frankly, *Hogan's Heroes* in general is a good sitcom that struggles to overcome its overelaborate plots. Instead of funny situations, the writers generally worked with compelling, dramatic situations, then added the comedy. Some episodes, however, transcend this tendency. "Casanova Klink" is one of them.
- Kathleen Freeman played Gertrude Linkmeyer in four different episodes of

Hogan's Heroes. This is certainly one of her finest performances in the role, but she was also quite excellent in the later episode "Commandant Gertrude," in which she takes over Stalag 13.

- Werner Klemperer twice won the Emmy Award as Best Supporting Actor for his role as Colonel Klink. His father, Otto Klemperer, was a renowned conductor of classical music.

99

"Class Reunion"
the andy griffith show

Episode 82
Original air date: February 4, 1963
Original series run: 1960–1968
Series total: 249 episodes

Credits
Open: Starring Andy Griffith. With Ron Howard. Also starring Don Knotts. End: Directed by Charles Irving. Written by Everett Greenbaum and Jim Fritzell. Produced by Aaron Ruben. Story Consultant: Aaron Ruben. Cast: Barbara Perry, Don Haggerty, Frank Behrens, Molly Dodd, Paul Smith, Virginia Eiler. Guest star: Peggy McCay. Executive producer: Sheldon Leonard. In Association with Danny Thomas Enterprises.

Episode Review
Andy and Barney come across "The Cutlass," their high school yearbook. Naturally, they get to reminiscing, especially about their "lost loves." Before you know it, they're organizing a high school reunion. In

THE BIG TV SATISFACTION FORMULA	
SyndicoDurability	9.9
Comic Valence	7.5
Emotional Resonance	9.8
Writing, Story	8.8
Writing, Characters	8.7
Acting	9.2
Quintessence	7.9
Series Originality	7.3
Episode Originality	8.1
Historical Significance	6.4
Celebrity	5.6
Gimmickry	5.6
Theme Song	8.7
Kitsch	7.1
BTVS Ratio	**77.01**

classic form, Barney's subplot provides the comedy, while Andy's is the emotional core of the story. Barney is worried that his former flame Ramona, now married, will still have it for him bad. "I hope Ramona exercises a little self-control and don't horse around . . . I don't want to wreck a marriage!"

When the big event arrives, both of them are having a heap of trouble recognizing their old classmates. And Ramona doesn't seem to remember Barney 'tall. Even when he quotes his love letter to her: "The tears on my pillow bespeak the pain that's in my heart." Barney is crushed, but Andy assures him she's fighting the pain in her heart. Andy is disappointed, too, because Sharon DeSpain didn't make it . . . and just then she arrives in romantic glory.

They dance, rekindle the romance as if not a day had passed, and then kiss outside in the garden. Everything seems so perfect. They can't remember whatever drove them apart until they start to talk about whether they are serious about getting back together.

She likes the big city of Chicago and "trying to be a big fish in a big pond." It's all coming back to them. As much as they like each other, they value different lifestyles and will remain "old friends."

In the final scene (or coda, as it is known in dramatic structure), Andy and Barney agree it was an emotion-packed evening. Barney asks, "Do the tears on your pillow bespeak the pain that's in your heart?" And Andy can't deny it.

Notes

- Even for an *Andy* episode, a 9.8 is a very high Emotional Resonance score, more than overcoming the modest 7.5 Comic Valence.
- This episode is a sentimental journey that explores many of the themes of the series: Andy's romantic life, the value of small-town life, and, of course, Andy and Barney's all-abiding friendship.
- The "Molly Dodd" in the cast was the inspiration for the 1987 series *The Days and Nights of Molly Dodd*, which was about the travails of a bit player in the world of 1960s Hollywood television production. (Okay, maybe not.)
- Andy's yearbook entry reads: Andrew Jackson Taylor. Philomathian Literary Society. Barney's is: Bernard Milton Fife. Board of Directors Tinfoil Drive, Hall Monitor, Volleyball Court Maintenance Crew, Spanish Club.
- The Mayberry High School anthem— "The orange and blue will try try try"— was written by the show's resident music composer, Earle Hagen, who scored all the episodes and arranged the musical performances that took place within the show.

98

"Up in the Air"
three's company

Episode 125
Original air date: May 4, 1982
Original series run: 1977–1984
Series total: 172 episodes

Credits

Open: Starring John Ritter, Joyce De Witt, Priscilla Barnes, Richard Kline, Jenilee Harrison, and Don Knotts. Produced by Martin Rips & Joseph Staretski and George Sunga. Executive Producers: Michael Ross, Bernie West, George Burditt. End: Directed by Dave Powers. Written by Shelley Zellman. Developed by Nicholl/Ross/West. Script Consultant: Shelley Zellman. Story Editor: Ellen Guylas. Barry Williams . . . David Winthrop. Lauree Berger . . . Nancy Winthrop. Gertrude Flynn . . . Mrs. Peabody. Paul Marin . . . Mr. Peabody. Rick Edwards . . . Mark. Thom Fleming . . . Robert. Dean Taliaferro . . . Bridgit, The Maid. Choreographer: Don Crichton. "Three's Company" music by Joe Raposo. Lyrics by Don Nicholl. Sung by Ray Charles & Julia Rinker. Based on a Thames Television Production "Man About the House." Created by Johnnie Mortimer & Brian Cooke

Episode Review

Janet needs a date to impress the man she really wants, dreamy and wealthy David (a

THE BIG TV SATISFACTION FORMULA	
SyndicoDurability	7.3
Comic Valence	8.8
Emotional Resonance	8.4
Writing, Story	7.6
Writing, Characters	7.9
Acting	9.4
Quintessence	8.8
Series Originality	7.7
Episode Originality	8.2
Historical Significance	7.2
Celebrity	7.2
Gimmickry	8.8
Theme Song	8.8
Kitsch	9.1
BTVS Ratio	**77.13**

man who looks suspiciously like Greg Brady). She and Terri decide that Jack "would do" if he were dressed up a little. After first objecting—"I feel so used"—Jack is talked into going along with the plan. Then he learns that the party he will be attending is on an island and requires a flight on a small plane. Problem. He is afraid of flying.

Jack tries to fob the date off on Larry, but he can't go. Larry does try to cure him of his fear of flying, by using a chair to simulate takeoff. It doesn't work at all, as Jack "bails out at 4,000 feet." As a last resort, Larry offers to give him some tranquilizers; a desperate Jack accepts. In a "very special" moment, Terri warns him not to do it. After all, he has no idea what the effect will be. "And never take any medication that a doctor doesn't prescribe for you!" At her insistence, Jack promises not to take one . . . (he'll take two!).

David is at the party with his sister Marcia . . . I mean Nancy. We now know that Janet's jealousy is mistaken. Nancy is his sis-

ter, not his girlfriend. But it will take most of the episode before Janet comes to this realization.

Jack and Janet arrive, and it is quickly apparent that both pills are kicking in. Impressed by the monied guests, Janet asks Jack not to say that he is a chef. He is annoyed, but also feeling no pain. To various different groups he introduces himself as a Jesuit priest, a brain surgeon, and a congressman.

Out of control, he embarrasses himself and Janet. At one point, feeling groggy, he accepts a drink, a concoction that does not contain alcohol but is nonetheless called "The Rocket." He claims that it "does nothing for him," but then his eyes open wide and we are about to witness five of the wildest minutes any sitcom has ever seen. He can't stop dancing. After being dragged to the patio, he grabs an older woman and dances her back inside: "Strut with me, Mama!" (That line was a Ritter ad-lib, according to the writer.) Every comic convention available is run through, from a spit take to a double entendre. He kissed Janet, and she says, "Sometimes he just can't help himself," to which David responds, "It looks like he just did!" A toupee is knocked off an old man. Tripper becomes Fred Astaire, then Carmen Miranda. The party music suddenly (inexplicably) shifts from rock to a soft-shoe Broadway show tune. He smashes a potted plant, then wears the "crockery" on his head. He finally flings himself over a chair into parts unknown.

While this is going on, David talks to Janet on the patio, and she realizes her mistake. The comedy of errors concludes, and

Jack and Nancy flirt and connect, although Jack proceeds to fall asleep on her shoulder. In the coda, Jack and Janet arrive home at the apartment, where Jack is under the delusion that he really is a brain surgeon and due at the hospital for a 5:00 A.M. surgery.

Triple

There are a number of simple triples in this episode ("It's so immature, so devious . . . I like it!"); *Three's Company* worked this form heavily. But there is also a tragic missed opportunity to execute a full triple in this episode. The bit still works, but it might have been even better if the rules of comedy mathematics had been more strictly adhered to. During his intoxicated rampage, Jack describes himself as a priest, surgeon, and congressman. When he is talking to Nancy, postrampage, she tells him that she is a home economics major, and he says he is a chef! They have so much in common! But then other guests in turn come by and ask him about his surgery ("I can explain that") and his congressional work ("I can explain that") but no one mentions his Jesuit priest role! It was a natural triple just waiting to be executed. In any case, Nancy completed the moment by saying, "You just told me you were a chef!" and stomping off, indignant that he would say "anything" to get what he wanted.

Notes

• Casual students of *Three's Company* may be surprised that the one episode to make the Top 100 is from the post-Chrissy years, and from so late in the series.

Others might have expected a Roper- or Furley-enhanced episode. But to the serious aficionado of the series, the ascendancy of this episode will come as no surprise. This show was always John Ritter's vehicle. His timing, physical comedy, and energy brought life to even the most formulaic jokes and predictable story lines. This particular episode is simply Ritter at his unbridled best. The "Rocket" launch and subsequent dance are what made this episode so special.

• The first pilot for *Three's Company*—which adapted it from the British *Man About the House*—was written by veteran comedy writer Larry Gelbart, the creator of *M*A*S*H*. However, his version (starring Ritter, Valerie Curtin and Suzanne Zenore) did not make it to TV; a second pilot was commissioned, this one produced by the Nicholl/Ross/West team that would go on to produce the successful series.

• In explaining their reliance on sexual humor and double entendre, the makers of *Three's Company* would often suggest that what they were doing was classical farce, as exemplified by the nineteenth- and early-twentieth-century French playwright Georges Feydeau, whose work used mistaken identities, slapstick comedy, and titillating sexual themes. Of course, this is all based on the highly questionable assumption that anything done by the French a hundred years ago is respectable. And we won't even bring up the fact that the French consider Jerry Lewis a genius.

97

"What Makes Sammy Run?"

the jeffersons

Episode 218
Original air date: January 1, 1984
Original series run: 1975–1985
Series total: 253 episodes

THE BIG TV SATISFACTION FORMULA

SyndicoDurability	7.9
Comic Valence	7.7
Emotional Resonance	8.1
Writing, Story	8.5
Writing, Characters	8.5
Acting	8.1
Quintessence	8.9
Series Originality	7.6
Episode Originality	8.2
Historical Significance	9.2
Celebrity	9.4
Gimmickry	8.9
Theme Song	9.4
Kitsch	9.4
BTVS Ratio	**77.24**

Credits

Open: Starring Isabel Sanford, Sherman Hemsley, with Roxie Roker, Franklin Cover, Paul Benedict, and Marla Gibbs. Executive Producer: Michael G. Moyer. Co-executive Producers: Jerry Perzigian & Donald L. Seigel. Produced by Peter Casey & David Lee. Developed by Norman Lear. End: Directed by Tony Singletary. Written by Sara V. Finney. Created by Don Nicholl, Michael Ross, Bernie West. Co-Producer: John Maxwell Anderson. Special Guest Appearance by Sammy Davis, Jr. William Schilling . . . Harold O'Steen. And Ned Wertimer as Ralph the Doorman.

Episode Review

Sammy Davis, Jr., has picked the wrong floor of the wrong building on Manhattan's posh Upper East Side to hide out and take a break from the showbiz grind. Louise Jefferson is so bored that she is trying to bribe the doorman to come talk to her, when she spots Sammy as he gets off the elevator with an armful of packages.

Louise isn't shy. "I'd like to invite all my friends over and have you sing 'Candyman.' " And even after Sammy confides in her, begging her to keep his secret, Louise isn't going to let go easily, "I promise not to tell anyone, if you sing one verse." And Sammy complies reluctantly.

Meanwhile a reporter from *The Examiner*—a *National Enquirer*–type magazine—has arrived in the building, hot on the trail of rumors that Sammy is holed up somewhere close. The farce doesn't take long to get into full gear. Sammy is hidden and rehidden and finally locked out on the patio as a cold rain begins to pour down. (Oddly, the Jeffersons' high-rise seems to have one of the rare "uncovered" patios in New York.)

In the end, Louise saves the Greatest Entertainer in the World by sending the *Examiner* reporter off on a "hot tip" that Sammy is in Zimbabwe. For this one act of altruism, all is forgiven. And at least Sammy's secret is still known only by Louise . . . as George and Florence enter! Handshakes and snapshots all around, as another fine celebrity guest episode draws to its inevitable conclusion.

Notes

- Isabel Sanford named this episode as her very favorite.
- The high ranking of this episode may come as somewhat of a surprise to the casual *Jeffersons* observer, who would expect that an episode with very little George would have a hard time comparing. Indeed, overall, the episodes that featured George ranked higher than those focused on Weezie. The following are the next five highest-ranking episodes overall, all falling outside the BTVS Top 100 list:

178. "One Flew Into the Cuckoo's Nest": George is mistaken for a mental patient at an asylum.
267. "Brother Tom": Tom wants to learn to be black.
412. "George and the President": As a publicity stunt, George claims to be related to Thomas Jefferson and even dresses in eighteenth-century costume.
445. "Every Night Fever": George goes disco crazy, dancing all night every night.
571. "Jefferson Airplane": George takes up flying as a hobby.

96

"Chico and the Van"
chico and the man
Episode 24
Original air date: October 17, 1975
Original series run: 1974–1978
Series total: 88 episodes

Credits

Open: Jack Albertson starring in . . . Created by James Komack. Also starring Freddie Prinze. Music performed by Jose Feliciano. Produced by Michael Morris and Ed Scharlach. Written by Ann Gibbs & Joel Kimmel. Directed by Jack Donohue. End: Executive Producer: James Komack. Guest Stars Scatman Crothers as "Louie," Ralph Manza, and Penny Marshall.

Episode Review

It's the big applause era, as the live audience welcomes Chico to the stage. A building inspector has arrived and is causing Ed (the Man) all sorts of trouble. The end result is that Chico can't sleep in his parked van anymore. Somehow, Chico convinces Ed to let him move in upstairs. Naturally, the proximity quickly leads to conflicts. Ed wants to watch TV, but they can't agree on a show. Chico wants to play his guitar. Ed stomps out of his own place.

Ed is eating at a diner talking over his troubles with Louie. He ends up making a speech: "I hope someday he has his own

THE BIG TV SATISFACTION FORMULA	
SyndicoDurability	6.1
Comic Valence	8.5
Emotional Resonance	8.3
Writing, Story	8.5
Writing, Characters	8.8
Acting	8.6
Quintessence	9.4
Series Originality	8.4
Episode Originality	8.2
Historical Significance	7.3
Celebrity	7.1
Gimmickry	7.3
Theme Song	7.6
Kitsch	9.3
BTVS Ratio	**77.26**

garage and hires a mechanic who gives him as much trouble!" The people sitting in the diner burst into applause. With the matter resolved, Ed jumps up and exits. The waitress (Penny Marshall) is left to make one final mournful comment: "Nobody paid."

All ends well, as sentimentality, love, and brotherhood reign. The building inspector's complaints are all taken care of, and Chico returns to his happy little van.

Notes

- The essence of this series was the chemistry between Freddie Prinze and Jack Albertson. They managed to convey both their cultural differences and a grudging respect. This episode stands out because it focuses on that relationship.
- Although it was the first sitcom about Chicano culture, the series was criticized at launch because it included no Chicanos in the cast. Freddie Prinze was half Puerto Rican and half Hungarian. Later, some Mexican Americans were added to the cast.
- If you get a chance to watch the series, it is sad but fascinating to watch Freddie Prinze transform from chubby-faced and upbeat—the first season—to gaunt, haggard, and morose. In his last episodes, there is a clear difference in his affect; he smiles only when the script calls for it.
- During the run of the show, which propelled Prinze to stardom, the depressed and troubled actor took his own life. NBC attempted to continue the series the next fall, adding to the cast a young illegal immigrant boy named Raul (Gabriel Melgar) and later in that final season a

character named Aunt Charo (played by Charo). It has been Charo's only regular series role to date.

95

"Think Deep"
family affair

Episode 14
Original air date: December 26, 1966
Original series run: 1966–1971
Series total: 138 episodes

Credits

Open: Starring Brian Keith, and Sebastian Cabot. Produced by Edmund Beloin and Henry Garson. Written by George Tibbles. Directed by William D. Russell. End: Executive Producer: Edmund Hartmann. Cissy . . . Kathy Garver. Buffy . . . Anissa Jones. Jody . . . Johnnie Whitaker. Gail . . . Diane Mountford. Robert Reed as Julian Hill. Created by Edmund Hartmann and Don Fedderson.

Episode Review

A "dreamy" psychology lecturer, Professor Hill (Reed) is holding Cissy in thrall. Under his influence, she introduces some radical new ideas about equality and power into the household. She suggests, among other things, that they should rotate the places where they eat at the table, because having Uncle Bill sit at the head of the table all the time implies a dominating hierarchy.

Mr. French is one of her causes. He explains to Bill that she has "incited him to

THE BIG TV SATISFACTION FORMULA	
SyndicoDurability	6.9
Comic Valence	7.9
Emotional Resonance	9.2
Writing, Story	7.8
Writing, Characters	7.6
Acting	7.9
Quintessence	9.6
Series Originality	5.6
Episode Originality	8.3
Historical Significance	7.1
Celebrity	7.7
Gimmickry	7.1
Theme Song	7.2
Kitsch	9.4
BTVS Ratio	**77.41**

rebel" and insists on his addressing him by his given name, Giles. Bill quickly isolates the source of the problem and visits school to chat with Professor Hill. He finds that the professor is a bit persnickety—obsessive-compulsive might be a good guess, as he sharpens his pencils and straightens his hanging pictures. Seeing an opportunity, Bill invites the professor to dinner.

At first, all goes well and Cissy is more smitten than ever. But sure enough, Hill reveals his true colors. Buffy and Jody do what they do so well—jump around in excitement—and the foreseen disaster happens. The professor's coffee is spilled all over him: "Look what they've done! The little monsters. Cream and sugar almost never comes out." Cissy snaps awake as if from a dream. Her ideal man has revealed himself as human, all too human. A little resolution talk with Uncle Bill, and all is well.

Triple

When Cissy is describing what a wonderful and important person Professor Hill is,

she says he is "like Leander or Voltaire or . . . Cary Grant."

Notes

- Brian Keith's performance is really a thing of beauty; it's as if Marlon Brando has been a sitcom dad. He's all understatement and smoldering power.
- In an unusual case of playing against type, Robert "Mr. Brady" Reed dons a goatee and guest-stars as nemesis to the wise father figure that is Uncle Bill.
- This is the sole episode of *Family Affair* to make the BTVS Top 100, but among the other high-ranking episodes of this series: the time that Buffy and Jody win a lamb, but then have to give it up; the guest-starring turn by Butch Patrick (not in Eddie Munster makeup); the time that French played the role of Henry VIII in a low-budget film; and the time Eve Plumb, another very Brady guest star, appears in the holiday episode "Christmas Came a Little Early."

94
"What Goes Up"
welcome back, kotter

Episode 65
Original air date: February 9, 1978
Original series run: 1975–1979
Series total: 95 episodes

Credits

Open: Gabriel Kaplan starring in . . . Co-starring Marcia Strassman, and John Sylvester White as

Mr. Woodman. Also starring in alphabetical order, Robert Hegyes as Epstein. Lawrence-Hilton Jacobs as Washington. Ron Palillo as Horshack. John Travolta as Barbarino, and Melonie Haller as Angie. Created by Gabriel Kaplan & Alan Sacks. Developed for television by Peter Meyerson. Produced by Nick Arnold and George Bloom. Supervising Producer: Peter Meyerson. Teleplay by Nick Arnold. Story by George Tricker & Neil Rosen. Directed by Jeff Bleckner. End: Creative Consultant: Eric Cohen. Executive Story Editor: Beverly Bloomberg. Story Editors: Garry Ferrier and Aubrey Tadman. Based on Characters Created by Eric Cohen, Gabriel Kaplan & Alan Sacks.

Episode Review

We begin, as we so often did, with Mr. Kotter telling his wife, Julie, about one of his purported relatives. "Did I ever tell you about my uncle George?" It seems this fellow gift-wrapped his trash so it would be stolen.

It seems Freddie, after a basketball injury, has become addicted to "painkillers." Kot-

THE BIG TV SATISFACTION FORMULA	
SyndicoDurability	7.3
Comic Valence	9.1
Emotional Resonance	8.9
Writing, Story	7.5
Writing, Characters	8.1
Acting	8.8
Quintessence	8.5
Series Originality	7.4
Episode Originality	8.3
Historical Significance	7.4
Celebrity	7.8
Gimmickry	8.7
Theme Song	9.3
Kitsch	9.7
BTVS Ratio	**77.45**

ter catches Freddie taking drugs out of his shoe: "I don't mean to pry, but do you always take your shoe off to go the bathroom?" Later, Freddie is obviously stoned in class. Horshack is childishly disbelieving: "Freddie says they're vitamins; Freddie's never lied to me!"

Kotter pays Freddie another visit. He tries to get him to "look in the mirror".but Freddie dramatically tells him to get out of his life. Even Woodman is wondering what is happening to this particular student. After all, the signs are pretty easy to see. "This morning in the cafeteria he planted his feet in a plate of peas and said, 'Ho ho ho, I'm the jolly black giant.' "

The sweathogs try to talk to their pal. Barbarino, unforgettably, attempts to dramatize the plight of the drug-addicted by marching back and forth saying "gimme drugs" over and over. Of course, it makes no impact.

Then Arnold arrives, behaving strangely. He free associates about this and that, then opens the window and says he's going to jump! The sweathogs are terrified and try to talk him down. He ends up falling off the ledge back into the room, and hurting his leg. They realize that he is stoned. But little Horshack just took some "vitamins." That's right, he got some "vitamins" from the same guy who gave them to Freddie. Heavy. Seeing what happened to his friend, Freddie swears he will get clean.

Despite the dramatic turn of this episode, the coda is just another old-time joke, this one about Uncle Luther, a dietitian and inventor. You don't really want to hear the joke, do you? Good.

Whee Wohn

It's not a whee wohn cut, but there is a whee wohn entrance. Epstein suggests that whatever is going on with Freddie, Mr. Woodman will never figure it out. At that moment Mr. Woodman enters and says, "What's going on with Washington?"

Notes

- When Kotter arrives, the other three guys do a little Marx Brothers bit—as they often did—and pop their heads around the corner one after another, forming a sort of totem pole.
- Becoming addicted to painkillers after a sports injury was undoubtedly the most "acceptable" drug problem for a sitcom to take on. And as people who were around in the seventies knew, painkillers were just the first step, possibly leading to the misuse of No-Doz and even anti-inflammatory ointments!
- When we began to apply the BTVS formula to television shows in hopes of finding the best episodes, we certainly never expected that a "very special" episode would rank anywhere near the top. In general, episodes of sitcoms that attempt to take on important or uncomfortable social issues tend, among other things, to be ill-crafted and not funny.

Nonetheless, "What Goes Up" did very well, but this can be explained. The humor is, unfortunately, the result of just how bad and awkward the special message is. Witness the rarely seen 9.7 Kitsch score! It's a classic case of "so bad it's good." The show never recognized that it didn't have characters, it had caricatures.

To ask this crew to pull off an emotionally charged story, about a serious issue? They must have been dipping into Boom Boom's vitamins.

93

"Tiger Dance"
the adventures of ozzie & harriet

Episode number unknown
Original series run: 1952–1966
Series total: 435 filmed; approximately 100 shown in syndication

Credits

Open: "The Adventures of Ozzie and Harriet . . . starring the entire Nelson family: Ozzie, Harriet, David, and Ricky. Here's Ozzie who plays the part of Ozzie Nelson, and, of course, his lovely wife, Harriet, as Harriet Nelson. The older of the Nelson boys, David Nelson, plays David, and the younger, Ricky, is played by Ricky Nelson." End: Produced and Directed by Ozzie Nelson. Screenplay by Perry Grant, Don Nelson, Dick Bensfield. Ozzie . . . Ozzie Nelson. Harriet . . . Harriet Nelson. Dave . . . David Nelson. Rick . . . Ricky Nelson. Barry . . . Barry Livingston. Pat . . . Pat Thompson. Kim . . . Kim Tyler. Janet . . . Janet Waldo. Jack . . . Jack Wagner. Ronnie . . . Ronnie Dapo. Suzy . . . Laurie Nelson. Jimmy . . . Gil Smith.

Episode Review

Barry and Pat are collecting money from Ozzie, his dues for membership in the

THE BIG TV SATISFACTION FORMULA	
SyndicoDurability	8
Comic Valence	7.6
Emotional Resonance	9.4
Writing, Story	8.9
Writing, Characters	8.5
Acting	8.5
Quintessence	9.7
Series Originality	7.2
Episode Originality	8.7
Historical Significance	6.5
Celebrity	5.5
Gimmickry	8.8
Theme Song	5.6
Kitsch	9.2
BTVS Ratio	**77.51**

Tigers Club. It's for the Jimmy Dugan fund. You know, dance school. What's that? Are they raising money to send a pal to dance school? No, Jimmy is being forced to go, and they're raising money to pay Eddie Benson to take his place.

Meanwhile, Harriet is working at cross-purposes, organizing a dance for all the children to attend! Now Ozzie has to convince his fellow Tigers to help him. He needs them to attend the dance. After all, "When one Tiger is in trouble, the others help him out." This, despite the fact that there is a well-established penny fine for saying the word "dance."

The Tigers consult, over chocolate malts provided by Ozzie's largess. The soda jerk listens in and reports back to Ozzie: "I never heard such language! 'Doggonit,' 'nerts,' 'fer gosh shakes,' and about four 'holy mackerels.' " But the Tigers cave and promise to show up.

But not to dance. So Ozzie has to go back to the Tigers one more time to make sure they will actually dance. And come the day of the dance, the boys all arrive. They even dance to a rock 'n' roll number, and a twist, too. However, Harriet uncovers Ozzie's subterfuge: "You bribed them!" But all is forgiven, and a wonderful time is had by all.

Triple

Even in the early days of television, the triple was a well-established formula. There is a nice one in this episode as three little boys arrive at the dance, looking very spiffy, and take turns boasting:

BOY #1: This is a new suit.
BOY #2: I even took a bath in hot water.
BOY #3: I shaved!

Notes

• Nowadays "Ozzie and Harriet" has become easy shorthand for a world that is passé, the old-fashioned world of fifties clichés. But this is unfair. The show is certainly a product of its era, but it is hardly a fairy tale, and it is full of humanity and humor.

• This particular episode features Barry Livingston, who, in typical Nelson style, plays "Barry." He went on to greater glory under the moniker "Ernie"—the fourth son of *My Three Sons*.

• Janet Waldo (playing "Janet") went on to become famous in the animation world as the voice of Judy Jetson, Penelope Pitstop and Josie, of *Josie and the Pussycats*.

• There has been much debate and misinformation about the famous question of which show was the first to break the "double-bed barrier." Was it *Ozzie & Har-*

riet? In most television shows of the fifties and sixties, network censors did not allow married couples to occupy a double bed. The standard bedroom was appointed with separate twin beds.

Today, of course, most TV couples' bedrooms have one large bed. When did it change? There are a number of answers, depending on your definitions. Many say *The Brady Bunch* (which premiered in 1969), but Oliver and Lisa Douglas occupied an extravagant king-size bed in *Green Acres* prior to that (1965). Lily and Herman Munster beat them by a year (1964)—but were not a "human" couple, if you want to get technical about it. Fred and Wilma Flintstone were also shown in a double bed—human, but animated. In *I Love Lucy,* Lucy and Ricky were seen in a double bed in occasional episodes, while traveling, or, famously, while handcuffed together. But in the New York apartment, they, too, had separate beds.

For a long time, we believed that *The Adventures of Ozzie & Harriet* was the real answer. The network censors intended to prevent actors and actresses who were not married to be seen in bed, but Ozzie and Harriet Nelson were married in real life. Thus, in many of their shows, they have a large double bed: There is even one episode in which, through a series of misunderstandings, Ozzie thinks that Harriet wants him to start sleeping in another room, and in the happy conclusion, they are back in bed together—and after the lights are out we hear a joke about how cold Harriet's feet are! Quite scandalous for a show with the reputation for "old-fashioned family values."

In our TV Land to Go! on-air segments, we gave just that answer, but we were soon corrected, with yet an earlier example! Apparently, one of the very earliest sitcoms on television, a fifteen-minute domestic comedy called *Mary Kay and Johnny* (1947!) showed its two leads—also married in real life—sharing a tiny Greenwich Village apartment and one bed. The show aired live, and apparently there are not even any kinescope tapings of it. Let the historical record show, however, that it was *Mary Kay and Johnny,* on the DuMont Network, that first broke the double-bed barrier.

92

"Rendezvous at Big Gulch"

police squad

Episode 3
Original air date: July 1, 1982
Original series run: 1982
Series total: 6 episodes

Credits

Open: "In Color" Starring Leslie Nielsen. Also starring Alan North, and Rex Hamilton as Abraham. Special Guest Star: Florence Henderson. "Tonight's Episode: Terror in the Neighborhood." Executive Producers: Jim Abrahams, David Zucker, and Jerry Zucker. Produced by Robert K. Weiss. Teleplay by Nancy Steen and Neil Thompson. Story by Pat Proft.

Directed by Reza S. Badiyi. End: Created by Jim Abrahams, David Zucker, and Jerry Zucker. Executive Script Consultant: Pat Proft. Executive Story Editor: David Misch. Story Editors: Tino Insana and Robert Wuhl, Nancy Steen and Neil Thompson. Featuring Ed Williams as Mr. Olson, William Duell as Johnny, Peter Lupus as Norberg, and Al Ruscio as Dutch. Robert Costanzo . . . Leo. John Ashton . . . Rocky. Connie Needham . . . Jill, and Rebecca Holden as Stella.

Episode Review

It is beside the point and practically impossible to encapsulate a show like *Police Squad*, whose very genius lies in the fact that it is more a rapid-fire collection of jokes than a story. There is a linear thread, but it is largely irrelevant. Nonetheless, here are some of the things that happen: Mobsters are collecting protection money, and they beat up a ballet teacher, while her class imitates each move she makes. We see the Eiffel Tower out the window of the police station. When a woman leaves, they put a tail on her, literally. Al walks by, a cop who is so tall his head doesn't appear.

They set up a little business as locksmiths, to see if they get hit on for protection payments. They offer all sorts of keys: Florida Keys, monkeys, turkeys, pot roast. While they are at it, Nordberg is intent on improving service, focusing his energies more on the business than the crime fighting.

Mr. Olsen, down at the lab, is always in the midst of explaining some bit of science to a young child, like Mr. Wizard. They need a rock analyzed. He has a theory: "Billions of years ago, the earth was a molten mass . . ."

The mobsters arrive and beat up another victim, first hanging a polite sign: SORRY, OWNER BEING BEATEN. BACK IN FIVE MINUTES. There is also some hard-boiled dialogue: "Why don't you lie there till Tuesday; that's when they pick up the garbage."

Act II. Gesundheit.

A beautiful dame arrives to have a key duplicated. She needs forty-nine copies, one for each of the Chicago Bears. She suggests Drebin keep a copy for himself and stop by sometime.

Drebin provides the narrative voice-over: "It took me two weeks to find Stella's apartment; she had neglected to give me her address."

As always, the Police Squad turns to Johnny the shoeshine informer who knows everything, for a price. He tells Drebin all about his suspect. And adds, "This doesn't excuse what he does, but I think we understand him a little better."

After Drebin joins the bad guys under-

THE BIG TV SATISFACTION FORMULA	
SyndicoDurability	6.2
Comic Valence	9.6
Emotional Resonance	7.1
Writing, Story	9.5
Writing, Characters	7.6
Acting	8.5
Quintessence	9.4
Series Originality	9.7
Episode Originality	8.8
Historical Significance	7.2
Celebrity	7.9
Gimmickry	9.5
Theme Song	5
Kitsch	7.1
BTVS Ratio	**77.93**

cover, he is given the task of hitting the old tailor, but at the last minute a switch is made and they hit the dance teacher! Where the protection has been called off (policemen in leotards who had left earlier).

In the end, justice prevails, no thanks to the Police Squad!

Triple

The fast-moving comic stylings of the Zucker/Abraham/Zucker team utilizes every formula known to modern comedy science. Their work depends more on quantity than quality. During the fight scene, they execute a nifty absurd non sequitur triple. The damsel in distress warns our heroes of approaching thugs and their weapons, one by one:

"He's got a knife!"

"He's got a club!"

"He's got a signed Picasso!"

Notes

- Though unsuccessful as a TV series, running just six episodes (legend has it that a TV executive declared that it took too much attention to watch), the series did spawn the successful *Naked Gun* movies.
- Yes, the episode title does not match the title as it is announced by the voice-over. Just another random joke.
- In the final credits each week, *Police Squad* would employ the classic freeze-frame technique, with a twist. The actors would freeze, but the criminal would wander off and escape, or a monkey would jump around the office. In this episode, Drebin is being poured a cup of coffee when they freeze . . . and the coffee just pours and pours, filling and overflowing the cup.

91

"Rhoda's Wedding"
rhoda

Episodes 8 and 9
Original air date: October 28, 1974
Original series run: 1974–1978
Series total: 109 episodes

Credits

Open: Starring Valerie Harper. Created by James L. Brooks and Allan Burns. Developed by David Davis and Lorenzo Music. End: Directed by Robert Moore. Written by James L. Brooks, Allan Burns, David Davis, Lorenzo Music, Norman Barasch, and Carroll Moore, David Lloyd. Executive Producers: James L. Brooks and Allan Burns. Executive Story Consultants: Norman Barasch, Carroll Moore. Story Editor: James L. Brooks. Produced by David Davis and Lorenzo Music. Co-starring David Groh as Joe, Julie Kavner as Brenda, and Guest Stars (In Alphabetical Order) Edward Asner as Lou Grant, Georgia Engel as Georgette Franklin, Harold Gould as Martin Morgenstern, Cloris Leachman as Phyllis Lindstrom, Gavin MacLeod as Murray Slaughter, Mary Tyler Moore as Mary Richards, Nancy Walker as Ida Morgenstern. With Bernard Barrow as the Judge, Bella Bruck as the Neighbor, Paula Victor as Joe's Mother, and L. Music as Carlton the Doorman.

Episode Review

"This is Carlton, your doorman . . . in the lobby?"

He is calling up to say a strange lady is coming up. Shouldn't he have found out

155

THE BIG TV SATISFACTION FORMULA	
SyndicoDurability	7.1
Comic Valence	7.8
Emotional Resonance	9.4
Writing, Story	7.4
Writing, Characters	7.3
Acting	7.5
Quintessence	7.8
Series Originality	6.5
Episode Originality	9.6
Historical Significance	9.9
Celebrity	8.5
Gimmickry	9.4
Theme Song	7.6
Kitsch	9.2
BTVS Ratio	**78.17**

who it is? "I know who it is; it's your mother."

Rhoda has been planning a small wedding, just a few friends in the judge's chambers, but with just two days to go, Ida is here to change her mind. She lays on the guilt, until Rhoda caves in. Good thing, since Ida has already invited seventy-nine people, not including the band. (The Morgensterns' Bronx apartment must be bigger than it looks.)

Rhoda is excited for Mary to meet Joe, but when he comes home in a rotten mood, he brushes past Mary with a cursory "hi." He is ranting about the stupidity of the people he works for and the people of the city in general. He then storms into the bathroom. Rhoda and Mary stare at each other awkwardly, until Rhoda says, "So, what do you think?"

Rhoda then goes into the bathroom. They yell and fight while Mary tries not to hear. "How could you! That was my best friend in the world!" Joe comes out and tries to apologize.

The big day arrives. Somehow, Phyllis—the whole Minneapolis crew have arrived to join the festivities—ends up in charge of picking up Rhoda, and forgets to get her! Rhoda, bedecked in her full gown, is waiting, and waiting. . . . She goes outside, then gives up and tries to hail a cab. She can't get one, so she starts walking. She eventually gets on the subway, then walks from the subway stop to her parents' house.

At the Morgensterns', the mood is somber. At last, Phyllis arrives, and there is a collective sigh of relief, until Mary asks where Rhoda is. "I don't know," says Phyllis blithely. "I just got here." Then her face falls as she realizes her grievous error. (There is no real explanation for why she was an hour late to a wedding, but details, details.) Everyone is horrified, and in a scene too tragic to be comic, Phyllis begs for forgiveness.

When Rhoda finally arrives—after letting off some steam—she is left alone in the building hallway. She begins walking, wedding-style, down the aisle. Then a next-door neighbor opens a door, taking out some trash. And they have a short conversation:

"Hi, Rhoda, what's new?"

"Not much."

The neighbor walks off, and Rhoda continues, down the hall, into the apartment, and to her wedding. She and Joe are duly married and hugs and celebration fill the room.

Triple

Early on, as they talk about the upcoming wedding, Rhoda says to her sister Brenda that this will all happen for her one day: "You'll fall in love, you'll decide to get married, and then you'll feel as nauseous as I do right now."

Notes
- For its original airing on October 28, 1974, the show received huge ratings, as 51 million viewers tuned in.
- As a historical landmark, this episode ranks high, but, frankly, it doesn't hold up as well as most of the others on the list. Note the high 9.9 Historical Significance and low writing scores. Why? The arrival of Phyllis and her forgetting to pick up Rhoda is simply unbelievable. Just as unlikely is Rhoda's three-hour trek from Manhattan to the Bronx. Ida's last-minute changing of the wedding is also a big stretch. The romance between Rhoda and Joe, which seems intended to be realistic and combative, like a James L. Brooks version of the Kramdens, is actually quite sad. Perhaps knowing that the characters will eventually divorce informs one's viewing, or perhaps the seeds of discord were already sown. Still, this was the ultimate Rhoda episode, and full of great guest stars, too.
- Joe and Rhoda wrote their own vows, and they promise to stay together "as long as you both shall love," which is a pretty open-ended vow if you think about it. Although, "as long as your character seems to be contributing to our Nielsen ratings" would have been even more accurate.
- This episode was originally a one-hour-long special episode. It was screened and judged, as it is now generally shown in syndication, as two separate half hours.

- Under the final credits there is special end theme music that intermingles the *Rhoda* theme with "The Wedding March."
- Rhoda's route from Manhattan to the Bronx, filmed on location, is a bit circuitous. Her apartment is at 332 West Forty-sixth (not a great neighborhood, then or now). However, she walks past three subway stops before going below ground at Seventy-second and Broadway. But once she gets inside, she is at a different subway platform, which looks a lot like Fiftieth and Broadway. Finally, she does end up in the Bronx near Fordham Road at 3517 Grand Concourse. She probably would have made better time going over to Sixth Avenue and taking a D train directly to Grand Concourse.
- Creator-Producer James L. Brooks appears as the bearded man who gives her a long, bemused look on the subway platform.

90

"Ed the Beachcomber"
mister ed

Episode 45
Original air date: April 1, 1962
Original series run: 1961–1965
Series total: 143 episodes

Credits
Open: Starring Alan Young. Co-starring Connie Hines. Co-starring Larry Keating. Produced and Directed by Arthur Lubin. Written by Lou

Derman and Robert O'Brien. End: Executive Producer: Al Simon. Script Consultants: Norman Paul, William Burns. Featuring Edna Skinner as Kay Addison. Larry Merrill . . . Buzz Dixon. Nancy Lee . . . Zelma Beasley. Jay Berniker . . . Harry. Gail DaCorsi . . . Gertie. Joe Conley . . . Photographer. Mister Ed . . . Himself. From characters created by Walter Brooks.

Episode Review

Ed reads a newspaper editorial about how the need for the horse is "extinct" and how they are no longer important. Why exactly a local newspaper editor in 1963 would be taking such a stance is entirely unclear, but one thing is for sure: He is no friend to Mister Ed. Ed's going on a hunger strike until Wilbur lets him respond to the editor.

Meanwhile, Addison wants to chase some beatnik kids off his beach property—they hang out and hurt the property value! Two of the kids, Buzz and Zelda, arrive and beg him to let them stay, to no avail. They get nothing but "rejection rejection rejec-

tion. Cast out by a world we didn't make!" They share their latest—"Buzz's Rejection Poem"—about their pain, and the feeling that youth itself is extinct! They are "a nothing, a zero, a hole in the cheese."

These words cut Ed to the quick! They echo his pain. Ed resolves to become a beatnik painter, complete with a beach hat and sunglasses, and write his own "beat" poetry. Ed's "Ode to Life" expresses these feelings through metaphor. "Life is a feedbag, without any oats."

Feeling rejected, Ed heads for the beach where he will find kindred spirits, and, indeed, even without saying a word he makes new friends. "I think that horse reads us!" "You said it, Daddy-o." Wilbur is working on convincing Addison to let the kids stay, but when Addison's latest deal to sell the property falls through, he storms off to the beach to throw them all off. However, he arrives to find a newspaper writer who congratulates him on his selfless efforts to support the young people. Addison's ego responds, and all's well on that front.

Also, Wilbur has discovered that Ed has run away, and they are reunited at the beach. Are horses useless relics of a time gone by? As Wilbur puts it: "Anyone who is loved is never useless." That's all Ed needed to hear . . . off they go. And he has revised his "Ode to Life" to express his undying affection for Wilbur.

Notes

- Despite the quality of Mister Ed's poetical works, the 1963 Pulitzer Prize for Poetry went to William Carlos Williams.
- How did Mister Ed talk? Amazingly

THE BIG TV SATISFACTION FORMULA	
SyndicoDurability	8.9
Comic Valence	8.9
Emotional Resonance	9.1
Writing, Story	9.2
Writing, Characters	8.5
Acting	8.4
Quintessence	8.2
Series Originality	8.8
Episode Originality	8.1
Historical Significance	6.7
Celebrity	5.9
Gimmickry	8.2
Theme Song	9.7
Kitsch	9.2
BTVS Ratio	**78.42**

enough, the answer remains a secret to this day. Some say peanut butter on the roof of the mouth, others say nylon lines, others say he was just incredibly well trained and would move his mouth on off-camera cues from his trainer.

- The wonderful gravelly voice of Mister Ed was provided by Allan "Rocky" Lane, the star of many B-movie Westerns.
- This episode earned its stature as the highest-ranking episode of *Mister Ed* without the high gimmickry ratings employed by episodes such as "Mister Ed Plays Baseball," and the ones in which Ed surfs and flies a plane. Its score came from consistently high marks across the board, as well as particularly high writing marks for the poetry.
- The second-highest ranking episode of *Mister Ed* was the one in which Clint Eastwood guest-starred. He was then famous for his work on the television Western *Rawhide* but, interestingly enough, was one of the few actors to work with both Mister Ed and his film precursor Francis the Talking Mule. Eastwood appeared in *Francis in the Navy* (1955).

89
"Opie and the Bully"
the andy griffith show
Episode 34
Original air date: October 2, 1961
Original series run: 1960–1968
Series total: 249 episodes

THE BIG TV SATISFACTION FORMULA	
SyndicoDurability	9.9
Comic Valence	7.2
Emotional Resonance	8.9
Writing, Story	8.7
Writing, Characters	9.2
Acting	9.1
Quintessence	9.5
Series Originality	7.3
Episode Originality	7.9
Historical Significance	7.3
Celebrity	6.2
Gimmickry	5.6
Theme Song	8.7
Kitsch	7.5
BTVS Ratio	**78.51**

Credits

Open: Andy Griffith, Ron Howard, Don Knotts. End: Directed by Bob Sweeney. Written by David Adler. Produced by Aaron Ruben, Frances Bavier, Terry Dickinson. Executive Producer: Sheldon Leonard. In Association with Danny Thomas.

Episode Review

Opie is getting his lunch for school. He gets a nickel for milk from Aunt Bee. Then, without her knowing, he gets another nickel for milk from Andy. On his way to school, Opie runs into Sheldon, who offers him the classic "knuckle sandwich."

Meanwhile, Andy is on to the second nickel. He has a little talk with Opie, who pretends to fall asleep. Andy lets him off the hook. The next day, Andy and Barney talk it over. Turns out Barney has supplied a nickel now and then. Barney decides that he will solve the "mystery" and trails after Opie the next day. Using a newspaper with a hole cut out, he witnesses the crime and reports back to Andy.

"It's extortion, that's what it is!" He suggest fightin' lessons. Andy is torn. "I don't want him to be the sort of boy who's looking for fights, but I don't want him to go runnin' from them either."

Andy's solution is to take Opie fishing; while they're at the fishing hole, he gets the idea to tell a little parable. It's his own story of how he dealt with Hodie Snitch. First he crawled off liked a whipped pup, but he found out that tough talk is just talk. He got in a fight all right, but it wasn't so bad: "I lit into him like a windmill in a tornado," and as for getting hit, well, he didn't even feel it.

So now there's nothing to do but wait. Andy and Barney are at the station, pacing. Barney keeps trying to leave so's he can go and watch, but Andy won't let him. The boys have to handle it on their own. Opie returns with a whopping shiner and a big smile. He can't hardly feel it, and he got his licks in. And he knows one thing for sure: "A sandwich sure tastes better with milk!"

Notes

- Talk about your quintessential episodes. Since this one was made, there have probably been five hundred kid-dealing-with-a-bully episodes, but none have topped it for sheer charm.
- Naming the bully "Sheldon" was no doubt a nod to the executive producer, Sheldon Leonard, who, before his television producing career, was an actor frequently cast as a tough guy or mobster. He takes a memorable guest-starring turn as the mob leader in the *Dick Van Dyke* episode "Big Max Calvada" (another show for which he was executive producer).

- The snippets of regional southern diction make this show unique. Listen to Andy when he'd talking to Aunt Bee about her cooking: "Aunt Bee, you're a burden in this world. You have to have a little braggin', dontcha?"

88

"The Greatest Entertainer in the World"

i dream of jeannie

Episode 53
Original air date: February 27, 1967
Original series run: 1965–1970
Series total: 139 episodes

Credits

Created by Sidney Sheldon. Written by Sidney Sheldon. Directed by Claudio Guzman. Executive Producer: Sidney Sheldon. Starring Barbara Eden as Jeannie, Larry Hagman as Major Anthony Nelson. Featuring Hayden Roarke as Dr. Bellows, Bill Daily as Major Roger Healey, General Peterson . . . Barton MacLane, Charles . . . James J. Walters, Mack . . . George Rhodes, Master of Ceremonies . . . Bob Melvin, Man in Hotel . . . Murphy Bennett, Sammy Davis, Jr. as Sammy Davis, Jr. A Sidney Sheldon Production.

Episode Review

The quintessential "need a big star" plot line that Lucy invented and Marcia Brady and Davy Jones perfected takes form with the usual celerity of *Jeannie* plots. Tony is

THE BIG TV SATISFACTION FORMULA	
SyndicoDurability	8.6
Comic Valence	8.8
Emotional Resonance	7.3
Writing, Story	9.1
Writing, Characters	9.2
Acting	7.9
Quintessence	9.2
Series Originality	8.1
Episode Originality	8.7
Historical Significance	7.1
Celebrity	9.7
Gimmickry	9.2
Theme Song	8.3
Kitsch	9.2
BTVS Ratio	**78.61**

put in charge of arranging entertainment for General Peterson's big birthday party. Dr. Bellows consents: "Well, it's in your hands now. It's the most important day in General Peterson's life. Don't disappoint me."

Tony decides that he will try to get Sammy Davis, Jr., and sneaks out of the house to go to Miami, where Sammy is playing two "gigs" a night. Meanwhile, Roger lets slip to Bellows that Sammy is being asked and actually gives the impression that Sammy has already agreed to appear. Tony makes it as far as Sammy's hotel room/rehearsal space, but Sammy's manager, though polite, basically tells Tony that the world's greatest entertainer is booked solid for the next year or so.

After a downcast Tony has left, the manager tells Sammy that Major Tony Nelson just stopped by. "The astronaut!?" says an impressed Sammy Davis, Jr. (Who knew Major Nelson was such a celebrity?) "If that cat's not too busy to go the moon for me, then I'm not too busy to stop a rehearsal and talk to him." He insists that his manager go bring Nelson back. After all, Sammy's met the Queen of England and the President of the United States, but never a real live astronaut. Blink!

Jeannie, imagine it, has gotten impatient and is taking matters into her own hands. But after blinking Sammy to the house, she finds that Tony is missing. She blinks Sammy back, where he decides that he definitely needs to take some time off.

Tony returns to Jeannie, and after some explanations on both sides, the Rat Pack crooner is reblinked back to Cocoa Beach. A little more composed this time, Sammy says he'd love to lay his talent on the general, but he's booked solid. He'd do it if he could.

"I think I could arrange it," pipes up Jeannie merrily, and she promptly blinks up a second Sammy Davis, Jr. (Or is he the third?) That Friday, Sammy Davis performs "That Old Black Magic"—fittingly—at both the Miami night club and in Cocoa Beach at General Peterson's birthday bash. Naturally, he wows both audiences.

Notes

- This is the second of the three episodes rated among the BTVS Top 100 that feature a guest-starring turn by singer-dancer Sammy Davis, Jr. His appearance on *The Jeffersons* came in ninety-seventh, while his famous appearance on *All in the Family* ranked thirteenth. What is it about him that elevates seemingly any episode? Perhaps it's his sheer talent. The man loved to entertain, and he did so with unflagging energy coupled with endless humility. They do call him the greatest entertainer in the world, you know. He was certainly the busiest member of the Rat Pack, in terms of TV guest-starring roles. In addition to the series above, he was in episodes of *The Patty Duke Show, Dick Powell Theater, The Beverly Hillbillies, Mod Squad, The Rifleman, Ben Casey, Here's Lucy, Chico and the Man, Charlie's Angels* and *One Life to Live*. Frank, in case you're wondering, never appeared on any of those shows.

• In the coda scene, Sammy stops by Tony's place to request that Jeannie blink away his double. . . . It's unclear why, exactly, since it seems as if they could have cut a very cool album of Sammy-Sammy duets. Can't you hear it? "Anything I can do, I can do better, Anything I can do, I can do, too."

87

"Christmas Show, 1952"

the george burns and gracie allen show

Episode number not available
Original series run: 1950–1958
Series total: 239 episodes made;
130 shown in syndication

Credits

Open: The George Burns and Gracie Allen Show. End: "Featured in tonight's show were Sarah Shelby as Mamie; Jerry James, Melinda Ploughman, and Jill Oppenheim as Jerry,

Melinda, and Jill; and Kathleen O'Malley as Julie." Produced and Directed by Ralph Levy. Written by Paul Henning, Sid Dorfman, Harvey Helm, and Willy Burns. Supporting Cast: Harry Von Zell, Bea Benadaret, Fred Clark. Gracie Allen's gowns by Ward Greer. The George Burns and Gracie Allen Show was presented by Carnation, "Milk from Contented Cows."

Episode Review

Harry and Blanche Morton, the neighbors, are each trying to hide the other's Christmas gift over at George and Gracie's. In turn, Harry explains the red alligator purse with shoes to match. Gracie thought alligators were brown. He explains that they're dyed. She hopes so, since they made a bag and shoes out of it. Blanche shows her the fish creel, to hold fish in, but Gracie warns her that it won't hold water. Blanche explains that it's for dead fish, and Gracie gives a "whatever" look and says, "It's your house, Blanche."

Cousin Mamie Kelly and her three daughters are invading . . . er, visiting for

THE BIG TV SATISFACTION FORMULA	
SyndicoDurability	6.5
Comic Valence	8.5
Emotional Resonance	7.8
Writing, Story	9.4
Writing, Characters	9.4
Acting	8.5
Quintessence	9.2
Series Originality	7.8
Episode Originality	8.8
Historical Significance	8.4
Celebrity	6.8
Gimmickry	6.5
Theme Song	6.1
Kitsch	8.4
BTVS Ratio	**78.64**

the holidays. After they arrive, with Harry and Blanche helping, they all gather in the living room; Gracie works out the sleeping arrangements. She has room for everyone but Harry and Blanche. Harry says, "Gracie, we live next door. Maybe we could sleep there?" To which Gracie responds, "That's a wonderful idea!"

There is a great bit where George is sent up and down the stairs to get suitcases, constantly getting "the wrong one" or "you were right the first time." Harry Morton is trying to get the three girls to stop their incessant drumming. They won't take no for an answer, so he says, "Besides, if you hit it all the time you'll spoil the candy that's inside." They run off to open it as he grins. Harry Von Zell and Julie talk to Cousin Mamie, who leaps to the conclusion that they're married. She exits before she can be corrected, and Gracie enters moments later, excited about the news!

The best scene of all comes when the three little girls ask Gracie to tell them a good-night story. They want Dickens's *A Christmas Carol*. She tries to recall it. "George, is that the one that starts 'Once upon a time' and ends 'they all lived happily after?' " Could be. "Now I just have to remember that part in the middle."

George gives her a hint, "It's got Scrooge, Bob Cratchitt, and Tiny Tim in it." With that, she launches into the story: "Once upon a time, Scrooge, Bob Cratchitt, and Tiny Tim went for a walk in the woods while their breakfast cooled. . . ." George tries to interject and correct her. She responds with, "Who told you that story?" He answers, "My mother." Gracie

has found the problem. "*This* is by Dickens." She manages to finish the story. In the final bit, George gets into his Santa suit, which doesn't fool the girls at all. "How could they tell he was trying to be Santa," suggests Gracie, "behind all those whiskers?"

Triple

At one point, the three little girls are asked to run off and do something else. As they leave, they torture Harry one last time. The eldest says, "Poke the elephant," as she pokes him in the belly; the second says, "Poke the elephant," and pokes him in the belly; the littlest one says, "Poke the elephant," but because she can't reach up as high, she stomps on his foot instead. Verbally, it's simply a thrice-repeated phrase; but physically, it is a fine triple, indeed.

Notes

- In this era, the sponsor's commercials are not only done by the actors, but the plugs are actually worked into the story lines of the show. When they sit down for some coffee, Gracie offers "Carnation?" Later when Harry Von Zell arrives, as part of the overall story, he brings with him Julie, a secretary from the Carnation company, and talks about the first time he saw her. She was typing the script for a Carnation commercial. Beautiful! (Not her, the script!) And he recalls the copy: "I remember just how it went . . . 'Carnation is the perfect choice for babies because . . .' " And he proceeds to read the sponsor's entire message.
- In an era of observational comedy, a

show with traditional joke structures can seem dated, but Burns and Allen had a deft touch, and Gracie's oblivious character brings such absurdity to the show that it does indeed hold up.

- When Gracie enters for the first time, not only is there applause, but she acknowledges it with a smile and small bow. What came to seem like such an annoyance in the seventies, when Barbarino was collecting applause for his entrances, seems quaint and friendly in this context.

- Paul Henning, here a writer, went on to create that classic TV triumvirate *Petticoat Junction, The Beverly Hillbillies* and *Green Acres.* With this in mind, it becomes clear that George and Gracie were the most influential antecedents to Oliver and Lisa. The woman lives in a logical world of her own, while the man tries to bring reason to bear on the situation. (Men are from Mars, women from Venus?) Of course, in *Green Acres* the difference is that they were living in a world that daily confirmed Lisa's absurd beliefs and statements. Hooterville was a world in which farmers raise pigs as if they are children, outboard motors fly, real jewelry can be found in cereal boxes, and hens lay eggs that have opening credits written on them. In *The Burns and Allen Show,* the rest of the world was on George's side.

86

"Richie Fights Back"
happy days

Episode 45
Original air date: October 14, 1975
Original series run: 1974–1984
Series total: 255 episodes

Credits

Open: Starring Ron Howard, Henry Winkler, Co-starring Marion Ross, Anson Williams, Donny Most, Erin Moran. Also Starring Tom Bosley as Mr. Cunningham. Producers Mark Rothman, Lowell Ganz. Executive Producers Thomas L. Miller, Edward K. Milkis, Garry K. Marshall. Produced by Tony Marshall. Created by Garry Marshall. Written by Arthur Silver. Directed by Jerry Paris. End: Executive Script Consultants Lowell Ganz, Mark Rothman. Executive Story Consultant Bob Brunner. Script Consultants Marty Nadler, Joe Glauberg. Guest Star Pat Morita as Arnold. Featuring Ken Lerner as Frankie, Jeff Conaway as Rocko, Susan Lawrence as Vivian.

Episode Review

Richie is humiliated down at Arnold's by Frankie and Rocko, two hoods who force him to act as a human sound-effect machine to replace the broken bumpers on the pinball machine. Fonzie enters (to applause) and scares them off, but Richie runs off to the men's room where he throws things around. Fonzie goes in. "Can I ask you a question? Why are you beating up the bath-

THE BIG TV SATISFACTION FORMULA	
SyndicoDurability	7.5
Comic Valence	9.3
Emotional Resonance	9.2
Writing, Story	8.9
Writing, Characters	8.8
Acting	8.9
Quintessence	9.2
Series Originality	6.3
Episode Originality	8.1
Historical Significance	7.5
Celebrity	5.6
Gimmickry	8.3
Theme Song	8.3
Kitsch	8.8
BTVS Ratio	**78.76**

room?" After some conversation, Richie, Ralph, and Potsie decide to take jujitsu lessons.

Arnold is the one giving the lessons, and Joanie, who has also signed up, flips Richie. He's humiliated again. She flipped him twenty times! Richie turns to Fonzie for help. Fonzie teaches him to act tough, although "with that Howdy Doody face, you could only be so tough." But he gets him to clench his teeth, talk in low voice. Saunter.

Richie tries it the next morning at breakfast and gets the oatmeal he wants. Then he explains that this is his new system. Mr. C is annoyed with everyone and decides to leave and have breakfast at the store. But Mrs. C, adopting the Fonzie style, tells him he's not going anywhere and to sit right back down again. Mr. C follows her orders, and she says, "Chalk one up for the Fonz."

But Richie's real test will be at Arnold's. Rocko and Frankie are there. Richie acts tough: "The name's Richie; don't ever call me anything else." He says, "When I turn back around, you guys better be gone." But

they don't back down. The Fonz forgot one detail. To act tough, you first have to have a reputation. "That's not a good detail to leave out, Fonz," says a panicky Richie.

Backed to the wall, Richie attacks. He grabs Rocko to throw him, but gets only his leather jacket and whips it to the ground. Then Richie goes bonkers, running all over and leaping on tables, until Rocko becomes convinced that he's crazy and runs away. Victory.

Triple

There is an interesting physical triple in this episode. It happens when Richie hits up his dad for the twenty bucks to pay for the martial arts lessons. Mr. C gets the whole story and says Richie doesn't need lessons, because he himself can teach his son everything he needs to know. He learned martial arts in the army. He has Richie grab him around the neck, then tries to flip him or get free. Mr. C says, "Here we go," and strains to no effect (the first element of the triple). Again: "Here we go." No progress (second element). Then: "Richard?" "Yeah, Dad?" "The twenty dollars is in my back pocket." (The triple, executed.)

Notes

- Jeff Conaway, the secondary hood in this episode, is best known to TV fans as *Taxi*'s would-be actor, Bobby Wheeler. However, his best-known "hood" role is Danny Zuko from *Grease*. He played the role on Broadway for eight years, turning in 3,388 performances. (In the movie, he played the role of Kenickie, aced out for Danny by some kid named Travolta.)

- Erin Moran got her start on *The Don Rickles Show* (1972), playing his young daughter, Janie.

85

"Spewey and Me"
get a life

Episode 33
Original air date: February 9, 1992
Original series run: 1990–1992
Series total: 35 episodes

Credits

Open: Starring Chris Elliott, Brian Doyle-Murray, Robin Riker. Executive Producer: David Mirkin. Created by Chris Elliott, Adam Resnick, David Mirkin. Produced by David Latt. Producers: Chris Elliott, Adam Resnick, Steve Pepoon, Jace Richdale. Written by Jace Richdale. Directed by David Mirkin. End: Guest Starring Arturo Gil as Spewey. Frank Welker as Voice of Spewey. Taylor Fry as Amy Potter. Dave Florek as Brooks. Michael Frances Clarke as Mason. Rick Fitts as Pebo Griffin. Executive Story Editor: Bob Odenkirk. Main Theme: "Stand" by R.E.M.

Episode Review

If the Episode Review you are about to read seems a little disconnected and strange, welcome to the world of *Get a Life*, where the writer's whimsy was always more important than motivations, consistency, or logic.

Chris is knitting when a spacecraft crashes in his backyard. He knows almost immediately that it is an "unidentified flying

thing—a UFT!" Perhaps it contains a lifeform? Perhaps it contains a cute little furry creature with a caustic wit, like ALF or Ray Walston.

Indeed, it is an alien, and not only that, it's *his* alien. No matter how vile, nasty, and malodorous, Chris sees only the good side of Spewey. When the creature bites him and hits him, well, our puny minds cannot comprehend his meaning. Spewey vomits on him; Chris suggest perhaps this is a gift? If it is, it is the first of many, for Spewey vomits, streams, and sprays on pretty much everyone he meets throughout the rest of the episode. Chris attempts to communicate with Spewey: "Do you want to phone home?"

The government arrives, but they hide Spewey. The redoubtable Gus Borden suggests selling Spewey for profit. Chris then discovers that a yellow goo pours out of Spewey's elbow. Well, what would you do if a strange creature from another planet suddenly emitted something of a puddinglike consistency? Assuming this is another "gift" and not wanting to offend him, Chris drinks it.

Chris still believes that Spewey is here on a mission of compassion and hope, so he takes him to visit his old high school pal, the Pope. Uh-oh! Spewey really goes after the pontiff. Gus tries to sell him to the circus, but they find that he is too disgusting.

Gus has alerted the government, hoping to squeeze a little money out of them. They arrive seconds later, but Chris and Spewey flee to his neighbor's house. There, he introduces Spewey to Amy, a little girl: "Get ready to be transformed by love and by magic!" She takes one look and attacks Spewey, hitting him over and over, saying, "I want to kill it. I want it dead!" Chris nods sagely, "Leave it to the children to understand his special language."

But now Spewey is spewing more than ever, through his mouth and "eyes." Chris puts Spewey in the front basket of his bicycle and rides off—in front of a huge moon, à la E.T.—and then plummets to the ground. He returns, battered and bruised. Gus asks, "What'd you do, try to make out with it?"

Chris is really worried. "Something seem to be wrong. . . . His pudding is an odd color, and it tastes garlicky—especially after the fifth helping." He leaves to get him some medicine at the supermarket, first eliciting a promise from Gus that he won't sell him to the government. Gus promises.

Chris returns, and indeed Gus did not sell him. Instead, he beat Spewey to death with a rake and cooked him. He is in the midst of eating him. Chris is disconsolate for almost fifteen seconds, then joins in the meal. "I'd probably be a tad more upset, if he weren't so darn tasty."

But all is not lost! Spewey regenerates from his own leftovers! And the mother ship returns, "levitates" him (using a big rope), and carries him away, splattering Chris and Gus with one last dousing of goo.

Notes

- This was a sad story of a show cut down in its prime, with this high-ranking episode coming at the end of its run. The show elicited a strong response. Some hated it; others loved it. We believe that in time it will be recognized as a groundbreaking and underappreciated series.

- Chris Elliott was a writer for David Letterman. His on-screen appearances on *Late Night* in such roles as "the guy beneath the stairs" led to this series. A cult classic, it ran for two years on Fox, until the success of the movie *Cabin Boy* led Elliott to give up television and devote himself exclusively to film, nightclub appearances, and charity work.

- Chris Peterson's parents never got out of their bathrobes. Fred Peterson, his father, was played by Chris's real father, Bob Elliott, who was famed for his radio and television work in the comedy team Bob & Ray. (He was Bob.)

- Gladys Peterson, his mother, was played by Elinor Donahue, whose sitcom career thus spanned the eras from perhaps the most idyllic and innocent when she was "Princess" on *Father Knows Best* to the most cynical and dark to date; see above. Donahue has had, in fact, perhaps the single most varied and active TV career of any actress. In addition to those roles, she was Sheriff Andy Taylor's early romantic interest, Ellie Walker, and she played Felix Unger's girlfriend Miriam on *The Odd Couple*. As if that's not enough, she also played Spock's mother on *Star Trek*.

- Brian Doyle-Murray is Bill Murray's brother, and worked with him on *National Lampoon*'s various radio shows.

84

"The Case of the Hooterville Refund Fraud"

green acres

Episode 139
Original air date: February 28, 1970
Original series run: 1965–1971
Series total: 170 episodes

Credits

Open: Eddie Albert, Eva Gabor. Created and Produced by Jay Sommers. Executive Producer: Paul Henning. Story by Arnold Horwitt. Teleplay by Arnold Horwitt, Jay Sommers and Dick Chevillat. Directed by Richard L. Bare. End: Pat Buttram as Mr. Haney. Tom Lester . . . Eb. Alvy Moore as Hank Kimball. Frank Cady as Sam Drucker. Hank Patterson . . . Fred Ziffel. Kay E. Kuter . . . Newt Kiley. Hal Smith . . . Colby. Jay Jostyn . . . Harold Gilmour. Tom Lowell . . . Fred Feldinger. Robert Carson . . . Senator Hanson. Story Consultant . . . Dick Chevillat. "This has been a Filmways Presentation, Darling."

THE BIG TV SATISFACTION FORMULA

SyndicoDurability	7.7
Comic Valence	9.4
Emotional Resonance	7.6
Writing, Story	9.4
Writing, Characters	8.9
Acting	8.7
Quintessence	7.9
Series Originality	8.1
Episode Originality	8.9
Historical Significance	7.2
Celebrity	6.6
Gimmickry	9.1
Theme Song	9.7
Kitsch	8.5
BTVS Ratio	**78.91**

Episode Review

This episode takes the form of a documentary, hosted by one Harold Gilmour, chief of division twelve of the sixtieth Internal Revenue District. With Gilmour narrating, we are taken back to the fateful day when Oliver received his income tax refund at Sam Drucker's store. The townsfolk have never heard of refunds, or income tax for that matter. Before long, word is out that Oliver has got a sure-fire method of getting free money from the government. They all write in for refunds, even though they've never paid any taxes in the first place. A quick spin cut later, practically everyone is Hooterville has been given huge checks from the government! (Gilmour is a bit disingenuous about the government's role in this obvious blunder.) Fred Ziffel got $62,000, while Newt Kiley got $45,000!

Naturally, the IRS sends a man to Hooterville to straighten things out. Just as naturally, he makes no headway. In any case, it is too late to get the money back. Almost all of it has been invested in Mr.

Haney's newest project: a monkey-racing track. Oliver is flabbergasted, as always, but Lisa assures him that monkey-racing is quite popular. It's the second-biggest sport in Hungary, behind goulash-betting. The only solution our beleaguered IRS team can figure out is to join the rest and invest in the track, and in a stunning final scene, we actually see little monkeys in silks chasing a wooden banana.

Notes

- Since this episode originally aired, monkey-racing has gone from a quaint country custom to a national phenomenon. What? You haven't been out to the monkey-racing track? You really ought to go. The sight of those little simians in their jaunty silks tearing after the wooden banana will make even a skeptic's heart race. If there is no monkey track in your local area, you might tune in for the annual Chiquita Stakes, the July classic that aired on ESPN 3.

83

"How to Succeed in Television Without Really Trying"

green acres

Episode 83
Original air date: January 24, 1968
Original series run: 1965–1971
Series total: 170 episodes

THE BIG TV SATISFACTION FORMULA	
SyndicoDurability	7.7
Comic Valence	9.3
Emotional Resonance	7.2
Writing, Story	9.6
Writing, Characters	8.9
Acting	8.8
Quintessence	8.4
Series Originality	8.1
Episode Originality	8.5
Historical Significance	6.9
Celebrity	6.7
Gimmickry	9.7
Theme Song	9.7
Kitsch	8.5
BTVS Ratio	**78.92**

Credits

Open: Eddie Albert, Eva Gabor. Created and Produced by Jay Sommers. Executive Producer Paul Henning. Written by Jay Sommers and Dick Chevillat. Directed by Richard L. Bare. End: Pat Buttram as Mr. Haney. Tom Lester . . . Eb. Frank Cady as Sam Drucker. Alvy Moore as Hank Kimball. Hank Patterson . . . Fred Ziffel. Barbara Pepper . . . Doris Ziffel. Christopher Sheal . . . Dilly Watkins. Tom Browne Henry . . . Mr. Malone. Story Consultant . . . Dick Chevillat. "This has been a Filmways Presentation, Darling."

Episode Review

Another wonderful postmodern experiment disguised as a rural sitcom. This one begins with Eb suggesting that Oliver invest money in the business of a local inventor, Dillingham Watkins, president of his own electronics firm and ten-year-old boy genius. Oliver is skeptical.

To prove Dilly's worth, Eb has the boy "electronificate" the house while Oliver and Lisa are away, adding a "burglar discourager" that gives them an electric shock when they touching their own front door. Oliver goes to call Dilly, and he finds that he doesn't have to climb the pole because Dilly has put in a "phone-come-to-er." Now this actually seems to be an improvement, and Oliver is warming up to the boy until the phone whips him up into the air and drops him thirty feet.

More havoc has been done. Oliver finds that his TV's insides are gone, used to create a monitor in the barn. And they can't get into the barn because the door is now "moo-activated." Eb suggests they will need the cow to get in and calls Eleanor on her two-way radio. Eleanor gets the door open, and Oliver gets in; but the door closes behind him, and he is locked inside. He has to crow like a rooster to get the door open.

Meanwhile, the monitor that was installed has actually been made into a TV transmitter. So all of Oliver's struggles to get out are being viewed by Arnold and the Ziffels on their TV set at home. They think he's trying to teach his cow to crow like a rooster and agree that the show will never be a hit.

Oliver finally gets out and brings the camera into the bedroom (not aware that it is broadcasting) for Dilly to turn it back into a TV set. But the next day a Mr. Malone from the FCC comes to arrest Oliver for illegally broadcasting. Oliver protests, of course, but just then Mr. Haney arrives to give him his royalty for the sale of polka-dot underwear as seen on his "Man Getting Undressed" show. "Oh, selling commercials!" accuses Malone.

Somehow, Oliver manages to avoid prison, but in a classic "here we go again" ending, another of Dilly's inventions is broadcasting on a radio frequency. Oliver is explaining his tax write-offs to Lisa, and we see that Sam Drucker down at the store is listening in. "Shh, I'm listening to *The Income Tax Evasion Hour* on the radio . . ."

Triple

Fittingly, *Green Acres* delivers a triple in which the first two elements are absurd, and the interruptive third is not. When Mr. Haney arrives, he also has great news, the overnight ratings are in and in the Hooterville area *Man Getting Undressed Show* was number one, followed by *Barnyard Imitations Show*, and third *The Beverly Hillbillies*.

Notes

- There is one particularly obscure joke in this episode that is worth explaining. Eb suggests that Oliver is being pessimistic: "You must have been the fellow who told Fulton that his fish market wouldn't work." This intricate malaprop is based on the fact that while there is a Fulton Street Fish Market in New York City, the more reasonable claim to fame for a Fulton would be that of Robert Fulton, inventor of the first profitable steamboat.
- In a cosmic coincidence of absolutely no meaning or import, this episode is both eighty-third in the series and eighty-third in the BTVS Top 100.

82

"Miss Jekyll and Hide"
my favorite martian

Episode 35
Original air date: May 17, 1964
Original series run: 1963–1966
Series total: 170 episodes

THE BIG TV SATISFACTION FORMULA

SyndicoDurability	8.3
Comic Valence	9.1
Emotional Resonance	9.3
Writing, Story	8.5
Writing, Characters	8.4
Acting	7.2
Quintessence	9.4
Series Originality	7.1
Episode Originality	8.9
Historical Significance	7.2
Celebrity	9.2
Gimmickry	9.2
Theme Song	7.1
Kitsch	9.2
BTVS Ratio	**78.94**

Credits

Open: Starring Ray Walston as The Martian, with Bill Bixby as Tim O'Hara. Produced by Jack Chertok. Written by Al Martin and Bill Kelsay. Directed by Oscar Rudolph. End: Pamela Britton appeared as Mrs. Brown. Paula . . . Marlo Thomas. Edgar . . . Tom Skerritt. Young Man . . . Peter Brooks. Created by John L. Greene.

Episode Review

Mrs. Brown's niece Paula Clayfield is visiting, and she's a brilliant scientific prodigy. She is immediately intrigued by Martin's spaceship plans, which he carelessly left out. "This must be your oxygen recycler and waste moisture conversion unit!"

The next day, Paula comes by again, breathlessly excited about the possibilities of this design. Uncle Martin worries that she will figure out where he is from. He insists that Tim distract her with romance. Tim is reluctant, since his impression is that she is an unattractive nerd. They go on a date anyway, but there's no magic.

Paula returns to Martin to work with him on his engineering plans. Martin points his finger, and magically remakes her hair, ties the bow on her dress, adds makeup and, voilà . . . the librarian has become gorgeous! Tim is wowed! He immediately asks her out to a romantic restaurant. She is surprised, after the lukewarm first date, but accepts.

After the date is over, Martin undoes his artistry. Tim comes upstairs and reveals that he has proposed to her! "But Tim," protests Martin, "this girl has a super intellect!" And he responds righteously, "What do you think attracted me to her in the first place?"

Come morning, she's a nerd again. But Martin tells her that she's just hiding behind her intellect, that she can be beautiful if she wants to be. This time instead of magic, he shows her how much better she would look with her hair up, glasses off, etc.

She is thankful, but has also scooped up a rare Martian mineral to analyze down at the university labs. Furthermore, her sometime boyfriend Edgar arrives in town. He is an intellectual like her, and he hardly recognizes her. They go off, despite Tim's proposal, to the university. (The whole marriage proposal thing is taken rather lightly.)

Martin realizes that his mineral is missing and that if they analyze it, they will be on to him. They rush down to the university to recover it and do so in the nick of time.

Notes

- While one may expect an episode of this show to score high in Gimmickry and Kitsch, this episode's overall score depended more on its impressive 9.4 mark in Quintessence and 9.3 in Emotional Resonance.
- One of Paula's theories about the craft is that with the proper shield to take the first heat-wave impact, one could overcome that initial heat loss with microminiature electronic impulses. This is, of course, preposterous. As we now know, microminiature impulses would only increase the shield's conductivity!
- The special effect when Marlo Thomas is transformed is actually quite impressive for its era. In fact, we can't quite figure out how it was accomplished.
- Ray Walston has a clever bit part in the 1999 theatrical film version of *My Favorite Martian*, starring Christopher Lloyd.

81
"Soul Club"
the partridge family

Episode 18
Original air date: January 29, 1971
Original series run: 1970–1974
Series total: 96 episodes

Credits

Open: Starring Shirley Jones. Co-starring David Cassidy, Susan Dey, Danny Bonaduce, Jeremy Gelbwaks, Suzanne Crough, and Dave Madden as Reuben Kincaid. Created by Bernard Slade. Written by Harry Winkler & Harry Dolan. Directed by Paul Junger Witt. End: Executive Producer: Bob Claver. Produced by Paul Junger Witt. Story Consultant: Dale McRaven. "Bandala" Music by Wes Farrell. Lyrics by Edward Singleton. The voices and music of the Partridge Family were augmented by other performers. Guest Star Richard Pryor as A. E. Simon. Lou Gossett as Sam Simon. Co-starring Charles Lampkin as Heavy. Herbert Jefferson, Jr. as Black Leader. Baker . . . Morris Buchanan. Policeman . . . Ben Frank.

Episode Review

It's Detroit Rock City. The Partridges arrive on their bus for their "gig." And none other than Richard Pryor slides down the fire pole of the club: "Are you folks lost?" In fact, they are. They are supposed to be in Tucson; the Temptations are supposed to be here.

That's a real big problem, because A. E.

THE BIG TV SATISFACTION FORMULA	
SyndicoDurability	8.1
Comic Valence	9.1
Emotional Resonance	8.6
Writing, Story	8.3
Writing, Characters	7.9
Acting	8.1
Quintessence	7.5
Series Originality	8.2
Episode Originality	9.8
Historical Significance	8.1
Celebrity	9.7
Gimmickry	9.1
Theme Song	8.9
Kitsch	9.7
BTVS Ratio	**79.01**

Simon (Pryor) and his brother Sam (Lou Gossett, Jr.) have borrowed money from a loan shark to keep their operation afloat. It's a community thing—the name groups play for expenses, just to help them out. It's "a place for our people to go." If they can just get through this week, James Brown will be in town next weekend, but the loan shark, who goes by the name "Heavy," is merciless.

Shirley suggests that the Partridge Family could play anyway, but A. E. is skeptical: "I just don't think you're our kinda group." Then comes the heavy, relevant dialogue. . . .

SHIRLEY: You mean because we're white?

PRYOR: Oh wow, no. Our people like soul music, and I don't know if they'd turn out.

It's not because you're white; it's because you play white music. It's a subtle distinction, but they decide they've got nothing to lose. They go on, but their audience is exactly one person. A. E. is enthusiastic: "It's Albert, you'll love him. He's a big fan of yours."

All seems lost, but the Partridges are

nothing if not resilient. Laurie announces: "We're gonna have a block party." They all pitch in to raise interest and get the things they need for this last, desperate fund-raising event. They get food. Keith has an idea for a song—"it's sort of an afro thing"—and A. E. helps him score it. The only problem is that he's just got to have some violins.

Danny sneaks off (as usual, he gets the funniest subplot) and wanders into the Afro-American Cultural Society, where a large group of tough-looking black men are practicing martial arts: "I saw you were a cultural club, so I thought you might know where we might find some violin players?" Sure enough, they find him three "fiddlers."

R&B meets Bubble Gum Pop, and with all the berets and afros, the crowd is looking every bit like a meeting of the Black Panthers. They collect enough money to pay off the loan shark—who proceeds to begin roughing them up—but the Cultural Society members step in to protect them. They say their farewells, exchanging "soul shakes." And Danny is made an honorary member of the Afro-American Cultural Society—and even gets his own beret! Man, those Partridges can do it all, musical harmony and racial harmony, too!

Whee Wohn

The Partridge Family directors made frequent use of the "whee wohn" device, although they often did so without the use of a classic sound effect. Instead, they chose the "parallel dialogue" effect. In this classic episode, when they first arrive at the Detroit venue, Reuben sizes it up hopefully: "On the outside it looks like a condemned fire-house." We then cut to Reuben inspecting it from the inside: "On the inside, it still looks like a condemned firehouse."

Notes

- What was the difference between *The Brady Bunch* and *The Partridge Family*? As Louis Armstrong said about jazz: If you have to ask, you'll never know, but watching this very groovy and relevant episode might help.
- The revered and beloved Richard Pryor made his name on the stand-up stage, and in the movies that captured those performances, but he tried the TV thing, too. He wrote several *Sanford and Son* episodes. Later he guested on *SNL* and created a famously censored special for the networks.

80

"Zombo"

the munsters

Episode 60
Original air date: February 17, 1966
Original series run: 1964–1966
Series total: 70 episodes

Credits

Open: Starring Fred Gwynne as Herman. Yvonne De Carlo as Lily. Al Lewis as Grandpa. Pat Priest as Marilyn. Butch Patrick as Eddie. Produced by Joe Connelly and Bob Mosher. Written by Dennis Whitcomb. Directed by Ezra Stone. End: Special Guest Star: Louis Nye as Zombo, with Mike Barton as Frank, Jimmy Stiles as Billy, Jackie

Minty as Tommy, and Digby Wolfe as The Director. Developed by Norm Liebman and Ed Haas. From a Format by Al Burns and Chris Hayward.

Episode Review

On SCTV it was Count Floyd, but on many local channels nationwide there were other ghoulish hosts of weekend horror movie slots. In the particular corner of TV Land that the Munsters inhabit, the host is a ghoulish-looking fellow named Zombo. And Zombo's number-one fan is an innocent lad named Eddie Munster.

Herman arrives home and can't get Eddie to stop staring at the set. Herman is unhappy, although the horrifying films are "good wholesome entertainment."

Then, Eddie wins the Why I Like Zombo contest. Herman is jealous, believing a father should be a son's hero. Grandpa bucks him up, only to overhear Lily and Marilyn speaking of how wonderful and handsome Zombo is.

More drastic measures are called for.

THE BIG TV SATISFACTION FORMULA	
SyndicoDurability	8.8
Comic Valence	9
Emotional Resonance	8.8
Writing, Story	8.9
Writing, Characters	9
Acting	8.3
Quintessence	8.7
Series Originality	8.5
Episode Originality	8.9
Historical Significance	7.1
Celebrity	6.1
Gimmickry	9.3
Theme Song	8.6
Kitsch	9.3
BTVS Ratio	**79.06**

Grandpa gives Herman a secret formula to make him devastatingly gorgeous. He turns hideous—but in the backward land of Munsterville, they believe he has succeeded. He runs upstairs to "impress" Eddie's friends. But they don't go for it— "What's with the corny makeup?" (And they haven't noticed that their buddy Eddie is a little odd-looking himself?)

As part of the prize, Eddie gets to appear on Zombo's show. Eddie and Lily arrive to find that Zombo is a fake—an ordinary man who puts on makeup! Don't that beat everything? Grandpa and Marilyn literally drag Herman to watch Eddie on the TV. Meanwhile Eddie is finding that everything is fake!

Then Eddie is pushed in front of the camera by the desperate Zombo. "Is there anything you'd like to say to all your friends and fiends in television land?"

As a matter of fact . . .

"I'd like to tell everybody that Zombo is nothing but a big fake."

Apparently, this shocking revelation is not a mere blip in the world of live TV, but the deathblow to Zombo's successful run at the top. But he's not angry, he's been looking to get out of this gig for a while. All's well that ends well, and the upside-down world of the Munsters returns to "normal."

Triple

Louis Nye's Zombo is grateful that his show has been destroyed. Why? His answer concludes with a nifty comic triple. "I've been trying to get out of my contract for a month. I am made for much better things . . . *Macbeth, Hamlet, My Mother the Car.*"

Whee Wohn

When Grandpa is trying to cheer up the despondent Herman, he suggests: "What can Zombo give him that his father can't give him?" And we get a perfect whee wohn cut to Marilyn, looking over all the fabulous loot that the contest has provided: "A TV set, and a bicycle . . . I had no idea how many prizes Eddie won!"

Notes

- What makes every *Munsters* episode work is the inversion of almost all our expectations. (Beauty is ugly, tasty food is repugnant, etc.) What makes this episode stand out is the ultimate inversion. It's the twisted self-referential nature of having Eddie become a fan of a TV monster. That premise alone makes this episode a peculiar delight from beginning to end.
- Guest star Louis Nye first made his mark as one of the regulars on *The Steve Allen Show*, and he went on to make frequent guest-star appearances on TV and in the movies.

79

"In Society"
the abbott and costello show

Episode 29
Original series run: 1951–1953
Series total: 52 episodes

Credits

Open: Starring Bud Abbott and Lou Costello.
End: Executive Producer: Pat Costello. Written by
Clyde Bruckman. Cast: Hillary . . . Hillary
Brooke. Mrs. Van Goo . . . Isabel Randolph.
Landlord . . . Sidney Fields. Mike . . . Gordon
Jones. Joyce . . . Sheila Bromley. Mrs. Ashton . . .
Alix Talton. Digby (Butler) . . . Jack Rice. Foote
. . . Tristram Ruffin. Produced and Directed by
Jean Yarbrough.

Episode Review

Mike the Cop is running Lou in for non-payment of rent and somehow gets talked into showing Lou how helpless he would be if he had his hands handcuffed behind him. Mike insists that Lou cuff him.

Finding himself free, with Mike hand-cuffed, Lou takes advantage—poking him, then slapping him. Then he goes to town, slapping him over and over. Lou obviously lives for the moment, never pausing to consider the future. Delighted at the situation, he runs in to get Abbott; while he is gone a

passerby frees Mike. When Lou and Bud return, Mike keeps his hands behind him, so Lou assumes he is still cuffed. In a hilariously lengthy revelation, Lou first gets Bud to slap the cop, then thinks he sees Mike straighten his own cap with a free hand. He slaps Mike again—testing, and yes, he straightens his hat. Lou is chortling with glee the whole time, but as the truth dawns on him, he slowly make the transition from laughter to crying.

We never see Lou beaten senseless, but we can assume that Mike works him over thoroughly. The notion of police brutality is a long way off; and after all, when you slap a cop silly, the only possible retribution is a beating. It's schoolyard justice.

Meanwhile a society dame—Mrs. Van Goo—has hired Bud to take the place of the Duke of Glutton (pronounced Glueton), who was supposed to attend her party, since he bears an uncanny likeness to said nobleman. What about Lou? "Bring him as your friend, the Earl of Waldo."

When we arrive at the party, Abbott has apparently been holding court. It seems that imitating a British nobleman is not that difficult. Costello is jealous of Abbott's attention and is finally given the floor to tell a story. In a bit from their vaudeville acts, he tells a long suspense-building shaggy-dog story about Buzzards.

They go in to dinner, where Lou, in a classic timing sequence, can't finish his soup because the butler keeps removing it. The boys face artichokes for the first time, and they fling the leaves around the table as they try to get to the edible part. Finally, they are served dessert. Lou chases a cherry from his sundae all over the table, and inevitably incites a huge ice cream fight.

Whee Wohn

At the open of the episode, Mr. Fields bursts in and gives Lou ten seconds—literally—to pay the rent. Lou has no money, but he's confident that he won't get thrown out; after all, Mike the Cop is an old friend.

"Do you think my pal Mike will take me down to the station?" There is a whee wohn cut to Lou getting the bum's rush by Mike.

Notes

• Sure, "Who's on First" is more memorable, and Lou's fencing duel is a favorite of many, but this episode, in which the boys successfully masquerade as British nobility, scores highest according to the BTVS ratio.

• Jerry Seinfeld is a big fan of Abbott and Costello, and he served as host to a tribute special on the two. On the face of it, it's hard to see the connection. Seinfeld's comedy, both in stand-up and on his show, is verbal, observational, wry; Abbott and Costello's comedy is physical, slapstick, broad. On closer observation, however, there are parallels.

Both exist in an absurd, almost cartoonish world. Reality exists only as a backdrop for the set pieces. Mr. Fields is forever on the prowl for the forever late rent payments; Kramer can exist forever without visible means of support. The boys can cash a check for a million dollars and fourteen cents; Seinfeld can sell NBC on a show about nothing. Who is stranger and less wholesome: Stinky or Newman?

Are the series of jobs and get-rich-quick schemes that Lou takes on any more strange and unlikely than George's jobs and schemes? Are the stand-up interjections of the early years of *Seinfeld* so different from the Abbott and Costello performances in front of the curtain?

More than mere parallels, something at the essence of each show is the same. They are characters who, despite the extravagant and ludicrous situations in which they find themselves, are never anything but real. Lou's hunger is real. His frustration at chasing the cherry off his sundae is real. Lou's ineptness as waiter/delivery boy/exterminator/salesman is always real. The same is true of all the characters in *Seinfeld*. Whether inventing the "Bro" or dating Keith Hernandez or stealing a loaf of marbled rye, their hopes, passion, embarrassment, and anxiety are always genuine. It's the miracle of both shows that the actors can bring humanity to a world that is so blatantly contrived—and it's what ultimately makes the shows so brilliant.

78
"Hash"
barney miller

Episode 46
Original air date: December 30, 1976
Original series run: 1975–1982
Series total: 125 episodes

THE BIG TV SATISFACTION FORMULA

SyndicoDurability	8.2
Comic Valence	9.2
Emotional Resonance	7.1
Writing, Story	9.5
Writing, Characters	9.2
Acting	8.7
Quintessence	7.8
Series Originality	6.6
Episode Originality	8.7
Historical Significance	8.1
Celebrity	6.6
Gimmickry	6.7
Theme Song	7.5
Kitsch	7.6
BTVS Ratio	**79.12**

Credits

Open: Starring Hal Linden, Abe Vigoda, Max Gail, Ron Glass, Jack Soo. End: Directed by Noam Pitlik. Written by Tom Reeder. Created by Danny Arnold and Theodore J. Flicker. Produced by Danny Arnold. Story Editor: Tony Sheehan. Guest Starring Ed Peck, Walter Janowitz, George Perina, Michael Tucci, and Ron Carey as Officer Levitt.

Episode Review

Wojo enters with a shoe box and asks Barney to guess what's inside. Barney plays with him and asks, "Is it bigger than a shoe box?" Wojo slowly takes this in, and then responds: "It couldn't be."

It turns out to be homemade brównies baked by his new girlfriend. He hands some around. He eats some, so do Yemana, Harris, and Fish. They get a call reporting a couple of guys having a duel with sabers in Washington Square Park.

A police officer named Mike Slater shows up to say hello to Fish. They went through training together. Fish does not re-member, but Mike remembers, and he asks if Fish is still married to Bernice. Slater reveals that he once had a big crush on her. Fish takes all this in without reacting. Slater plans a lunch with all three of them.

Wojo and Fish are sent to investigate a prowler. Meanwhile, the men are beginning to act oddly. Yemana is showing how when you dip the brownie in the coffee, it gets mushy. "Mushy, mushy, mushy." Harris is feeling good: "Wha's happening baby . . ." and now Yemana is breaking into an impromptu song to the captain: "Barney, Barney, Barney, is your mother from Killarney?"

Barney suspects there is something in the brownies, and he sends them out to be tested. Harris concurs. He thinks, just from the way he's feeling, that they have hash in them. (But how would he know . . . ?) Then Barney asks: "How's Nick?" and Harris answers slowly: "I like him." Nick emerges from the back room to ask, "Anybody seen my legs?" Barney sends them both home for the day.

Wojo and Fish return with their man. In fact, the alleged thief tells them it was unbelievable, that Fish and Wojo were leaping twelve feet between buildings to catch him. Barney tells them of his suspicions. The lab returns the results. It is indeed hash. As Fish says: "First time in twenty years I feel really good, and it has to be illegal."

Then his old acquaintance Slater drops by to tell him that he had lunch with Bernice, and that it was too bad Fish couldn't make it. He then proceeds to make suggestive remarks about Bernice. Detective Fish, who spent a career complaining about his wife, gives a long passionate speech telling Slater off, telling Slater to steer clear of his woman, and telling him in no uncertain terms that she is the woman of his life.

Slater runs off, chastised. Fish turns back to the room.

"Oh my God, what am I talking about?"

Notes

- Danny Arnold began as a stand-up and comic actor, appearing in films with Dean Martin and Jerry Lewis. He began writing for early TV shows like *The Rosemary Clooney Lux Show,* and later series like *Bewitched* and *That Girl.* He also cocreated the critically acclaimed series *My World and Welcome to It.*
- At the same time Danny Arnold was creating *Barney Miller,* he and his team were also working on a female cops sitcom entitled *Ann in Blue,* which was also set in New York City. The pilots for both shows aired in the summer of 1974. The series *Barney Miller* was picked up and launched as a midseason replacement in January 1975.

77

"The Groovy Guru"

get smart

Episode 75
Original air date: January 13, 1968
Original series run: 1965–1970
Series total: 138 episodes originally aired;
117 shown in syndication

THE BIG TV SATISFACTION FORMULA

SyndicoDurability	7.3
Comic Valence	8.9
Emotional Resonance	7.2
Writing, Story	8.9
Writing, Characters	8.1
Acting	9.1
Quintessence	9.2
Series Originality	9.1
Episode Originality	9.1
Historical Significance	7.2
Celebrity	7.3
Gimmickry	9.1
Theme Song	8.4
Kitsch	8.8
BTVS Ratio	**79.15**

Credits

Open: Starring Don Adams, and Barbara Feldon as "#99." Edward Platt as "Chief." Created by Mel Brooks with Buck Henry. Produced by Burt Nodella. Executive Producer: Leonard Stern. End: Directed by James Komack. Written by Norman Paul and Burt Nodella. Story Consultant: Norman Paul. Guest Star: Larry Storch as the Groovy Guru. Ellen Weston as Dr. Steele. Sharon Vaughn as Wanda. Mickey Morton as Cab Driver. Bob Karvelas as Larrabee. Barry Newman as Assistant Guru.

Episode Review

Max survives a sneak bombing attack, then reports in for his assignment. The Chief reports that the Groovy Guru is hypnotizing teenagers with his music. "Do you have any idea how much damage ten million teenagers can do to this country?" To which Max replies dryly, "I thought they'd already done it."

First stop is to meet Dr. Steele, one of CONTROL's top chemists. She also turns out to be a stripper, who is working tonight in a Bo Peep outfit.

At the Groovy Guru's lair they are quickly captured by the old bug-in-the-rug trick. The floor opens up, and they are dropped into the Groovy Chamber, where they have an audience with the Guru himself, behind glass. As evil villains so often do, the Guru tells them his whole plan. Using the popular rock group the Sacred Cows (see below) he will hypnotize all the nation's teenagers. "Tonight all of television land's teenagers are gonna be on my wavelength. And when I say go, they are gonna attack the establishment!"

The Sacred Cows begin to play, with their irresistible beat, and 99 is drawn to dance. Max resists, but is eventually disarmed and left with 99 to die in a special chamber that amplifies every sound a thousand times. A mosquito makes a deafening roar, and flicking it makes a huge sound. Luckily, as any well-accoutered spy would, Max has a tiny tuning fork with him, and it makes a tone too high for the human ear but, when amplified, is enough noise to shatter the glass. They escape, beat up the Guru, and foil KAOS again.

Triple

In a series that was replete with running jokes, this episode is relatively light. There is one "the old ____ trick," two "don't tell me . . . I asked you not to tell me that," and a variation on the "would you believe . . ." formula, which itself is a specific variation on the basic triple. Max says, interrupted only by doubtful looks from the Chief,

"Have I ever failed you? Have I failed you recently? How about today?"

There is also a classic example of the "long-winded triple with a reverse." In this particular joke form, the speaker elaborates in three building statements, then reverses himself in some form, either admitting he doesn't know, or was lying, or just changed his mind. In this case, Max is forced to admit he doesn't know. 99 exclaims, "The Sacred Cows!" And Max agrees, "Of course it's the sacred cows. Who else could it be but the sacred cows? The sacred cows. One question, 99: Who are the sacred cows?"

Notes

- Larry Storch is best known as *F Troop*'s Corporal Agarn, but he was a frequent guest star throughout the sixties and seventies. He and Don Adams were actually childhood friends who grew up in New York City, along with another pal, James Komack, who went on to produce *Welcome Back, Kotter* and *Chico and the Man*.

- Barry Newman, who plays the minor role of Assistant Guru, is better known today as Petrocelli, the big-city lawyer who fought crime in San Remo, somewhere in the American Southwest.

76

"Mama's Little Pirates"
the little rascals

Episode 33
Series total: 79 episodes compiled
from the original theatrical shorts

Credits

Open: Hal Roach Presents *Our Gang.* "Mama's Little Pirate." Directed by Gus Meins. Photography by Art Lloyd A.S.C. End: "The End." No credits appear, but the following were the players: George "Spanky" McFarland, Scotty Beckett, Matthew "Stymie" Beard, Jerry Tucker, Marilyn Bourne, Gilbert Hullett, Paul Rodriguez, Billie "Buckwheat" Thomas, Claudia Dell as Spanky's mom, and Joe Young as Spanky's dad. Billy Bletcher was the voice of the giant; R.E. "Tex" Madsen was the giant.

Episode Review

Spanky is planning to lead an expedition to search for pirate treasure in a cave. But his mom catches him trying to take his dad's flashlight. Then he is smart-alecky, and gets sent to his room. There, in classic film optical fashion, his "bad boy" self splits from him, and his id and ego have a conversion. Spanky-id calls Spanky-ego a sissy. He says, "Well, what are we, mice or men?" At that, Spanky cleaves his two opposing parts together and heads for the cave.

We next see the gang inside the cave with candles. To avoid getting lost, Spanky ties a string to Buckwheat, who is sitting at the entrance to the cave. It'll leave a trail for them

THE BIG TV SATISFACTION FORMULA	
SyndicoDurability	9.2
Comic Valence	9.3
Emotional Resonance	8.9
Writing, Story	8.9
Writing, Characters	9
Acting	7.8
Quintessence	9.4
Series Originality	8.7
Episode Originality	8.6
Historical Significance	7.4
Celebrity	6.1
Gimmickry	9.4
Theme Song	8.5
Kitsch	9.1
BTVS Ratio	**79.19**

to get back out. But soon enough Buckwheat climbs in and starts following them.

Just when they run out of string, they find it. A truly giant treasure chest. They kick it open and treasure pours out, practically burying them up to their waists. They gather it in various comical ways. Spanky stuffs his pants full of gold and jewels. They start to head out. But Buckwheat has arrived . . . yoo-hoo!

Now they don't have a trail to follow! As they try to find their way out, they come across a giant door, and a giant chair, and giant footprint. . . . Then they hear the giant! He really does look quite giant compared to them. The kids try to hide around his cave and end up on a ledge inside his chimney. Coins slipping from Spanky's pants reveal them. Laughing and humming, the giant collects them all. At one point he uses a giant snap mousetrap to capture a boy. And flypaper gets Spanky! But Spanky doesn't give up, and he leads a merry chase ending up on the giant's bed . . . the giant pulls the sheets out from under him and, as Spanky crawls frantically away on the unending scroll of bed sheet, he recalls his mother's warning and all the mistakes that led to this fate.

Then he awakens in his own bed. It was all a dream, but the gang has gathered at his window. They are ready to go to the cave. Spanky-id returns and repeats, "Are we men or mice?" and Spanky gets up and gives him a swift kick. The end.

Notes
- The Little Rascals films, or Our Gang comedies, were originally created to be seen as movie shorts, but their long history in television syndication made them eligible for consideration, and this classic episode cracked the BTVS Top 100.
- As with all the Little Rascals episodes, the musical score adds brilliantly to the comedy, especially the up-tempo selection as the giant chases the little robbers.
- Tex Madsen, the actor who played the giant, was 7'6" tall.
- Leonard Maltin has suggested that this episode might have been, consciously or unconsciously, an inspiration for Steven Spielberg's *The Goonies*. The parallels are easy to see, especially the glorious discovery of pirate treasure. However, even more fascinating are the parallels between Spielberg's *Saving Private Ryan* and the episode in which Spanky baby-sits for a houseful of two-year-olds, including one kid who just keeps saying, "Remarkable!"
- In 1990 the actor who played Buckwheat was interviewed on ABC's news magazine *20/20*. One problem, though: The

real actor had passed away a decade earlier. ABC had been duped by an impostor.

75

"The Return of Father Lundigan"
the flying nun
Episode 34
Original air date: October 24, 1968
Original series run: 1967–1970
Series total: 82 episodes

Credits
Open: Starring Sally Field, Madge Redmond, Madeline Sherwood. Also Starring Alejandro Rey. Executive Producer Harry Ackerman. Written by Lee Erwin & Stan Dreben. Directed by Jerry Bernstein. End: Produced by Ed Jurist. Created for Television by Max Wylie & Harry Ackerman. Based on a Novel by Tere Ríos. Developed by Bernard Slade. Story Consultant: Michael Morris. Shelley Morrison as Sister Sixto. Sister Ana . . . Linda Dangcil. Stewardess . . . Stefani Warren. Sid Haig as Señor Quesada. Guest Star: Paul Lynde as Father Lundigan. Guest Star: Bernie Kopell as Dr. Paredes. In cooperation with the National Catholic Office for Radio and Television.

Episode Review
Sister Bertrille is avoiding a trip to the dentist, despite her evident need. She floats off midconversation with Sister Jacqueline. Next we meet a salesman of nuns' vestments, who is pitching the very latest thing, the "mini habit," a shorter skirt outfit. Nat-

THE BIG TV SATISFACTION FORMULA	
SyndicoDurability	7.6
Comic Valence	8.4
Emotional Resonance	8.2
Writing, Story	8.7
Writing, Characters	8.7
Acting	8
Quintessence	9.3
Series Originality	9.8
Episode Originality	8.7
Historical Significance	7.1
Celebrity	8.8
Gimmickry	9.4
Theme Song	7.1
Kitsch	9.7
BTVS Ratio	**79.25**

urally, the Reverend Mother is having none of it. The final establishing event is the arrival of Father Lundigan. Apparently, a year ago he had spent some time with the convent, dealing with the "delusional" thinking that a nun could fly, and he left after a breakdown of sorts. After a year's therapy he has returned, healthy and happy.

Carlos decides that what Sister Bertrille needs is Dr. Paredes, a dentist who uses hypnosis to help his patients deal with pain and anxiety. The Reverend Mother takes Sister Bertrille to him. The hypnosis works, and despite his reluctance ("Carlos, I'm a dentist, not a nightclub performer!"), he is also talked into showing what hypnosis can do. He hypnotizes Sister Bertrille and the Reverend Mother so that each will act like the other when they hear the word "red." Then he rushes off because his wife is having a baby, and (Let's see a show of hands, who saw it coming? Hmm, always the same hands.), he forgets to remove the posthypnotic suggestion!

Hoo boy! The Reverend Mother tries to

fly, she plays basketball exuberantly and decides that the whole convent should wear mini-habits, "Those crazy mini-habits!" Why? "A girl's entitled to change her mind, isn't she? Mini-habits for everybody!" In stark apposition, Sister Bertrille has lost her sense of fun entirely.

All this, combined with the usual flying, is enough to push Father Lundigan right back over the edge, as he continues taking notes about the situation for his "report." He runs away, leaving the convent "before it regresses to a violent phase." Actually, the most pressing danger is that the Reverend Mother will fling herself over the wall in an attempt to fly. But everything is straightened out. The dentist returns and breaks the spell.

Sister Bertrille runs after Father Lundigan to explain, and since he is already on the plane . . . well, she flies up to his window to say good-bye. Naturally, like William Shatner's passenger on the classic *Twilight Zone* episode, Father Lundigan immediately suffers a psychotic break.

Notes
- With hypnosis as a gimmick, a classic role-reversal plot, and quintessential guest star Paul Lynde, there was never a doubt that this would be the highest-ranking *Flying Nun* episode.
- Despite Lynde's sneering, prattling presence, the really spectacular performance in this episode is turned in by actress Madeline Sherwood as the Reverend Mother Plácido, who for most of the series was called upon to do nothing but scowl, disapprove, glower, and occasion-

ally look shocked. As she transforms into the giggling, energetic "Bertrille" personality, it is hard not to be stunned. Her characterization of the Reverend Mother as a severe authoritarian was so thorough and convincing, we found ourselves thinking "Boy, I can't believe the Reverend Mother agreed to do this script!"

- As noted in the credits, the series is based on a novel by Tere Ríos. That book, entitled *The Fifteenth Pelican* in its original form, was also republished in 1965 as *The Flying Nun*. The first episode of the TV series (an hour-long origin story) is relatively faithful to the text, including many events and characters more or less as written. The one major change is that, in the book, Sister Bertrille was very dependent on a group of fourteen pelicans who took a special interest in showing her around and guiding her long "glides." Perhaps this idea was being saved for the episode "With Love from Irving" in which a pelican falls in love with Sister Bertrille.

- By the way, though many sources list the Mother Superior's name as "Plaseato," this is probably a corruption of the name Plácido from the original novel.

- Although the episode is entitled "The Return of Father Lundigan," our research turns up no previous episodes with either Father Lundigan or Paul Lynde. Perhaps there is a "lost" episode waiting to be found? Or perhaps the "return" was simply a plot device?

- The character Sister Bertrille's given name was Elsie Ethrington.

- A running joke of the show was Sister Sixto's error-prone use of English idiom.

There is a fine example in this episode, as she suggests: "That kid's ready for the laughing ranch." Sister Jacqueline, everybody's straight nun, corrects her: "Funny farm."

74
"Lucy's Italian Movie"
i love lucy
Episode 150
Original air date: April 16, 1956
Original series run: 1951–1961
Series total: 179 episodes

Credits
Open: Lucille Ball, Desi Arnaz, Vivian Vance, William Frawley. End: Produced by Jess Oppenheimer. Directed by James V. Kern. Written for Television by Jess Oppenheimer, Madelyn Pugh, Bob Carroll, Jr., Bob Schiller, Bob Weiskopf. Director of Photography: Karl Freund, A.S.C. Executive Producer: Desi Arnaz, Jr. Uncredited: Vittoria Fellipi . . . Franco Corsaro. Bellboy . . . Saverio Lo Medico. Woman in Vat . . . Teresa Tirelli. Vineyard Boss . . . Ernesto Molinari. Grape Picker . . . Rosa Barbato.

Episode Review
Thanks to Fred's cheapness (who put him in charge of the European trip anyway?), they are taking a thirteen-hour trip in tight train seating. Like sardines, except "the sardines are better off—they've got all that oil to wiggle around in."

Lucy thinks a masher has been eyeing

THE BIG TV SATISFACTION FORMULA	
SyndicoDurability	10
Comic Valence	8.5
Emotional Resonance	7.5
Writing, Story	8.8
Writing, Characters	8.5
Acting	9.1
Quintessence	9.1
Series Originality	6.4
Episode Originality	8.4
Historical Significance	6.7
Celebrity	6.6
Gimmickry	9.3
Theme Song	7.1
Kitsch	8.9
BTVS Ratio	**79.45**

her, but it turns out to be Vittorio Fellipi! Lucy's seen all of his pictures. He asks innocently: "Tell me, Mrs. Ricardo, have you ever considered acting?" He is casting for his next film. Well! "The calla lilies are in bloom again!" Lucy musses her hair to demonstrate the sexy, rumpled look that she thinks will be perfect for a Fellipi leading lady. Arrangements are made to meet in Rome.

Lucy can't be bothered with sight-seeing; she must prepare for her role in *Grappolo Pungente* (*Bitter Grapes*). She gets hold of some peasant garb, then heads out to do some method-acting preparations. Lucy manages to get past suspicious coworkers and into the big grape stomping tub. After stomping grapes for a while, Lucy is pooped, but the other woman insists that she keep up the pace. The argument escalates into a full-scale brawl in the grape juice.

When Lucy returns—although still in black-and-white to us at home—she is apparently dyed blue. "Boy, when it comes to soaking up local color, you don't mess around."

Worst yet, Fellipi had wanted her for the role of a typical American tourist, so, not altogether surprisingly, another effort to make it big in show business goes by the boards. Worse, he picks Ethel to fill the role!

Notes

- Though many people perceive of *I Love Lucy* as the quintessential sitcom, an extension of vaudeville and radio comedy styles, there are other levels of resonance that have allowed it to survive while other series from the era have been more or less forgotten. The passage of time allows us new perspectives. For one, there is the underlying postmodern irony of a show that is all about trying to be "in the show." Desi plays the star; but Lucy is the star. The dissonance between their perceptions and ours create a compelling comic tension throughout.
- Not too surprisingly, *I Love Lucy* is the only series to score a perfect 10 in SyndicoDurability, the category that measures the long-term strength of a show. Below are the closest contenders among the BTVS Top 100. These are the shows that have continued to draw audiences long after their first run.

I Love Lucy	10
The Andy Griffith Show	9.9
The Brady Bunch	9.9
Gilligan's Island	9.8
The Honeymooners	9.7
The Flintstones	9.7
The Beverly Hillbillies	9.5
The Abbott and Costello Shaw	9.5
Leave It to Beaver	9.3
Bewitched	9.3

73

"Brewster's Baby"
the beverly hillbillies

Episode 127
Original series run: 1962–1971
Series total: 216 episodes

Credits

Open: Starring Buddy Ebsen, Irene Ryan, Donna Douglas, Max Baer. Created and Produced by Paul Henning. Written by Paul Henning and Mark Tuttle. Directed by Joseph Depew. End: Executive Producer: Al Simon. Featuring Mr. Drysdale . . . Raymond Bailey. Jane Hathaway . . . Nancy Kulp. Frank Wilcox as Mr. Brewster. Lisa Seagram as Edythe Brewster. Kitty Kats . . . Phyllis Davis, Joyce Nizzari, Christine Williams.

THE BIG TV SATISFACTION FORMULA	
SyndicoDurability	9.5
Comic Valence	8.4
Emotional Resonance	7.3
Writing, Story	9
Writing, Characters	9.2
Acting	8.5
Quintessence	8.9
Series Originality	8.8
Episode Originality	8.1
Historical Significance	8.7
Celebrity	7.3
Gimmickry	8.1
Theme Song	9.8
Kitsch	8.9
BTVS Ratio	**79.56**

Episode Review

Granny is going home to hillbilly country to midwife a birth. Mrs. Brewster's time is nigh, and there's nobody better at assisting in such matters than Granny. Mr. Drysdale is worried that they'll never come back and he will have lost his bank's largest depositor. "Granny's the key! Stop her and you stop them all."

Drysdale is too late to get Granny before the train leaves, so they drive ahead, where he actually makes Miss Jane Hathaway lie across the railroad tracks. It works, and they manage to get Granny back, convincing her that she is needed to help with a baby here. They have to scramble to create such a need, and the best they can do is another client of the bank who is about to adopt a baby.

Granny, however, misunderstands and thinks that the couple are just very naive and confused. That they don't know the facts of how babies are born. When they say, "We're picking him up at three o'clock," Granny thinks they're going to a baby store—to buy a baby.

She has Ellie get them a baby monkey—to take the place of the baby until Granny can "explain the facts" to them. But much to her surprise, they come home with a beautiful baby! Granny is dumbfounded: "It appears things have moved ahead considerable since my day."

Notes

• The cultural misunderstandings that were the core of *The Beverly Hillbillies* were never in better form, as they took on the potential disturbing subject matter of "birthin' babies."

- Granny reveals that Jethro was a physiological anomaly: "Funny thing about Jethro, he was born with a full set of teeth, like a beaver."
- In the B plot, Jethro drives home with three "Kitty Kats"—the TV version of Playboy Bunnies—but Jed won't let them stay.
- Max Baer was the son of heavyweight champion boxer Max Baer, Sr.

72

"Flower Power"

gomer pyle, u.s.m.c.

Episode 147
Original air date: March 28, 1969
Original series run: 1964–1970
Series total: 150 episodes

Credits

Open: Starring Jim Nabors. Also Starring Frank Sutton. End: Directed by John Rich. Written by Bill Idelson & Harvey Miller. Created by Aaron Ruben. Story Consultants: Duke Vincent and Bruce Johnson. Ronnie Schell as Duke Slater. Guest Artists Leigh French . . . Michelle. Rob Reiner . . . Moondog. Christopher Ross . . . Geordie. Forrest Compton . . . Colonel Gray. Ed Rice . . . Marine. J. Gilbert . . . Lieutenant Swanson. Executive Producers . . . Aaron Ruben and Sheldon Leonard.

THE BIG TV SATISFACTION FORMULA	
SyndicoDurability	7.8
Comic Valence	8.8
Emotional Resonance	8.8
Writing, Story	8.7
Writing, Characters	8.7
Acting	8.5
Quintessence	9.3
Series Originality	8.5
Episode Originality	8.4
Historical Significance	6.5
Celebrity	8.8
Gimmickry	8.8
Theme Song	8.1
Kitsch	8.9
BTVS Ratio	**79.71**

Episode Review

In order to win a maneuver, Sergeant Carter tries to find the most innocuous possible assignment for Gomer. So while the others are all moving, scouting, and covering possible targets, Gomer is set the task of painting the mobile command unit in camouflage. Gomer is disappointed, but Carter reminds him: "They also serve who only stand and paint."

Gomer sets to his appointed chore, and he's soon interrupted by three flower children: Michelle, Moondog, and Geordie. They "rap" and find that Gomer is just "doing his thing." Gomer agrees, "It is the thing Sergeant Carter gave me to do." They are a little upset that the truck is parked on some daisies.

The hippies share their philosophy of life, that possessions just hold you down. Gomer suggests that maybe they should try joining the Marines: "Well, I was just thinking, if you don't have a job or anything? You just got time on your hands? Maybe the service might be your answer." They don't

187

really think it's for them. They sing "Blowin' in the Wind" together. Enjoying their time with Gomer (or Greensleeves, as they have renamed him) and his "good vibrations," they volunteer to help him finish painting the camouflage on the truck.

Uh-oh! While Gomer finished one side, they did the other, with crazy hippie flowers! It's too late to repaint it now. The next morning at dawn, Sergeant Carter and Gomer return to find that the mobile command unit is gone! Sergeant Carter tries calling the unit's radio, and he reaches the hippies, who "crashed" in the truck for the night.

Through a happy circumstance, the moving of the truck actually kept it from being "captured" by the other team. Then the hippies themselves turn up. Inexplicably, the colonel thinks that the hippie painting, and "soldiers disguised as hippies" are part of a brilliant scheme hatched by Sergeant Carter. Those poor deluded army brass! You never know what they'll think.

Triple

There is a simple triple with what is technically called a "motivated third" early in this episode. Sergeant Carter was chosen to run the communications during the big maneuvers: "And why not? I got the experience, I got the know-how . . ." At that Gomer Pyle enters with a "Sergeant Carter!" And Carter completes the thought with a lower-tone third: "And I got Pyle."

Notes

- Episodes in which the Hollywood establishment attempted to represent the counterculture always score well in BTVS. There is something inherently amusing about the effort to sanitize the phenomenon. It's hippies, but there are no drugs, no anger at the Vietnam War, and only a pale imitation of acid rock. When this particular trio of flower children first enter, we know that they are hippies because the music suddenly veers into a cheesy melange of electric guitar psychedelia.

- Rob Reiner was apparently still wandering the country before settling down to mooch off Archie in Queens. "Moondog" looks very much like a young Meathead in his hippie clothes.

- In the coda scene, Gomer delivers a string of "peace beads" as a gift from Moondog to Sergeant Carter. And just at the moment Gomer slips them on to Carter, their commanding officer arrives; Carter must stand at attention with no time to remove the necklace. "Peace beads, Sergeant Carter?"

- The opening to the show, in which Gomer is seen marching with a large group of real-life Marines, was shot in North Carolina. Jim Nabors has soberly noted that many of the soldiers seen in the open were on their way to Vietnam, and many would not return.

- For all its innocence, perhaps this episode from late in the series was intended as a legitimate statement, if a rather soft one, about the war in Vietnam, which the show otherwise ignored. When they sing "Blowin' in the Wind," Gomer takes a solo verse. Quite an ironic image, as the naive Marine sings, "How many times must a man look up, before he can see the sky? How many ears must one man have before he can hear people cry? How many deaths will it take 'til he knows that too many people have died?" Wonder if Bob Dylan caught this episode?

71

"That's Show Biz"
f troop

Episode 58
Original air date: February 9, 1967
Original series run: 1965–1967
Series total: 65 episodes

Credits

Open: Starring Forrest Tucker, Larry Storch, Ken Berry, Melody Patterson, Frank DeKova. Written by Arthur Julian. Directed by Hollingsworth Morse. End: Produced by Herm Saunders. Hannibal Dobbs . . . James Hampton. Crazy Cat . . . Don Diamond. Trooper Vanderbilt . . . Joe Brooks. Trooper Duffy . . . Bob Steele, and "The Factory," Lowell T. George, Warren S. Klein, Richard T. Hayward, Martin F. Kibbee, as The Bedbugs. Executive Producer Hy Averback.

Episode Review

It's a classic exercise in anachronism as rock 'n' roll makes its way to 1870s Fort Courage. The men are learning to waltz for the Military Ball when the musical group arrives. It's the Bedbugs, and they launch into a rockin' version of "Camptown Races" as the faces of the men fall.

THE BIG TV SATISFACTION FORMULA	
SyndicoDurability	7.8
Comic Valence	9.2
Emotional Resonance	7.1
Writing, Story	8.8
Writing, Characters	8.5
Acting	8.8
Quintessence	8.6
Series Originality	8.9
Episode Originality	9.4
Historical Significance	7.2
Celebrity	8.7
Gimmickry	9.4
Theme Song	9.2
Kitsch	9.1
BTVS Ratio	**79.82**

But Agarn is smitten with them. In fact, he buys his way out of the army to become the manager of the Bedbugs. Why? To get rich quick! Agarn has become a whole new character, a rhyme-spouting agent who calls everybody "chicky baby." He plans to take them out on the "saloon circuit." "We'll start dazzling the hicks in the sticks, then work our way west to the coast, because it's the most."

O'Rourke has to figure a way to get his old pal back. His first plan is to set them up to play at the Fort Courage saloon and plant the audience with saboteurs. They hardly give the band a chance to start when they boo, holler, and then pelt them with assorted vegetables, fruit, and even sausages.

It could have worked, except that it turns out that the Hekawi like the Bedbugs' sound. Agarn's hopes arise again: "They could make a lot of money on the teepee circuit!"

O'Rourke's next plan is more subtle. Everyone knows Agarn is a hypochondriac, so they decide that if he thinks he's losing his hearing, because of how loud his band plays, that he'll give it up

The plan almost works, but Vanderbilt spoils the plan by calling out after he thinks Agarn is gone. Jane has the next plan: to come up with a group that's even better than the Bedbugs and try to sell Chief Wild Eagle on them. And so the Termites are born. They arrive on a buckwagon at the Hekawi camp, and Wrangler Jane sings "Lemon Tree." (Miraculously, Dobbs, the incompetent bugler, is a wonderful flutist.)

They're a smash, and Agarn falls for it. He decides to manage the Termites, promptly sending the Bedbugs packing. The members of the group then pepper him with demands until he quits and says he's going back to F Troop. The Termites close with "Mr. Tambourine Man."

In the coda, it seems that the Bedbugs have pulled a "Spinal Tap." Agarn is standing in front of the cannon begging someone to shoot him because he got a letter from his former protégés, who were a smash in Liverpool and London!

Notes

- This episode couldn't really have happened in the 1870s, because Bob Dylan didn't write "Mr. Tambourine Man" until 1964. Oddly enough, the previous episode (*Gomer Pyle, U.S.M.C.*) and this episode are the only two in the BTVS Top 100 that features songs written by Dylan, and they rank right next to each other.
- The front man for the Factory was Lowell George, who gained his greatest fame as slide guitarist for the country-rock group Little Feat, and died of unnatural causes in 1979.
- During the first saloon performance, when the band is pelted with food, there is one particularly astonishing moment that you can really enjoy only with a VCR. If you get a chance, tape the episode and watch this scene. For one thing, they are throwing real food, and throwing it with some gumption. But the wildest moment comes when a set of three link wieners come whipping up from the audience like a mace, and wrap themselves around Lowell George's face. It's particularly gratifying in frame-by-frame slow motion.

70

"It May Look Like a Walnut"

the dick van dyke show

Episode 51
Original air date: February 6, 1963
Original series run: 1961–1966
Series total: 158 episodes

Credits

Opening: Starring Dick Van Dyke, Rose Marie, Morey Amsterdam, Larry Mathews, and Mary Tyler Moore. End: Directed by Jerry Paris. Written by Carl Reiner. Produced and Created by Carl Reiner. Featuring Richard Deacon as Mel Cooley. Guest Starring Danny Thomas. Executive Producer: Sheldon Leonard. In Association with Danny Thomas.

THE BIG TV SATISFACTION FORMULA	
SyndicoDurability	8.1
Comic Valence	9.3
Emotional Resonance	7.2
Writing, Story	9.3
Writing, Characters	8.5
Acting	9
Quintessence	5.7
Series Originality	6.7
Episode Originality	9.9
Historical Significance	6.8
Celebrity	8.3
Gimmickry	9.8
Theme Song	8.4
Kitsch	8.8
BTVS Ratio	**80.14**

Episode Review

Much to Laura's chagrin, Rob is watching a late-night horror movie. He insists on telling her all about what she missed by hiding her head under the pillow. She doesn't want to know because she doesn't want to have nightmares, but he can't resist. It seems that invaders from Twylo come. They eat only walnuts, and bring with them particles of absorbatron which take away man's imagination and his thumbs! They sent an emissary who looks really scary . . . like Danny Thomas!

Eventually, Rob tells all there is to tell and they go to bed. Then the next morning he finds walnuts on the floor of the living room. He accuses Laura of planting them, but she plays dumb. He then watches as she gives Richie walnuts for lunch, and then offers him breakfast. Fried, poached, or scrambled . . . walnuts!

Frustrated that she won't give in and admit that she's mad, he goes to work, but things there are just as strange. Buddy is eating walnuts, and it seems that Danny

Thomas is the guest star. Everyone seems to think that Kolak is a real person. Strangest of all, Buddy and Mel are acting like good friends.

They all leave Rob alone when Danny Thomas makes his guest appearance; but he doesn't know who or what a "Danny Thomas" is, he is Kolak from the planet Twylo!

Rob finds that he has lost his thumbs! He decides to rush home so that he can wake himself up from this nightmare. Once there he opens the closet and a thousand walnuts pour out, with Laura surfing atop them: "Darling, what are you doing home from work so early?"

But it is too late, as he soon discovers that his Laura has been transformed into Lolak of Twylo. Rob is panicking when Buddy, Sally, Mel, and Danny all come into the room surrounding him and laughing when at last . . . the alarm clock rings and Rob awakens from his nightmare. Laura was also having a nightmare. They talk it over. Then try to find something soothing to watch on TV. The closest thing they can find (since this is before the dawn of TV Land!) is an exercise show. And we fade out as they begin touching their toes.

Triple

When Rob first arrives at the office, there is a simple, effective dialogue triple.

ROB: Hi, gang. I'm sorry I'm late.
BUDDY: I'm sorry I'm short.
SALLY: I'm sorry I'm single.

Notes

• Dick Van Dyke recalls that during the filming of this episode, they were all snacking on the props all week . . . which led to digestive problems all around.

- When Danny Thomas, one of the producers of *The Dick Van Dyke Show*, exits from his scene, he is humming the song "Oh Danny Boy," which is the theme song for his own long-running series, *Make Room for Daddy*.
- Rose Marie has been in show business practically from birth. She was "Baby Rose Marie," a precocious vaudeville tot. She has logged guest-starring appearances on *The Jackie Gleason Show; Dobie Gillis; Gunsmoke; Hi Honey, I'm Home,* and the underappreciated nineties series *The Good Life.*
- The suggestion of casting Morey Amsterdam as Buddy was Rose Marie's.
- For a while, the working title of *The Dick Van Dyke Show* was *The Full House.* A version of the show was made with creator Carl Reiner taking the lead role. That pilot was entitled *Head of the Family.*

69

"Too Many Girls"
the monkees

Episode 15
Original air date: December 19, 1966
Original series run: 1966–1968
Series total: 58 episodes

Credits
Open: Micky, Mike, Davy, Peter. Teleplay by Dave Evans and Gerald Gardner & Dee Caruso. Story by Dave Evans. Directed by James Frawley. End: David Jones, Micky Dolenz, Michael Nesmith, Peter Tork. Produced by Robert Rafelson and Bert Schneider. Developed by Paul Mazursky and Larry Tucker. Gerald Gardner & Dee Caruso, Script & Story Editors. Mrs. Badderly . . . Reta Shaw. Fern Kelly . . . Jean Peters. Hack . . . Jeff De Benning. Music Supervision: Don Kirshner. Background Music composed and conducted by Stu Phillips. "I'm a Believer," written by Neil Diamond and produced by Jeff Barry.

Episode Review
The Monkees are rehearsing "Steppin' Stone," but Davy is in a trance, a girl-induced catatonic state. He vows no more girls, but every time they turn around, there is another girl staring longingly at "the cute one."

They are lured into a gypsy tea room, where the matron, Mrs. Badderly, is a show-biz mom intent on nabbing a partner for her daughter, Fern. She uses a nail and some pepper to make her predictions come true, and also predicts that within twenty-

THE BIG TV SATISFACTION FORMULA	
SyndicoDurability	8.2
Comic Valence	8.9
Emotional Resonance	7.9
Writing, Story	8.7
Writing, Characters	8.9
Acting	8.6
Quintessence	9.6
Series Originality	9.1
Episode Originality	8.1
Historical Significance	6.6
Celebrity	7.6
Gimmickry	8.3
Theme Song	9.1
Kitsch	9.2
BTVS Ratio	**80.50**

four hours Davy will fall in love. (Well, that happens every day!)

The boys try to isolate Davy, finally chaining him to a chair. But he makes his escape when he gets an invitation to judge a beauty contest. "But how far can he get, dragging a chair?" They run after him. At one point, they think they've found him, but, no, it's another young man dragging a chair chained to his foot.

Sure enough, Davy has made his way into the clutches of Fern. He thinks he is in love, and he agrees to be her partner in the talent show amateur hour. The boys decide to sabotage his act. Also, they all enter the talent show as well. Peter does a bad magic act, culminating in his crying over spilt milk. Michael does a bad folk singer, Billy Ray Hodstetter. Micky does a rotten comedian-impressionist named Locksley Mendoza. Finally, Fern and Davy come out, and, thanks to bad throat spray and a breakaway cane, their song-and-dance number is a disaster.

The host then throws to his sponsor, but the Monkees correct him. "His sponsor? No, our sponsor!" When we return, the host is doing a commercial for the sponsor, a product named Sdrawkcab. "Remember, Sdrawkcab spelled backwards is backwards."

The final entry in the talent show is the Monkees, who sing "I'm a Believer."

Mrs. Badderly is foiled. Although, then Fern and Davy are announced as the winners!

Notes
- During the scene while Davy and Fern fall in love, don't think your eyes have gone bad. Apparently, the network censors decided that Fern's decolletage was too much for the 1966 audience. She has been discreetly blurred throughout the scene.
- "I'm a Believer" was a number-one hit, and the Monkees' all-time top-selling single.
- Michael Nesmith was independently wealthy because his mother invented the once-popular office supply product Liquid Paper.
- It's easy enough to make fun of the Monkees as the prefab four and all that, but long before the dawn of MTV, the guys at Screen Gems had tapped into the potent combination of television and rock music. The number-one and -two top-selling albums of 1967 were "More of the Monkees" and "The Monkees." Wallowing down at number ten was something the Beatles had thrown together called "Sgt. Pepper's Lonely Hearts Club Band."

68
"Hot Lips Hannigan"
the flintstones

Episode 9
Original air date: October 7, 1960
Original series run: 1960–1966
Series total: 166 episodes

THE BIG TV SATISFACTION FORMULA	
SyndicoDurability	9.7
Comic Valence	9.2
Emotional Resonance	8.1
Writing, Story	9.5
Writing, Characters	8.9
Acting	8.6
Quintessence	9.1
Series Originality	6.6
Episode Originality	8.1
Historical Significance	7.3
Celebrity	5.4
Gimmickry	9.3
Theme Song	9.7
Kitsch	9.1
BTVS Ratio	**80.51**

Credits

Open: Executive Producers: William Hanna and Joseph Barbera. End: Written by Warren Foster. Fred . . . Alan Reed. Barney . . . Mel Blanc. Wilma . . . Jean Vander Pyl. Betty . . . Bea Benadaret. Hot Lips . . . Jerry Mann.

Episode Review

Like many early *Flintstones* episodes, this one packs in a lot of plot. The lodge is having the annual talent show. Fred is planning to sing, but Barney has something up his sleeve that turns out to be a trampoline act. After a disastrous first try with it, Fred gets the hang of the trampoline ("Hey, hey, hey, these trampolines are all right!") and borrows it to surprise Wilma at the second-floor dress shop. He surprises her all right, peeping in at someone else in the changing room! And he can't stop bouncing! Luckily, Wilma has, for some reason, brought a frying pan with her to the dress shop, and lets her hubby have it.

That's all just preamble. Fred borrows a magic kit from Rockstone the Great. Wilma protests sensibly, "But, Fred, you don't know anything about magic!" He'll show her! After a failed effort to make an egg disappear, he ushers Wilma and Betty into a full-size "disappearing cabinet." He says the magic words and, alakazam! They're gone. (They found the back exit and snuck out to go along with the gag.)

Barney is impressed, and says, "Now bring them back." But Fred, in a classic bit of smug misjudgment, suggests they be less hasty. He made them disappear, so why not take advantage of their absence with a boys' night out on the town? As Wilma and Betty listen in, Fred and Barney plan on a night at Rockland Dance Hall.

The girls suspect the worst, but Fred is really interested in the music, not the dancing or women. His old high school chum Hot Lips Hannigan is playing. Soon after they arrive, Fred connects with his old pal, and they talk about the old songs. Then, for old time's sake, Hot Lips gets Fred to sing, and Barney takes a turn on the drums. "Dig Freddy Flintstone, the Golden Smog. And on the skins? Barney Rubble to give us trouble." They do "When the Saints Come Marching In" and after some initial skepticism from the young audience, they are a big hit.

Wilma and Betty are in the dance hall in disguise. They see the guys performing and watch the gathering storm of teenyboppers. Sure enough, Fred and Barney are stormed by screaming fans. They run for it, and are "rescued" by two ladies (Wilma and Betty in their hep outfits and wigs) who then come on to them. The boys are faithful as can be and run for it.

They race home, glad that Wilma and Betty will never know what happened. The girls have beaten them home, and when Fred summons them from the magic box, they appear . . . but still in teenybopper guise! Fred and Barney run and hide. When they think the coast is clear, they come out to face Wilma and Betty, now in their own clothes and hair. At first Fred faints dead away, rather than explain himself. Later he feels better, but when Wilma speaks in "hep talk," Fred, dazed and confused, goes back to bed.

Notes

- It is left unclear whether Wilma ever explains to her naive hubby what really happened. It is this sort of intentional ambiguity that gives *The Flintstones* its deep emotional resonance.
- *The Flintstones* is the series, according to the BTVS, that had the most extreme variance in episodes. This one obviously ranked very high, but as the series continued, the flights of imagination of the early episodes slowed to a trickle, and the show became dull. Even the addition of Pebbles and Bamm Bamm could do only so much to help.
- In addition to providing the voice of Betty and establishing her trademark giggle, Bea Benadaret played Cousin Pearl Bodine, who occasionally appeared on *The Beverly Hillbillies*, as well as Aunt Kate on *Petticoat Junction*.
- Fred and Barney's lodge is here called the "Loyal Order of Dinosaurs," although later it was the "Royal Order of the Water Buffalo." Maybe they switched allegiances?
- Long before Homer Simpson, Fred brought a wonderfully insouciant ignorance to television. Think about his reactions in the episode . . . he has somehow made his wife disappear in a magic box, and rather than being concerned about bringing her back, or what he has done, he sees it as an opportunity for a night out on the town!

67

"Christmas"
the wonder years
Episode 9
Original air date: December 14, 1988
Original series run: 1988–1993
Series total: 115 episodes

Credits

Open: Fred Savage, Dan Lauria, Alley Mills, Olivia d'Abo, Jason Hervey, Danica McKellar, Josh Saviano. Co-executive Producer: Bob Brush. Created by Neal Marlens and Carol Black. Supervising Producer: Steve Miner. Producer: Jeffrey Silver. Written by Bob Brush. Directed by Steve Miner. End: Executive Producers: Carol Black and Neal Marlens. Executive Story Editor: Matthew Carlson. Story Editor: Dave Stern. Featuring Liz Torres . . . Mrs. Gambino. Mary Gregory . . . Woman. Ty de Kierney . . . TV Salesman. Michael Landes . . . Kirk McCray. Gary McGurk . . . Tree Man. Robina Suwol . . . Perfume Lady. (Uncredited: Daniel Stern as voice-over of Kevin).

THE BIG TV SATISFACTION FORMULA	
SyndicoDurability	7.3
Comic Valence	8.7
Emotional Resonance	9.9
Writing, Story	9.1
Writing, Characters	9.2
Acting	7.8
Quintessence	9.8
Series Originality	9.1
Episode Originality	7.6
Historical Significance	6.5
Celebrity	6.2
Gimmickry	8.5
Theme Song	9.3
Kitsch	5.6
BTVS Ratio	**80.52**

Episode Review

Kevin and Wayne stare at it. It's incredible. Mesmerizing. It's *color* television. Maybe Dad will choose this Christmas to buy one for the family. It is a question that consumes both boys and threatens to ruin the holidays.

That's not all. Winnie has given Kevin a present, not to be opened until Christmas. Now he has to figure out exactly what she meant by it and get a present for her that will be neither too romantic nor too mundane. "I had to find a present for Winnie. It had to be perfect. It had to say everything without saying anything, and it had to be under six bucks." After some difficulties, time runs out and he gets her a snow globe.

The psychological war that Kevin is fighting with his dad keeps getting set back to square one by Wayne, who brings brute force to a subtle operation. As the family watches TV, Wayne rattles off comments about the lack of color. "That's the ocean, could it be orange? Probably it's blue, but how would I know?" And "Ew, that man is eating a gray banana." Dad is buried in the paper. Even Mom is too sad to help bring any holiday cheer to the group.

Kevin walks his gift over to Winnie's, running through a fantasy in his mind of what it will be like. Winnie, dressed as a sort of snow princess, standing in the warm glow of her open door and starting to kiss . . . The door opens, and Kevin returns to reality. It is an older woman he doesn't recognize. Winnie's family is away. It was a last-minute decision. The woman at the door explains, and says, "Gwendolyn said you would understand." Then she adds, "You know about her brother Brian, right? He was killed last fall, in Vietnam?"

Kevin feels stupid. How could he have forgotten what her family was going through. What difference did a color television really make? He rejoins his family, who are outside caroling with some other neighbors when it starts to rain . . . pour. For some reason, while the others run for cover, Mr. Arnold doesn't. He stands, and his family stands with him. Then after a few moments, he starts to laugh. And they all join in.

That night Kevin opened his present from Winnie: a four-leaf clover. In reflection, a reminder that we should wish the best for those around us.

And they got the color TV set . . . two years later.

Whee Wohn

There is a subtle whee wohn cut in the department store as Paul helps Kevin shop for Winnie. Paul suggests a snow globe, but Kevin decides to find the intoxicating scent he had smelled on Winnie. It's hard to describe. "Leaves . . . in the ocean . . . at night?" One after another he smells practically every scent in the store and finally finds it! Then Paul bursts his bubble. "If she already has it, why get her more?" Whee wohn cut to Kevin buying the snow globe, hoping that it really is the thought that counts. It's not an over-the-top cut with a full sound effect, but it still counts, technically.

Notes

- Like many episodes in the BTVS Top 100, this one contains many of the key elements that defined a series. In this particular case, it is the two key relationships—Kevin-Father and Kevin-Winnie—along with the quintessential childhood memories of Christmas and shopping for a present. Plus there are the era-specific details that make the show so resonant for baby boomers: Vietnam and the advent of color television.
- The use of a narrative voice in *The Wonder Years* is not unlike the great film *A Christmas Story,* so it's fitting in some way that this Christmas story would be the highest-ranked holiday episode of *The Wonder Years,* and the only one to crack the BTVS Top 100.
- Writer Dave Stern is the brother of voice-over narrator Daniel Stern.
- It has often been debated whether this series should even be measured against "sitcoms," since it is so unconventional, but the BTVS allows us to compare. It ranks high in series originality, naturally, as well as in emotional resonance, but definitely has enough humor to measure up.

66
"Caged Fury"
the bob newhart show
Episode 99
Original series run: 1972–1978
Series total: 120 episodes

Credits

Open: Bob Newhart in . . . *The Bob Newhart Show.* Also starring Suzanne Pleshette. Created by David Davis and Lorenzo Music. Written by Gordan & Lynne Farr. Directed by Michael Zinberg. End: Produced by Gordan & Lynn Farr and Michael Zinberg. Story Consultant: Sy Rosen. Executive Producers: Tom Patchett and Jay Tarses. Also starring Peter Bonerz as Jerry Robinson. Bill Daily as Howard Borden. Marcia Wallace as Carol Kester Bondurant. Will Mackenzie as Larry Bondurant. And Jack Riley as Mr. Carlin.

THE BIG TV SATISFACTION FORMULA	
SyndicoDurability	8.7
Comic Valence	9.5
Emotional Resonance	7.6
Writing, Story	9.2
Writing, Characters	9.1
Acting	8.6
Quintessence	8.3
Series Originality	6.8
Episode Originality	9.1
Historical Significance	7.7
Celebrity	5
Gimmickry	9.1
Theme Song	8.1
Kitsch	7.3
BTVS Ratio	**80.54**

Episode Review

The year is 1976, and in honor of our nation's bicentennial, Jerry decides that he will railroad Bob into throwing a Fourth of July party. Howard decides that he will host this little wingding but, of course, has to get everything he will need from Bob. In setting up for the party, Bob and Emily go to their basement storage room to get a card table and punch bowl. While there, Emily starts going through old stuff. She finds their wedding album. When she suggests that her mother was happy for them, Bob recalls things a bit differently than Emily: "Your mother wore black to our wedding." Emily replies: "That was dark gray . . . only her armband was black."

As Bob grows increasingly impatient, Emily comes across Bob's old exercise contraption and sets it up. Pulling on the cords to try it out, Emily pulls the door closed and the doorknob off. Bob immediately realizes they're locked in.

Looking for a way to pass the time, Bob asks Emily if they should tell jokes. Sure, she replies. So he starts with a riddle: Why did the moron lock herself and her husband in the storage locker? Emily waxes philosophical: Did you ever wish we had kids? And Bob responds, "Right now I wish we had a kid . . . that was a human mole."

Meanwhile, the party upstairs is getting started. Jerry shows up in a full Uncle Sam suit, bright jacket, top hat, and red-striped pants—and Howard answers the door in the same suit. "They said they only rented one of these," says Jerry. Howard: "I didn't rent this, I own it." Then Carol and her husband arrive, both also in the same suit.

Downstairs, Bob and Emily have faced the possibility of spending the night and have gotten into sleeping bags. Emily is still trying to take advantage of this opportunity to talk; Bob is still single-minded. Emily asks, "If I died, would you remarry?" Bob responds thoughtfully that, yes, he might: "Someone different than you. Someone big enough to break through that door."

Then, rescue! Howard arrives looking for the punch bowl. He can't believe what he sees. "If you didn't want to come to my party, why didn't you just say so. You didn't have to hide." He stomps off, having closed the door on them again. In the coda, the whole group from upstairs has arrived in their Uncle Sam costumes. Bob: "I feel like I've been rescued by a vaudeville act."

Notes

- This episode is a perfect representation of the later period of *The Bob Newhart Show,* in which Dr. Hartley has evolved from a stuttering, deadpan observer full of self-doubt into a stuttering, deadpan observer brimming with self-confidence. His jokes are tinged with a cynicism bordering on bitterness. There were still many classic episodes to come—the nudist camp, the elevator shaft, and the ex-cons—but it was becoming clear that someday Bob would have to leave the frenzied, neurotic city and escape to the gentility and calm of Vermont.
- Isn't it a little odd that Bob and Emily store their wedding album in the basement?
- This series landed two episodes among the BTVS Top 100, and, oddly enough,

each of them is centered around a holiday that is generally ignored by sitcoms. The other episode is the Thanksgiving-themed "Over the River and Through the Woods" (ranked fifty-eighth).

- Eerily, this episode is number ninety-nine in the series, and ranked as number sixty-six on the BTVS Top 100. We're turning the world of television upside down!

65

"Never Trust a Little Old Lady"

green acres

Episode 48
Original air date: December 28, 1966
Original series run: 1965–1971
Series total: 170 episodes

Credits

Open: Eddie Albert, Eva Gabor. Created and Produced by Jay Sommers. Executive Producer: Paul Henning. Written by Jay Sommers, Dick Chevillat, and Al Schwarz. Directed by Richard L. Bare. End: Pat Buttram as Mr. Haney. Tom Lester . . . Eb. Alvy Moore as Hank Kimball. Frank Cady as Sam Drucker. Smiley Burnette . . . Charley Pratt. Rufe Davis . . . Floyd Smoot. Hank Patterson . . . Fred Ziffel. Kay E. Kuter . . . Newt Kiley. Jack Bailey . . . Announcer. Story Consultant: Dick Chevillat. "This has been a Filmways Presentation, Darling."

Episode Review

Oliver is once again attempting to till the good earth, starting with tiny little seeds

THE BIG TV SATISFACTION FORMULA	
SyndicoDurability	7.7
Comic Valence	9.2
Emotional Resonance	8.2
Writing, Story	9.4
Writing, Characters	9
Acting	8.7
Quintessence	8.8
Series Originality	8.1
Episode Originality	9
Historical Significance	6.8
Celebrity	6.3
Gimmickry	9.5
Theme Song	9.7
Kitsch	8.8
BTVS Ratio	**80.78**

that push up through the soil seeking out the sunlight that will allow them to grow and flourish . . . (please provide your own patriotic music). This time, it's tomatoes, and the question is when exactly to harvest them. When is the first frost coming? Rather than turn to "Ye Olde Farmer's Almanac," the locals rely on either Walter or the little old lady. Oliver would rather have a more trustworthy meteorologist, but the choices in Hooterville are limited. Oliver's anxieties manifest themselves in a dream, in which he and Lisa become life-sized figures in a giant Bavarian clock.

In the end, Oliver's failure to heed the wisdom of the little old lady leads him to leave his tomatoes in the field too long. How can he possibly save them? As they so often do, Lisa's famous "hotzcakes" save the day, converted into tomato plant warming "crêpes suzette." The final triumphant scene shows the Douglases in their field amid the flames. The tomatoes are saved!

Notes

- Though many casual TV viewers lump the story of Lisa and Oliver Douglas's dislocation to Hooterville in with all the other rural comedies of that era—*Gomer Pyle, U.S.M.C., The Beverly Hillbillies, Petticoat Junction,* et al.—in fact, *Green Acres* was a strange and wonderful show like none other. It combined surrealism and nonsense that Salvador Dalí and Lewis Carroll would have admired, and never more so than in this episode, the highest ranking of the three episodes that made the BTVS Top 100.
- Lisa Douglas's incredible inedible pancakes have served in other episodes as handy roofing shingles and as spare parts for the automobile engine.

64

"The One After the Super Bowl, Part II"

friends

Episode 37
Original air date: January 28, 1996
Original series run: 1994–
Series total: 146 episodes through 1999,
still in production for 2000–2001 season

Credits

Open: Jennifer Aniston, Courteney Cox, Lisa Kudrow, Matt LeBlanc, Matthew Perry, David Schwimmer. Created by David Crane and Marta Kauffman. Written by Michael Borkow. Directed by Michael Lembeck. End: Executive Producers: Kevin S. Bright, Marta Kauffman, David Crane.

Executive Story Editors: Ira Ungerleider & Adam Chase. Executive Story Editor: Alexa Junge. Executive Story Editors: Jeff Astrof & Mike Sikowitz. Executive Story Editors: Michael Curtis & Gregory S. Malins. Special Guest Stars Julia Roberts as Susie, and Jean-Claude Van Damme as himself. Guest starring Lisa Roberts as Cathy. Co-starring Seth Isler . . . Monkey Trainer. Steven M. Porter . . . Security Guard.

Episode Review

The episode begins with a brief synopsis of Part I, which basically explains that they have come down to the set of a movie to find Marcel the chimp. There Chandler sees an old acquaintance, Susie Moss (Julia Roberts), whom he doesn't really remember until she prompts him that they were in grade school together. She has really grown up, and the two flirt.

Meanwhile, Monica is confiding in Rachel her deep and abiding crush on Jean-Claude Van Damme. Rachel prods her to go introduce herself, but Monica is too shy. Rachel agrees to go and talk to him, but

THE BIG TV SATISFACTION FORMULA	
SyndicoDurability	7.3
Comic Valence	9.5
Emotional Resonance	7.2
Writing, Story	9.3
Writing, Characters	8.3
Acting	8.8
Quintessence	8.5
Series Originality	7.1
Episode Originality	8.8
Historical Significance	8.8
Celebrity	9.9
Gimmickry	8.8
Theme Song	6.5
Kitsch	7
BTVS Ratio	**80.84**

"speak for yourself, John Alden!" Van Damme hits on Rachel. Monica is devastated.

Susie is Chandler's dream come true. Sexy, assertive, not afraid to try anything. In fact, she convinces Chandler to wear her panties out to dinner because it would be sexy. Why? Well, after all, then what would she wear?

Rachel and Monica are home, where they get into a major forehead-flicking fight, which turns into an actual fight that Phoebe must break up physically by pinching their ears. It is settled that Rachel will "give" Jean-Claude back to Monica.

So Monica gets her date, and she walks arm-in-arm with the action movie hero, asking him, "Can you beat up that guy? Can you beat up that guy?" But they get to talking, and Monica asks why he agreed to switch from Rachel to a blind date with her. He answers: "Rachel said you were dying to do a threesome with Drew Barrymore . . ."

Cut to Rachel and Monica hitting again. Then they destroy each other's things. Monica unravels Rachel's favorite sweater while Rachel pours marinara sauce into Monica's handbag.

At dinner, Susie coaxes Chandler to leave the table and meet her in the men's room. Hot and bothered, he complies. In fact, he also goes along when she suggests that he take off all his clothes but the panties in the stall. She then proceeds to take all his clothes and leave him stranded, all part of an elaborate revenge for a long-forgotten (by him!) prank in elementary school that left her with the nickname "Susie Underpants." As Joey later puts it,

with his standard partial comprehension: "Talk about bad luck! The first time you try panties and someone walks off with your clothes."

Marcel's done with filming, and Ross guesses that he has big parties to go to, but no! Marcel is there at the window! Waiting for his old pal! What follows is a sappy montage of Ross and Marcel to Barry Manilow's "Looks Like We Made It."

Triple

It's actually a quadruple, rarely attempted, but glorious when executed properly. Over the end credits we get to see Joey acting the small part he had landed with Jean-Claude Van Damme. During Joey's death scene, Van Damme's line is, "This man is dying . . ." to which Joey reacts with a piece of hammy coughing and gasping. They take it again. "This man is dying . . ." more overacting. One more try. "This man is dying . . ." a smaller, but still failed, effort to look natural. The fourth take, and the line has been rewritten, "This man is dead." Joey is perfectly still. Dead, he can do.

Notes

• This is the second half of a two-parter that was originally an hour-long episode that aired, as you might well assume, after the Super Bowl. We have judged it in the two half-hour versions created for syndication. Part I is a fine episode featuring Brooke Shields as a delusional soap opera fan who has confused Joey with his role on *Days of Our Lives*, but it doesn't quite stack up to Part II.

• Many shows have occupied the much-desired time slot right after a Super Bowl, when everybody in the world has their TV set on (although, frankly, they have probably nodded off, given the usual on-field drama of the Super Bowl). Some years, this slot is used to launch a new series, such as *The Wonder Years*. This particular year, the network chose to give their hit show a boost rather than expose some untried rookie.

- Almost all *Friends* episode titles begin with "The One Where . . ." in a nod to the way most people talk about TV episodes. Frankly, we're shocked that more viewers don't do the proper research to know the proper titles of episodes, but perhaps we're prejudiced on the matter.

63

"Bubble Boy"
seinfeld

Episode 47
Original air date: October 6, 1992
Original series run: 1990–1998
Series total: 180 episodes

Credits
Open: Jerry Seinfeld, Julia Louis-Dreyfus, Michael Richards, and Jason Alexander as George. Supervising Producer: Larry Charles. Supervising Producer: Tom Cherones. Executive Producer: Andrew Scheinman. Created by Larry David & Jerry Seinfeld. Written by Larry David and Larry Charles. Directed by Tom Cherones. End: Executive Producer: Larry David. Executive Producers: George Shapiro & Howard West.

Producer: Jerry Seinfeld. Story Editor: Peter Mehlman. Program Consultants: Jon Hayman, Bob Shaw. Program Consultants: Bill Masters, Steve Skrovan. Guest Starring Heidi Swedberg as Susan. Jessica Lundy as Naomi. Brian Doyle-Murray as Mel. Carol Mansell as Mother. O-Lan Jones as Waitress. Also Starring Jon Hayman as Donald. George Gerdes as Man #1. Tony Pappenfuss as Man #2.

Episode Review
George and Jerry plan on going to Susan's place in the country for the weekend, and not with Kramer. Luckily, he's got big golf plans. He gave one of the "cubanos" to a golf pro and got an invite to the Westchester Golf Club in return. Still, he would like to go. Is there any golf up there? Nope, pies, the boys say. It's pie country. Lots of pies. Somehow, Kramer is deterred.

Jerry has no date, so he asks Elaine. While they're talking in the diner, Mel Sanger comes over and introduces himself. He's a Yoo Hoo truck driver, but, more to

THE BIG TV SATISFACTION FORMULA	
SyndicoDurability	6.8
Comic Valence	9.3
Emotional Resonance	7.5
Writing, Story	9.3
Writing, Characters	9.1
Acting	8.7
Quintessence	9.4
Series Originality	7.5
Episode Originality	8.9
Historical Significance	7.5
Celebrity	7.7
Gimmickry	9.7
Theme Song	7.1
Kitsch	6.8
BTVS Ratio	**80.85**

the point, his son has an immunological disorder and must live inside a bubble. It seems that "our little bubble boy" saw Jerry on *The Tonight Show* and that Jerry is his favorite comedian. It would mean a whole lot if Jerry would come visit him for this birthday this weekend. Jerry hesitates, but Elaine insists that he must.

At first it seems that the weekend plans will be scotched, but Susan knows the town the Bubble Boy lives in and it's right on the way! However, as they drive up the Saw Mill River Parkway out of New York, George's insistence on "making good time" causes him to lose Jerry, who is trying to follow him but can't keep up and doesn't have any directions.

Hopeless, Jerry and Elaine pull into a diner. There, Jerry is recognized, and Elaine, just to torment him, goes and gets a photo for him to sign. She knows that one of his pet peeves is his inability to come up with anything clever to write on such photos. After he writes the short couplet "There is nothing finer than being in your diner," he has second thoughts (Elaine says it's incredibly lame, and asks if he wants that hanging in this diner forever); he tries to get them to give it back. Nothing doing. A fight breaks out.

George and Susan made it to Bubble Boy's house, and she insists they go in. They sit with his parents, explaining that Jerry is lost. We hear the Bubble Boy off-screen, not a cute little guy at all, but a belligerent adult: "What do I have to do to get some food around here!"

They go in to meet him. "Who are you? Where's Seinfeld?" But George tries to be friendly, and they get into a highly competitive game of Trivial Pursuit. The Bubble Boy is beating George when the question "Who invaded Spain in the eighth century?" comes up. Bubble Boy knows and says, "The Moors." But the card reads, "Moops." Bubble Boy protests angrily, but George insists that it is "Moops." Their argument escalates into a physical fight, and Bubble Boy gets his arm extenders locked around George's neck, when suddenly the bubble springs a leak. A loud hissing sound.

Meanwhile, Kramer has arrived—after buying a lot of pies—at Susan's family house with Naomi, Jerry's girlfriend. They prepare to go for a swim, and when they do Kramer leaves a lit cigar on a pile of newspapers.

The events accelerate. Elaine and Jerry's brawl at the diner is interrupted by two angry men, who come in to raise up a rabble. It seems someone hurt the Bubble Boy! Jerry and Elaine follow the mob to his house, where Bubble Boy is being taken away in an ambulance. The mob turns on them, but they make their escape. At last, they walk through the woods toward Susan's house, which her father built himself in 1947.

It is engulfed in flames. As she looks on in horror, boyfriend George says, "I just remembered, you didn't give me the change from the tolls."

Notes

- A true epic among Seinfeld episodes, this both picks up on certain ongoing story lines, Kramer's Cuban cigars, and tells a full tragic tale all its own.

- Among the character-flawed girlfriends of Jerry, this episode is the end for Naomi, who has a bad laugh but doesn't know it until she overhears George's snickering message on Jerry's phone machine: "She's got that laugh, what did you say? It's like Elmer Fudd sitting on a juicer."
- If the writers of this episode got together with the creators of *Taxi* to form a production company, they could call themselves John Charles Walters Larry David Larry Charles Productions.
- The voice of the Bubble Boy was provided by writer Jon Hayman.
- Tony Pappenfuss, who plays one of the angry townspeople, was one of the Darryls of *Newhart*'s Larry, Darryl, and Darryl. His lines in this episode are: "He got in a fight with some guy" and "Some little bald guy from the city!"
- Brian Doyle-Murray makes his second appearance in the BTVS Top 100; he was also in the top-ranked *Get a Life* episode.

62

"Mork's Mixed Emotions"

mork & mindy

Episode 19
Original air date: February 22, 1979
Original series run: 1978–1982
Series total: 91 episodes

Credits

Open: Robin Williams, Pam Dawber, Elizabeth Kerr and Conrad Janis. Starring in *Mork and Mindy*. Produced by Dale McRaven and Bruce Johnson. Executive Producers Garry K. Marshall, Tony Marshall. Created by Garry K. Marshall, Dale McRaven, Joe Glauberg. Written by Tom Tenowich & Ed Scharlach. Directed by Jeff Chambers. End: Executive Story Consultant: Jim Parker. Story Editor: April Kelly. Story Editor: Ed Scharlach. Story Consultant: Bruce Johnson. Also Starring Jeffrey Jacquet. Guest Starring George Pentecost as the Maître d'. Co-Starring Peter Elbling as the French Waiter, and Bill Kirchenbauer as the "Customer." Featuring Ralph James as Orson.

Episode Review

Mork has had a bad dream (the entire cast of *The Untouchables* was there); this is a bad sign, because Orkans don't dream. They stopped bleems ago when they cut off their emotions. That's right, Orkans don't have emotions. "That's a no-no no-no for a nanoo nanoo."

Mindy is appalled and insists that Mork get "in touch" with his emotions. In fact, she kisses him to show him how great emo-

THE BIG TV SATISFACTION FORMULA	
SyndicoDurability	7.7
Comic Valence	8.9
Emotional Resonance	8.8
Writing, Story	8.6
Writing, Characters	8.5
Acting	9.7
Quintessence	9.4
Series Originality	7.5
Episode Originality	8.2
Historical Significance	7.2
Celebrity	6.3
Gimmickry	8.4
Theme Song	7.2
Kitsch	9.3
BTVS Ratio	**80.90**

tional attachments can be. Zing! Mork's emotions, long shut away, are now let loose all at once! Fear, anger, love, hate, lust, despair . . . it all hits him at once, as Mork transforms into a seething cauldron bubbling over with random feeling. It's quite a performance. Finally, he goes flying out of the apartment as if dragged by his emotions, screaming for help.

Later, he arrives at the record shop, a disheveled mess. (On the way in he says, "Well, excuuuse me," to a Steve Martin poster.) He is in a momentary lull, back in partial control of his emotions. He is in a fugue state, unclear as to what he has been doing.

They go to celebrate Mindy's birthday at a fancy restaurant, Chez Michelle. However, it is quickly apparent that Mork is not yet in control of his newfound emotions. In another manic scene, he chews out the Maitre d', screams, "Sell my clothes, I'm going to Heaven!" and steals two lobsters from a nearby table to work them into his improvisational frenzy.

In the end, Mork huddles with his emotions—like a football huddle—and they try to agree to work as a team. Robin Williams leaps in and out of character, Anger is a Texan, Disappointment is wimpy, Fear is Peter Lorre, Disgust is fey, and Hope is— "Thanks for the Memories"—Bob Hope. The ending is romantic; all the emotions agree they care for Mindy very much.

In the coda, Mork provides the little moral to the story, that you can't feel fully alive without emotions, and he convinces Orson not to report his transgressions to his superiors.

Notes

- Sorry, Pam and the rest, but *Mork & Mindy* was all about Robin Williams and his manic free association comedy. No episode made better use of that performance style than this one. The plot is thin, but a perfect device to wind up Mork and then let him go—although the metaphor of a windup toy is far too slow and mechanical. It would be better to say that the episode is like letting go the valve of an inflated balloon and watching it skitter and bounce off the walls with a loud, constant raspberry sound until it finally collapses, a small, empty version of its former glory.

- Bill Kirchenbauer appears in an early scene as the guy with the bad toupee in the record shop. He was frequent guest Tony Roletti from *Fernwood 2-Nite* and *America 2-Nite,* then parlayed his role as Coach Lubbock on *Growing Pains* into the starring lead role on *Just the Ten of Us.*

- Peter Elbling plays the waiter, which seems to have been something of a specialty. He later played the Maitre d' in the 1987 films *Baby Boom* and *Some Kind of Wonderful;* he was a waiter in 1981's *Private Lessons;* and he began as a cook in 1977's *The Absent-Minded Waiter.* He also played a memorable guest-starring role as Mascha in the two-part *Taxi* episode that featured the wedding of Latka and Simka.

- When Robin Williams makes his initial entrance as Mork, he and Pam Dawber are forced to hold the dialogue until the applause dies down. Many TV shows in different eras were filmed in front of a live audience, but the phenomenon of big applause when the stars made their entrances reached epidemic proportions during the seventies. Naturally, the responsibility for this must fall to producer Garry Marshall and network executive Fred Silverman, whose programming defined that era.

61

"Illegal Separation"
bewitched

Episode 32
Original air date: May 6, 1965
Original series run: 1964–1972
Series total: 254 episodes

Credits

Open: Starring Elizabeth Montgomery, Dick York, and Agnes Moorehead as Endora. Written by Richard Baer. Directed by William Asher. Produced by Jerry Davis. Executive Producer: Harry Ackerman. End: Gladys Kravitz . . . Alice Pearce. Abner Kravitz . . . George Tobias. Salesman . . . Dick Balduzzi. Production Consultant: William Asher. Created by Sol Saks. Script Consultant: Danny Arnold.

Episode Review

Sam and Darrin are planning a quiet, uneventful, romantic evening. Naturally, it lasts all of ten seconds as Abner arrives, in his pajamas. "Good evening, Mr. Stevens, Mrs. Stevens. I dropped by to give you some neighborhood gossip. Mrs. Kravitz and I just broke up."

The two have had a row, and Abner stormed out to go to his club, forgetting that

THE BIG TV SATISFACTION FORMULA	
SyndicoDurability	9.3
Comic Valence	9.1
Emotional Resonance	9.3
Writing, Story	8.8
Writing, Characters	9.1
Acting	8.8
Quintessence	8.1
Series Originality	8.9
Episode Originality	9.4
Historical Significance	7.5
Celebrity	5.3
Gimmickry	9.5
Theme Song	9.1
Kitsch	8.9
BTVS Ratio	**81.14**

he doesn't have one. He is invited to stay, and becomes a "man who came to dinner." Darrin first tries simply to convince him to go back to Gladys. Sam is here "because she's my wife. And Mrs. Kravitz is your wife." To which Abner quips: "I know, want to trade?"

They can't get rid of him. Gladys explains her side of the story to Samantha: "He's so neurotic," she explains, as only Gladys could. Gladys later drops off a note that Darrin gives to Abner. He looks at the note and says, "This is shocking. She has the penmanship of a ten-year-old child." Nothing seems to be moving Abner, including Gladys's effort to wear "sexy" clothes and pose at the front door of her house. Darrin finally says (as he actually does quite frequently) that he wants Sam to use magic. "In this case, I'll make an exception!"

Sam hits on the idea of having them each dream of the day he proposed. To do so, she uses neither the nose twitch nor the arm wave, but the most unusual twinkling-finger magic effect. What follows is one of the most ludicrous dream sequences ever, as Alice Pearce and George Tobias attempt to play Gladys and Abner as lovesick youngsters at a soda shop. But the dream has its desired effect, and just for fun, Sam puts them into slow motion as Gladys and Abner run toward each other from the two separate houses.

Notes

• This is an episode that highlights Abner Kravitz, one of the most underappreciated characters of the many who peopled *Bewitched* throughout its long network run. He is the perfect dour realist to complement the piteously "delusional" Gladys, and he brings his philosophy of deeply felt complacency to everything he does. As he says, while trying to fill in a crossword in an earlier episode: "Five letters for the ultimate happiness, tranquillity, and peace. Ah yes, D-E-A-T-H." It's no wonder that Sam has to resort to magic to rouse Abner from his stupor and put the Kravitz marriage back together.

• The original casting of Elizabeth Montgomery to play Samantha the suburban witch was a natural. What other actress could capture the perky sexiness of the role, and also utilize her own mystic powers to perform the magic stunts? That's right, in the audition and pilot episodes, Montgomery performed all the magic herself. But when the show went into production, they hit a snag. As so often happens in Hollywood, the unions made the going difficult.

It seemed that Montgomery was not a member of the powerful Witches and Warlocks Associated Union. A settlement was reached, and for the rest of the series production, a union witch was on hand to perform all the necessary magical transformations and levitations. Oftentimes, for convenience, Montgomery still performed her own magic. As long as their own witch was on hand, and being paid, the union was content.

60

"The Soup Nazi"
seinfeld

Episode 116
Original air date: November 25, 1995
Original series run: 1990–1998
Series total: 180 episodes

Credits

Open: Jerry Seinfeld, Julia Louis-Dreyfus, Michael Richards, and Jason Alexander as George. Producer: Peter Mehlman. Producer: Marjorie Gross. Co-producer: Carol Leifer. Producer: Tim Kaiser. Produced by Suzy Mamann-Greenberg. Supervising Producers: Tom Gammill & Max Pross. Created by Larry David and Jerry Seinfeld. Written by Spike Feresten. Directed by Andy Ackerman. End: Executive Producer: Larry David. Executive Producers: George Shapiro & Howard West. Producer Jerry Seinfeld. Executive Story Editors: Alec Berg, Jeff Schaffer. Story Editor: David Mandel. Story Editors: Gregg Kavet, Andy Robin. Program Consultant: Spike Feresten, with Wayne Knight as Newman. Guest Starring Heidi Swedberg as Susan. Alexandria Wentworth as

Sheila. Larry Thomas as Soup Nazi. Steve Hytner as Bania. John Paragon as Ray. Yul Vazquez as Bob. Also starring Thom Barry as Super. Vince Melocchi as Furniture Guy. Ana Gasteyer as Woman. Mike Michaud as Customer. Buddy Quaid as Customer.

Episode Review

Kramer has discovered "The Soup Nazi," as he is called behind his back, and George, Elaine, and Jerry head over, reviewing the rules: Make no extraneous comments, have your money ready, move to the left. Once there, George slips up and gets no bread. When he questions this, his soup is taken away. "No soup for you!"

Elaine never makes it. She gets distracted by an armoire for sale on the sidewalk. She has it delivered to her building but isn't allowed to move it inside until Monday, the next day. Her solution is to hire Kramer to stay on the sidewalk and watch it. He asks only that she get him some soup from the soup man. She tries, but she breaks every rule in the book. Not only does she get no

soup, she is banned for one year. What's more, by the time she returns, her armoire has been stolen. Kramer was unable to stop two incredibly fey, but also very threatening, men who "took a liking to it" and didn't care who it belonged to.

Later, Jerry is back for more soup, this time bringing with him his girlfriend Sheila (her flaw: ostentatious displays of affection). Despite being "on deck," she kisses Jerry. The Soup Nazi says no kissing, and she fires back that she'll kiss wherever she wants. The Soup Nazi throws her out, and she says fine, let's go, Jerry. Faced with this difficult choice, Jerry says, "Do I know you?"

Kramer, unlike the rest of the world, as usual, is allowed to chitchat with the soup man. He tells him the horrifying armoire story, and the Soup Nazi says: "You have been a good friend." Then he offers Kramer the armoire in his basement.

Kramer delivers the armoire to Elaine. She is delighted and simply has to go and thank that nice soup man in person. He is less than charitable. "If I had known it was for you, I would have taken a hatchet and smashed it to pieces." His mistake. Later, Elaine finds his soup recipes in the armoire. She goes running back to flaunt them in front of his face. She says she's giving them to anyone and everyone; she's publishing them. Now he's done, history.

She stares at him triumphantly and says: "No soup for you!"

THE BIG TV SATISFACTION FORMULA	
SyndicoDurability	6.8
Comic Valence	9.4
Emotional Resonance	7
Writing, Story	9.5
Writing, Characters	9.1
Acting	9.4
Quintessence	9.3
Series Originality	7.5
Episode Originality	8.1
Historical Significance	7.3
Celebrity	8.1
Gimmickry	9.5
Theme Song	7.1
Kitsch	8.4
BTVS Ratio	**81.18**

Notes

• The attempt to condense a episode of *Seinfeld* points out its virtues. Each episode is dense with motivations, shifts, and plot changes, many of which make very little sense. But as you watch, the sheer comic energy of the moments carry you through without ever getting caught up in the inconsistencies. There's no time to stop and think; the next event is already here. This episode is just as rich and thick as the Soup Nazi's mulligatawny, and we didn't even try to include the entire subplot in which George deals with Sheila and her "schmoopiness."

- The Soup Nazi is based directly on a real New York City soup vendor located on Fifty-fifth Street near Eighth Avenue. The proprietor, Al Yeganah, who looks very much like his TV self, does indeed maintain a strict reward system for those who order promptly and simply, and move immediately to the left. Make a mistake, and you will be asked to step out of line. Small slipups mean no bread. If you are perfect, you can get, in addition to your soup, bread, fruit, and some chocolate, too. The soup is very good, if a bit pricey. Despite the potential for abuse, there is almost always a line.

59
"Beaver the Magician"
leave it to beaver
Episode 90
Original series run: 1957–1963
Series total: 234 episodes

THE BIG TV SATISFACTION FORMULA	
SyndicoDurability	9.3
Comic Valence	8.9
Emotional Resonance	9.1
Writing, Story	8.9
Writing, Characters	9.6
Acting	8.8
Quintessence	9.5
Series Originality	7.2
Episode Originality	8.2
Historical Significance	6.2
Celebrity	7.2
Gimmickry	8.7
Theme Song	7.4
Kitsch	8.1
BTVS Ratio	**81.44**

Credits
Barbara Billingsley, Hugh Beaumont, Tony Dow, and Jerry Mathers as the Beaver. End: Directed by David Butler. Written by George Tibbles, Joe Connelly, and Bob Mosher. Created and Produced by Joe Connelly and Bob Mosher. Cast: Rusty Stevens, Madge Kennedy, Ann Dopan, Edward Marr, and Joey Scott as "Bengie."

Episode Review
Open on Larry and the Beaver in the local magic and novelty shop. After much debate, they buy a slide trick to make a penny disappear and reappear. Sadly, the Beaver finds on arriving home that Dad, Mom, and Wally all know the trick.

Luckily, for every little kid, there is always a littler kid. There's Bengie (pronounced "Benjy," but the credits have it as Bengie, so that must be his name) a kid who collects ants "so's he can talk to them."

Bengie is impressed by the magic. Larry and Beaver up the ante. Using a blanket hung over a rope as a curtain, they show the little boy how they can turn Beaver into a rock. Beaver scoots inside a door, and Bengie is astonished. Then June arrives to summon Larry, who should have been home an hour ago! Beaver is inside, Larry leaves in a hurry, and Bengie is left with the rock that he earnestly believes is the transformed Beaver. "Change him back!" he calls after Larry, but the older boy is too intent on getting home. Bengie picks up the rock and assures Beaver (the rock) that he'll take care of him.

Later, Bengie's mother is trying to get Bengie to see the light: "If the boys said they changed Beaver into this rock, they were just fooling you." She calls to see if June and Beaver can help her dissuade her son from his mistaken belief. But now Beaver is out of town staying at his aunt's house!

They come over anyway, and Bengie, in an incredibly sweet moment, brings the rock over to June, thinking that she would want to hold her son. They have Bengie talk to Beaver on the phone. He believes it's Beaver. Everyone is relieved . . . until he says he thinks that Beaver must have been calling from heaven.

Wally has an idea. He shows Bengie the trick, how the blanket on the rope worked—and he seems to understand, but then he says, "Now turn the rock back into Beaver."

In the end, only Beaver's arrival back home can reassure Bengie. As Wally and the Beaver reflect on little kids, they talk about things that scared them when they were little. Beaver talks about how a fear of tigers is healthy: "Well, tigers are pretty good to be scared of, if they're walking around loose, so if you ever see a tiger, get

on a bus or something." Wally admits that when he was little he was creeped out by the wooden cigar-store Indian.

Notes

- One of the many brilliant achievements of *Leave It to Beaver* was the creators' ability to have their characters mature and grow naturally over the series. Beaver was great as the totally innocent, grammar-bending waif of the first years, but he was equally real and wonderful as he grew into the more knowing near teen of the series's final seasons. They didn't get stuck in the conventions that they had established for any of their characters. (With the possible exception of Larry Mondello, who just never really changed.)

- In what seems at first blush a very strange transition, the creators of *Leave It to Beaver* went on to create *The Munsters*. However, the two shows are alike in the underlying emotional and moral tenor of their stories. They are about doing the right thing, helping one another deal with life's little tribulations, and maintaining the strength of family. They simply had two different gimmicks. *Beaver* was about the world from a boy's point of view; *Munsters* was from a ghoul's.

58

"Over the River and Through the Woods"

the bob newhart show

Episode 83
Original air date: November 22, 1975
Original series run: 1972–1978
Series total: 120 episodes

Credits

Open: Bob Newhart in . . . *The Bob Newhart Show.* Also starring Suzanne Pleshette. Created by David Davis and Lorenzo Music. Written by Bruce Kane. Directed by James Burrows. Produced by Gordan & Lynn Farr and Michael Zinberg. End: Story Consultants: Gordan & Lynn Farr. Associate Producer: Michael Zinberg. Produced by Tom Patchett and Jay Tarses. Also Starring Peter Bonerz as Jerry Robinson. Bill Daily as Howard Borden. Marcia Wallace as Carol Kester Bondurant. David Himes as Delivery Boy. Janet Meshad as Elaine, with Jack Riley as Elliot Carlin.

Episode Review

Using the needs of his patients as an excuse, Bob begs out of a Thanksgiving trip to visit Emily's family in Seattle. So off Emily goes, and through the usual sitcom-fluence of circumstances, the following group gathers at Bob's apartment for Turkey Day. Bob (sans Emily), Jerry (the orphan), Mr. Carlin (who has nowhere else to go), and Howard (whose son, Howie, is in Maui with his mother). Jerry is watching the football game and following his old school tradition of drinking a swig of booze each time his team is scored upon. The others join in, and soon the merry revelers are all sauced to the gills.

They realize that drinking on an empty stomach might not be such a good idea, so they get out the turkey, which is frozen solid. They figure that instead of five hours at 400 degrees they could cook it for one hour at 2,000 degrees. But the oven goes only to 500, so they'll have to use four ovens. Giving up on cooking, they decide to order Chinese food. Bob is on the phone taking orders from the rest and ends up ordering "Moo Goo Gai Pan" for everyone.

"More goo to go!!"

Emily *ex machina*. She decided to cut short her family trip. Bob answers the door with a tellingly aspirate, "Hi, Emily, wha's happening?" In the coda, the Chinese food is delivered in the mass quantities Bob unwittingly requested.

Triple

As the drunks sit around in a stupor, they accidentally speak in song lyrics that also form a triple

BOB: I love coffee

JERRY: I love tea.

CARLIN: I love the Java Jive, and it loves me.

Notes

• After they are drunk, this episode becomes an intricate, interwoven dance of physical jokes, non sequiturs, and callbacks to earlier jokes to which no synopsis could truly do justice. Here's one small example. Mr. Carlin attempts to be jovial and tells the following joke: "Knock knock." Jerry responds, "Who's there." Carlin: "I don't know, do I have to come up with everything?" Later, there is a real "knock, knock" at Bob's door, and Carlin, in a stupor, responds, "Who's there?" "Carlin, get the door." "Carlin get the door who?"

• Every successful TV series has Christmas episodes, sometimes one each season, but Thanksgiving-themed episodes are a somewhat rarer breed. Rarer still is a Thanksgiving episode in which the plot does not involve unwanted relatives visiting. "Over the River and Through the Woods," perhaps better known as "The Moo Goo Gai Pan One," is such an episode.

57

"Barney and the Choir"
the andy griffith show

Episode 52
Original air date: February 19, 1962
Original series run: 1960–1968
Series total: 249 episodes

Credits

Open: Andy Griffith, Ron Howard, Don Knotts. End: Directed by Bob Sweeney. Written by Charles Stewart and Jack Elinson. Story Consultant: Aaron Ruben. Produced by Aaron Ruben, Frances Bavier, Olan Soule. Betty Lynn as Thelma Lou. Executive Producer: Sheldon Leonard. In Association with Danny Thomas.

Episode Review

There is a crisis in the town choir! The first tenor has a new job that takes him out of town two weeks out of three. As Andy

THE BIG TV SATISFACTION FORMULA	
SyndicoDurability	9.9
Comic Valence	9.6
Emotional Resonance	8.2
Writing, Story	9.1
Writing, Characters	9.4
Acting	9.3
Quintessence	7.1
Series Originality	7.3
Episode Originality	9.2
Historical Significance	6.8
Celebrity	5.5
Gimmickry	7.5
Theme Song	8.7
Kitsch	8.8
BTVS Ratio	**81.64**

and Aunt Bee watch helplessly, Barney insinuates himself, volunteering his services to the choirmaster, who doesn't know that the deputy can't sing a lick but thinks he can.

The choirmaster quickly realizes his error, and everyone begins trying to find a way to spare Barney's feelings. They try to hold a secret rehearsal (secret, that is, from Barney) so that they can have at least one rehearsal that isn't spoiled by his horrific caterwauling. But Barney wanders by and hears the singing.

Andy gets another idea at dinner. He draws short, grabs Barney, and looks down his throat. Will you look at that?! He's got a big lump. Yeah, it's all red. They send him off to go to bed and stay there; although he doesn't feel sick, "Or not very" he adds, in his confusion.

It seems to have worked, but Barney stops by the doc's since he was so concerned about disappointing the choir, and it turns out his throat is just fine. In fact, that lump that Andy saw, well that was nothing but a uvula. "I've got a uvula. You've got a uvula. She's got a uvula. All's God's children got a uvula!"

Andy's penultimate idea is to have Barney do dramatic recitations in lieu of singing! Anything would be better than his warbling. They rehearse, but as Barney goes into his dramatic read, he can't help himself and bursts into tuneless howling. "It's no use, Andy. Can you tell a bird to talk? Can you tell a bird to just say chirp, chirp, chirp. No, Andy, I was born to sing."

Luckily, though it's as elaborate as you could make it, the ultimate idea works. They make Barney a soloist, with a separate microphone. Andy then coaches Barney on how to use this particularly powerful mike. You've got to barely whisper, or you'll make everyone deaf! In a wonderful scene, Barney starts singing, and Andy keeps telling him to lower his volume, lower, lower, lower. A bit of dialogue and then, yup, keep going lower, lower, lower, until finally not a sound can be heard. Perfect! Barney is skeptical (but not skeptical enough). That night, when Barney opens his mouth to sing at this incredibly low volume, another singer backstage belts out the song—on key, too! Barney, the innocent dupe, thinks that he is hearing his own voice, magnified to great volume. Without knowing what he is doing, he lip-synchs the entire number, with increasing swagger and finally a dashing show-biz bow at the finale.

Whee Wohn

When Barney is first asked to join the choir, he says, in a close-up, "Wait'll Thelma Lou hears about this! She'll be thrilled!" And there is a perfect reaction whee wohn cut to a close-up of a disbelieving, horrified Thelma Lou: "Barney's going to sing in the choir!?" She proceeds to count out his many virtues, but as she puts it, "He can't sing a lick."

Notes
- This episodes hinges on the very unlikely fact that Barney is completely oblivious to his own lack of singing ability, and also oblivious to the machinations surrounding his membership in the choir. But no

one in the world is better at playing sincere, convincing oblivion than Don Knotts.

- This is an unusually complex plot for Mayberry, where generally the second or third idea works.
- It's *The Andy Griffith Show,* but it's Barney who makes the show. Episodes that feature Barney in the main story rank an average of 3.8 points per episode better than those featuring others—and that's not even counting the episodes after Don Knotts had left the cast!
- This episode represents the most times the word "uvula" was used in a single television program until a suggestive *Saturday Night Live* sketch in 1977.

56

"Job Switching"
i love lucy
Episode 39
Original air date: January 15, 1952
Original series run: 1951–1961
Series total: 179 episodes

Credits

Open: Lucille Ball & Desi Arnaz, William Frawley & Vivian Vance. End: "The part of Mr. Snodgrass was played by Alvin Hurwitz, the forewoman by Elvia Allman, and the chocolate dipper by Amanda Milligan." Produced by Jess Oppenheimer. Directed by William Asher. Written for Television by Jess Oppenheimer, Madelyn Pugh, Bob Carroll, Jr. Director of

Photography: Karl Freund, A.S.C. Executive Producer: Desi Arnaz.

Episode Review

Ricky enters and calls "Lucy!" What better way to begin? It seems her bank account is always overdrawn, and their argument escalates into a classic scenario that would be repeated in many variations throughout the history of sitcoms: the role reversal episode. He says holding a job is a lot harder than lying around the house. She says he never appreciates how much work goes into cooking and housekeeping. With Fred and Ethel joining in, they all agree to trade places. Fred and Ricky will take care of the house; Ethel and Lucy will find jobs.

After some other missteps, Lucy and Ethel end up at Kramer's Kandy Kitchen. Meanwhile, Ricky and Fred aren't doing so well at home; ironing and cleaning aren't so easy. But they plan a big dinner, Ricky will make his old family favorite *arroz con pollo,* and Fred will bake a cake.

Can Lucy dip chocolates? Oh yes. "I'm a

THE BIG TV SATISFACTION FORMULA	
SyndicoDurability	10
Comic Valence	9.4
Emotional Resonance	7.9
Writing, Story	8.4
Writing, Characters	9.2
Acting	9.3
Quintessence	8.8
Series Originality	6.4
Episode Originality	8.3
Historical Significance	7.8
Celebrity	6.7
Gimmickry	8.7
Theme Song	7.1
Kitsch	7.1
BTVS Ratio	**81.71**

dipper from way back. They used to call me the big dipper." Lucy plays in the chocolate happily for a while, then tries to slap a fly and incites a major brawl. Are the boys doing any better? No, they have cooked enough rice to feed an army, and it overflows, threatening to fill the kitchen.

Back to the factory, where Lucy and Ethel will get one last chance. They are on the chocolate-wrapping assembly line. Anyway, you probably know the rest. In a brilliant series of events, the girls appear to be handling the situation, only to have the cruel forewoman "speed it up a little!" They end up hiding chocolates everywhere, including down their blouses and in their mouths.

They return home, feeling defeated, only to find that the boys are also willing to concede defeat. Not only that, but they bought the girls a nice present: a big five-pound box of chocolates!

Notes
- So many memorable moments all packed into one episode, which is somehow both quintessential and totally unique.
- One small flaw in the story has always seemed obvious to us: how fair is it really that in order to compare their lives with a nightclub singer and a landlord, the girls have to go work on an assembly line?
- According to Lucy legend, she decided to get a realistic performance from her fellow candy dipper (not an actress, but an actual candy factory employee) by whacking her solidly on camera, after going easy in rehearsal. Watching it on film today, the swat certainly looks convincing.

- In 1994, Nick at Nite celebrated Cinco de Mayo by airing four episodes that had been dubbed into Spanish. We used the episodes that had been created years before for Spanish-speaking markets, and chose to show "Job Switching." There was one particularly odd moment in the translation. See page 79, "10 Wacky Stunts That May Have Gone Too Far" for more details.

55
"A Day in the Life"
night court
Episode 72
Original air date: February 5, 1987
Original series run: 1984–1992
Series total: 193 episodes

Credits
Open: Starring Harry Anderson, Markie Post, John Larroquette, Charles Robinson, Richard Moll, Marsha Warfield. End: Directed by Thomas Klein. Written by Nat Mauldin & Teresa O'Neill & Bob Stevens. Created by Reinhold Weege. Produced by Bob Stevens. Co-Producer: Tim Steele. Supervising Producer: Jeff Melman. Executive Producer: Reinhold Weege. Guest Starring Fred Applegate . . . Ted Boswell. Dannel Arnold . . . Delivery Boy. Norman Bartold . . . Mr. Reynolds. Leslie Bevis . . . Sheila. Raye Birk . . . God No. 1. Mark Blankfield . . . Magician. Jim Doughman . . . Jason the Pleading Man. John Dullaghan . . . Mr. Tuttle. Alix Elias . . . Sue Boswell. Gary Grossman . . . Man in a Dryer. Phil Leeds . . . God No. 2. Jeannette Nolan . . .

Mrs. Smith. Raymond Singer . . . The Monk. B. Donald Tartikoff . . . Brandon Tartikoff. Executive Script Consultant: Tom Reeder. Executive Story Consultant: Dennis Koenig. Executive Story Editor: Tom Straw. Story Editor: Teresa O'Neill. Story Editor: Linwood Boomer. Starry Night Productions (Laughing Sound).

Episode Review

It's comedy at the speed of sound, as the court finds itself with the difficult task of getting two hundred cases heard by midnight. It would not only prevent a number of criminals from being set free, it would also set a new record. They figure it's worth a shot, and it makes for a frenetic, fantastically funny episode.

D.A. Dan Fielding's current girlfriend is leaving town: "I've got a new position," she says. "Does it involve a loss of consciousness?" he asks. They plan a tryst during the dinner break. But the dinner break is canceled because of the huge docket of cases. Dan begs her to wait; he'll be done at midnight.

THE BIG TV SATISFACTION FORMULA	
SyndicoDurability	7.9
Comic Valence	9.7
Emotional Resonance	8.1
Writing, Story	9.6
Writing, Characters	8.3
Acting	8.6
Quintessence	8.8
Series Originality	7.7
Episode Originality	9.2
Historical Significance	7.3
Celebrity	9.1
Gimmickry	9.8
Theme Song	6.3
Kitsch	7.2
BTVS Ratio	**81.72**

Everyone not sentenced by midnight is to be set free. Bull brings up the first case, a guy in handcuffs and a hockey mask, who is happy to hear they are rushing: "Gee, I'd kill to be out of here by midnight." Next is a monk who's taken a vow of silence. Then they quickly forgive a public book burning of twelve hundred copies of *The Genius of Barry Manilow.* An elderly prostitute appears with character witnesses—four elderly men in wheelchairs whooping and cheering. "Were these men as happy as this before they met Mrs. Smith?" asks the defense. The prosecution responds: "No, but they could walk."

More cases: A magician who disappears. A man accused of indecent exposure, who flashes Judge Stone when asked to show the evidence. "No need to tag this one." Two old men who both claim to be God.

Also, a man who tried to commit suicide by stuffing himself in a dryer. When he is asked what could make him despondent enough to attempt "laundricide," he speaks of his misery at being so short, only five-foot-six. Christine looks over, and down, and says, "You can't be, I'm five-six." And with slowly dawning horror, he realizes that he shrunk himself.

Astonishingly, they are close to achieving their goal. "Nothing will stop us now! Two cases. Fifteen minutes to go." Then the next case begins. A man whose IRS return was due at midnight who attacked a postal employee because he was so annoyed with his pace. The postal employee begins to speak . . . i-n-c-r-e-d-i-b-l-y s-l-o-w-l-y: "So . . . I . . . switched . . . to decaf . . . but . . . I . . . digress."

They manage to get past him and move on: one last case. It's a felony that simply needs to be turned over to a grand jury, but the accused refuses to dispense with the formal reading of the charge. Dan speed-reads with the time counting down. And makes it! But his rendezvous is not going to happen. What his girlfriend really wants is a man who takes his time; she goes off with the postal employee.

Triple

When the elderly prostitute explains herself, she does so in a classic triple: "Sometimes I do it for pudding; sometimes I do it for green stamps; sometimes I do it for kicks."

Notes

- During one scene a character is asked, "How do you plead?" The accused demonstrates with a desperate, whining, "Oh please, oh please, oh please . . ." When the character goes into this bit, John Larroquette can be seen turning away to hide his out-of-character laughter.
- There is a special walk-on appearance by Brandon Tartikoff, then the head of programming for NBC. He posts bail for a man accused of killing Lucy, Punky Brewster, and the Jetsons. Aside he says, "I'll have you out of here in time to see *Misfits of Science.*"
- This episode of *Night Court* was one of the five that tied for the highest score in the Comic Valence category. This figure represents, roughly speaking, an isolated measure of how pure and outright funny

an episode is. So these are the ten funniest episodes ever.

All in the Family, "The Bunkers and the Swingers"	9.7
The Simpsons, "The Crepes of Wrath"	9.7
Mary Tyler Moore, "Chuckles Bites the Dust"	9.7
The Bob Newhart Show, "Over the River and Through the Woods"	9.7
Night Court, "A Day in the Life"	9.7
The Andy Griffith Show, "Barney and the Choir"	9.6
Gilligan's Island, "The Producer"	9.6
The Dick Van Dyke Show, "Coast to Coast Big Month"	9.6
Seinfeld, "The Contest"	9.6
Car 54, Where Are You?, "How Smart Can You Get"	9.6
Police Squad, "Rendezvous at Big Gulch"	9.6
Get a Life, "Spewey and Me"	9.6

54
"Steinberg and Son"
sanford and son

Episode 97
Original air date: October 1, 1975
Original series run: 1972–1977
Series total: 136 episodes

Credits

Open: Starring Redd Foxx, and Demond Wilson. Written and Produced by Saul Turteltaub and Bernie Orenstein. End: Directed by James Sheldon. Executive Producer: Bud Yorkin. Story

Supervisor: Ted Bergman. Story Editor: Jerry Ross. Co-starring Whitman Mayo as Grady. La Wanda Page as Aunt Esther. Nathaniel Taylor . . . Rollo. Don Bexley . . . Bubba. Jack Somack . . . Gabey. Robert Guillaume . . . Albert Brock. Corey Fischer . . . Anthony Marvinowsky. Rik Pierce . . . Mac John. John Larroquette . . . Murray Steinberg. Albert Hall . . . Bernie Taub. Jane Lambert . . . Aunt Ethel. Larry Wilde . . . Saul Green, and Lou Jacobi as Steinberg. Based on *Steptoe and Son* created by Ray Galton & Alan Simpson.

Episode Review

Fred is planning to sue a TV network that seems to have adapted his life story into a sitcom about a Jewish junk dealer that is entitled *Steinberg and Son*. The gang gets tickets to see this TV version of themselves. "If we can prove they're basing the show on our life, we can sue for one million dollars." It's applause-era TV (the show, not the show within the show) and Esther, Grady, and even Bubba all get applause for their first entrance.

THE BIG TV SATISFACTION FORMULA	
SyndicoDurability	7.9
Comic Valence	8.6
Emotional Resonance	7.2
Writing, Story	9.4
Writing, Characters	8.7
Acting	8.9
Quintessence	8.6
Series Originality	7.7
Episode Originality	9.3
Historical Significance	8.2
Celebrity	8.9
Gimmickry	9.9
Theme Song	8.1
Kitsch	9.2
BTVS Ratio	**81.80**

The show is indeed about a junk dealer and his son who live in a ghetto. And it's their theme song. The "Fred" character grabs his heart and says, "You hear that, Naomi?" Then the "Aunt Ethel" flubs a line. She asks for a line from the script supervisor, but instead she gets the real thing. Aunt Esther leaps up and yells, "Fish-eyed fool," then makes a ruckus. The shoot is over for the day.

Later, Fred meets with lawyers and producers to straighten it all out. Turns out that it was indeed their story, and that it had "inspired" their cousin Rollo, who had sold the idea to them. Still, the network execs want to "do the right thing." So they talk to Fred. He makes demands for a dressing room with lots of windows. He settles for $200 a week and a minor role in each episode. After all, a show called "*Sanford and Son*? It would never make it." At that, Fred breaks the fourth wall with a quick, meaningful look to camera.

His TV debut quickly goes to Fred's head. He sports a red dressing gown and sunglasses. Plus, he's got lots of ideas for shows, for example a police show based on his life: "Kojunk," he suggests, holding up a lollipop. If that doesn't work, he's got a dynamite idea about a family of pioneer plumbers . . .

Notes
• This classic episode from late in the series is a roller coaster as fiction and reality blend, overlap, and reference each other. The plot also hinges on references to Redd Foxx's well-publicized disputes with the show's producers about money, but

also about things like windows in his dressing room, and other minor details. He had walked out on the show for long periods, during which they continued production with episodes that revolved around other characters, like Grady. Demond Wilson also got caught up in "contractual differences" and missed episodes. After the 1975–76 season, both costars left. NBC felt that there was still mileage in the supporting cast and milieu, and created *Sanford Arms,* a show centered on Aunt Esther's boardinghouse. It limped through a few weeks and was mercifully canceled.

- The high-concept self-reference in this episode of *Sanford and Son* pushed it well above the show's usual mediocre BTVS rating. In fact, along with *Hogan's Heroes* and *The Flying Nun, Sanford and Son* is one of the few shows that managed to place an episode in the BTVS Top 100 while having an episode average below 50; it averaged a scant 36.5. For comparison, here are some other BTVS series averages, a figure that measures a show's consistency:

Mary Tyler Moore	71.3
The Honeymooners	70.8
The Dick Van Dyke Show	69.9
I Love Lucy	69.4
The Odd Couple	69.3
Car 54, Where Are You?	68.2
The Andy Griffith Show	64.0
The Beverly Hillbillies	58.7
The Munsters	52.1
Gilligan's Island	52.1
My Mother the Car	37.3
The Flying Nun	37.1
Sanford and Son	36.5
Hogan's Heroes	35.8

What's interesting here is that even though *The Andy Griffith Show* placed more episodes in the BTVS Top 100 than *Mary Tyler Moore,* the latter still managed to have a significantly higher average. In fact, it is the highest series average ever recorded, reflecting the show's consistency over the years. They say that records were made to be broken, but *Mary Tyler Moore's* total average is, to many observers, a figure that may remain unchallenged.

The low score for *Sanford and Son* may seem surprising, but don't forget that every episode counts, and many episodes of that series were made while Redd Foxx was not participating due to contractual disputes. Those episodes brought down the average score considerably.

53

"Turkeys Away"
wkrp in cincinnati
Episode 8
Original air date: October 30, 1978
Original series run: 1978–1982
Series total: 90 episodes

Credits
Open: Starring Gary Sandy, Gordon Jump, Loni Anderson, Richard Sanders, Frank Bonner, Jan Smithers, Tim Reid, and Howard Hesseman as Dr. Johnny Fever. Created by Hugh Wilson. Written by Bill Dial. Directed by Michael

Zinberg. End: Story Editors: Tom Chehak, Bill Dial, Blake Hunter. Produced by Hugh Wilson. With Michael Fairman . . . Shoe Store Owner.

Episode Review

Jennifer is being her usual hypercompetent self, making Mr. Carlson feel useless. Herb, Les, Johnny . . . no one will engage Carlson. Andy drops by, interrupting a pencil rocket launch. Carlson asks him the big question: "What do I do?" Andy hems and haws, but it's clear that being "at the helm" doesn't mean a thing. Andy is nervous because Carlson is itching "to be involved in the day-to-day details."

They are all looking for a big promotional stunt. Nothing seems quite right. But Carlson has a plan, and, taking Herb as his sole confidant, he sets it in motion. Les is placed at a local mall, to provide live coverage.

He notes that there is a helicopter high above the mall parking lot, and then, this is his report: "There is something coming out, skydivers? No parachutes yet . . . I can't tell

what they are. Oh my God, they're turkeys! They're plummeting to the ground. One just went through the windshield of a parked car! Oh the humanity! The turkeys are hitting the grounds like sacks of wet cement. I don't know how much longer I can hold my position. The Palmdale shopping mall has just been bombed with live turkeys."

What else is there to say? They field calls from the mayor and the humane society. Carlson and Herb return, covered with scratches and feathers. The turkeys apparently resisted. Les arrives shell-shocked; he describes how Carlson landed and tried to free the rest of the turkeys, and then the turkeys, as if organized, counterattacked. But the final word is Carlson's classic plea for clemency: "As God is my witness: I thought turkeys could fly."

Triple

When Carlson first takes Herb into his confidence about the "big plan" he says: "All it's gonna take is your complete cooperation, absolute secrecy, and twenty live turkeys."

Notes

- Some episodes are about the intricate farce that sitcoms can weave; others are about an acting tour de force, as a character takes over; and some are simply about one big idea. This was one of the big-idea episodes as reflected by high BTVS scores in the categories of Writing, Episode Originality, and Gimmickry. But getting there is half the fun.
- According to some sources, the turkey

THE BIG TV SATISFACTION FORMULA	
SyndicoDurability	7.7
Comic Valence	9.3
Emotional Resonance	7.6
Writing, Story	9.5
Writing, Characters	8.7
Acting	8.8
Quintessence	8.7
Series Originality	8.1
Episode Originality	9.8
Historical Significance	8.8
Celebrity	6
Gimmickry	9.3
Theme Song	7.3
Kitsch	7.2
BTVS Ratio	**81.84**

story is based on a real-life incident that took place at a Texas radio station, but we have been unable to verify this. It is our suspicion that this may be an "urban legend," which has been spread around as a true story but has either no basis or only a slim basis in fact. If you've ever stood next to a live turkey, you know it's readily apparent that this great, fat bird with tiny wings could never get airborne.

- ESPN recently borrowed the concept for an on-air promotion. Sportcenter anchor Dan Patrick is seen in a helicopter, from which he is dropping "collectible, souvenir baseball bats" and suggesting that some lucky viewers will get them.

- In an unusual experiment, *WKRP in Cincinnati* was revived for first-run syndication in 1991, nine years after its initial cancellation, airing, among other places, on cable TV's VH1. The new episodes featured Tarlek, Carlson, and Nessman (all played by the original actors) and a new group of characters. Dr. Johnny Fever (Howard Hesseman) made several appearances in these episodes, then finally rejoined as a regular.

52

"Krusty Gets Kancelled"

the simpsons

Episode 9F19
Original air date: May 13, 1993
Original series run: 1989–
Series total: 248 episodes produced through 1999, still in production as of 2000–01 season

Credits

Open: Created by Matt Groening. Developed by James L. Brooks, Matt Groening, Sam Simon. Executive Producers: Al Jean and Mike Reiss. Supervising Producer: George Meyer. Producer: Jon Vitti. Producer: John Swartzwelder. Producer: Jeff Martin. Producer: Conan O'Brien. Producer: Frank Mula. Written by John Swartzwelder. Directed by David Silverman. End: Executive Producers: James L. Brooks, Matt Groening, Sam Simon. Starring Dan Castellaneta, Julie Kavner, Nancy Cartwright, Yeardley Smith, Hank Azaria, and Harry Shearer. Special Guest Voice: Johnny Carson. Special Guest Voice: Hugh Hefner. Special Guest Voice: Bette Midler. Special Guest Voice: Luke Perry. Special Guest Voice: Red Hot Chili Peppers (Anthony Kiedis, Flea, Chad Smith, Arik Marshall). Special Guest Voice: Elizabeth Taylor. Special Guest Voice: Marcia Wallace. Special Guest Voice: Barry White. Also Starring Pamela Hayden. Animation Executive Producer: Phil Roman. Animation Producers: Bill Schultz, Michael Wolf. Story Editors: Bill Oakley and Josh Weinstein. Story Editor: Dan McGrath.

THE BIG TV SATISFACTION FORMULA	
SyndicoDurability	8.8
Comic Valence	9.1
Emotional Resonance	7.8
Writing, Story	8.4
Writing, Characters	8.9
Acting	8.8
Quintessence	8.8
Series Originality	9.3
Episode Originality	8.4
Historical Significance	9.2
Celebrity	9.9
Gimmickry	9.8
Theme Song	7.6
Kitsch	6.2
BTVS Ratio	**82.10**

Episode Review

Bart and Homer are watching *The Springfield Squares* when a tidal wave sweeps Charlie Weaver away. The next tidal wave is the marketing campaign for Gabbo, who turns out to be a Doody-esque dummy whose show will air in direct competition against Krusty! His hook line? "I'm a bad widdle boy." He sings a big number showing how and why he will take the country by storm. "I'll give out shiny dimes; I'll travel back in time!"

Krusty's not afraid, but his efforts to compete flop horribly, especially his own ventriloquist dummy, which falls apart in front of his horrified young audience. Itchy and Scratchy have moved to Gabbo's show, leaving Krusty to show an Eastern European, animated "cat and mouse" cartoon. Krusty is kancelled. He visits Johnny Carson for advice. He auditions for *Melrose Place*. He is the victim of a Gabbo prank call, beating himself on the head with the phone in the hopes of landing a Japanese

commercial. Finally, he is out on the street holding a sign: "Will drop pants for food."

Bart and Lisa find him. Is he making any money? "No," says Krusty. "That guy is giving it away for free," pointing to a crazy old man singing "The Old Gray Mare" with his pants around his ankles. But when the kids see all Krusty's show-biz photos, they see hope. If all these big stars will appear in a special, Krusty could make a comeback. They run off to gather the stars, while Krusty's hopes rise. He proclaims, "I'll claw my way back onto TV!" Then he turns on the TV, where the crazy old man is singing his song with his pants around his ankles. The announcer says: "And now, the crazy old man singers!"

Bette Midler is found chasing litterers, grabbing their cars and sending them spinning over cliffs. She's willing to do the show. Hugh Hefner gives Bart a short tour of the mansion, including the seldom-seen alternative energy research facility. He's game, too. Luke Perry, Krusty's no-good half-brother, really wants to be part of the show. Krusty has something special planned for him.

The Krusty Komeback Special begins with "Send in the Clowns." Luke Perry is shot out of a cannon. Screaming all the way, he smashes through the studio walls, through a sandpaper factory, through a large stack of bottled acid Apu is stacking in his store, and finally comes to rest safely on a large stack of pillows in a pillow factory. However, just at that moment a demolition team implodes the building and he is crushed.

Johnny Carson's act is spinning a 1987 Buick Skylark over his head while singing opera. Hefner plays music by rubbing his fingers on crystal glasses. The Red Hot Chili Peppers play in their underwear. Finally, Bette sits on Krusty's desk and serenades him, just as she did Johnny on his farewell week.

Celebrating at the bar, they all toast Krusty, the greatest entertainer in the world. Except maybe that guy! And Bart points to a man tap-dancing, playing the accordion, and balancing two old men on his head.

Triple

With Gabbo's arrival, Krusty boasts that he has beaten every challenger so far: "hoboes, sea captains, Joey Bishop . . ."

Notes

• As even casual viewers probably know, the opening sequence to *The Simpsons* has slight variations in it. In this episode Bart's blackboard sentence is "I will not charge admission to the bathroom." And the final moment of the open finds the Simpsons swept up into a net trap.

• The huge cast of celebrity voice-overs is one of the reasons that this episode, which is certainly not as tightly constructed or as outright funny as many *Simpsons*, was vaulted onto the BTVS Top 100 list. It was tied with two other episodes for the highest "Celebrity" factor. Here are the top seven:

The Simpsons, "Krusty Gets Kancelled"	9.9
Friends, "The One After the Super Bowl, Part II"	9.9
All in the Family, "Sammy's Visit"	9.9
The Partridge Family, "Soul Club"	9.7
The Many Loves of Dobie Gillis, "Best Dressed Man"	9.7
The Phil Silvers Show "Hillbilly Whiz"	9.7
I Dream of Jeannie, "The Greatest Entertainer in the World"	9.7

• The phenomenal success of *The Simpsons* has spawned many imitators and variations on animation that appeal to adults—*King of the Hill, The PJs, Futurama, Baby Blues*—but few have found the success of this original. However, there were progenitors in the realm of prime-time animation. Both *The Flintstones* and *The Bullwinkle Show* were produced for prime-time network television. *Wait Till Your Father Gets Home* (1972–74) was another interesting experiment that tried to graft the issue-oriented comedy, popularized by *All in the Family*, onto an animated series. In reviewing this genre, however, it becomes apparent that what is unique about *The Simpsons* is not the form, but the substance and comic voice of the series.

• Staff writer Conan O'Brien left the show to take over the late-night slot on NBC vacated by David Letterman.

51

"Fat Farm"
the odd couple

Episode 33
Original air date: November 12, 1971
Original series run: 1970–1983
Series total: 114 episodes

Credits

Open: Starring Tony Randall. Starring Jack Klugman and based on the play *The Odd Couple* by Neil Simon. Developed for Television by Garry Marshall and Jerry Belson. Produced by Frank Buxton. Written by Albert E. Lewin. Directed by Mel Ferber. End: Executive Producer Garry Marshall. Executive Consultant Jerry Belson. Script Consultants Bill Idelson and Harvey Miller. Co-starring Joan Hotchkis as Nancy. Dave Ketchum as Jock. Thelma Pelish as Lady. Norbert Schiller as Dr. Burger. David Warren Duclon . . . Waiter. Edward Fury . . . Patient. Wardrobe furnished by Worsted Tex.

THE BIG TV SATISFACTION FORMULA	
SyndicoDurability	9.1
Comic Valence	8.9
Emotional Resonance	9.1
Writing, Story	8.7
Writing, Characters	9.2
Acting	9.6
Quintessence	8.6
Series Originality	7.7
Episode Originality	8.4
Historical Significance	7.1
Celebrity	6.3
Gimmickry	9.2
Theme Song	8.7
Kitsch	7.1
BTVS Ratio	**82.18**

Episode Review

Felix convinces Oscar that he needs to improve his physical fitness and drags him to his "health farm" for two weeks of healthful living under the mandates of Dr. Burger. Their first meal is almost nothing. Their "soup" is water enhanced with a few key minerals. Then they get served make-believe dessert. Felix explains that they're supposed to imagine eating it. While Oscar is holding up his empty plate, a very large woman comes over and asks, "Don't you want your dessert?" and takes his empty plate.

At the gym, Felix works out while Oscar sleeps on the mat. Then Burger, the leader of the institution, comes in, talking while eating a peach. As he waves his hands around, the starving Oscar is mesmerized by the peach and finally attacks it, stuffing it in his mouth regardless of Burger's hand.

That night Oscar and the very large woman sneak out of camp and get loads of food. Oscar can't believe it, but Felix turns him in. Security rushes in and grabs the contraband. He is punished with no movie and no unbuttered popcorn. And if he gets caught again, he's to be thrown out.

After the movie Felix comes in with popcorn and won't give any to Oscar. "You're being punished," says the righteous Unger. Oscar attacks him, and the guards are summoned. Oscar is sent home and Felix goes with him.

Notes

- In the opening scenes Oscar's girlfriend is a Dr. Nancy Cunningham. And after Felix expresses concern about his roommate's health and eating habits, Oscar goes in and gets a physical from Nancy. But aren't you not supposed to do that? Doesn't the Hippocratic Oath say anything about mixing romance and medical advice? It works out fine, because she finds that he's basically okay, but that he'd be "sexier" if he were in better shape. Now that's not a diagnosis you hear every day.

- Tony Randall once described the Felix character as essentially a Jewish mother, more than a Mr. Belvedere. He found that the show's writers would sometimes let his character become more of a snooty aesthete, while he felt Felix should be more of a meddlesome noodge.
- Dave Ketchum is perhaps best-known as Agent 13, the oft-hidden spy of *Get Smart*. He is certainly better known for that role than the guest-starring role of Jock above, a part that has been completely edited out of the version of this episode that airs in syndication. He was also a comedy writer and worked on the next episode in our BTVS Top 100. See below.
- In other episodes Felix's son, Leonard, is seen briefly. The role was played by both Leif Garrett and Willie Aames, in turn.
- In the 1982–83 season Ron Glass (Felix) and Demond Wilson (Oscar) starred in an all-black version of the series.
- The doctor's name is not "Berger" but "Burger," as written in the credits. This was either a pun relating to Oscar's hunger, or an effort to distance this character from Dr. Stuart Berger, the real-life dietitian who has written books about diets he espoused to improve the immunological system.

50

"The Dating Game"
laverne & shirley
Episode 118
Original air date: December 30, 1980
Original series run: 1976–1983
Series total: 178 episodes

Credits
Open: Penny Marshall, Cindy Williams. Supervising Producers: Tony Marshall, Milt Josefsberg. Executive Producers: Garry K. Marshall, Thomas L. Miller, Edward K. Milkis. Produced by Gary Menteer, Marty Nadler. Created by Garry K. Marshall and Lowell Ganz, Mark Rothman. Written by Al Aidekman. Directed by Penny Marshall. End: Creative Consultant: Robert L. Boyett. Executive Script Consultant: Marty Nadler. Executive Script Consultant: Jeff Franklin. Executive Story Consultants: Dave Ketchum, Tony DiMarco. Executive Producer: Frank Alesia. Story Editors: Al Aidekman, Ruth Bennett. Story Editor: Joanne Pagliaro. Also Starring Betty Garrett as Edna DeFazio. Co-starring Michael McKean as Lenny. David L. Lander as Squiggy. Phil Foster as Frank. Eddie Mekka as Carmine. Leslie Easterbrook as Rhonda. And Ed Marinaro as Sonny St. Jacques. Special Guest Star: Jim Lange. Guest Stars: Ilene Graff as Monique. Frank Ashmore as Bob Gatenby.

Episode Review
The boys are taking the girls to an audition for *The Dating Game*. Their demand?

THE BIG TV SATISFACTION FORMULA	
SyndicoDurability	8.1
Comic Valence	9
Emotional Resonance	7.3
Writing, Story	9.1
Writing, Characters	9.2
Acting	9.1
Quintessence	6.4
Series Originality	6.1
Episode Originality	9.4
Historical Significance	7.2
Celebrity	8.9
Gimmickry	9.3
Theme Song	7.5
Kitsch	9.3
BTVS Ratio	**82.56**

"In exchange for us being gallant enough to drive you down to this *Dating Game* thing, we would like to have all your used vacuum cleaner bags." Laverne wants to know for what, but Shirl' cuts her off: "Don't ask." They agree; but at the show it is not the girls but their bizarre alliterative male counterparts who somehow get selected.

The big night arrives. (Oddly enough, this particular episode of *The Dating Game* seems to be airing live.) In order to get reception on their television (since we are, after all, only up to the mid-1960s in this carefully detailed depiction of another era) Laverne, Shirley, Big Ragu, and Sonny have to get into outrageous and ridiculous positions while forming a human chain that touches the rabbit ears.

But the real comedy is happening on the show within the show. Jim Lange plays the role of Jim Lange perfectly.

"Bachelor Number Two is an ice cream vendor, who plays the guitar, and a champion shadow boxer; he enjoys Bosco and Squiggy. Say hello to Leonard Kosnowski."

"Bachelor Number Three is a top Hollywood agent whose hobbies include hang gliding, deep-sea fishing, and building a bridge to Japan; he's very proud of his collection of beautiful women and moths. Here is Andrew Squiggman."

It's a perfect situation for the bizarre non sequitur comedy of the boys. Also, it provides one more chance for Squiggy to employ his "catchphrase.": "Please say hello to our bachelorette." Squiggy: "Hello."

Then they field the questions of Monique, the leggy bachelorette, like no one else could.

"What sort of vegetable would you be?" Lenny: "I would be a sauerkraut. It was my only toy as a child."

"If you could invent a machine that would make me fall in love with you, what would it be?" Squiggy answers without hesitation: "A lawn mower." (Another of Squiggy's answers gets bleeped out, but even the part that is spoken is too racy for this family-friendly book.)

Len is asked, "What's the most romantic word you can think of?" He, too, answers without hesitation: "Lint." She chooses to follow up the question, "What does that mean?" To which, Lenny sagaciously replies: "Have you never been in love?"

When Squiggy is chosen over Lenny at the end, Lenny is broken up—he throws himself at her but is met only with rejection. Squiggy steps in to defend his pal, with the following speech: "You little harlot, you little trollop. All right, I want you take a look at his face. This is a shell of a man. This used to be a happy face, the face of a child at play. But no, not no more. You know why? You know why? You used him like a worn-out old Kleenex box. You just took your turned up nose and blew it right in his face."

After that, Monique basically runs for her life, but Jim is ready for anything: "Monique forfeited your date, so according to the rules you can choose anyone you want." Naturally, Squiggy chooses his buddy, Lenny. Lange then says, as he so often did, "You're going to Acapulco." And the boys couldn't be more excited: "We're going to France!"

Notes

- This is one of the rare episode in which the girls occupy the B plot, and Lenny and Squiggy take center stage. Nonetheless, it begins with some classic Laverne and Shirley physical comedy. Laverne has gotten into an outrageously sexy green gown. It rips, and then the zipper sticks. Shirley gets a candle to wax the zipper and ends up with a cramp in her shoulder . . . okay, it's basically impossible to describe without resorting to charts or animation, so we'll just move on.
- The key to understanding Squiggy is to realize that he is sleazy, dim-witted, egotistical, and disconnected from the world, just like Lenny, but unlike Lenny he has no redeeming qualities (except his loyalty to Lenny). Most important, he is a truly filthy pervert. The fact that he was on a family-hour sitcom made it difficult for this aspect of Squiggy to fully manifest itself, but if you study him long enough, you realize that he is one sick puppy.
- When you go through all the episodes in

TV history, as we have, you have to pause and wonder why it took four writers, a producer, and a director to make an episode of *I Love Lucy,* while it took twenty-two various consultants, producers, and story editors to make an episode of *Laverne & Shirley.*

- Dave Ketchum, one of those many writers for the series, began his career as a comic actor. He had regular roles in the shows *I'm Dickens—He's Fenster* and *Camp Runamuck,* and, most memorably, played Agent 13 in *Get Smart.*
- Though Penny Marshall is better known for directing such major motion pictures as *Big, A League of Their Own,* and *Riding in Cars with Boys,* she still says that this episode represents her finest work behind the camera. This is, of course, not true, but she never said it wasn't her finest work.
- One of the running jokes of this series was the lines that led to Lenny and Squiggy's entrances. This episode includes a classic example. The girls comment about Rhonda: "Besides there's worse people we could have as neighbors . . ." which is the cue for Lenny and Squiggy to enter with their trademark: "Hello."
- The character of Sonny, Laverne's boyfriend, was played by Ed Marinaro in one of his first regular series roles. The former Ivy League football star—he set numerous rushing records as a halfback for Cornell University—went on to fame as Officer Joe Coffey on *Hill Street Blues.*

49

"Vivian's First Funeral"

maude

Episode 94
Original series run: 1972–1978
Series total: 142 episodes

Credits

Open: Starring Beatrice Arthur, Bill Macy. Co-starring Adrienne Barbeau, Conrad Bain, Rue McClanahan, Hermione Baddeley. Produced by Charlie Hauck. Created by Norman Lear. End: Directed by Hal Cooper. Written by Samuel Greenbaum. Executive Producers: Rod Parker & Hal Cooper. Script Consultant: Charlie Hauck. Story Editors: William Davenport & Arthur Julian. Script Supervisor: Rod Parker. Arny Freeman as Mr. McDonald. Richard McMurray as Malcolm Flanagan. Production Supervised by Norman Lear. A Bud Yorkin–Norman Lear–Tandem Production.

Episode Review

Maude is getting ready to go to Hattie Flanagan's funeral. It becomes apparent that no one liked her. Vivian doesn't want to go. Carol won't go. Mrs. Naugatuck isn't going either. Walter comes home. He's not going. As they make preparations, they discuss that Maude had borrowed a brooch from Vivian—one that had been a gift from Arthur—and then lent it to Hattie Flanagan. Arthur arrives and asks where the deceased is being laid out. Maude answers, "McDonald's." (The name of the funeral home.) Arthur thinks it's nice she's at McDonald's: "She deserves a break today."

Maude, Vivian, and Arthur arrive at the funeral. Maude and Vivian notice, to their horror, that the brooch in question is actually on the deceased! Maude tells Vivian not to worry, he won't even notice it, but Arthur takes one look and practically yelps.

The three confer. Arthur insists that Maude get the broach, which was a "family heirloom!" Maude tries to figure out a subtle way to do it, while getting into a conversation with Hattie's bereaved husband. When Maude makes her next approach to get the brooch, she finds the casket is closed. Undeterred, she pretends to be grieving, opens it, and throws herself into the coffin.

The brooch is back in Vivian's hands at last. Then Arthur accidentally reveals it was originally a gift he had given his deceased wife on their first anniversary. This is news to Vivian, who decides she wants no part of it. She promptly returns the brooch to Hattie Flanagan, may they both rest in peace.

THE BIG TV SATISFACTION FORMULA

SyndicoDurability	7.4
Comic Valence	9
Emotional Resonance	7.8
Writing, Story	9
Writing, Characters	7.7
Acting	8.8
Quintessence	7.1
Series Originality	5.5
Episode Originality	9.4
Historical Significance	6.7
Celebrity	7.3
Gimmickry	9.3
Theme Song	8.9
Kitsch	8.7
BTVS Ratio	**82.58**

Triple

A simple triple with a reverse occurs early in the episode. The doubtful Vivian is worried about going to the funeral; after all, "there are so many unanswered questions." Maude replies: "What to do? What to say?" To which, Vivian answers: "No, what to wear."

Notes

- Deaths and funerals often seem to bring out the best in sitcoms. Other classic examples are Mary Tyler Moore's outstanding performance in "Chuckles Bites the Dust," the *Bob Newhart* episode "Death of a Fruitman," Ed Norton's wonderful eulogy for Ralph in "A Matter of Life and Death," and George Costanza's attempt to get free airfare for having attended a funeral.
- Bea Arthur had never done regular TV work before this series. She was a theatrical actor who starred in the original productions of *The Threepenny Opera* and *Gentlemen Prefer Blondes*. She won a Tony Award for playing Vera Charles in *Mame*.
- Bill Macy was in the original Broadway cast of *Oh! Calcutta*.
- At the very end of the series, Maude's political career became more and more the focus and the producer planned to have her be elected to Congress and move to Washington, but the irreplaceable Bea Arthur decided to leave the series. Interestingly, the producers tried to launch a new series based on the ideas that they had about a sitcom that took on the world of politics, and finally did briefly air a series called *Hanging In,* which starred Maude's costar Bill Macy as the lead.

48
"Ego-a-go-go"
gidget

Episode 20
Original air date: January 27, 1966
Original series run: 1965–1966
Series total: 32 episodes

Credits

Open: Sally Field, Don Porter. Written by Barbara Avedon. Directed by Jerrold Bernstein. End: Produced by William Sackheim. Executive Producer: Harry Ackerman. Creator & Script Consultant: Frederick Kohner. Gidget . . . Sally Field. Russell Lawrence . . . Don Porter. Larue . . . Lynette Winter. Anne . . . Betty Conner. John . . . Pete Deuel. Norman . . . Richard Dreyfuss. Chuck Batson . . . Ed Griffith. Shari Sue . . . Susan Yardley. Marilyn . . . Leslie Towner. Surfing Technical Consultant . . . Phil Savers.

Episode Review

Gidget is competing with Sherry Sue, a new girl, over the available boys. Larue runs through all the dreamy possibilities for who might be taking her to the Spinster's Ball. But she is shocked to hear that it is . . . Norman Durfner!

Norman is the ultimate nerd, and Gidget is taking him as a way of building up his ego. It was a bet with her brother-in-law, the psychologist. She is testing her theory that a single positive experience can mend a shat-

229

THE BIG TV SATISFACTION FORMULA	
SyndicoDurability	5.9
Comic Valence	7.8
Emotional Resonance	8.8
Writing, Story	8.8
Writing, Characters	8.7
Acting	8.3
Quintessence	9.5
Series Originality	5.8
Episode Originality	8.7
Historical Significance	7.9
Celebrity	8.8
Gimmickry	7.5
Theme Song	7.3
Kitsch	9.2
BTVS Ratio	**82.78**

tered ego like Norman's, or at least put him back on the path to mental health.

Then, Chuck Batson arrives. He is a studly athlete who has been assigned to special tutoring with Gidget's father to mend his horrible grammar. Despite his problems with syntax, and insistence on calling her "Gadget," Gidget has found the perfect guy to show up Sherry Sue. She also gives her father the helpful tip that Chuck will probably do better working with sentences that are about football, and, more specifically, about "star quarterback Chuck Batson."

But breaking the date with Durfner is harder to do than she thinks. She falls back into her original plan, of building up his confidence, and Durf thinks that she is getting serious. He's not ready for that. He can't let a little high school romance get in the way of his plans to become a brain surgeon. He breaks the date with her!

Furthermore, Durf's newly engorged ego is running rampant. He arrives with new clothes and slicked-back hair (apparently this is supposed to be a major transfor-

mation). "Mom was pretty excited about that. Kept calling me her late-blooming Valentino." And the girls at school are actually beginning to buy it. Sherry Sue has her eyes on Durf "the Surf." Now, Gidget has to get Durf to take her to the dance, or the truth will be revealed.

Gidget invites Durf over to talk, to somehow bring his ego back down to size. She is getting nowhere until Durf overhears Chuck, who is inside with Professor Lawrence, parsing sentences that have Chuck Batson as the subject. What an apparently bloated ego Chuck has—and with a little nudging from Gidget, Durf realizes that someone else around here has sounded like that. He realizes in an epiphany that he has had a swelled head. He asks her out to the dance, and all's well.

Notes

- The ideal heartthrob for teenage girls has changed considerably since mid-1960s. When Larue is trying to imagine the perfect guy, she suggests to Gidget that he should be "a cross between Prince Charming, Ringo, and Sandy Koufax."

- Don Porter spent a lifetime on television dealing with dizzy dames of one sort or another. He was Ann Sothern's long-standing boss and foil on her eponymous series.

- Richard Dreyfuss was a frequent guest star in sixties television series, appearing on such series as *Bewitched*, *Gunsmoke*, *The Mod Squad*, *The Young Lawyers*, *Room 222*, *The Ghost and Mrs. Muir* and *Please Don't Eat the Daisies*. He also had a regular role on the 1964–65 series *Karen*. Like *Gidget*, that series was also about the travails of a teenage girl in southern California. *Karen* was part of an interesting experiment on NBC entitled *90 Bristol Court*. They created three sitcoms that were all set in the same apartment complex. The superintendent, for example, was a recurring character in all three series, and other cross-over events could occur. However, the plug was quickly pulled on the other two sitcoms, *Harris Against the World* (starring Jack Klugman!) and *Tom, Dick and Mary,* leaving Karen to carry on alone for one full season before joining them in the purgatory of short-lived sitcoms.

- Pete Deuel played Gidget's brother-in-law, the young psychologist, but he is perhaps best known for his role in the popular Western *Alias Smith and Jones,* and, unfortunately, for his tragic suicide in 1971. That show, which was a sort of TV version of *Butch Cassidy and the Sundance Kid,* was doing well in its first season when, for reasons known only to himself, Deuel shot himself. He had a reputation for being a demanding actor, often critical of the material he was given, but he had not seemed depressed or despondent. His role in *Alias Smith and Jones* was recast, and the show continued for another year.

47

"Sam's Women"
cheers

Episode 2
Original air date: October 7, 1982
Original series run: 1982–1993
Series total: 275 episodes

Credits

Open: Starring Ted Danson, Shelley Long, Nicholas Colasanto, Rhea Perlman, and George Wendt. Created by Glen Charles & Les Charles and James Burrows. Co-Produced by Ken Levine & David Isaacs. Written by Earl Pomerantz. Directed by James Burrows. End: Produced by James Burrows, Glen Charles, Les Charles. Guest Starring Donnelly Rhodes as Leo. Donna McKechnie as Debra. Keenen Wayans as Customer #1, and Jack Knight as Jack. Angela Aames as Brandee, and John Ratzenberger as Cliff. Executive Script Consultant: David Lloyd.

Episode Review

Norm arrives. "Beer, Norm?" He replies, "Don't know the stuff. Better give me a tall one in case I like it." A blond bombshell enters. Carla tells them to forget it. Once Sam sees her, no one else will have a shot. Diane questions this; she has the impression that Sam has a little more depth than that. Carla demonstrates, knocking on the office door. Sam emerges. "Don't bother me . . ." Then he sees the bombshell. ". . . unless there's a customer." Sam goes to work, and Brandee ("with two E's") is easy prey. But Diane is

THE BIG TV SATISFACTION FORMULA	
SyndicoDurability	7.4
Comic Valence	9.3
Emotional Resonance	7.2
Writing, Story	8.9
Writing, Characters	9.4
Acting	9.2
Quintessence	9.9
Series Originality	7.1
Episode Originality	8.7
Historical Significance	7.1
Celebrity	7.6
Gimmickry	6.7
Theme Song	9.1
Kitsch	6.5
BTVS Ratio	**82.82**

snorting and laughing at Sam's lines and Brandee's dim-witted replies: "No, no Australian films. I hate subtitles."

Sam takes Diane aside to ask what her problem is. While they argue, someone else snags Brandee and exits. Sam warns Diane that she better not show any sign of enjoying this, so she is careful not to smile . . . while he is looking. They do a nifty little bit where he can tell that she is smiling each time he looks away, and he finally catches her.

Sam brings Deborah (his ex-wife) by, trying purposefully to make her look smart. They are pretending they came from a Mozart concert, but then Diane notices that the program from the concert is two years old. "I didn't say we came straight from the concert," explains Sam.

After Deborah leaves, Diane corners Sam and asks why he is so unhappy. He resists, but he finally admits that this week he's been out with every woman he really enjoys; now all he can think about is how dumb they are. It's Diane's fault. They get

into a name-calling fight, in which Diane criticizes Sam's values, while he calls her a snob. She says his phony come-ons would never work on an intelligent woman anyway.

Later they apologize to each other. Then Sam says something about the color of Diane's eyes. "What? Is there something wrong with it?" No, in fact he's never seen a color quite like it, oh wait, yes he has. As Diane mouth hangs slightly open, he spins a lavish tale of a certain sunset when the sky's color took on an unearthly hue that he never thought he would see again, etc., etc. He lets it sink in, then says . . . "An intelligent woman would see right through that, right?" Diane catches herself, pretends she had, but then drinks one of the shots off her tray as she leaves.

Triple

Early in the episode, Norm asks Carla a benign question: "How are the kids?" Her answer takes the basic triple form: "Two of 'em are ugly, one's obnoxious, and one's just stupid. He's my favorite."

Notes

- *Cheers* didn't take any time at all to hit its stride with the ineffable mix of barroom banter and the Sam and Diane sexual tension. This episode was the second in the series.
- In addition to the central plot, there is a fine B plot revolving around Coach's efforts to match up to the former bartender in giving wise advice.
- John Ratzenberger was not yet a regular cast member, just a featured player. The

character of Cliff Clavin was not one originally envisioned by the show's creators. Ratzenberger had suggested it after he had auditioned for the role of Norm. After he pitched the "know-it-all" character, he was signed for seven episodes. At first he was going to be a security guard, but at the last minute he was made a postman, the thinking being that a postman would come across lots of information that could inspire plot turns.

- Keenen Wayans plays a bit part in the beginning of this episode. In the cold open, Diane is still getting the hang of waiting tables. She delivers a long, complicated series of orders, taking them off her tray and placing them all around a group of six customers. But Wayans's character tells her she's got the wrong group of six. She hesitates, looks over the situation, and then asks if the two groups would mind just switching tables—a request they all accommodate.

- There were three episodes among the BTVS Top 100 that scored a nearly perfect 9.9 in Quintessence, the ineffable measure of how much the individual episode captured the core values of the series. It's amazing that such an early episode of *Cheers* could already be so close to the bull's-eye, but with the tension between Sam and Diane driving this episode, the show was already in peak form. Below are the top scoring episodes.

46

"When the Good Fellows Get Together"

get smart

Episode 68
Original air date: November 18, 1967
Original series run: 1965–1970
Series total: 138 episodes originally aired; 117 shown in syndication

Credits

Open: Starring Don Adams, and Barbara Feldon as "#99." Edward Platt as "Chief." Created by Mel Brooks with Buck Henry. Produced by Jess Oppenheimer. Executive Producer: Leonard Stern. End: Directed by Sidney Miller. Written by C. F. L'Amoreaux. Story Editor: Norman Paul. Guest Star: Dick Gautier as Hymie. Ted de Corsia as Spinoza. Jim Boles as Dr. Ratton. Martin Ashe as Agent 42. Byron Morrow as Dr. Harris. Pete Sotos as Guard. Bob Karvelas as Larrabee. In Charge of Production: Burt Nodella.

Episode Review

KAOS has created Gropo, a superpowered robot with one mission: to seek out and destroy Hymie, the CONTROL robot. But Hymie is looking forward to meeting Gropo. Hymie is sensitive and lonely; he hopes that he can make Gropo turn from evil and be his friend.

Hymie is given a complete overhaul to improve his capabilities in meeting the Gropo threat, but it is taking him some time to get used to his new internal workings. In order to give him time to adjust, Max takes him to a Western-style ghost town that CONTROL built. (Handy way to reuse the existing sets, too.)

With the threat of Gropo, along with Hymie's talk of friendship and "buttercups," they realize there is only one solution: reprogramming Hymie to be mean instead of good and nice. But, tragically, it would be a permanent change. There is no choice. They'll do it in the morning.

Hymie has overheard and runs away to avoid this fate. Max is left to fight Gropo on his own. Though the odds against him are impossible, they prepare him with boots that are guns and cuff links that are power-ful grenades. However, when Gropo arrives and Max attempts to arrest him, these weapons are quickly disposed of. Gropo eats the grenades and suffers only minor indigestion.

When all looks bleakest, Hymie arrives calling out, "Gropo! Gropo!" as he walks through the town not unlike the boy in the movie *Shane*. Hymie does his best to use the "nice and friendly approach," but Gropo is unresponsive. Hymie keeps up the idle chitchat ("perhaps we have some mutual friends?") as Gropo pounds him

Then Max rejoins the fray and is thrown aside by Gropo, an act that finally brings out the aggression in Hymie. They battle. Gropo is about to smash him when we enter the last commercial break. And when we return, Max pushes Gropo down a well. End of Gropo.

Triple

When Max is first approached by Gropo, he plays it by the book . . . and turns in a nifty triple. "All right, Gropo, you're under arrest. Assault with a deadly weapon, operating without a robot's license . . ." At that Gropo pushes him, so Max continues ". . . and pushing."

Notes

- Dick Gautier, who played Hymie the Robot, is an accomplished caricature artist.
- Mel Brooks and Buck Henry are credited with creating the show, but executive producer Leonard Stern was a comedy writer, too, on *The Honeymooners* and *The Phil Silvers Show*. Buck Henry served as

head writer for the first two years of production, but Mel Brooks basically left for other projects after the pilot, doing some contracted script work from New York. During the development process, Mel Brooks had toyed with the idea of trying to play the role of Maxwell Smart himself.

- The pilot was funded by ABC, but it passed on the series. NBC picked it up and aired it for its first four seasons. Then CBS took a turn, airing it for its final season. In 1995, Fox got in on the act, airing a brief revival of the series about the adventures of Zach, the son of 86 and 99.
- Barbara Feldon had been a winner on *The $64,000 Question,* answering questions about Shakespeare.

45

"The Fist Fighter"
the many loves
of dobie gillis

Episode 18
Original air date: December 15, 1959
Original series run: 1959–1963
Series total: 147 episodes

Credits

Open: Starring Dwayne Hickman. End: Featuring Bob Denver as Maynard G. Krebs and Tuesday Weld as Thalia Menninger. Warren Beatty as Milton Armitage. Writers: John Kohn and Mel Diamond. Director: Ralph Francis

Murphy. Created by Max Shulman. Produced by Rod Amateau.

Episode Review

Thalia explains to Dobie that what she wants is an athlete—after all, Ted Williams made $100,000 last year for playing baseball two hours a day—and he got a nice suntan, too! Milton, captain of the football team, arrives, and aces Dobie out, inviting Thalia to see *The Monster Who Devoured Cleveland* at the local drive-in theater, which in Dobie-land is always showing movies about monsters devouring municipalities of one sort or another.

Desperate for Thalia's affection, Dobie stages a fake fight with a local boxing legend in the hopes of impressing her with his brawny athletic prowess. The scheme works, and Dobie is transformed overnight into Top Fist, a legendary fightin' man replete with his own personal theme song, which is played whenever he enters Sam Wong's Ice Cream Shoppe. All men fear him. All women get squishy at the sight of

THE BIG TV SATISFACTION FORMULA	
SyndicoDurability	7.5
Comic Valence	9.5
Emotional Resonance	8.5
Writing, Story	8.9
Writing, Characters	8.3
Acting	8.8
Quintessence	7.2
Series Originality	6.3
Episode Originality	9.8
Historical Significance	3.5
Celebrity	9.3
Gimmickry	9.2
Theme Song	7.4
Kitsch	9.1
BTVS Ratio	**82.85**

him. Even the fickle Thalia swoons, awe-stricken by the moneymaking potential of his "swift but terrible hands." Despite the hype over Dobie's blazing fists of steel, the jealous Milton Armitage (a varsity wrestler) calls his bluff and challenges Top Fist to a boxing showdown. They both turn chicken in the end, arriving at the appointed time with matching casts on their arms. Thalia is left to continue her search for a husband with breeding, athletic ability, and oodles and oodles of money.

Notes

- Known as *The Many Loves of Dobie Gillis* in its initial network run on CBS, it became simply *Dobie Gillis* for syndication.
- The character Dobie Gillis was originally created by Max Shulman as a character in a series of stories published in the *Saturday Evening Post*. These were also collected and published in book form. In 1953, a movie musical version of the stories entitled *The Affairs of Dobie Gillis* was made starring Bobby Van as Dobie and Debbie Reynolds as Thalia. In that film, Hans Conried played Professor Pomfritt. It also includes a young Bob Fosse and Kathleen Freeman in supporting roles.
- Although many sitcoms feature wacky schemers with wannabe complexes, only *Dobie Gillis* would go that extra postmodern mile by parodying the whole idea with a self-referential theme song. Fresh from his (staged) annihilation of Monster Moose McCulloch, Dobie swaggers into Sam Wong's while the Western-style song "Top Fist" is sung. According to this cowboy Western–style croon, he never hits

women or children, or women of the opposite gender, or kittens or puppies or squirrels. Later in the episode, the song is reprised, with the redoubtable Maynard lip-synching the song to encourage Dobie not to chicken out.

44

"Her Sister's Shadow"
the brady bunch

Episode 59
Original air date: November 19, 1971
Original series run: 1969–1974
Series total: 117 episodes

Credits

Open: Starring Robert Reed, Florence Henderson, and Ann B. Davis as Alice. Created by Sherwood Schwartz, Executive Producer. Produced by Howard Leeds. Teleplay by Al Schwartz and Phil Leslie. Story by Al Schwartz and Ray Singer. Directed by Russ Mayberry. End: Maureen McCormick as Marcia. Eve Plumb as Jan. Susan Olsen as Cindy. Barry Williams as Greg. Christopher Knight as Peter. Mike Lookinland as Bobby. Lindsay Workman as Principal. Gwen Van Dam as Mrs. Watson. Peggy Doyle as Teacher. Julie Reese as Katy. Nancy Gillette as Pom-Pom Girl.

Episode Review

It begins with Jan's teacher complimenting her essay: "What a lovely title! 'What America Means to Me.'" (Frankly, any teacher who would compliment such a

THE BIG TV SATISFACTION FORMULA	
SyndicoDurability	9.9
Comic Valence	8.5
Emotional Resonance	9.6
Writing, Story	9
Writing, Characters	9.2
Acting	8.7
Quintessence	9.7
Series Originality	6.5
Episode Originality	8.1
Historical Significance	8.2
Celebrity	5
Gimmickry	6.7
Theme Song	9.9
Kitsch	9.8
BTVS Ratio	**82.87**

banal turn of phrase is suspect anyway, but we must remember that we have entered the Brady universe, a purer, simpler place.) However, her sweet compliment turns to ashes in Jan's mouth as the teacher proceeds to compare Jan to Marcia. Yes, wonderful Marcia, "the best student she ever had."

In a fit of pique, Jan throws Marcia's awards and trophies in the closet. When Marcia later finds the empty shelf, she is devastated: "A whole lifetime of achievements was on that shelf . . . gone, gone, gone!" (Note the tripartite repetition, a literary foreshadowing.)

When Jan finally admits her misdeed, she calls for pity with her famous (if short) soliloquy: "All I hear all day long at school is how great Marcia is at this or how wonderful Marcia did that. Marcia, Marcia, Marcia." She storms off, and the central theme is established. Now the Bradys try to fix the problem.

Jan is given advice: "Find what you do best, and do your best at it." Her first idea is to become a pom-pom girl. Alice cuts up newspapers to make pom-poms, while Greg and Bobby help—each trying a cheer. While Jan is practicing, the sad truth is apparent to the others: "Boy is she bad." And indeed, whatever it takes to be a good pom-pom girl, Jan clearly lacks. Diffident, Marcia claims, "If there was any way I could make her feel better, I'd gladly give back all my trophies."

When all seems lost, Jan is suddenly a success. Her scores in school have won her the Honor Society award! Finally, she'll have a trophy of her own. Or will she? While proudly looking it over, Jan realizes that there is a mistake in tabulation. She didn't win; she finished second. Jan struggles with her conscience but says nothing until the big day.

Everybody congratulates her, celebrates her. Then, as the ceremony proceeds, Jan's conscience comes to life. At the last second, Jan runs out and admits the truth to Mrs. Watson. After this consultation, the beloved teacher returns to the microphone to make the most stunning announcement in Fillmore Junior High history: "The winner of the Honor Society award is not Jan Brady."

However, as throats tighten and tears well, she goes on to praise Jan's courage and integrity: "She has set a standard today of sportsmanship and honesty that truly gives meaning to the words 'Honor Society.' "

Jan has accomplished her goal and received special recognition. Will the circle be unbroken? Now Cindy has a complaint: "All I heard all day is what a great sister I have. Jan, Jan, Jan." A classic "here we go again" coda.

Triple

Regarding the absent awards, the three boys perform a team triple:

GREG: I didn't take them.

PETER: I wouldn't touch them.

BOBBY: I couldn't reach them.

By the way, the groupings of the Bradys can be considered in sets of comic triples. Recall that the basic formula calls for two items that establish a pattern, followed by a comic deviation. There is Mike, Carol . . . and Alice! Marcia, Cindy . . . and Jan! And Greg, Peter . . . and Bobby! Okay, maybe the boys don't make as much sense, but Bobby could have been more eccentric. Or you could think of it as Greg, Peter/Bobby . . . and Oliver!

Notes

- This is the ultimate Brady episode, an emotional roller coaster that includes many classic, well-remembered quotes and moments. "Marcia, Marcia, Marcia" is a line that has become a pop-culture catchphrase.
- The Kitsch factor is always high in *Brady* episodes, but this particular episodes scores a stunning 9.6 in Emotional Resonance, thanks largely to the tearjerking moments surrounding Jan's onstage heroics.
- Marcia is supposed to be a wonderful student, and the others seem to be above-average achievers. But if the Bradys are such wonderful students, why don't they get A's? Their report cards are replete with mediocrity. Perhaps it was the show's creators making sure that the kids would

never be too "intimidating" to the young viewing audience.

- When Jan wrestles with her conscience, she actually hears the voice of "evil Jan" in her head: "Jan, everybody thinks you won. Nobody but you and I know. . . ." You and I? Who are these two people? Can it be that Jan is actually teetering on the point of a schizophrenic break? Perhaps it was some similar psychic crisis that later led to her strangely uncharacteristic bout of "irrepressible practical joking."

43

"Margie and the Shah"
my little margie

Episode 85
Original air date: May 12, 1954
Original series run: 1952–1955
Series total: 126 episodes

Credits

Open: Starring Gale Storm as Margie. Charles Farrell as Vern. End: Directed by Hal Yates. Teleplay by Frank Gill, Jr. and G. Carleton Brown. Story by Alan Woods and John Kohn. Characters Created by Frank Fox. Gale Storm as Margie. Charles Farrell as Vern, with Don Hayden, Clarence Kolb, Edgar Barrier, Donna Martell, Henry Corden, Ralph Sanford. Produced by Hal Roach, Jr. A Roland Reed Production. Wardrobe for Gale Storm by Junior House of Milwaukee.

THE BIG TV SATISFACTION FORMULA	
SyndicoDurability	6.2
Comic Valence	9.1
Emotional Resonance	9.1
Writing, Story	8.5
Writing, Characters	8.4
Acting	8.6
Quintessence	9.5
Series Originality	6.3
Episode Originality	9.1
Historical Significance	7.5
Celebrity	6.8
Gimmickry	9.1
Theme Song	5.2
Kitsch	9.2
BTVS Ratio	**83.15**

Episode Review

The Shah of Zena is in town to make an oil deal, but he's also an old college pal of Vern's: old "Beaver." Margie is fascinated by the idea of meeting a shah, a man with sixty-five wives in his harem. Vern bribes Margie not to get involved, by offering to buy her a new convertible.

We see the shah and realize that his secretary, Ahmed, is manipulating him to sign certain leases. In fact, he prevents Vern's phone message from getting to the shah.

Vern, unaware of this, walks up to the shah's suite, where there is a classic Irish cop on duty. Vern talks his way past him: "It's all right, Officer; I'm an old friend of the shah. And I'm a commissioner in the traffic department." But the shah's bodyguards give him the bum's rush. Finding Vern on the floor, the cop can't help rubbing it in, in his delightful brogue: "Did you want me to call ye a car, Commissioner?"

Margie finds out about this turn of events and decides, as usual, to take matters into her own hands. After all, a new con-

vertible is at stake! Boyfriend Freddy helps her sneak into the suite. But they are forced to hide in closets and linen baskets when four harem girls arrive.

Meanwhile, the shah has uncovered Ahmed's treachery and has dealt with it forthwith. And Vern has uncovered Margie's meddling. They decide to give Margie a little taste of her own medicine. She is dressed as a harem girl, and, trying not to get caught, she plays along, introducing herself as "Shah Shah." Vern demands "Shah Shah, peel me a grape." Then Vern excuses himself. Then the shah scares her by declaring that she will be his sixty-sixth wife! Back with the other harem girls, Margie panics, but one of the girls explains that if she fails to pass the test of "grace and beauty," perhaps she will not be chosen to be his wife.

She then is asked to dance for the shah. She does a purposefully horrible dance, a strange mix of Charleston and hootchie kootchie. But the shah claims to love it. Then she tries to fail the test of beauty, by displaying a mouthful of blacked-out teeth. He is visibly taken aback, but pretends to find her gorgeous. Just when all seems lost, Margie catches sight of Vern, hiding in the background. All becomes clear.

Margie immediately turns the whole prank around. She throws herself at the shah, declaring her love! "From now on, I'll get my kicks as wife sixty-six!" Even when he tries to explain that it was a joke, and even when Vern emerges, she insists that she must have the shah as her husband, and proceeds to chase them around the room lashing at them with a whip, until finally she decides that the jest has been amply repaid.

Notes

- Margie has been called a poor man's Lucy, but we believe that she wasn't really a markedly inferior character. If you actually sit down and watch the two shows today, the schemes, verbal parries, and physical comedy seem very similar. Margie is charming, frankly more lovable than Lucy. There is a tendency for success to breed praise. *I Love Lucy* was a bigger hit, stayed in syndication longer, became better known by more and more generations, overcame critics' early disdain through sheer popularity, and ultimately emerged as a pop icon. So *I Love Lucy*, a show that is probably 5 or 10 percent better than *My Little Margie*, becomes 2,000 percent more popular. It's simply the nature of our entertainment culture. Perhaps in five hundred years, when both shows are ancient relics, some student of our culture will be able to judge them more objectively. Or, more likely, people will still be chuckling appreciatively at the chocolate factory scene, and saying "Margie who?"
- In the reverse of the usual pattern of the era, *My Little Margie* was adapted from a TV original into a radio show that become a top-ten hit.
- Gale Storm's real name is Josephine Owaissa Cottle, and she was thirty-one years old when she began playing the twenty-one-year-old Margie.
- Despite Charles Farrell's distinctive Boston accent, the show took place in New York City. Their apartment was in the Carlton Arms on East Fifty-seventh Street.

42
"Perfect Hostess"
the patty duke show
Episode 54
Original series run: 1963–1966
Series total: 104 episodes

Credits

Open: Starring Patty Duke as Cathy Lane and Patty Lane. William Schallert as Martin Lane. Jean Byron as Natalie Lane. Written by Arnold Horwitt. Produced by Stanley Prager. Directed by Don Weis. End: Paul O'Keefe as Ross Lane. Eddie Applegate at Richard. George Gaynes as Gaylord. Frances Heflin as Cissy. Jeff Siggins as George. Don Scardino as Timmy. Sammy Smith as Sammy. Gerald Peters as Roger. Scott Glenn as Harry. Todd Everett as William. Guest Star: Patty Duke as Betsy. Created by Sidney Sheldon and William Asher. Story Supervisor: Sidney Sheldon.

Episode Review

It's time for breakfast in Brooklyn Heights, and the Lanes have just heard from Cousin Gaylord Lane, of the Atlanta Lanes, who has asked if his daughter can spend some of her vacation with her northern cousins. However, the letter has only *just* beaten the arrival of . . . Betsy Lane!

Sure enough, Patty and Cathy meet yet another cousin who looks exactly like them,

THE BIG TV SATISFACTION FORMULA	
SyndicoDurability	8.3
Comic Valence	8.6
Emotional Resonance	9
Writing, Story	8.7
Writing, Characters	8.8
Acting	9.2
Quintessence	8.4
Series Originality	9.2
Episode Originality	9.6
Historical Significance	8.3
Celebrity	7.1
Gimmickry	9.9
Theme Song	9.9
Kitsch	9.1
BTVS Ratio	**83.19**

except with blond hair. The other difference is her southern accent. She is welcomed by the Lanes. As she sets up her room, she unpacks the photos of all the boys she dates back home. Patty and Cathy are impressed.

So are the boys at the Shake Shop. Using her beguiling southern charm, she "accidentally" steals George Tutweiler from Cathy. Then she proceeds to move in on Patty's guy. When Patty finds out, she exclaims: "Why, that Confederate Cleopatra!"

In a strange little soliloquy, as Betsy addresses her doll, Sarah Jane, the new cousin decides that she wants to stay permanently, as Cathy does. She decides that it will never happen while Cathy is there, and further that she can plant the idea in Cathy's head that Cathy is unwanted and would be better off in Europe with Daddy.

Betsy suggests to Cathy that sometimes relatives can be a drag, that it can be tiresome if they never leave. Then Betsy tries to sow discord in Patty, too. Cathy and Patty argue. At first it seems that Betsy's plan will work, but then the two get suspicious. Patty decides to be sneaky to find out what Betsy is doing, and she makes the Patty-to-Cathy transformation in front of a mirror, hair back, hairband on. Sure enough, Patty-as-Cathy hears from the horse's mouth how Betsy is trying to split them up.

In the end, Martin Lane has a talk with her. Cousin Gaylord is on her way to pick her up, but Martin has uncovered her real desire: a family. Her parents work all the time and ship her off during vacations. But the parents arrive, and, somehow, they've mended their ways. They are going to take her out of boarding school and have her live at home. All's well, and Patty says good-bye with a jaunty, "Y'all come back now."

Triple

This entire episode is one big comic triple! Patty, Cathy . . . Betsy!

Notes

- Sidney Sheldon created this show and then *I Dream of Jeannie*, along with dozens of best-selling novels. He was widely known in Hollywood as the fastest writer ever. He would dictate an episode of *Patty Duke* in the morning, then knock out a *Jeannie* in the afternoon. On the latter show he wrote so many episodes that he invented four pseudonyms for himself. One supposes he was hoping to create the impression that lots of people were contributing their collective talents, but no, Sidney was just cranking out stories and dialogue.
- In 1989, Nick at Nite created a special salute to the unsung hero of *The Patty*

Duke Show: the Back of Patty Duke's Head. In a series of humorous vignettes, the network interviewed a woman who was forever facing away from the camera.

- The measurement for total originality, the Originality quotient, is a rather complex one that attempts to balance episodic originality with series originality. In any case, the episodes below amply demonstrate that the formula works. Each is a highly unique episode of a highly unique show.

The Patty Duke Show,
    "Perfect Hostess"   18.8
Gilligan's Island, "The Producer"   18.6
Get a Life, "Spewey and Me"   18.6
The Beverly Hillbillies,
    "The Giant Jackrabbit"   18.5
Bewitched, "Divided, He Falls"   18.5
The Flying Nun, "The Return of
    Father Lundigan"   18.5
Police Squad, "Rendezvous at
    Big Gulch"   18.5
Bewitched, "Illegal Separation"   18.3
F Troop, "That's Show Biz"   18.3
Get Smart, "The Groovy Guru"   18.2

41
"The Foundling"
the donna reed show
Episode 6
Original air date: October 22, 1958
Original series run: 1958–1966
Series total: 274 episodes

THE BIG TV SATISFACTION FORMULA	
SyndicoDurability	7.2
Comic Valence	7.5
Emotional Resonance	9.9
Writing, Story	9.2
Writing, Characters	9.6
Acting	9.1
Quintessence	9.9
Series Originality	6.6
Episode Originality	8.3
Historical Significance	7.1
Celebrity	5.8
Gimmickry	8.8
Theme Song	8.2
Kitsch	9.2
BTVS Ratio	**83.25**

Credits

Open: Starring Donna Reed, Carl Betz, Shelley Fabares, Paul Peterson. End: Directed by Oscar Rudolph. Written by John Whedon. Based on characters created by William Roberts. Associate Producer Williams Roberts. Produced by Tony Owen. Donna Stone . . . Donna Reed. Dr. Alex Stone . . . Carl Betz. Mary Stone . . . Shelley Fabares. Jeff Stone . . . Paul Peterson. Milkman . . . Paul Picerni. Kathleen . . . Fintan Meyler. Policeman . . . Don Hildreth. Hairstyles by Helen Young of Beverly Hills. Wardrobe by Ohrbach's. A Todon-Briskin Production.

Episode Review

If you were going to leave your baby with a note on someone's doorstep, Donna Stone, the perfect American mom, is certainly a fine choice. The note suggests that she take him in and raise him as her own: "Dear Mrs. Stone, His name is Willie. He's a good boy and hardly ever cries." Donna, Alex, and Kathleen, her Irish maid (who, apparently, was let go later in the series, otherwise why would Donna have ever vacuumed while wearing pearls?) discuss the matter. Just then the milkman arrives, in fine 1950s fashion. His advice? "You sure are lucky, Mrs. Stone. Most people go through all kinds of trouble to have a baby, right, Doc? And here you got one for nothing."

Eventually, the local constabulary are alerted, but Donna simply can't part with the baby. She just wants to keep it until the parents are found. Alex is sure that the authorities are the best ones to deal with the situation, but he finally caves in to the pressure and agrees to let the baby stay.

Jeff is the one member of the family who is not so sure about having a new addition. It's never too late for a little sibling rivalry. But, left alone to mind the baby, his nurturing side reveals itself, and he soon warms up to the idea. Babies are just so darn cute.

Meanwhile, Donna is doing a little detective work, trying to figure out who in Hilldale might have left her a baby. Then she cracks it, realizing that a baby whose birth certificate reads "Guillermo" might be called "Willy" by his Americanized parents. And whose son is Guillermo? The milkman's.

Donna goes to his home to find out why he abandoned his baby. She thinks he is such a nice man; there must be some good reason. Sure enough (bring up the mournful, slow version of the show's theme music) there is a reason, and it's a real tearjerker. It seems that his young wife passed away shortly after having the baby. He's been doing his best to take care of the baby and hold down his milk route, but he is running himself ragged. He was desperate. Why did he choose Donna?

"You know, a milkman, he . . . he gets to know his customers' homes pretty well. And I know you've got a happy home, Mrs. Stone."

He knows he did the wrong thing, but a baby needs a mother. (Ah, those fifties assumptions.) But he asks Donna please not to bring this to the authorities, and, of course, she says she won't. Meanwhile, Donna's eyes are welling with emotion at this sad tale. The milkman says, "I'm going to bring you a present, Mrs. Stone, something you'll really like. Some cheese . . ."

At this, Donna loses it, and tears begin to flow. "Oh, cut it out, Mrs. Stone. I see a woman cry, and I go all to pieces. What are you crying about?" To which Donna replies with the definitive *The Donna Reed Show* sound bite "Oh, I don't know. I guess it's just that I like cheese."

As good as cheese may be, it's not the answer to all their problems, but Donna has another idea. In a few deft moves, she manages to make a little match between the milkman and her maid. There had been a few romantic sparks earlier in the episode; all she did was help it along a little. After all, Willy does need a mother of his own.

Notes

- In these early episodes, Bill Roberts is given credit for "creating" the characters. While Roberts is undoubtedly a talented television writer and executive, how much effort exactly did it take to create these "characters"? Let's see, there's the mom, she's really nice and thoughtful. The dad is nice, too. It would be nice if he were a doctor, because doctors help people; in fact, let's say he's a pediatrician because that's the nicest sort of doctor. The daughter? Nice! And the son, nice, but in a more boyishly nice way. And we'll put them in a nice house in a nice town, and while it may seem like things aren't so nice at times, they will always end up nice. This is not to say that *The Donna Reed Show* is not a well-crafted television achievement, but the characters weren't exactly huge leaps of imagination.

- Was it some sort of strange sitcomic foreshadowing? The theme song to *The Donna Reed Show* is entitled "Happy Days," by William Loose and John Seely. (However, neither of the two theme songs to *Happy Days* is called "Donna Reed.")

- In the years after her show left the air, Donna Reed became involved in the women's liberation movement and regretted the limitations and ethic that her show seemed to espouse. She felt she had helped create a male fantasy of what a woman should and could be.

- Shelley Fabares and Paul Peterson followed Ricky Nelson's lead in dabbling in recording careers. Both had songs that cracked the Top 40 after being performed as part of episodes. Fabares sang "Johnny Angel" in an episode about visiting the college that Donna had attended. Peterson sang "My Dad"—a real tearjerker—in an episode about Dr. Stone's busy schedule, but his ultimate devotion to his family.

40

"This Little Piggy Had a Ball"

that girl

Episode 28
Original series run: 1966–1971
Series total: 136 episodes

Credits

Open: Starring Marlo Thomas. Also Starring Ted Bessell. Produced by Jerry Davis. Created by Bill Persky and Sam Denoff. End: Executive Producers: Bill Persky and Sam Denoff. Script Consultant: Jerry Davis. Bonnie Scott as Judy. Dabney Coleman as Leon. Jane Dulo . . . Nurse. Murray Roman . . . Bowling Manager. Marc London . . . Doctor. Jerry Fogel . . . Fireman. Burt Taylor . . . M.C. Shirley Bonner . . . Sharon Hackett. Rob Reiner . . . Carl. Terry Garr . . . Date. Gene Tyburn . . . Young Man. Diane Quinn . . . Teenage Girl. Executive in Charge of Production: Ronald Jacobs

Episode Review

Ann Marie has a small role in a play with rising young actress Sharon Hackett, who has been nominated by the Drama Guild as most promising young actress of the year. However, Sharon must be in Hollywood for a screen test and won't be able to attend the awards ceremony. (Who's her agent, anyway?) Sharon lines up her friends for a quick round of "catch a tiger by the tail" to decide who will represent her at the cere-

THE BIG TV SATISFACTION FORMULA	
SyndicoDurability	6.6
Comic Valence	9
Emotional Resonance	8.6
Writing, Story	8.3
Writing, Characters	8.1
Acting	8.7
Quintessence	9.7
Series Originality	7.2
Episode Originality	9.7
Historical Significance	7.6
Celebrity	6.8
Gimmickry	8.8
Theme Song	8
Kitsch	9.4
BTVS Ratio	**83.53**

mony and finishes with, "My mother said to choose 'That Girl!' "

In any case, Ann and Donald have a bowling date. She is trying to get him to write the acceptance speech, since Sharon didn't provide one. While he works something up, she reads a fascinating article in a bowling magazine about a man who can bowl 118 with his toe. Well, what would you do? She tries it and finds that her toe is firmly wedged in the ball and won't come out.

First, they try the manager of the lane, who throws the bowling magazine in the trash; apparently Ann is the fourth person this week to try it and get stuck. He applies grease, then tries to tug it off with no luck. They leave a deposit for the ball and head home. Ann decides that the fire department might be the answer because, "When I was five years old, we called the fire department when I got my elbow stuck in a peanut butter jar."

That makes sense, but the fire department rescue squad is out on a call. Only the underwater specialist is available, and he can't think of a solution that doesn't involve putting her toe in serious peril—drilling, acetylene torches, fire axes, etc. They go to the hospital next. The doctor's prognosis? "What we have here is a case of an excited toe." Ann's response? "Well, it's never been in a bowling ball before." Hmm, paging Dr. Freud!

He gives her muscle relaxants to calm down the toe, and, since we're in TV land, it's basically okay that she then overdoses on them in the hopes that more pills will make the toe relax more quickly. Soon, the pills have kicked in, making her positively goofy. She is feeling no pain.

The award ceremony approaches, and no one else can take over Ann's task. In order to make it at least a bit safer for her, they slice the ball in half. The actual process of sawing through the ball is skirted over. It couldn't have been easy.

Ann gets dressed. There is some discussion of how to get her pants off, but naturally Donald has nothing to do with that. They arrive at the big event with the half ball still firmly in place. There they are met and mocked by an obnoxious friend named Carl.

Naturally, Sharon (remember her?) wins the award and Ann begins clomping stageward. Obviously the half ball is a very light "stunt" ball created for the show, because rather than really drag it, she lifts it off the floor with each step. Even half a bowling ball weighs eight pounds. (Try it.) In any case, she is most of the way there when the toe finally relaxes, the ball comes off, and the award is accepted.

Notes

- Do you ever wonder if the creators of the show regretted that they had set themselves the challenge that every opening sequence would be constructed to end with the words "That Girl"? This open was a relatively logical one. Sharon's impending stardom has already gone to her head, and she's already forgotten the names of the little people like Ann. But it only got more and more contrived.
- The obnoxious fellow at the award ceremony is played by Rob Reiner. The character is named Carl; his date, although she is credited only as "date," is referred to as Stella. This is surely an in joke about Rob's illustrious father, Carl, whose wife is named Estelle.
- Stella, by the way, is played by "Terry" Garr, but yes, it's the Teri Garr we know and love.
- Alas, Dabney Coleman's role here is forgettable. But his presence did add to the Celebrity quotient.

39

"TV or Not TV?"
murphy brown
Episode 26
Original air date: October 16, 1989
Original series run: 1988–1998
Series total: 247 episodes

Credits

Open: Starring Candice Bergen. Also Starring Pat Corley, Faith Ford, Charles Kimbrough, Robert Pastorelli, Joe Regalbuto, Grant Shaud. Producers: Tom Seeley & Norm Gunzenhauser. Producer: Russ Woody. Producers: Gary Dontzig & Steven Peterman. Producer: Barnet Kellman. Co-Producer: Deborah Smith. Consulting Producer: Korby Siamis. Created by Diane English. Written by Craig Hoffman. Directed by Barnet Kellman. End: Executive Producers: Diane English & Joel Shukovsky. Story Editors: Sy Dukane & Denise Moss. Guest Starring Morgan Fairchild as Julia St. Martin. Keith Amos as Secretary #23. Sanford Jensen as Mark. Jeff Mooring as Stage Manager, and Connie Chung.

Episode Review

It's an episode of a TV series (*Murphy Brown*) about a TV series (*FYI*) becoming an episode of a TV series (*Kelly Green*). Here's how it works: the network's entertainment division wants *FYI*'s help in developing a sitcom. They pretend it's an "amalgam," but the working title character is Kelly Green. Everyone is skeptical. Jim says, "I

THE BIG TV SATISFACTION FORMULA	
SyndicoDurability	8
Comic Valence	9.3
Emotional Resonance	7.8
Writing, Story	8.7
Writing, Characters	8.3
Acting	8.7
Quintessence	7.2
Series Originality	6.2
Episode Originality	9.5
Historical Significance	8.5
Celebrity	9.3
Gimmickry	9.8
Theme Song	8.2
Kitsch	8.2
BTVS Ratio	**83.57**

better get back to work before the network decides to give me a wacky sidekick."

The star, Julia St. Martin, is coming to observe the real doings at *FYI*. Only Murphy doesn't fawn or put on airs. Frank shows up looking like Indiana Jones. Murphy says, "Hi, Frank, the Temple of Doom is that way." Julia asks Corky for advice. Murphy aside: "The blond leading the blond."

But when Julia finally gets Murphy to give her a chance, she proves she know her stuff, by being familiar with the underlying political issues surrounding the Korea River Dam Project. With Murphy's defenses down, Julia pleads to be allowed to shadow her.

Murphy gives an inch, and Julia runs wild. She repeats a phone call Murphy makes to a senator as a "sense memory acting exercise." Then Julia has a great idea: "Murphy Brown meets Kelly Green. We'll have a real-life newswoman walk into our fictional world. Now tell me this isn't the best!" Murphy is reluctant, but beginning to get caught up in the ego trip.

At the sitcom, Murphy is absolutely terrible. The TV director is that perfect mix of aesthete and drill sergeant found running many a set, bitchy but also forever optimistic. Murphy has to search for her mark. Her line reading is flat. Her line is: "I got your letter of apology, Kelly. Now I'm sorry I filled your car with herrings." As Julia says in an aside after take four, "The woman is a redwood."

The gang gathers at Murphy's place to watch the premiere of *Kelly Green*. Only Murphy is laughing. Jim is appalled: "I braved three wars and eight administrations so that I could see myself become a comic tour de force for Peter Graves?"

Then, as life meets art meets life meets art, or something like that . . . Connie Chung walks onto the set, just as Murphy had onto Kelly's show. They chat a bit, then Connie says, "Murphy, can I be honest with you? I think it's wrong for a journalist of your stature to appear in a sitcom."

Notes

- These sorts of twisted self-referential episodes seem to do very well in the BTVS ratio scoring system. The other episode of *Murphy Brown* that did particularly well, though it didn't crack the BTVS Top 100, was the infamous episode in which she decided to raise her baby on her own. Dan Quayle's use of the sitcom story line to critique the morality of television backfired and made him look more ridiculous than usual.
- Murphy's new secretary is a very "fly" rapper. She eventually fires him in a short "rap."
- There was a real news show entitled *F.Y.I.* Airing on CBS in 1960, it was a short-lived Sunday morning (then evening) public affairs and news program hosted by Douglas Edwards.

38

"Amnesia in the Addams Family"

the addams family

Episode 22
Original air date: February 19, 1963
Original series run: 1964–1966
Series total: 64 episodes

Credits

Open: Starring Carolyn Jones, John Astin. Written by Phil Leslie and Keith Fowler. Directed by Sidney Lanfield. End: Produced by Nat Perrin. Developed for Television by David Levy, Executive Producer. Based on Characters Created by Charles Addams. Featuring Jackie Coogan as Uncle Fester, with Ted Cassidy as Lurch. Blossom Rock as Grandmama. Lisa Loring as Wednesday. Ken Weatherwax as Pugsley.

THE BIG TV SATISFACTION FORMULA	
SyndicoDurability	8.5
Comic Valence	8.4
Emotional Resonance	7.9
Writing, Story	9.1
Writing, Characters	9.2
Acting	9.4
Quintessence	9.6
Series Originality	9.1
Episode Originality	8.9
Historical Significance	7.1
Celebrity	7
Gimmickry	9.7
Theme Song	9.5
Kitsch	9.6
BTVS Ratio	**83.61**

Episode Review

Gomez is working out with some old Indian clubs. "Where does anyone get old Indian clubs? From an old Indian!" But at that moment, he whacks himself on the head. When he comes to, he is Gomez, but a strangely "normal" version who, like so many visitors, finds the decorating dismal, the food repulsive, and Morticia's fashions to be dreary at best.

We then tour the classic Addams devices. Pugsley wrecks the train; Fester has his head in a vise; Mama suggests a little time on the rack might put Gomez back to normal. Naturally, Gomez becomes convinced Morticia's trying to kill him, to collect his insurance. But in a calmer mood he buys her a whole new wardrobe of pretty dresses that appall her.

Thing has a suggestion, and mimes hitting. Morticia reads from a medical handbook that amnesia caused by a blow on the head "can sometimes be cured by a similar blow," but she is reluctant to try it for fear of hurting him. Of course, in TV land, the "second-blow" cure always works. But leave it to *The Addams Family* to take it further than that.

First, Fester takes it upon himself to smack Gomez on the head—and the real Gomez returns. He's cured! Morticia is delighted to find that he is horrified by the "pretty dresses" she is trying on.

But what we have here is a failure to communicate. Lurch, unaware that the cure has been delivered, gives Gomez another whack, intoning, "It's for his own good!" Back to the milquetoast Gomez: "Perhaps I am too strict with you. You are my wife. You may call me Honeybun or Doll-boy."

Next up, Mama knocks him in the head. The real Gomez is back. But only briefly . . . Wednesday and Pugsley approach. His daughter says she has a surprise. Gomez closes his eyes, and Pugsley wallops him. Lurch arrives with some grisly Addams fare, but our all-American Gomez persona requests a slab of apple pie with cheese.

Meanwhile, Morticia has decided that action must be taken, but she doesn't want to see his dear sweet face when she hits him. She gets Fester to get Gomez to play hide-and-seek in the draperies. But naturally, things go awry and—like *Hamlet* through the arras—she hits not Gomez, but Fester!

Gomez runs away when he see the club—"I thought it was you!" But Morticia protests, "I'm only trying to make you well!" In his panic Gomez runs into the wall, and knocks himself all better at last.

In the coda, Thing is using sandpaper to take the "knots" out of Gomez's head, and they discover that Morticia's mistaken wallop has had consequences for Fester. As Fester says: "Who's Fester?" Here we go again!

Notes

- As usual, *The Addams Family* packs three times the plot twists into their take on the classic "amnesia" story line. Furthermore, the amnesiac Gomez provides the perfect foil for the show's quintessential "the normal way vs. the Addams way" comedy.
- *The Addams Family* was launched the same week as *The Munsters*, ran for two years, and ended within two weeks of the final

episode of *The Munsters*. Surely one of the most fitting coincidences in TV history.

- However, those who lump *The Munsters* and *The Addams Family* together creatively are not paying close enough attention. While both shows play off many of the obvious possibilities, *The Munsters* is much gentler, a goof on the movie versions of monsters. *The Addams Family* was much more perverse, more of a vision of the exact opposite of *The Donna Reed Show* at every level: moral, emotional, even sexual.
- Thing was generally played by Ted Cassidy, whose Lurch role left him with extra time on his hands, or hand, as the case may be.
- In 1973, a pilot for a musical version of *The Addams Family* was tested but rejected before it was made into a series. Hard to imagine. (The show, not the cancellation.)

37

"A Shirt Story"
the cosby show

Episode 5
Original air date: October 8, 1984
Original series run: 1984–1992
Series total: 201 episodes

Credits

Open: Bill Cosby in . . . Starring Phylicia Ayers-Allen, Lisa Bonet, Malcolm Jamal-Warner, Tempestt Bledsoe, Keshia Knight-Pulliam. Produced by Caryn Sneider. Co-Executive Producer: Earl Pomerantz. Written by John

Markus. Created by Ed Weinberger and Michael Leeson, and Dr. William H. Cosby Jr., Ed.D. Directed by Jay Sandrich. End: Executive Producers: Tom Werner and Marcy Carsey. Guest Stars: Sonia Bailey, Kadeem Hardison, Cassandra Murry. Co-Producer: Jerry Ross. Executive Story Consultant: John Markus. Executive Script Consultants. Karyl Geld Miller and Korby Siamis.

Episode Review

Theo and his mom return from shopping. They had only one fight . . . it began when they left and lasted the whole time. In any case, Theo has come home with a $95 Gordan Gartrell shirt. Cliff takes a stand: "No fourteen-year-old boy should have a ninety-five-dollar shirt, unless he is onstage with his four brothers."

Denise says that she could make a shirt that looked exactly like a Gordan Gartrell. And by Saturday, too. Theo, in a moment of naive trust, hands her the thirty dollars and dances off, sure that his problems are solved. The folks question her willingness to complete this job. They give a long list of all the things she has given up on once the going got tough. But she promises them that she won't fail. She will finish the shirt, on time and beautifully.

The day arrives, and the shirt is done. Denise hands it off to Theo in a box, and sits on the bed, pulling in Vanessa for moral support. Sure enough, after a few moments, Theo enters wearing the most unbelievably misshapen and bizarre-looking agglomeration of pockets, odd lengths and patches of color that you have ever seen. He is horrified. And doomed.

Theo comes to Dad, who laughs and tells Theo an instructive story about how he once wore a truly horrible tie to speak at a medical convention because it was given to him by little six-year-old Theo. Cliff says, "I think you've learned your lesson." Theo responds immediately: "Oh, I've learned my lesson; I've learned my lesson. Whatever it is, I learned my lesson." Cliff has the original shirt upstairs. He never returned it because he thought that Denise's might not work out.

Theo is ecstatic and heads out into the living room, saying, "I was *that* close to one of the most embarrassing days of my life . . ." only to find all his friends have already arrived and he's still wearing Denise's creation.

Cliff goes in to save him, but Theo, in a moment of grace, admits, "This is my shirt." And is amply repaid when Christine loves it! It's very "Ichi Ammarata" or something. Before they head out, Theo runs upstairs to tell Denise the good news.

THE BIG TV SATISFACTION FORMULA	
SyndicoDurability	7.9
Comic Valence	8.9
Emotional Resonance	9.2
Writing, Story	9.3
Writing, Characters	9.4
Acting	8.9
Quintessence	9.7
Series Originality	7.7
Episode Originality	9.3
Historical Significance	7.4
Celebrity	6.1
Gimmickry	6.1
Theme Song	6.2
Kitsch	7.6
BTVS Ratio	**83.68**

Triple

At one point, while Denise works, Theo comes into her room, anxious to know if the shirt will be done in time. She reassures him but needs to get back to work. Her concluding comments are in nifty response-infused triple.

DENISE: Believe me?

THEO: Yeah.

DENISE: Feel better?

THEO: Yeah.

DENISE: Get out.

Notes

- This was one of the earliest episodes of the incredibly popular series that went on to reign as the number-one show from 1985 to 1989.
- The expensive shirt episode was no doubt a conscious declaration that this was a show about the upper middle class. Bill Cosby wasn't going to produce another *Good Times*.
- The only episode of *The Cosby Show* to rank higher in Comic Valence is the one in which Rudy has a new friend she calls "Bud." (Pronounced "Buuud.")
- Bill Cosby ranks slightly ahead of Bob Newhart as the actor with the most confusing number of different TV shows. He was in *The Bill Cosby Show* (1971, sitcom in which he was a gym teacher), *The New Bill Cosby Show* (1972, comedy variety), *Cos* (1976, comedy variety for kids), *The Cosby Mysteries* (1994, detective drama), *The Cosby Show*, and most recently, *Cosby*, and, of course, Nick Jr.'s *Lil' Bill*. Then there was his work hosting remakes of *You Bet Your Life* and *Kids Say the Darndest Things*.

He also created *Fat Albert and the Cosby Kids* and *The New Fat Albert Show*. By comparison, Bob Newhart has *The Bob Newhart Show* (a 1960 variety series), *The Bob Newhart Show* (psychologist), *Bob* (cartoonist), *Newhart* (innkeeper), and then *George and Leo* (Bob's real name is George Robert Newhart). Newhart has no plans at this time to produce a preschool show entitled *Lil' Bob*.

36
"Best Dressed Man"
the many loves of dobie gillis

Episode 5
Original air date: September 22, 1959
Original series run: 1959–1963
Series total: 147 episodes

Credits

Open: Starring Dwayne Hickman. End: This show was . . . Produced and directed by Rod Amateau. Written and created by Max Shulman. Starring Dwayne Hickman. Featuring Frank Faylen, Florida Friebus, Bob Denver, and Tuesday Weld as Thalia Menninger. Warren Beatty as Milton Armitage. With William Schallert, Mel Blanc, Jim Johnson, Tom Orme, Paul Von Schreiber

Episode Review

Like many of the early episodes, this one begins with Dobie in the classic pose of Rodin's *The Thinker*. As usual, he is thinking about his current obsession, in this case, Thalia Menninger. Fashion is the problem. If only Dobie had enough wherewithal, then he could dress as well as Milton Armitage. Gillis Pater is no use at all, suggesting that Dobie work (work!) for the money.

As Dobie and Maynard look in the window of Ziegler's men's clothing store, he is inspired. He makes a deal with Ziegler (Mel Blanc) to serve as a sort of walking advertisement. Ziegler provides "loaner" clothing, and Dobie wears them; as a role model and leader, he inspires imitation among the teen set.

It works like a charm. Thalia is positively mad for Dobie's outfits. But Milton Armitage is not taking this challenge lightly. He fights back, stepping up his fashion statement to be bigger, bolder, more extravagant. When Milton goes to Mohair "from real goats," Dobie tops him with cashmere. Thalia loves expensive clothes: "It shows you've got money, and that's what's important: money!"

In the end, Dobie triumphs! His suit is so outrageous and fabulous that Thalia passes him a note: "You are the most . . . will you be my steady?"

Milton is not through yet, and he finds his way to Ziegler's in search of something to top Dobie. There, he uncovers the deceit when he finds Thalia's note in the pocket of the suit. Milton rushes to Thalia to tell all, but he is rebuffed again. The sweet siren of Central High explains that Milton's money is nice, but that Dobie's initiative in creating this business arrangement shows that Dobie will be making scads of money later, when she's ready to marry.

Dobie glows, until Thalia asks how much Ziegler was paying him. He tries to explain, but she insists that he should be getting the clothes to wear, plus an advertising fee. She pushed Dobie into Ziegler, who naturally tosses Dobie right back out. The deal is off, and Dobie is back to square one.

Notes

- There are many elements that make *The Many Loves of Dobie Gillis* stand out. As with *Burns and Allen*, the fourth wall was regularly transgressed. The characters are purposefully single-minded. Dobie's world is filled with running jokes and little absurdities, like the fact that the local Bijou is always showing a movie that involves a monster devouring some municipality or another, or that they hang out at Charlie Wong's Ice Cream Parlor where the treats offered include such combinations as Pistachio Lo Mein and Chocolate Egg Fu Yung Sundaes.

However, the single characteristic of the show that truly makes it an original is the wonderfully baroque writing. No attempt is made to make the characters sound real or natural. They are players on the stage, out of whom flow words that are more poetry than dialogue. Dobie on the girl of his dreams: "Thalia Menninger! Why, that's not a name, it's a poem; it's a song!" Thalia to Dobie: "What bothers me is that you're cute and I'm helpless and disconnected, and I could fall for you no trouble at all" because "Dobie, you're a doll socially, but you'll never make a merchant prince." Annabelle is no kinder: "Dobie, you're a nice boy, but you simply don't have the divine fire." While Mignon wants to remake him, arguing that Dobie should choose her instead of another: "Will *she* propel you up the ladder of success like I will? Will *she* forge a solid rock of achievement out of the gooey clay of your mediocrity?" Even Herbert T. Gillis is prone to verbosity: ". . . you are Maynard G. Krebs, a fine, warm-hearted, self-sacrificing young man, and tonight you are going to play the bongos with Thelonious Monk, whatever that means." Then there is Chatsworth Osbourne, Jr. (the Latin on his family crest spells out the Osbourne motto: "Never touch the capital"), who decides in one episode to democratize his social life: "By gad, I shall palaver with the hoi polloi, no matter what the cost to my feelings!" Now that is writing!

- In this episode, as she so often does, Thalia explains why she must be so preoccupied with money: "My father is sixty with a kidney condition. Mother isn't getting any younger. My sister married a loafer, and my brother shows every sign of becoming a public charge." She does not, however, give her other classic line: "My father always says: 'Love doesn't butter any parsnips.' "
- Though Yvonne "Batgirl" Craig did a fine job as Linda Sue Faversham, the second recurring *objet de crush*, no one did it better than Tuesday Weld. By the bye, Craig actually started on the show playing another love interest for Dobie, Aphrodite Millican of the Flying Millicans.

35

"Divided, He Falls"
bewitched

Episode 69
Original air date: May 5, 1966
Original series run: 1964–1972
Series total: 254 episodes

Credits

Open: Starring Elizabeth Montgomery, Dick York, and Agnes Moorehead as Endora. Written by Paul Wayne. Directed by R. Robert Rosenbaum. Produced by Jerry Davis. Executive Producer: Harry Ackerman. End: Sanford Stern . . . Frank Maxwell. Francie . . . Joy Harmon. Joe the Diver . . . Jerry Catron. Girl . . . Susan Barrett. David White as Larry Tate. Production Consultant: William Asher. Created by Sol Saks. Script Consultant: Bernard Slade. Wardrobe and furnishings for Tabatha provided by Babycrest. Dick York's wardrobe furnished by Michaels-Stern.

THE BIG TV SATISFACTION FORMULA	
SyndicoDurability	9.3
Comic Valence	9.2
Emotional Resonance	8.4
Writing, Story	8.6
Writing, Characters	9.4
Acting	9.2
Quintessence	8.8
Series Originality	8.9
Episode Originality	9.6
Historical Significance	8.1
Celebrity	6.1
Gimmickry	9.3
Theme Song	9.1
Kitsch	9.1
BTVS Ratio	**83.79**

Episode Review

Darrin is forced to cancel a long-planned and well-deserved vacation to work on still another "big account"—this one the Stern Chemical Company. Samantha, forever resilient, is disappointed for all of three seconds. Endora is feeling pretty relaxed this episode, so instead of letting loose with her hex-howitzer, she thoughtfully splits Darrin into his happy-go-lucky side (surprised to hear he has one?) and his diligent, responsible side. The id and the superego.

Darrin-id proceeds to replan the vacation, much to Sam's delight. Moments later, Sam encounters Darrin-superego, still hard at work in the den. She knows whom to call: "Mother!" Endora pops in, smoking a hookah no less. Samantha says, "I only want one Darrin," to which Endora shoots back, "I know exactly what you mean. It's humiliating to look as if you've made the same mistake twice." Nonetheless, Samantha's usual charming lack of resolve allows her to be convinced to go on vacation with Darrin-id.

And what a vacation! Her hubby is a young buck again, dancing, flirting, sipping mai tais by the pool, and showing off his Al Jolson imitation. He even dives in the pool—forgetting that he can't swim—and Sam has to blink him into reverse motion to put him back onto the diving board. Meanwhile, back in the city, Darrin-superego is so unrelentingly industrious that Larry and the client are ready to throttle him.

Meanwhile back at the resort, Darrin is out of control. When Sam disbelievingly asks if he really wants her to use magic, he says, "Sure, why not, the kids'll love it!" Enough is enough. Sam summons Endora and, shortly thereafter, Darrin the Dull. The two Darrins want nothing to do with each other, but they're tricked into running headlong into each other: flash, boom, mono-Darrin.

The coda? Sam says she loves both sides of her mortal mate's personality, and Endora is disgusted. A classic *Bewitched* ending to a classic *Bewitched* episode.

Whee Wohn

Early on, Samantha is packing for the long-awaited vacation and says to Endora, "Nothing short of a catastrophe can delay us now." Cut to the offices of McMann and Tate, where Larry is saying: "Darrin, you're just the man to save us from a catastrophe."

Notes

• On *Bewitched*, the eternal triangle was man, woman, and job. Darrin is forever torn between Larry Tate and Samantha, fired and rehired by Larry, imperiled and saved by Sam. In this episode—one of the last black-and-white shows—the triangle is solved by Endora applying multiplication to a geometry problem.

- When Dick York's health forced him off *Bewitched*, Dick Sargent became Darrin. In fact, the very first episode that Dick Sargent filmed was actually a remake of "Divided, He Falls." Episode 185, entitled "Samantha's Better Halves," was written (rewritten?) by Lila Garrett and Bernie Kahn and directed by William Asher. Talk about a challenge! They ask Sargent not only to fill York's role, but also to replicate what was arguably his finest performance.

Sargent's take on the dual role was interesting, but not nearly as satisfying as York's. Sargent was merely conflicted; York was schizoid. In fact, many of the lines in the episode—for example, "I only want one Darrin, Mother!"—made Dick Sargent understandably uncomfortable during production. They completed the episode, but it was not the first Dick Sargent episode to air. Instead, it was shelved and aired later in the season—as a flashback, because Adam had since been born.

Since that fateful transformation, the debate has raged: Which was the better Darrin? Unfortunately for Mr. Sargent, the results of our work with the BTVS ratio clearly demonstrate that Dick York was better. Not a single Sargent episode cracked the BTVS Top 100, while two Dick York–led episodes made it. For those still in doubt, the highest-ranked Dick Sargent episode came in at 675: "Samantha's Old Salem Trip," in which Esmeralda accidentally sends Sam back to seventeenth-century Salem. But, truth be told, maybe the debate wasn't really all that raging, after all. Dick Sargent's characterization was kinder and gentler, and the actor might have been a notch better looking; all in all, though, York defined the role, Sargent merely filled it.

34

"The Crepes of Wrath"
the simpsons

Episode 7G13
Original air date: April 15, 1990
Original series run: 1989–
Series total: 248 episodes produced
through 1999, still in production as of
2000–01 season

Credits

Open: Created by Matt Groening. Developed by James L. Brooks, Matt Groening, Sam Simon. Co-Producer Larina Jean Adamson. Produced by Richard Sakai. Written by George Meyer, Sam Simon, John Swartzwelder, Jon Vitti. End: Executive Producers James L. Brooks, Matt Groening, Sam Simon. Starring Dan Castellaneta, Julie Kavner, Nancy Cartwright, Yeardley Smith, and Harry Shearer. Also starring Pamela Hayden, Christian Coffinet, Tress MacNeille. Creative Consultant: George Meyer. Executive Story Editor: Jon Vitti. Story Editor: John Swartzwelder. Animation produced by Klasky-Csupo, Inc. Supervising Animation Producer: Gabor Csupo. Creative Supervisor: Sam Simon. Executive Creative Consultant: James L. Brooks.

THE BIG TV SATISFACTION FORMULA	
SyndicoDurability	8.8
Comic Valence	9.7
Emotional Resonance	8.3
Writing, Story	9.8
Writing, Characters	9.6
Acting	8.8
Quintessence	8.6
Series Originality	9.3
Episode Originality	8.1
Historical Significance	7.7
Celebrity	6.6
Gimmickry	9.3
Theme Song	7.6
Kitsch	7.9
BTVS Ratio	**83.81**

Episode Review

Bart has really done it this time. His toys cause Homer to fall down the stairs and throw his back out. Then he explodes a cherry bomb in the school toilets just when Principal Skinner's mother is in the facilities. The principal suggests that suspension or expulsion are not enough; that it's time to consider "deportation." By that he means granting a "big exception" to the criteria and letting Bart be chosen as a foreign exchange student, then sent to France. There is no cost so long as the Simpsons accept a student in their home. In return, the Simpson family takes in an Albanian lad.

After arriving, Bart is driven through a series of famous French paintings: Monet's pond of water lilies, Van Gogh's cornfield with crows, *Déjeuner sur l'herbe,* among others. As he approaches his destination, we see his host, César, telling his mule in French (with subtitles), "Ah Maurice, once the American boy arrives, your days of backbreaking labor will be over." Bart's adopted home is a decrepit farmhouse. His "family" includes

two scraggly low-life wine growers who figured this was a way to get some cheap migrant labor. "Quiet! When you work like a man, we will feed you like one!"

Back in America, Adil the Albanian boy is perfect, too perfect. And he's rather interested in Homer's work. In fact, he'd love to get a tour of the factory and take some photographs. While Bart picks and stomps grapes, Adil is transmitting classified information back to Albania.

Bart's captors now have three-day-old wine. Rather than wait for it to age, they decide to add a little antifreeze to it. Bart is sent to get more antifreeze, he finds a gendarme and tries to tell him of his plight, but the officer knows no English. Bart walks away, chiding himself for not having learned any French after two months of listening to it . . . when, miracle of miracles, he slips into French! He *can* speak French. He runs back to the policeman and tells all. The constable's response is swift and sure: "Antifreeze in the wine? That's a very serious crime!"

In America, the CIA has discovered "The Sparrow," who has been transmitting from the tree house. They quickly capture him. In France, the police quickly nab the wine sulliers, and Bart gets honored with a medal and ceremony.

Notes

- Bart's chalkboard sentence is "Garlic Gum is not funny." When the Simpsons gather in front of the TV, there isn't quite enough room on the couch and Homer pops out.
- Producer Jon Vitti was responsible for a

legendary *Saturday Night Live* sketch entitled "Amerida," a nightmarish vision of what our nation would be like after being taken over by Canada, a parody of the miniseries *Amerika*.

- When he was hired to write for *The Simpsons,* writer George Meyer was taking a sabbatical from television to edit and publish a small, photocopied "magazine" called *Army Man.* Though there were only three issues published, the eccentric and esoteric humor of the magazine has made it something of a legend, and in a *New Yorker* profile of Meyer, journalist David Owen suggests that *The Simpsons's* unique comic sensibility owes as much to *Army Man* as to the work of cartoonist Matt Groening.

- *The Simpsons* began its life as a series of animated shorts that appeared on *The Tracey Ullman Show.*

- Of all the series represented on the BTVS Top 100, *Bewitched* had the most episodes in syndication with 254, but after the rankings were computed, *The Simpsons* continued to produce episodes and are now the undisputed champion. Of course, some early series produced more episodes—*The Adventures of Ozzie & Harriet* filmed 435 in fourteen seasons, Jack Benny filmed 343 over fifteen seasons—but most of those episodes were not recorded for posterity.

33

"Ted Baxter's Broadcasters' School"

mary tyler moore

Episode 119
Original air date: February 22, 1975
Original series run: 1970–1977
Series total: 168 episodes

Credits

Open: Created by James L. Brooks and Allan Burns. Written by Michael Zinberg. Directed by Jay Sandrich. End: Executive Producers: Allan Burns and James L. Brooks. Executive Story Editor: David Lloyd. Produced by Ed Weinberger and Stan Daniels. Co-starring Edward Asner as Lou Grant. Gavin MacLeod as Murray. Ted Knight as Ted Baxter. With Georgia Engel as Georgette Franklin. Guest Star: Leonard Frey as The Student. Norman Bartold as Alan Marsh. Bernie Kopell as Tony. Guest Star: Betty White as Sue Ann Nivens. And Special Guest Star: Cloris Leachman as Phyllis Lindstrom. Executive Story Consultant: Treva Silverman

Episode Review

Ted is excited because Alan Marsh, an entrepreneur, has come into town and would like to start a broadcasting course. Ted will give lectures; Alan will organize it all. Naturally, this is a major ego trip for Ted, who sees it as his first step toward even greater things. He can see it now . . . "Ted Baxter, U.S. ambassador to Hawaii." And Georgette is just as excited: "One day Ted's

THE BIG TV SATISFACTION FORMULA	
SyndicoDurability	8.8
Comic Valence	9.3
Emotional Resonance	8.8
Writing, Story	9.4
Writing, Characters	9.3
Acting	9.2
Quintessence	9.1
Series Originality	6.8
Episode Originality	8.1
Historical Significance	8.1
Celebrity	6.4
Gimmickry	9.1
Theme Song	9.2
Kitsch	7.1
BTVS Ratio	**83.82**

name will be a household word . . . like spatula."

However, Alan is a con man who skips town without paying for his hotel or for the banquet room he has rented for the lectures, and with Ted's car. And who knows how many students paid $300 apiece to come! Ted is afraid he'll be thrown in jail for conspiracy to commit fraud.

Murray suggests they all pull together and act like the "faculty" for one night, which will give Ted a week to pull together something else. They arrive, and only one student has shown up. For a moment, Ted's problems seem to be solved. Ted will be out only the $300 it will take to pay back the one enrollee. But the young man tells a long (and hysterical) story of a lifetime of rejection, and he demands his class. So Ted proceeds with speeches written for a larger crowd and introduces the "faculty" as well as Georgette, his chick, and Tony, Mary's date. Each, in turn, gives a hilarious introductory lecture.

At the end of it all, the student has one final question: "Can I still get my three hundred dollars back?"

Notes

• While Mary was undoubtedly the core talent of her own show, her comedy came from how she reacted to the more outrageous behavior around her. And when it came to outrageous behavior, nobody on the show delivered more than Ted. That's why for pure comedy overall, it was the Ted episodes that ranked the highest. Sue Ann's episodes also stood out. Oddly enough, Rhoda's episodes underperformed even those episodes that focused on Murray. Yet she was the first to spin-off her own series.

• *Rhoda* was also the most successful in spinning off. *Lou Grant* was critically acclaimed but never found a big audience. *Phyllis* did well for a while but faded quickly. *The Betty White Show* (which also featured Georgia Engel) wasn't, strictly speaking, a spin-off, since it featured new characters, but it certainly was betting on viewers' fondness for those actors.

• In this episode Ted also writes a short school song for his abortive institution: "We have no gym and we have no pool, but we have a heart at Ted Baxter's Famous Broadcaster's School."

• Leonard Frey, who turns in the memorable soliloquy as the lone student, was a regular in the short-lived 1981–82 Western spoof *Best of the West*. He played Sheriff Sam Best's archnemesis Parker Tillman. He was also a regular on *Mr. Sunshine*, a 1986 sitcom that revolved around a leading character who was blind. The latter show was coproduced by Henry Winkler (The Fonz) and long-time TV directing great John Rich.

- With Bernie Kopell and Gavin MacLeod onboard, it's a wonder that love, exciting and new, didn't break out. They went on to play Captain Stubing (MacLeod) and Dr. Bricker (Kopell) on *The Love Boat*.

32

"The Golfer"

the honeymooners

Episode 3
Original air date: October 15, 1955
Original series run: 1955–1956
Series total: 39 episodes in the original
syndication package

Credits

Open: Jackie Gleason, Art Carney, Audrey Meadows, and Joyce Randolph. Director: Frank Satenstein. Writers: A. J. Russell, Herbert Finn. Executive Producer: Jack Philbin. Producer: Jack Hurdle. Entire Production Supervised by Jackie Gleason.

Episode Review

The rumor's going around—Ralph is going to be the new assistant traffic manager! Ralph tries to be humble and composed—but fails. However, it is quickly discovered that the rumor can be traced to one man: Ralph.

Frustrated, Ralph lectures Ed on the importance of "connections." Taking his own cue, he decides to chat up Mr. Harper—the

THE BIG TV SATISFACTION FORMULA	
SyndicoDurability	9.7
Comic Valence	9.4
Emotional Resonance	8.8
Writing, Story	8.8
Writing, Characters	9.5
Acting	9.4
Quintessence	9.4
Series Originality	6.6
Episode Originality	8.2
Historical Significance	6.9
Celebrity	5.6
Gimmickry	8.9
Theme Song	8.1
Kitsch	9.4
BTVS Ratio	**83.99**

traffic manager—to get in good with him on a personal level. Harper enters, carrying a bag of golf clubs. Inevitably, inexorably, Ralph is drawn into it—in this case, with a few firm shoves from Norton who insists that Ralph not be so shy about his excellent golf game.

By the time Mr. Harper has left, Ralph has a date to play golf. Luckily it's a month off. By then Ralph figures he'll have the promotion and can come up with any old excuse not to play. Oops! Mr. Harper wants him to play *this* Sunday—his regular partner can't make it. With two days to go, Ralph and Norton try to learn golf from a book—but they don't get much further than "address the ball." As interpreted famously by Norton: "Hellooo, Ball!" Norton then invents, and Ralph replicates, a loosey-goosey swivel-hipped swing that would probably get them banned from the PGA Tour.

Ralph is doomed. But at least he's learned never to shoot off his big mouth again. Then Mr. Harper is forced to cancel!

Saved, Ralph immediately shoots from the lip, bragging of his prowess on the links to Mr. Douglas, vice president of the company, who came to tell Ralph of Harper's injury. But now Mr. Douglas would *love* to have Ralph as his partner. He exits with a jaunty "See you tomorrow." Ralph is doomed again.

Notes

- The dreary black-and-white in which we watch *The Honeymooners* today is actually the perfect palette. Like the world Tom Stoppard circumscribed for Rosencrantz and Guildernstern, the world Ralph occupies is "light gray, from pole to pole."
- Art Carney made his first splash in show biz doing an impression of FDR. Not something you see much anymore.
- *The Honeymooners* was actually the second TV sitcom to star Jackie Gleason. He landed the lead role in the unsuccessful 1949–50 version of *The Life of Riley*. This was a show that originated on radio, where William Bendix had created the lead role. Bendix was not available to do the series, so Gleason got the job. Later, Bendix agreed to do the show, and his version ran for five years. It's interesting to watch Gleason play a character that is really not so far removed from Ralph Kramden, a bit less bold, a bit more mundane. In retrospect, it seems strange that he was not a success, but perhaps viewers didn't want a "replacement" Riley—even if it was Gleason. What a revoltin' development!
- The history of this show is endlessly complex; it made its way from a sketch on Gleason's *Cavalcade of Stars* show on the DuMont Network, to a regular sketch, to the stand-alone half-hour series that we know today as the Classic 39, to the many other episodes pieced together from kinescopes, to the many specials and reunions. The thirty-nine episodes upon which the legend of the show was built were one season's worth of shows, filmed using a new process called Electronicam in the 1955–56 season. Why didn't they make more? The truth is that the ratings weren't good—the story of many shows that go on to syndication glory. With the high cost of this process, the ratings were not enough to justify the expense.

31

"The Bunkers and the Swingers"

all in the family

Episode 44
Original air date: October 28, 1972
Original series run: 1971–1979
Series total: 204 episodes

Credits

Open: Starring Carroll O'Connor, Jean Stapleton. Co-starring Rob Reiner, Sally Struthers. Produced by John Rich. Developed by Norman Lear. End: Directed by John Rich and Bob LaHendro. Teleplay by Michael Ross & Bernie West and Lee Kalcheim. Story by Norman Lear. Script Consultant: Don Nicholl. Story Editors: Michael Ross, Bernie West. Executive Producer: Norman Lear. Vincent Gardenia . . .

Curtis Rempley. Rue McClanahan . . . Ruth Rempley. Isabel Sanford . . . Mrs. Jefferson. Based on "Till Death Us Do Part" Created by Johnny Speight. "All in the Family was recorded on tape before a live audience." A Bud Yorkin–Norman Lear–Tandem Production

Episode Review

Edith has found some pen pals in the back of a magazine she found in the subway. The ad reads: "Mature lonely couple seeking new friends. Warm, affectionate, fun-loving. Looking for company of lonely but compatible couple who want to swap good times." Edith's innocent response to this entry in the Swap column? "Ain't that sweet, people instead of things?"

The couple is coming to "visit" tomorrow. Archie isn't home yet, and he knows nothing about it. Mike and Gloria realize they have to stop the impending disaster, but they are running late to the ballet and don't have time to try to explain "wife swapping" to Edith. Instead they delay, leaving Edith with a vague feeling that something is wrong, but without any specific information. All they have is an address, so they send a telegram to the couple, the Rempleys. Thinking they have averted the crisis, they head out to the Russian ballet. Archie arrives as they leave. "Ain't that something. Wasting money to see some Communist fruit leaping around in his pantyhose."

Minutes later, the Rempleys arrive— Ruth and Curtis! They meant *this* day in the letter. "But I read the letter today," explains Edith, "and when you read tomorrow today, tomorrow is tomorrow." Archie comes downstairs and finds the situation hard to understand. He's all for sending them home until Curtis presents him with a pretty nice box of cigars, "each one in its own test tube dere." Edith is given perfume and is impressed. "Chanel Number Five! That's their highest number." Warming up, Archie decides to let the Rempleys stay for a while. He offers a drink, but Curtis turns it down: "It dulls the senses."

The double entendres fly as the Bunkers and Rempleys get to know each other. They start to dance. Then, "Louise *ex machina*." Mrs. Jefferson arrives to borrow a casserole dish, and in the kitchen she hears about the Rempleys and the want ad. She realizes that she must tell Edith, and she does: "They're here to change partners—but not for dancing."

Louise runs off, leaving Edith to stop the festivities. But she can't find a way to tell the oblivious Archie. Then Curtis, still thinking that they are all thinking what he's thinking, using a small viewer, shares with Archie a slide photograph of Ruth. Archie first assumes it's a mistake. This here is one of

THE BIG TV SATISFACTION FORMULA	
SyndicoDurability	9.1
Comic Valence	9.2
Emotional Resonance	9.1
Writing, Story	9.3
Writing, Characters	9.5
Acting	9.4
Quintessence	7.6
Series Originality	9.2
Episode Originality	8.6
Historical Significance	9.1
Celebrity	5.6
Gimmickry	6.5
Theme Song	9
Kitsch	6.5
BTVS Ratio	**84.13**

them stag photos. But no, Curtis says, that's Ruth! Archie looks again. Then Curtis is about to show Edith a photo when Archie stops the party: "I don't want no peepos, weirdos, or sexos in my house."

Then, after all the high comedy, comes pathos. The Rempleys try to defend their way of life, but Archie is having none of it. "Swinging, is that what you call it?" he says. "Yeah, what do you call it?" And Archie answers: "Communism!" The Rempleys take their leave, and Edith is banned from ever reading no magazines.

In the coda scene, Edith says she is going to mail back the present. Archie says he is going to do worse than mail it back—he is going to burn it. And he lights a cigar.

Notes

- When Louise explains that they want to change partners, the slow dawning on Edith's face is a truly classic take. It's a full twenty-two seconds of reaction as only Jean Stapleton could deliver it.

- The sound of the toilet flushing for comic effect is one of the taboos that Norman Lear fought, and he won the battle. It became a regular joke throughout the run of the series. It is used with impeccable timing in this episode, shortly after the Rempleys arrive.

  RUTHIE: When am I going to meet Archie?

  (Flush from upstairs)

  CURTIS: Well, Ruthie, it won't be long now.

- After *All in the Family*, Rob Reiner created, produced, and starred in an unusual 1978 comedy, *Free Country*. In it he played

Joseph Bresner, a Lithuanian immigrant. It was a dual role, as Reiner was both the young turn-of-the-century immigrant (for most of the show) and the old man of today narrating and recalling that world. Reiner also directed some movies.

- Apparently, the success of this episode was partially responsible for the creation of *Three's Company*, which is why it is ranked so high in historical importance. The creators of that show were the writers of this episode: Nicholl, Ross & West. They apparently took the success of the sexual double-entendre scene, with Archie and Edith missing the true meaning of the Rempleys' comments, and decided that it could serve as the comic backbone of an entire sitcom.

30

"Hillbilly Whiz"
the phil silvers show

Episode 79
Original air date: October 1, 1957
Original series run: 1955–1959
Series total: 138 episodes

Credits

Open: Starring Phil Silvers as M/Sgt. Ernest J. Bilko. Created by Nat Hiken. End: Phil Silvers as Sgt. Ernest Bilko, with Harvey Lembeck as Corporal Barbella. Paul Ford as Colonel Hall. Maurice Gosfield as PFC Doberman. Allan Melvin as Corporal Henshaw. The Platoon: Bernie Fein, Herbie Faye, Karl Lukas, Mickey Freeman, Maurice Brenner, Jack Healy, Terry

Carter, Billy Sands. Staged by Aaron Ruben. Writing Supervised by Billy Friedberg. Written by Coleman Jacoby, Arnie Rosen. Director Al De Caprio. Produced by Edward J. Montagne. "Also seen in tonight's cast were Dick Van Dyke as Hank Lumkin, Joe E. Ross as Sergeant Ritzik, Jimmy Little as Sergeant Grover, Joyce Flagmond as Lulubelle, Frank Campanella as the Scout, and Frank Milan as Dan Topping. Phil Rizzuto, Yogi Berra, Gil MacDougald, Whitey Ford and Red Barber played themselves."

Episode Review

Bilko discovers Hank Lumkin, a fresh recruit from out of the Tennessee hills, who don't see why the men are bothering to shoot at targets 150 feet away. Shucks, something that close you can hit with a rock.

It seems that he is used to hunting squirrels with rocks back home. After all, rocks is cheaper 'n ammunition. Not only that, he has a "bender" for getting squirrels that are hiding behind trees, and a knuckleball floater that's for confusing squirrels that are looking right at you. A lefty, he demon-

THE BIG TV SATISFACTION FORMULA	
SyndicoDurability	8.7
Comic Valence	9.3
Emotional Resonance	7.8
Writing, Story	9.1
Writing, Characters	9.1
Acting	9.4
Quintessence	9.2
Series Originality	7.7
Episode Originality	8.7
Historical Significance	7.1
Celebrity	9.7
Gimmickry	9.2
Theme Song	7.7
Kitsch	9.1
BTVS Ratio	**84.32**

strates them all, and hits the bull's-eye every time. Bilko coyly asks if he has ever thrown a baseball. Seems the first time he threw one, "I killed me a mountain lion."

Bilko immediately tricks the other platoon into raising the stakes on the next baseball game to $300. But the day before the game, his plans suffer a reversal! Doberman has accidentally closed the jeep hood on Lumkin's left hand. It's not broken, but it'll be a week. All is lost. But Lumkin doesn't understand the problem. Is there some rule to prevent him from using his right hand? He throws just as good that way. Bilko is back in heaven.

But he has bigger fish to fry. He gets his protégé a tryout with the Yankees. He don't rightly cotton to that. But Bilko talks him into it. Yankees is just a name, he explains. The players are really southern mountain boys. With names like Enos "Country" Slaughter, "Hill Billy" Skowron, Mickey "Moonshine" Mantle.

In New York, the Yankees are impressed. The Yankee GM, Dan Topping, boasts to his scout that he'll get him signed for fifteen thousand tops. Bilko arrives, and they go in the back room and come out with a deal for $125,000.

Now Bilko just has to get Lumkin to sign. Lumkin is still uneasy. He didn't hear a lot of southern accents down at the stadium. The master conniver is prepared. There is a knock at the door and a bevy of real New York Yankees enter. Each one says "Sho'nuff" when they are introduced as Colonel Philip "Calhoun" Rizzuto. Colonel Gilbert "Beauregarde" MacDougald, Colonel Whitey "Stonewall"

Ford, and Colonel Yogi "Ashley" Berra. After seeing that, Lumkin signs happily. As Yogi leaves, he says, "Arriverderci, you all."

But then Hank's girl Lulubelle arrives— a buxom, beautiful blonde—and demands that he come home and marry her; after all, folks are starting to talk, her being sixteen and still not hitched. Bilko tries to argue but gets "hushed up" by her each time. Lumkin asks Bilko what he would do, choose baseball or Lulubelle? Bilko, honest when he has to be, admits Lulubelle and tears the check into sad little pieces.

In the final scene, the platoon is gathered around the TV set where Lumkin is pitching a no-hitter for the Yankees against the Red Sox. Bilko still can't figure it. How did the Yankees get him to sign? Just then Red Barber (long-time Yankees broadcaster, and Alabama native) comes on the set and throws to his new announcing partner . . . Lulubelle.

Notes

- This has all the quintessential elements of a classic Bilko episode, sports, gambling, a get-rich-quick opportunity, plus sports celebrities, a trip to New York, and a great guest star, Dick Van Dyke.
- Nat Hiken, creator-producer of *Car 54, Where Are You?* and *The Phil Silvers Show,* was a sports fan. *Car 54* featured numerous guest-starring appearances by prizefighters, while many episodes of *The Phil Silvers Show* revolved around sports as well. In fact, the name "Bilko" was chosen both because of its Dickensian quality and also as a small tribute to a relatively obscure baseball player named Steve

Bilko. The hard-hitting first baseman, who came up with the St. Louis Cardinals and bounced around the majors without much success, was known primarily for his exploits as a minor-league hitter. He hit .388 for Winston-Salem in 1947.

- Dick Van Dyke is fine in the role of the backwoods hick, but his pitching motion is woefully unconvincing. Too bad Art Carney wasn't available. As a young man, Carney aspired to play in the majors, and he was said to have a pretty fair curveball.
- Phil Silvers, and his inimitable Bilko persona, have always been very popular in England, more so than other classic TV characters like Lucy Ricardo or Ralph Kramden. Hard to say why exactly, but perhaps his fast-talking, insincere manipulation touched on some English perceptions of the American stereotype, in much the same way that we enjoy *Monty Python's* upper-crust British twits.

29

"The Purr-Fect Crime . . ." and "Better Luck, Next Time"

batman

Episodes 19 and 20
Original air dates: March 16 and 17, 1966
Original series run: 1966–1968
Series total: 120 episodes

Credits

Open: Starring Adam West, Burt Ward, Alan Napier, Neil Hamilton, Stafford Repp, Madge

Blake. Executive Producer: William Dozier. Special Guest Villainess: Julie Newmar as The Catwoman. Written by Stanley Ralph Ross and Lee Orgel. Directed by James Sheldon. End: Jock Mahoney as Leo. Ralph Manza as Felix. Harry Holcombe as Mr. Andrews. Pat Zuriga as Guard. Special Guest Villainess: Julie Newmar as Catwoman. Executive Script Consultant: Lorenzo Semple, Jr.

Episode Review

Catwoman nabs one of two priceless Golden Cats, then plots how to get the other. Bruce Wayne and Dick Grayson are interrupted in a three-level chess game. "It's really quite rudimentary," says Bruce. "You just have to think fourteen moves ahead." Dick replies gamely, "I think I'll stick to Latin crossword puzzles."

The Catwoman has a pair of tomcats working for her. "Yours is not to question why, yours is to keep doing as I tell you." They lure the dynamic duo into a trap, then play with them, like a cat does with a mouse. When she threatens to dispose of him permanently, Batman replies verbosely: "I've heard that song before, but the last few bars are always the same . . . with the criminal behind them."

They are cast into a room whose spike-covered walls are closing in; they discover that the spikes are made of painted rubber. Then Robin is sucked into a giant pneumatic tube, while Batman is asked, "Are you a betting man?" To which he replies: "I never gamble." Nonetheless, he is given two doors from which to choose. Behind one is Catwoman; behind the other is a ferocious "Batman-eating tiger." The lady or the tiger. He picks a door. It's the tiger. Cliffhanger!

The next episode, same Bat-time, same Bat-channel, we see that Robin is suspended over a pit of ferocious big cats. But the duo make their escape and catch up with Catwoman, who is on her way to the treasure of Captain Manx. There, in the catacombs, she slips and falls, and finds herself clinging to the precipice. What happens is, frankly, too painful to talk about, but Batman and Catwoman first have a sultry conversation about the love that might have been. He tries to save her, but she plummets into the chasm.

THE BIG TV SATISFACTION FORMULA	
SyndicoDurability	8.5
Comic Valence	7.5
Emotional Resonance	8.9
Writing, Story	9.1
Writing, Characters	8.2
Acting	8.7
Quintessence	9.7
Series Originality	9.9
Episode Originality	8
Historical Significance	8.9
Celebrity	7.5
Gimmickry	9.6
Theme Song	9.3
Kitsch	9.5
BTVS Ratio	**84.46**

Notes

• This episode was the first appearance of Catwoman. She apparently landed on her feet at the bottom of the chasm; she was involved in six more plots to foil Batman. (Two of them as portrayed by Eartha Kitt.) Julie Newmar's Catwoman teamed up with Sandman in the other *Batman* episode to crack our BTVS Top 100.

- When the role of Catwoman was offered to Julie Newmar, she was convinced to take it by her college student brother who, along with his friends at Harvard, was a big fan of the show.
- Suzanne Pleshette was initially considered for the role of Catwoman.
- *Batman* is one of the most unusual television shows ever created, as indicated by the unmatched 9.9 rating in the Series Originality category. The underlying ironies of the scripts, which were parodies of comic-book writing, were even squarer and less vernacular than comic books. It was purposely bad in ways that one could never have imagined. The plots defied all logic; yet were completely formulaic. The acting was completely devoid of humanity, yet was somehow performed with such breathless sincerity that its failure to communicate, its failure to address reality became the message. In a hundred years, *I Love Lucy, Mary Tyler Moore, Cheers,* even *Seinfeld* may be relics—the *My Little Margie* and *The Jack Benny Program* of tomorrow—but we believe that *Batman* will continue to resonate and have meaning in the postmodern world.

28

"Man in a Hurry"
the andy griffith show
Episode 77
Original air date: January 14, 1963
Original series run: 1960–1968
Series total: 249 episodes

Credits

Open: *The Andy Griffith Show* "Starring Andy Griffith with Ronny Howard. Also Starring Don Knotts." End: Directed by Bob Sweeney. Written by Everett Greenbaum and Jim Fritzell. Produced by Aaron Ruben. Story Consultant: Aaron Ruben. Cast Frances Bavier, William Keene, Norman Leavitt, and Jim Nabors as Gomer Pyle. Guest Star: Robert Emhardt. Executive Producer: Sheldon Leonard. In Association with Danny Thomas Enterprises.

Episode Review

A car pulls over on the highway, a breakdown of some sort. A heavyset man in a suit gets out and finds a sign that he is two miles from Mayberry. He arrives, but not a soul is stirring in the town square. So far, it could be an episode of *The Twilight Zone;* for our motorist, Malcolm Tucker, a man accustomed to the hectic pace of city life, it might as well be, for his automobile trouble has sent him on a detour into . . . The Mayberry Zone.

We see where everyone was, as the

THE BIG TV SATISFACTION FORMULA	
SyndicoDurability	9.9
Comic Valence	8.7
Emotional Resonance	9.7
Writing, Story	9.3
Writing, Characters	9.7
Acting	9.3
Quintessence	9.2
Series Originality	7.3
Episode Originality	8.1
Historical Significance	7.9
Celebrity	6.3
Gimmickry	6.1
Theme Song	8.7
Kitsch	8.1
BTVS Ratio	**84.57**

church doors open and all the folks file out, complimenting the fine sermon. Mr. Tucker finds Andy to seek help. He needs to be in Charlotte in the morning. Andy expects that'll be hard to do because Wally don't work Sundays and Gomer Pyle's in charge down at the station.

Indeed, Gomer is not too helpful, suggesting only that he drive up and get some gas. "Sometime she'll tell you F when you really got a E. E means it empty. F means it—" Exasperated, Tucker demands to be taken to Wally.

Wally is settin' on his porch reading the funnies. He's happy to talk it over with Mr. Tucker, and by making a series of automobiles noises that Tucker identifies, Wally establishes that it must be a clogged fuel line. Fix it first thing tomorrow. Tucker stomps off, although Andy tries to explain: "If 'twere an emergency . . ."

Tucker has hopefully returned to Gomer. "Now your boss said it was a relatively simple repair," and finds out that Cousin Goober could probably fix it. But Goober is always out on his boat on Sundays. In a fit of insanity, Tucker jumps in the station's truck and drives off.

Andy brings him in and scolds him for stealing, but lets him off with a warning. Tucker wants to use the phone. However, it seems that every Sunday, since there is only one available line in town, everyone lets Maude talk to Cora all afternoon. After all, they're both in their eighties, and Cora lives all the way down in Mt. Pilot. . . .

While Andy, Barney, Opie, and Bee sit down for lunch, Mr. Tucker keeps on checking on the progress of the conversation to see if they are done yet. His ire bubbles back to surface as their inane babble about their medical ailments goes on and on. Finally, he bursts out with a diatribe against Mayberry: "You people are living in another world . . . a whole town is sitting still because two old women's feet fall asleep!"

Tucker is stymied. He goes out on the front porch where Andy is strumming his guitar, and then he and Barney sing a little old-time gospel song and Tucker lights a cigar. As they sing "Little Brown Church in the Vale," Tucker begins to relax, and then even sings quietly along. He is beginning to remember the virtues of small-town living.

But then Gomer comes back, with a report on the progress of the repairs; Goober is back, and he's working on it. But Gomer's inimitable personal style gets him all riled up again. Then Barney, in a truly classic Mayberry moment, runs through his plan for the rest of the afternoon: a nap, then go to Thelma Lou's, watch a little TV. He repeats the plan slowly three times until Malcolm Tucker just can't take it anymore and invents a great sneaker slogan: "Just do it!" Tucker barks. Then he repeats his admonition, "Just do it!"

Finally, Gomer comes back. The car is all repaired; it didn't need new spark plugs after all, and he won't take payment from Mr. Tucker, who is nonplussed. He insists they take payment for their work. Nope, it was an honor to work on such a fine car, and they kept him waiting and all, and they did take one liberty and had Goober's picture taken standing in front of the open hood.

Well, now Mr. Tucker can finally leave, and he makes his way out to the car. Aunt

Bee runs and packs him a lunch, chicken legs and cake for the road. Opie is sorry he's leaving because, if Mr. Tucker had stayed, Opie would get to sleep on the ironing board between two chairs: "That's adventure sleepin'!" Opie gives Mr. Tucker his lucky train-squashed penny.

He's all set to go, sitting at the wheel, but then, overcome by the goodness and humanity of these folks, he decides that all that pressing business in Charlotte can wait. He is going to stay the night. He pretends that there's something wrong with the sound the engine is making. Gomer is confused, but Andy catches his drift. "Oh yeah, that don't sound highway safe. Better stay and have Wally look at in the morning."

Mr. Tucker heads back inside to enjoy a little more of the Mayberry pace and the Mayberry life, before returning to his busy world.

Notes

- An extremely popular episode among fans of the show, with good reason, "Man in a Hurry" captures everything that made the show so brilliant. The quirky characters and behavior, the little timing jokes, the essential goodness and morality at the core. Maybe there never was such a place as Mayberry, but it never hurts to think about what would be ideal, and why.
- The phenomenon of shared phone lines is, of course, quite dated, but party lines were still in rural areas as late as the 1970s. If someone else was on the line, and you picked up, you would hear them talking and could join the conversation, if necessary.
- There is a wonderful line that is atypical of *The Andy Griffith Show* in its absurdity, but when Maude and Cora are blathering on, one of them says, "I know Charlotte Tucker. She married that man who fell down a lot."
- When Tucker returns from his first meeting with Gomer, he asks how they let a boy like that run the station. Andy says, "It's just a part-time job; he's saving up for college. Going to be a doctor." Hmm . . . Gomer Pyle, MD? Now that would have been quite a spin-off!

27

"Catch Me on the Paar Show"

car 54, where are you?

Episode 11
Original air date: November 26, 1961
Original series run: 1961–1963
Series total: 60 episodes

Credits

Open: Starring Joe E. Ross and Fred Gwynne. Special Guest Star: Hugh Downs. Written by Terry Ryan and Nat Hiken. Created and Directed by Nat Hiken. End: Starring Joe E. Ross . . . Toody. Fred Gwynne . . . Muldoon. Hugh Downs . . . Himself. Featuring Paul Reed . . . Captain Block. Beatrice Pons . . . Lucille. Mickey Deems . . . Fleischer. Al Henderson . . . O'Hara. Produced by Nat Hiken.

THE BIG TV SATISFACTION FORMULA	
SyndicoDurability	6.8
Comic Valence	9.3
Emotional Resonance	8.3
Writing, Story	9.1
Writing, Characters	9.1
Acting	9.1
Quintessence	8.4
Series Originality	6.7
Episode Originality	8.9
Historical Significance	7.3
Celebrity	9.5
Gimmickry	8.6
Theme Song	8.8
Kitsch	8.1
BTVS Ratio	**84.57**

Episode Review

Officer Charlie Fleischer is telling stand-up jokes in the locker room, and cracking up no one . . . except Toody, who is in absolute hysterics at such material as: "My girl. I call her my melancholy baby . . . she has a head like a melon and a face like a collie!" Captain Block comes in to hush the "hyenas."

On patrol, Toody is convinced that Charlie is a big talent just waiting for his break. Muldoon thinks he's just "a locker room comic," a dime a dozen. Toody tries to get Muldoon to agree that Charlie Fleischer is funnier than Jonathan Winters. No. Buddy Hackett? No. Phyllis Diller? No. Hugh Downs? Muldoon protests that he's an announcer, he's not supposed to be funny. Toody says he's sometimes funny. Okay, concedes his partner, every now and then he tells a joke. Triumphant, Toody says, there you go: every now and then, when Hugh Downs is funny, he's not as funny as Charlie Fleischer.

Just then, they pull over a speeder, who turns out to be Hugh Downs himself! Toody says that they were just talking about him, and tells him, "You've very funny now and then!" He really wants Downs to check out Charlie's act. Despite Downs being in a hurry, Toody calls Charlie on the radio to bring him over for an audition.

Downs watches reluctantly, watching the time click away. Finally, motivated by his desire to get going, he decides maybe it would be a novel idea . . . a New York policeman telling jokes. The arrangements are made, and Downs is released. Charlie wants Toody to be his agent. The two are caught up in their dreams of "the big time" and plan to turn in their resignations.

We then see *The Jack Paar Show*, with Hugh Downs sitting in as guest host. Hugh tells the story of being stopped on the highway and forced to hear an audition. Then Charlie freezes! Toody steps out from behind the curtain, saves the show, and goes over big! The crowd loves it.

The next day at the station, the gang gathers around their new hero, showering him with praise: "Did you ever hear such timing?" and "It's not what he says . . . it's how he says it!" But Muldoon says it was a fluke, that his appearance worked only because of the situation, with Charlie's freezing and Toody poking out from the curtains. After all, they've been riding in the patrol car for nine year and Toody never said anything funny.

But Toody gets invited to return to the *Paar Show*, and now Muldoon is changing his tune. After all, if an experienced show-business figure like Downs thinks Toody is talented, maybe he is. Muldoon takes over managing the act, and together they scour the neighborhood for jokes. Father Flanagan and Rabbi Eisenberg each tell them the same joke, about a little old lady and a kangaroo at the zoo.

The night of the show comes, and this time Toody freezes. It's a classic "here we go again," as Muldoon emerges from the curtain and tells the kangaroo joke . . . and slays them!

Notes

- Nat Hiken, producer of both *The Phil Silvers Show* and *Car 54, Where Are You?* was an early pioneer in efforts to integrate television. Both Bilko's barracks and the 53rd Precinct were manned by a mix of ethnicities, and Officer Anderson, who manned the radio at headquarters, was played by Nipsey Russell.
- On the night that Charlie is slated to debut, the other guests announced are Buddy Hackett and Zsa Zsa Gabor, but we never see them.
- Hugh Downs, today perceived as a TV journalist for his long-standing work on *20/20*, began his career in much humbler roles, and certainly not as a news reporter. He was an NBC announcer, part of *Caesar's Hour*, host of the classic game show *Concentration*, and, as seen above, he served as a regular on *The Jack Paar Show*, where he also was the fill-in host. And he hosted *The Tonight Show* occasionally in the interregnum between Paar and Johnny Carson.

26

"Lucy Does a TV Commercial"
i love lucy

Episode 30
Original air date: May 5, 1952
Original series run: 1951–1961
Series total: 179 episodes

Credits

Open: Lucille Ball, Desi Arnaz, Vivian Vance, William Frawley. End: "The part of the director was played by Ross Elliott, Joe by Jerry Hausner." Produced by Jess Oppenheimer. Directed by Marc Daniels. Written for Television by Jess Oppenheimer, Madelyn Pugh, Bob Carroll, Jr. Director of Photography: Karl Freund, A.S.C. Executive Producer: Desi Arnaz, Jr.

Episode Review

Lucy's latest idea for getting into show business is to become a commercial

THE BIG TV SATISFACTION FORMULA	
SyndicoDurability	10
Comic Valence	9.3
Emotional Resonance	7.6
Writing, Story	8.8
Writing, Characters	9.1
Acting	9.8
Quintessence	9.3
Series Originality	9.4
Episode Originality	8.6
Historical Significance	7.5
Celebrity	6.1
Gimmickry	9.1
Theme Song	7.1
Kitsch	8.3
BTVS Ratio	**84.81**

spokesperson. In order to show Ricky how good she can be, she removes the innards of their TV set and puts on a little show. As she gives her spiel, he goes behind her and, in a stunningly hazardous act, plugs in the set! Sparks fly, and Lucy is terrified but not electrocuted. Not only is Ricky unconvinced, but he is annoyed when it turns out that Lucy took out the insides piece by piece when she could have slid it all out of the chassis.

But for Lucy, opportunity is constantly rapping at her door. She takes a phone call from the actress who was going to do this particular job, so Lucy simply tells her the job is taken and heads down to the studio.

There she begins rehearsing her lines. In one of TV's best-known scenes, she samples the health tonic Vitameatavegamin (which contains 23 percent alcohol) over and over, becoming more and more inebriated and incoherent. The original script for the commercial, which she mangles in more and more fabulous ways, is as follows:

"Hello friends, I'm your Vitameatavegamin girl. Are you tired? Run-down? Listless? Do you poop out at parties? Are you unpopular? The answer to all your problems is in this little bottle: Vitameatavegamin. Vitameatavegamin contains vitamins, meat, vegetables, and minerals. Yes, with Vitameatavegamin, you can spoon your way to health. All you do is take a tablespoon after every meal. (Take a spoonful.) It's so tasty, too! Just like candy. So why don't you join the thousands of happy, peppy people and get a great big bottle of Vitameatavegamin tomorrow. That's Vita . . . meata . . . vegamin."

Notes

- Finding just the right substance to play the role of Vitameatavegamin was difficult. After a few unacceptable alternatives, they found apple pectin (whatever that is) was both syrupy and not too unpalatable for Lucille Ball to spoon herself.
- In an uncredited role, the show's script clerk Maury Thompson plays the role of the script clerk on Ricky's show.
- It was difficult to judge *I Love Lucy* episodes, even for the infallible BTVS system. So many of the classic moments have been sapped of all meaning as they were transformed from funny sitcom scenes into pop-culture icons: posters, advertisements, T-shirts, refrigerator magnets. Context and repetition inevitably alter our perceptions. The *Mission: Impossible* theme song is a great piece of jazz composition, but we can't hear it without associating it with the show. Mendelssohn's "Wedding March." *The Mona Lisa*. Rodin's *The Thinker*. Hamlet's "To be or not to be" soliloquy. Elvis singing "Blue Suede Shoes." The Beatles' "Can't Buy Me Love." "Lucy Makes a TV Commercial." They are all great works, but how great is almost impossible to say, because of their stature in our collective judgment. Luckily, the BTVS system lets us try, and it turns out that Lucy's "unpoopular" bit is not even in the Top 10 episodes. Shocking, but true.

25

"Captain Jack"
leave it to beaver

Episode 2
Original air date: October 18, 1957
Original series run: 1957–1963
Series total: 234 episodes

Credits

Open: Starring Barbara Billingsley, Hugh Beaumont, Tony Dow, and Jerry Mathers as the Beaver, End: Directed by Norman Tokar. Written and Produced by Joe Connelly and Bob Mosher. Executive Producer: Harry Ackerman, with Edgar Buchanan as Captain Jack, Connie Gilchrist, Irving Bacon, Penny Carpenter.

Episode Review

The boys order a "real live" alligator from the back of a comic book, and they await an eight-foot monster. An eight-inch

THE BIG TV SATISFACTION FORMULA	
SyndicoDurability	9.3
Comic Valence	9.1
Emotional Resonance	9.7
Writing, Story	9
Writing, Characters	9.1
Acting	8.5
Quintessence	9.6
Series Originality	7.2
Episode Originality	8.8
Historical Significance	8.3
Celebrity	8.3
Gimmickry	9.2
Theme Song	7.4
Kitsch	7.8
BTVS Ratio	**84.92**

alligator arrives. "Maybe if you put him in water, he swells up?" suggests Beaver.

The little critter's health seems to be fading. Ever resourceful, the boys pay a visit to the local alligator farm. At the farm Captain Jack, the proprietor, gives his stentorian spiel. They are cannibalistic by nature—the big beggars will eat the little beggars! And that an alligator would not bite the limb of a human off, no, he would "Saawww it off!" Afterward, he gives them loads of advice about the care and feeding of their pet. First he suggests milk, then adds his secret: "Put a little brandy in the milk. It not only makes for a healthy alligator, it makes for a happy alligator."

The boys name their gatorette Captain Jack in his honor and head home. Over the next few weeks (and months) they care for him and feed him, while June and Ward wonder where the raw eggs, beauty cream (Wally thinks it prevents his skin from cracking), and brandy are going. The boys also make a small business, charging other kids a dime to see their fierce pet, who has now grown to over a foot long.

Finally, Ward decides that Minerva the maid is perhaps singing a little too gaily, and he accuses her of nipping at the brandy. When she comes running up from the basement screeching that she has seen an alligator, his suspicions are confirmed. He takes her off to the bus stop; she can go home until she's feeling "more herself." Oh, those 1957 euphemisms.

While he is gone, a little girl arrives and tries to pay Mrs. Cleaver a dime to see the alligator. The jig is up. June finds the gator and sends Ward down to see it when he returns. He is doubtful, but a nip on the hand confirms that it is a real live alligator. Although, as Ward unwittingly notes: "The little fellow didn't actually bite me, he kind of sawed at me."

The boys are in bed speculating about their punishment, while Ward and June discuss the matter. The simple fact is that Ward is actually quite proud of how hard the boys worked and how careful they were, since raising an alligator to that size is practically impossible.

He comes upstairs, and the boys stand at attention, fearing the worst. But Ward tells them he is proud of them. But, with the emotional music underscoring his warm fatherly tones, in classic Ward style, he also tells them Captain Jack must go: "You can't hang on to things you love forever, Beaver. You have to turn 'em loose, give 'em a chance."

In their Sunday best, the whole family takes their overgrown pet to his namesake's farm, where the original Captain Jack assures them he will be well taken care of. They are content, but still quite sad to have lost their beloved pet. They arrive home still downcast, and Ward and June watch the boys trudge upstairs . . . to find a new puppy in their room! The sheer sweetness and joy of the moment is undimmed by the years.

Whee Wohn

At the very open of the episode, there is a classic fifties style whee wohn cut. We open on Ward digging lost items out of the seat cushions, all sorts of odds and ends, including "what appears to be a Peruvian nickel."

He and June exchange pleasantries, and he asks where the boys are. She says upstairs, and he says that no doubt they are doing "something childish . . . but harmless." Whee wohn! Cut to "Robot Monster Comic," which opens to the advertisement: BUY A REAL LIVE ALLIGATOR.

Notes

- The series got off to a brilliant start, immediately hitting its stride with this gem, which was the very first to be produced, although it was the second episode to air. The comedy is neatly crafted, the characters fully wrought, and the sentiment is truly touching.

- Edgar Buchanan is, of course, Uncle Joe from *Petticoat Junction*, and here he turns in a nifty, charming performance as the alligator impresario.

- The fact that the boys can wander down to the local alligator farm would seem to be evidence that Mayfield, their town, must be in a warm climate. The state is never named in the series.

- The episode did not air as the premiere episode because of a classic case of fifties-style censorship, which in retrospect seems positively quaint. The boys' first home for the baby alligator is the back of the toilet. However, the toilet was not to be spoken of, nor seen, according to the network standards of that era. The creators, Connelly and Mosher, insisted on leaving in the scenes that showed the toilet. The debates delayed the episode's broadcast, but in the end, the scene was allowed to play as it had been intended. Was it a blow for creative autonomy and realism? Or was it a first step down the slippery slope that would lead to Archie Bunker, *South Park* and *Jackass?* In any case, it was a historic television first.

24
"I Do, Adieu"
cheers

Episode 121
Original air date: May 7, 1987
Original series run: 1982–1993
Series total: 275 episodes

Credits

Open: Starring Ted Danson, Shelley Long, Rhea Perlman, John Ratzenberger, Woody Harrelson, Kelsey Grammer, and George Wendt. Created by Glen Charles & Les Charles and James Burrows. Produced by Peter Casey & David Lee. Produced by David Angell. Written by Glen Charles and Les Charles. Directed by James Burrows.
End: Executive Producers James Burrows, Glen Charles, Les Charles. Michael McGuire as Sumner Sloane. Walter Addison as Justice of the Peace. Steve Gianelli as Steve. Co-Producer: Tim Berry. Executive Script Consultant: Bob Ellison. Executive Story Consultants: Cheri Eichen & Bill Steinkellner. Story Editor: Phoef Sutton. Story Editor: Jeff Abugov. Creative Consultant: Tom Tenowich.

Episode Review

The fifth season of the show was coming to a close. Sam and Diane are planning the second of their three weddings when Sum-

THE BIG TV SATISFACTION FORMULA	
SyndicoDurability	7.4
Comic Valence	9.3
Emotional Resonance	10
Writing, Story	9.3
Writing, Characters	9.8
Acting	9.3
Quintessence	8.5
Series Originality	7.1
Episode Originality	7.9
Historical Significance	9.8
Celebrity	6.2
Gimmickry	9.2
Theme Song	9.1
Kitsch	6.2
BTVS Ratio	**85.12**

ner Sloane returns, the man who dumped Diane and left her at Cheers in the very first episode. (The circle is completed!) He has been reading Diane's old writings; now he thinks they hold great promise. In fact, he submitted one of her unfinished novels, *Jocasta's Conundrum*, to an editor who was impressed. Sumner offers her his place in Maine to write. When she protests that she has to stay and marry Sam, he convinces her that marriage will be the end of her writing. Nonetheless, she chooses to stay the course. (Sam has accidentally overheard this whole private conversation from underneath the pool table, where he had been making repairs.)

At home, they engage in a classic dance of motivations and second-guessing each other. Sam asks about the conversation, and Diane tells him the exciting news. He suggests she might want to postpone the wedding for six months. Now Diane, who thinks he's just getting cold feet, suggests that they get married right away. Sam suspects she is rushing only to avoid changing her mind.

She is certain, and while he thinks it over, she makes tea.

Sam envisions the future, and we see the aged Sam and Diane. They talk about their happy life together. Sam is too tired to get up, so Diane has to get the door, for both Cliff (still working!) and Norm, still making fun of Vera. Coming out of his blissful reverie, Sam says, okay, yes, and they decide to have the ceremony at Cheers.

The event arrives. Everyone in the bar is making side bets. As Carla weeps loudly, the ceremony proceeds. But just when Diane is set to say I do, the phone rings. Woody answers and calls for Ms. Chambers. She's kind of busy, so he takes a message, exclaiming as he does, "That's fantastic news!" Then he expects things to proceed.

The publisher has accepted the manuscript and will pay her a large advance to finish it! Undeterred, Diane says, "Yes, why wouldn't I? Yes," to the justice's question. Bets are paid. But then Sam reneges! "No wait, I want to change my answer." He withdraws his "I do" and tells her she has to write the book. She has to take her shot. Bets are unpaid. They restart the wedding, and each hesitation the gamblers all lean forward for a hint of the final answer, which is . . .

SAM: Do you agree that we shouldn't get married?

DIANE: I do.

Later, alone in the bar, they say farewell, planning to get back together in six months. But as Diane walks up the stairs, Sam calls out, "Have a good life." She turns back and insists she'll be back in six months. He goes along with her and watches her leave. But he knows better, and after she is gone, he repeats himself to her departing footsteps. "Have a good life."

When he comes home alone that night, he imagines coming home as an old man, to the old Diane. The couple, grown old together, dance a quiet waltz in their living room as the final fade draws the curtain on their love story.

Notes

- After the years of back and forth, the ongoing sexual tension, the greatest on-again, off-again romance in TV history, the conclusion managed to be believable and funny, satisfying and thoroughly sentimental.
- This was the final episode of the fifth season. Shelley Long's decision not to return to the series had been made and given to the producers just after she taped the engagement episode (Episode #109, "Diamond Sam"), which left precious little time to rewrite and create this episode.
- For Ted Danson, playing Sam Malone was a stretch, since he had almost no experience or interest in baseball. He had been a basketball player in his youth. George Wendt, on the other hand, is a major baseball fan, especially of the Chicago White Sox, as he grew up on Chicago's south side.
- In 1986, two TV icons came together in the film *Just Between Friends*, as Ted Danson and Mary Tyler Moore played husband and wife in an otherwise forgettable movie.
- Was it the most sentimental episode in the BTVS Top 100? It can be a very personal

matter. What kinds of episodes really get you? Reunions? Courage in the face of tragedy? Love triumphant? And how do you react? Maybe it's tears, maybe just melancholy, maybe you just want to call an old friend or go hug your kids. Whatever your reaction to an emotionally wrenching sitcom, here are the episodes from the BTVS Top 100 that are most likely to get you.

23

"The Eating Contest"
the phil silvers show

Episode 4
Original air date: November 15, 1955
Original series run: 1955–1959
Series total: 138 episodes

Credits

Open: Starring Phil Silvers as Master Sergeant Ernest T. Bilko, R.A. 15042699. Created by Nat Hiken End: "The Stomach was played by Fred Gwynne, Henderson by Vern Hoffman, the Sergeant by Murray Hamilton." Harvey Lembeck as Corporal Barbella. Paul Ford as Colonel Hall, and Allan Melvin as Corporal Henshaw. Produced and Staged by Nat Hiken. Written by Nat Hiken with Arnold Auerbach. Director: Al De Caprio. (Some regulars in the platoon appear in minor roles in this episode but are not credited: among them Mickey Freeman as Private Zimmerman, Gary Clarke as Sergeant Stanley Zewicki and Maurice Gosfield as Private Duane Doberman.)

Episode Review

Bilko is looking for a sports gambling angle, as always, when a young Fred Gwynne (fresh out of Harvard University) arrives as Ed Honnigan. Bilko looks up at the tall newcomer, hoping he's a football player or a basketball player—but no, he's just a soldier. "That's the last thing this platoon needs!"

But he is recognized by another soldier as

THE BIG TV SATISFACTION FORMULA	
SyndicoDurability	8.7
Comic Valence	9.3
Emotional Resonance	8.8
Writing, Story	9.1
Writing, Characters	8.3
Acting	9.5
Quintessence	9.5
Series Originality	7.7
Episode Originality	9.1
Historical Significance	7.2
Celebrity	8.8
Gimmickry	8.9
Theme Song	7.7
Kitsch	7.7
BTVS Ratio	**85.38**

"The Stomach," a renowned eating-contest champion. Company A is proud of its own eating champ, Hog Henderson, so Bilko practically runs to Company A and makes a big bet, $235 on a mano-a-mano eating contest. The stakes are put in a safe and given to the chaplain, under the pretense that it is a "benevolent fund."

Now, Bilko serves up dinner to an oblivious Honnigan as the whole barracks looks on enthusiastically. After exactly one bite, he lights up a cigarette. He's full. The platoon is up in arms. It turns out Honnigan has a big appetite only when he's miserable—his reputation was built in the period after he had received a "Dear John" letter. Now he's practically forgotten all about that girl—Hazel.

With money on the line, Bilko quickly hits on a solution: reminding him of his misery. He just needs to figure out which romantic song was "their song." They gather around Honnigan to play some likely favorites. Since it's TV land, they hit it on the second try. They play the song for him. His face falls, and nobody's face falls farther and longer than Gwynne's.

After some back and forth, the big contest has arrived. Honnigan is depressed; he arrives eating a banana. Hog Henderson, a pretty fair knife-and-fork man himself, is in awe of the legend that is "The Stomach."

They go to it, in a montage that shows them both eating voraciously. Hog finally quits; he can't take it anymore. Just at the moment, the chaplain brings Hazel into the restaurant. She tells Ed she is still crazy about him. Now Honnigan actually has to eat that last piece of cheese that Hog couldn't, or else it's a tie. But Ed's not hungry anymore. He's trying to get past Bilko to Hazel. Bilko holds the line; finally, just to get to Hazel, Honnigan eats the cheese and the company has won.

But Bilko never really wins. The chaplain has also brought along the "benevolent fund" that he has been holding, because he knows that Bilko will want to present it to Honnigan and his girl, who are going to need some cash to get started since they are going to be married. (Things move quickly, right?) Bilko's triumph is crumbling fast. The chaplain asks, "This isn't a gambling stake, is it?" Bilko answers "no," but in a brilliant line reading that perfectly echoes his internal conflict. He hands over the money.

Notes

- What's the actual menu the two men consume, for the total price of $65.88? They order . . .
  Ten dozen oysters. ("With plenty of crackers," adds The Stomach)

Five gallons of soup ("Maybe a little light consommé?" suggests Hog, but the Stomach says: "Cream of tomato, with plenty of croutons.")
Twelve chickens
Three bushel of salad
Fourteen steaks
Six pies ("With cheese," the Stomach requests.)
They are also seen eating corn on the cob during the contest, perhaps an afterthought, or perhaps it was included with the chickens.

- Buddy Hackett was in the original cast, but he left to do a Broadway show. (That's something you don't hear happening too often nowadays.)
- Neil Simon worked as a staff writer on the series.
- For its first year on the air, *The Phil Silvers Show* was known as *You'll Never Get Rich;* later, in syndication, it became *Sergeant Bilko.*
- When the show premiered in 1955, it was given an impossible time slot opposite the second half of Milton Berle's hour on Tuesday. Uncle Miltie had ruled the new medium with huge ratings. But after switching to 8:00 P.M. where it could take on the first half hour of *The Buick Berle Show,* Silver and company did the impossible and knocked the king off his throne. Milton Berle's reign was over, though his "lifetime" contract with NBC still had twenty-five years or so to go.

22

"The Lars Affair"
mary tyler moore

Episode 73
Original air date: September 15, 1973
Original series run: 1970–1977
Series total: 168 episodes

Credits

Open: Created by James L. Brooks and Allan Burns. Written by Ed Weinberger. Directed by Jay Sandrich. End: Executive Producers: Allan Burns and James L. Brooks. Produced by Ed Weinberger. Co-starring Edward Asner as Lou Grant, with Valerie Harper as Rhoda Morgenstern. Gavin MacLeod as Murray. Ted Knight as Ted Baxter. Guest Star: Betty White as Sue Ann Nivens, and Special Guest Star: Cloris Leachman as Phyllis Lindstrom. Executive Story Consultant: Treva Silverman.

THE BIG TV SATISFACTION FORMULA	
SyndicoDurability	8.8
Comic Valence	9.3
Emotional Resonance	9.3
Writing, Story	8.8
Writing, Characters	8.9
Acting	9.4
Quintessence	8.1
Series Originality	6.8
Episode Originality	8.8
Historical Significance	9.1
Celebrity	7.6
Gimmickry	8.6
Theme Song	9.2
Kitsch	6.8
BTVS Ratio	**85.46**

Episode Review

Mary is having a party. Always a sure sign of trouble. Sue Ann makes her debut as a character, arriving to save the day and tell Mary how to get a coffee stain out. Phyllis takes an immediate dislike to this peppy adviser: "Who's Little Bo Peep?" Mary explains that she is the host of *The Happy Homemaker Show* down at the station.

It soon becomes apparent that Phyllis's husband Lars (who was never seen on camera) is having an affair with Sue Ann. First Phyllis is in denial; then she decides that she wants to fight to keep her husband. Sometimes the saddest things are the funniest. She tries to bake a pie; Mary and Rhoda do their best to compliment the obviously terrible pie.

Since that angle clearly won't work, Phyllis enlists Mary to help her confront this Happy "Homewrecker" face-to-face. Her plan is to talk reasonably and, if that doesn't work, to rip her face off.

The confrontation takes place on the set of *The Happy Homemaker*, where Sue Ann is already fully in character as the steely warrior with the saccharine exterior, sweetly telling the director how to shoot the cooking sequence.

As they talk, Sue Ann is trying to bake a soufflé and asks that they keep it down. At that, Phyllis slams the oven door repeatedly. "Why you would destroy an innocent soufflé!"

Eventually Mary, who is really too busy with her own work to deal with this little cat fight, steps up and shows that she can be as assertive as the next career gal. She lets Sue Ann have it and basically threatens to have *The Happy Homemaker* jerked off the air if Sue Ann won't back off and leave Lars alone. Sue Ann caves in, not for herself, mind you, but for all the ladies out there who depend on her advice.

Notes

- As Sue Ann takes the murdered soufflé out of the oven, she does a brilliant little move where her ladylike behavior is put on hold and she uses her knee to shut the oven door. It's one of those little physical acts that can say so much about the character.

- Cloris Leachman won a well-deserved Emmy Award for this episode, for Supporting Actress, Single Appearance in a Continuing Series. Oh, those ever-changing Emmy categories!

- Sue Ann was such a great addition that Betty White was quickly brought back and made a semiregular on the series. Her program *The Happy Homemaker* lived on, bringing its viewers themed shows like "What's all this fuss about famine?"

- Betty White had a long career on television before she arrived at WJM. She was the lead in a 1957 sitcom called *Date with the Angels.* It was set in Los Angeles and revolved around the domestic doings of a newlywed couple, Bill and Vicki Angel. Richard Deacon and Burt Mustin appeared in supporting roles.

- When *Mary Tyler Moore* was in development, the producers wanted her to be divorced, but the network objected. Among other things, they worried that viewers would think that she had divorced Rob Petrie. Their concerns seem silly in retrospect, but one wonders if Mary Richards's frailty and anxiety might not have seemed as appealing if the weight of a divorce had been added to her history? Maybe the network prudes got it right.

- By the way, it is *Mary Tyler Moore,* and not *The Mary Tyler Moore Show.* The producers and Mary herself made that a distinct choice. They felt that the latter title would imply the show was all about Mary, while the former implied the ensemble show they were creating.

21

"The Puppy Episode"
ellen

Episodes 84 and 85
(Syndication numbers)
Original air date: April 30, 1997
Original series run: 1994–1998
Series total: 109 episodes

Credits

Open: Ellen DeGeneres, Joely Fisher, David Anthony Higgins, Clea Lewis, Jeremy Piven. Created by Neal Marlens, Carol Black, David S. Rosenthal. Executive Producer: Mark Driscoll. Executive Producer: Dava Savel. Executive Producer: Vic Kaplan. Co-Executive Producer: Matt Goldman. Supervising Producer: Jan Nash. Producer: Ellen DeGeneres. Consulting Producers: Tracy Newman & Jonathan Stark. Teleplay by Mark Driscoll, Dava Savel, Tracy Newman, Jonathan Stark. Story by Ellen DeGeneres. Directed by Gil Junger. End: Guest Starring Laura Dern as Susan. Guest Starring

Steven Eckholdt as Richard. Guest Starring k.d. lang as Janine. Guest Starring Oprah Winfrey as Therapist. Guest Starring Patrick Bristow as Peter. Jack Plotnick as Barrett. Featuring Patrick Harrigan as Waiter. Co-producer: David Flebotte. Co-producer: Alex Herschlag. Co-producer: Mark Wilding. Story Editors: Rob Lotterstein & Ellen Idelson. Music by W. G. Snuffy Walden.

Episode Review

Old college chum Richard is in town. He's at dinner with Ellen when they are interrupted and joined by his producer, Susan, with whom Ellen hits it off. Later, Ellen goes to Richard's hotel room, where he comes on to her. "You smell so great," he says, snuggling closer. Ellen excuses herself uncomfortably; after all, "we all know where smelling leads."

She leaves Richard and runs into Susan in the hall; she goes into her room to talk. She spills that Richard came on to her. Susan is surprised. Ellen talks about him and how sweet and handsome he is. "Why

THE BIG TV SATISFACTION FORMULA	
SyndicoDurability	6.2
Comic Valence	9.2
Emotional Resonance	9.6
Writing, Story	9
Writing, Characters	9.1
Acting	8.8
Quintessence	8.9
Series Originality	7.5
Episode Originality	9.1
Historical Significance	10
Celebrity	9.6
Gimmickry	9.3
Theme Song	6.8
Kitsch	6.1
BTVS Ratio	**85.48**

am I not interested?" she wonders aloud, and Susan laughs knowingly, "I can't imagine!"

Ellen is confused (in more ways than one), but she finally sees the light when Susan says that she is gay and she thought that Ellen was gay, too. Ellen is edgy and defensive. She says that she isn't gay. Ellen backs out of that room feeling uncomfortable; then, just to prove (to herself?) that she's not gay, she goes back to Richard's room and attacks him at the door.

The next day at the bookstore Ellen speaks of her conquest. "Men, men, men, why do I love men so much." She elaborates on their night of passion.

Cut to therapy: "Tell me what *really* happened." We see Ellen sitting on the end of Richard's bed: "I'm sorry, Richard, this has never happened to me before." Ellen talks about the person she met with who she really clicked, and after talking around it, admits that it was Susan.

Richard has left a message; he has to go back to Pittsburgh. Ellen runs to the airport to see Susan before she leaves but, once there, runs into Richard. They talk about their awkward night of not doing it. "Well, we'll always not have that."

Then Susan arrives. Ellen asks if they can talk. There in the airport, standing near a counter, Ellen talks around it. "Why can't I say it . . . why am I afraid to tell the truth? Be who I am. I'm thirty-five years old. Why do I have to be so afraid to tell people?"

She finally girds herself up, leans forward, and says, "Susan, I'm gay." And by leaning forward she has managed to say it into an open microphone, announcing herself to all the passengers waiting to board the departing flight.

Susan hugs her proudly. Ellen says with relief: "Well, I guess you have to get on a plane, don't you."

"No, I'm not leaving for another three days."

So Ellen can't just say it and run. She is nervous. Next we see an enactment of Ellen's dream; lesbian jokes are made as she is rolled through a grocery store, peopled by gay women like k.d. lang. In therapy Ellen talks about the dream, her anxieties and fears, and she jokes that you don't see too many cakes that say, "Good for you, you're gay." So her therapist says: "Good for you, you're gay. Now what are you going to do?"

"I'm going to Disneyland!"

But the next thing she needs to do is tell her friends. She has a party and manages to tell them. They accept in different ways, most with hugs and support. Joe asks . . . is it really what you want? Ellen says yes, and he then collects bets from everyone.

But it's not over yet. Susan comes by the store, where Joe and Audrey meet her excitedly. Ellen is positively beaming with her crush nearby. Ellen and Susan sit down for a coffee, and then it all comes apart. Susan tells Ellen that she is in a long-term relationship. Sadly, Ellen asks only for confirmation that she's not crazy, that there was "something" between them. Susan says she's not crazy. And leaves.

The gang has gathered at a lesbian coffeehouse. A folksinger is singing a feminist anthem, and Audrey joins in the song enthusiastically. Ellen comes in and joins them. Audrey says, "Surprise! It's a lesbian coffeehouse!" Ellen had figured that out. The singer, Janine, comes over, and Ellen assumes she is being hit on. She explains that she has only recently come out and isn't ready to start anything. Janine says, "Good for you, I'm your waiter. Do you want anything to drink?"

One more trip to the therapist. Ellen says that now that she's out there's no particular need for therapy and starts to leave, until her therapist asks if she is ready to start dating? Ellen sits right back down again.

Triple

Ellen executes an interesting variation on the classic triple while talking to Richard about how exciting it must be to report the news: "One day it's a whale getting washed up on a beach. The next day it's cloning. The next day it's two whales getting washed up on the beach." The traditional triple works to establish a pattern with the first two items, then to interrupt that pattern with the third. In this particular case, the first two establish a pattern, and the third not only interrupts that pattern, but does so by connecting the first two ideas.

Notes

- With all the publicity and prelude leading up to this historic episode, there was certainly plenty of pressure on the writers, producers, and cast to come through with something special. They did indeed.
- This is another episode that takes advantage of a full-hour length. In fact, at the very beginning of the show, they make reference to that fact. Ellen is in another

room getting ready for her date. Her friends know that she is preparing and call for her. "Are you coming out or not?" and "Quit jerking us around and come out already!" Ellen pops her head out and says, "What's the big deal, I've got a whole hour."

- Janine is played by popular singer k.d. lang and Ellen's therapist by talk-show host and megamillionaire Oprah Winfrey.
- To some, it's a scourge, but since the late nineties, television shows have not been content to simply run credits. In industry parlance, they are a "tune-out opportunity." Thus, viewers are given "credit crunch" or "squeeze credits." Luckily, the show creators are often given the opportunity to fill this time with added entertainment. In this episode, the credit crunch pays off an earlier joke in the show. When Ellen is still in denial and tells Susan how straight she is, she accuses Susan of "recruiting." Susan jokes that she'll have to call the home office and say that she lost her. "Darn, one more, and I would have gotten the toaster oven." Ellen responds stiffly, "What is that? Some sort of gay humor, because I don't get it." Much later, in the credit crunch, we see Ellen filling out forms at the bar, with Susan watching. Her forms are all stamped and approved, and Susan gets her toaster oven!
- This episode was the only one of the BTVS Top 100 to score a perfect 10 in the category of Historic Importance. Here are the top seven episodes that secured a permanent place in television and cultural history.

20

"The Income Tax Show"
the jack benny program

Episode 99
Original series run: 1950–1965
Series total: 343 episodes originally aired;
104 shown in syndication

Credits

Open: "From Hollywood, *The Jack Benny Program*, with his special guests Mr. and Mrs. Jimmy Stewart." End: Directed and Produced by Norman Abbott. Written by Sam Perrin, George Balzer, Hal Goldman, Al Gordon. Harold Gould as The 1st Tax Man. Bill Quinn as The 2nd Tax Man. Joan Marshall as Marsha. Scott Elliott as The Waiter. Jeanette Eymann as The Woman. Executive Producer: Irving Fein.

Episode Review

America's oldest thirty-nine-year-old is massacring some violin music when there is a knock at the door. Two gentleman from the Internal Revenue Service. A stunt double (we hope!) does a full-out faint straight back onto the floor.

When Benny awakens, he soon finds that, strangely enough, these gentleman are here because they think he may have paid too much tax. The fact is that they can't imagine that someone who made $375,000 last year only spent $19 on entertainment. "We feel you may unconsciously be cheating yourself." But, of course, that's all America's favorite cheapskate spent on business entertainment. As Benny recalls: "The year before, I spent $28 on entertainment? Hmm. Oh yes. That was the year I took a vacation in Las Vegas. Wow!"

THE BIG TV SATISFACTION FORMULA	
SyndicoDurability	7.6
Comic Valence	9.3
Emotional Resonance	7.5
Writing, Story	9.1
Writing, Characters	8.6
Acting	9.4
Quintessence	9.4
Series Originality	6.6
Episode Originality	9.1
Historical Significance	7.1
Celebrity	9.6
Gimmickry	8.8
Theme Song	5.8
Kitsch	8.9
BTVS Ratio	**85.71**

The IRS men press him. What about this dinner with Mr. and Mrs. Jimmy Stewart. The total was only $3.90! How can that be? Jack adds, "I brought a girl along, too." After chatting, the men go down the street to get the story out of the Stewarts.

They introduce themselves as from Internal Revenue Service. Stewart welcomes them, but then he, too, faints dead away. "At least he held out at first," they say. After he awakens, they explain the reason for their visit. But Stewart isn't surprised a bit. He hears $19 and says, "That much?" And then hears about the year before's $28 deductions and echoes Benny's response, "Wow."

Stewart then tells the story of that fateful dinner out. He and his wife were at a nice restaurant where Jack was eating with a young woman. They tried to hide from him but got roped into joining him. Astonishingly, Jack says that dinner will be on him. The Stewarts almost faint, but they gather themselves and have dinner. They also have this exchange.

JIMMY: I never told you this, but I saw the first TV show you ever did.

JACK: You saw the first show I ever did?

JIMMY: How have they been since then?

When the bill comes, Jack picks it up. Then he hesitates, adds it again. He then insists on talking loudly about "business" so that they can deduct it, and there will be witnesses. Then he suggests to Jimmy that deductions are hard to come by. Jimmy agrees, so Jack lets him have this deduction . . . and check.

We return to the present day, where the Stewarts are wrapping up the story to the IRS men. Jimmy Stewart paid the whole bill. So they only have one question left, what was the $3.90 for? "Oh, that was what it cost him to get his suit cleaned after getting a salad dumped on his head."

The men return to Jack Benny's, just to look at him one more time. After all, to penny-pinching bean counters like the IRS, Benny is a god.

Notes

- We don't precisely know what rules and regulations about privacy the IRS worked under in that era, but surely they must be breaking some rule by visiting Jack Benny's neighbors and telling them how much he made and deducted.

- Though Jimmy Stewart made very few television appearances, he was in two episodes of *The Jack Benny Program*. He was also the star of a short-lived 1971–72 family comedy *The Jimmy Stewart Show* and a 1973–74 crime drama called *Hawkins*.

- Harold Gould, who plays the IRS auditor, was a former tenured professor of drama at UCLA who left academia to devote himself to an acting career. He did just fine. He went on to play Rhoda's father in that series. He was also Richie Cunningham's father in the pilot for *Happy Days*, which was actually an episode of *Love, American Style*. He also played *Golden Girls* regular Miles Webber, Rose's sometime boyfriend.

- Some purists may object that *The Jack Benny Program* wasn't always a situation comedy at all, and shouldn't be compared to others. The fact is that some periods of the show found it to be more variety show, but for many years it was as much a sit-com as *The George Burns & Gracie Allen Show* or even *The Adventures of Ozzie & Harriet*. In any case, the BTVS allows us to measure it objectively, and this episode had enough story structure and character development not only to compare, but to rank high!

19

"Latka the Playboy"
taxi

Episode 64
Original air date: May 21, 1981
Original series run: 1978–1983
Series total: 114 episodes

Credits

Open: Judd Hirsch Also Starring Jeff Conaway, Danny DeVito, Marilu Henner, Tony Danza, Christopher Lloyd, and Andy Kaufman as Latka Gravas. Created by James L. Brooks, Stan Daniels, David Davis and Ed Weinberger. Produced by Glen Charles & Les Charles. Written by Glen Charles & Les Charles. Directed by James Burrows. End: Executive Producers: James L. Brooks, Stan Daniels and Ed Weinberger. Guest Starring George Wendt as The Exterminator. Robin Klein as Karen. T. J. Castranova as Tommy. Executive Script Consultant: Barry Kemp. Executive Story Editor: David Lloyd. Story Editor: Ken Estin. Associate Producer: Richard Sakai. Executive Consultant: James L. Brooks. Executive in Charge of Production: John Charles Walters Productions: Ronald E. Frazier.

THE BIG TV SATISFACTION FORMULA	
SyndicoDurability	7.1
Comic Valence	9.3
Emotional Resonance	9.4
Writing, Story	9.3
Writing, Characters	9.4
Acting	9.6
Quintessence	8.3
Series Originality	8.2
Episode Originality	9.7
Historical Significance	8.1
Celebrity	5.8
Gimmickry	9.7
Theme Song	7.3
Kitsch	7.8
BTVS Ratio	**85.73**

Episode Review

The gang is at Mario's, where Latka has a crush on a woman at the bar. They goad Latka into approaching her, but, not too surprisingly, he is shot down. Bobby goes over to tell her how wrong she was and ends up hitting on her and giving her a ride home.

Latka is intent on reforming himself. He studies *Playboy* magazine and immerses himself in it. He listens to tapes of an FM deejay to study his voice. As he repeats the line "Alter my lifestyle to fit the fast lane," the accent begins to disappear and the first glimmerings of Vic emerge.

Latka returns from a vacation. He is now fully submerged into the personality of Vic Ferrari. There is no trace of a foreign accent; instead there is a smarmy, smooth-guy voice. The scene is Mario's. He arrives, and while the gang watches, he approaches the bar. Almost immediately, "Vic" sees the woman who had rejected "Latka." This time, his approach is rather more successful.

"I can take one look at you and see that

you've heard every phony line in the book. So one more isn't gonna hurt you, right? But, seriously now, the first few moments of a relationship set the tone for the whole thing, if you know what I mean. So let's be honest. My name's Vic. I'm into Italian cars, Technics stereos, Australian films, and beautiful ladies. If you're interested, let's talk. If not, it's been beautiful."

She goes for it. As the two head out, the gang congratulates "Latka" but they only get a response from "Vic." Alex suggests that Latka can drop the act, but only Vic will answer: "I dropped my act."

Nobody likes the new persona. Even Louie seems to miss Latka. Everyone turns to Alex to solve the problem, but he can't get through Vic's cool exterior and snide putdowns. "Alex, with a heart as big as his schnoz."

Finally, Vic comes to Alex to beg for help. He doesn't like himself either. Somewhere beneath the surface, Latka is trapped, suffocating inside Vic. Alex tries to help him emerge. "You remember! Latka Gravas. Ibby dah?" But, at first, they make no headway. "I don't remember how I used to talk. I remember I was a cute little guy, had some kind of an accent."

But Alex is persistent, and finally, in a classic transformation, smug cockeyed Vic leans back on the sofa, and then vacant, innocent Latka leans forward. He's back!

Triple

In the B plot of this episode, there are insects in Louie's cage, which is redundant, so an exterminator is called in. George Wendt, who would later become Norm at Cheers,

plays the exterminator. Do the poisonous fumes that he works with bother him? He answers with a neatly executed triple. "Some people go in there the first day and get sick; others get a headache. . . . Me? I like it."

Notes

- According to legend—and the big-screen version of his life story, *Man in the Moon*—Andy Kaufman held his own *Taxi* work in disdain. He had not wanted to make a sitcom, and when Latka became a hit character, he was uncomfortable with the calls to do Latka that he would get in the comedy clubs. Despite all this, the producers of *Taxi* clearly knew what they had on their hands, and they wrote scripts like "Latka the Playboy" that took advantage of the full range of Andy Kaufman's abilities. It would have been very easy to turn Latka into a catchphrase-spouting phenomenon like Mork, Fonzie, or Vinny Barbarino. They didn't do that. Andy Kaufman's nonsitcom work was strange and confrontational, leaving many observers either angry or just confused. They didn't do that either. The tension between the sitcom form, and Andy Kaufman's ideas about performance, made Latka a unique creation that is still a wonder to watch. Vic Ferrari was a wonderful expression of Kaufman's self-loathing desire to tell the world how contemptible sitcoms are ("Oh, Alex's big heart!") and to show the world that he felt he himself was a shallow, self-consciously hip jerk.
- Vic Ferrari returned to inhabit Latka's

mind in a number of other episodes: #70, "Mr. Personalities"; #74, "Louie's Mom Remarries"; #77, "Louie Goes Too Far"; #80, "Tony's Lady"; and #81, "Simka Returns."

18

"PT 73, Where Are You?"

mchale's navy

Episode 4
Original air date: November 1, 1962
Original series run: 1962–1966
Series total: 138 episodes

Credits

Open: Ernest Borgnine in . . . Written by Joe Heller. Produced and Directed by Edward J. Montagne. End: Starring Ernest Borgnine as Lieutenant Commander Quinton McHale. Co-Starring Joe Flynn as Captain Binghamton and Tim Conway as Ensign Parker. Carl Ballantine . . . as Lester Gruber. Gary Vinson . . . as Christy. Billy Sands . . . as "Tinker" Bell. Edson Stroll . . . as Virgil. Gavin MacLeod . . . as Happy. John Wright . . . as Willy. Yoshio Yoda . . . as Fuji, with Bob Hastings . . . as Lieutenant Carpenter, Robert Kline . . . as Ensign Byrnes, Syl Lamont . . . as Yeoman Tate. Script Consultant: Si Rose.

Episode Review

Captain Binghamton is annoyed, and there is no better way to start a TV show. He is being forced by the admiral to reward McHale and his men with an easy assignment to run the reports to New Caledonia,

THE BIG TV SATISFACTION FORMULA	
SyndicoDurability	7.3
Comic Valence	9.1
Emotional Resonance	7.2
Writing, Story	9.4
Writing, Characters	8.9
Acting	8.1
Quintessence	9.6
Series Originality	5.1
Episode Originality	8.6
Historical Significance	7.4
Celebrity	8.9
Gimmickry	7.7
Theme Song	7.8
Kitsch	8.4
BTVS Ratio	**85.78**

a gravy run that means "wine, women, and hot showers."

However, when McHale returns to his men, he finds Virgil is being yelled at. He lost the PT boat. How do you lose a PT boat? He took a late-night cruise over to the village, took the chief's daughter for a little spin. Then pulled up and moored, went for a walk in the jungle, and couldn't find his way back.

"If Binghamton gets wind of this . . ." and soon enough, he does. Binghamton figures he will be able to get McHale thrown out of the navy. McHale may even need to make "restitution" and pay for the missing boat! "I've got forms that you never even heard of," boasts Binghamton. "I'm gonna make this one stick."

Meanwhile, the boys have stolen another PT boat and painted PT 73 on it. After all, the only difference between their boat and any other is that 73 carries beer cans in the Number 2 torpedo tube, and that Tinker keeps his comic books in the armor case.

Christy arrives and formally (in front of

an assistant) tells McHale PT 73 is ready. McHale bursts into Binghamton's office. "Have my boat, sir. It was never really lost." However, it's too late to get the New Caledonia run back, because it has been given to Carpenter. "He's real navy," says Binghamton proudly, but then Carpenter is forced to report that he has lost his boat! (Guess how?)

McHale, who knows exactly what happened, rushes out to the boat. They're trying to make it a bit sloppy to look like PT 73. The new paint is dry. Just then the real PT 73 pulls in—they found it! They rush it away. Meanwhile, back in the office, Carpenter and Binghamton are putting two and two together, slowly. They go out to check on their dawning suspicions, but McHale's men have done such a good job of making it look slovenly that they are fooled.

Just then, the 116, Carpenter's boat, pulls in. They have now renumbered that boat. Carpenter is sure it's his because it's tidy and shipshape. Then beer is found in Carpenter's torpedo tube. Shocking! And there are comic books in Carpenter's ammo case. Undone, Binghamton barks out to McHale to take his men away to New Caledonia now, before he reconsiders.

Notes

• Though this episode was written by novelist Joseph Heller and is a neatly crafted farce, it seems to have little of the satirical darkness that marked his other major work about World War II, the novel *Catch-22*. The closest parallel in tone might be seen as Binghamton threatens to use "forms you've never even heard of" and

the threat that McHale might actually have to make "restitution" and pay for the missing boat.

• John Wright, who played Willy Moss, was the son of the "Queen of Country Music," Kitty Wells, and Johnnie Wright, a successful country musician as well. Wells was one of the earliest solo female recording artists to make an impact, with hits like "It Wasn't God Who Made Honky-Tonk Angels" and "How Far Is Heaven."

• Previously Joe Flynn had played David Nelson's boss, Mr. Kelley, on *The Adventures of Ozzie & Harriet.*

• Tim Conway went on to greater acclaim for his work in the ensemble of *The Carol Burnett Show*, and, of course, for his popular "Dorf" videos.

17

"The Sandman Cometh . . ." and ". . . The Catwoman Goeth"

batman

Episodes 67 and 68
Original air date:
December 28 and 29, 1966
Original series run: 1966–1968
Series total: 120 episodes

Credits

Open: Adam West as Batman. Burt Ward as Robin. Alan Napier as Alfred. Neil Hamilton as Commissioner Gordon. Stafford Repp as Chief

O'Hara. Madge Blake as Mrs. Cooper. Executive Producer William Dozier. Special Guest Villain: Michael Rennie as Sandman. Extra Special Guest Villainess: Julie Newmar as Catwoman. Produced by Howie Horwitz. Teleplay by Ellis St. Joseph and Charles Hoffman. Story by Ellis St. Joseph. Directed by George Waggner. End: Richard Peel as Snooze. Tony Ballen as Nap. Valeri Kairys as Kitty. Pat Becker as Cattie. Jeanie Moore as Catarina. James Brolin as Reggie. Ray Montgomery as Dan. Lindsay Workman as Tuthill. Spring Byington as J. Pauline Spaghetti. Special Guest Villain: Michael Rennie as Sandman. Extra Special Guest Villainess: Julie Newmar as Catwoman. Associate Producer: William P. D'Angelo. Script Consultant: Lorenzo Semple, Jr.

Episode Review

Commissioner Gordon bemoans the "unholy alliance of Sandman and Catwoman," especially with Batman away on personal business. But he must call for him and up goes the Bat-signal, seen by Bruce Wayne, who is leading an expedition of teens in the woods. Gordon and O'Hara are trying to wait patiently for the caped crusader. "Grain by grain, the hen fills her belly, O'Hara. A pithy proverb about patience. Batman told it to me himself."

Catwoman is on TV plugging a cure for insomniacs: "Dr. Somnabula cured me." "Holy alter ego, Batman, you think Dr. Somnabula and Sandman are one and the same?" They begin deducing who their target might be, with the Bat-computer on hand to help. Batman asks, "Can you name some famous insomniacs?" Robin can.

"There was Olaf Cassad of Norway."

"He's been dead for eight hundred years."

"Then there's the famous Chinese historian Fu ha Chaung."

"Born with no eyelids."

"How about the French empress whose head stayed awake even after she'd been guillotined?"

"Poor creature."

At that the Bat-computer spits out spaghetti. The correct answer! "That's it: Spaghetti . . . J. Pauline Spaghetti."

The Dynamic Duo race to her rescue, and indeed the Sandman is already at work, putting her to sleep, and looking over her financial records. Batman and Robin climb the building, then break in and accuse him of being Sandman. But J. Pauline is happy with him; Sandman or no, she really could use a good night's sleep. Batman apologizes to her—and she angrily throws them out.

But the Sandman won't brook any interference, and his men attack Batman and Robin. During the battle, the following on-screen graphics appear: "Klonk! Clash!

THE BIG TV SATISFACTION FORMULA	
SyndicoDurability	8.5
Comic Valence	9
Emotional Resonance	7.1
Writing, Story	9.1
Writing, Characters	8.7
Acting	9.2
Quintessence	9.1
Series Originality	9.9
Episode Originality	7.6
Historical Significance	7.2
Celebrity	8.8
Gimmickry	9.2
Theme Song	9.3
Kitsch	9.3
BTVS Ratio	**85.82**

Slopp! Wham! Vronk! Uggh! Zowie!" Just when you think it's over, the fighting continues with "Zzwap! Biff! Bam! Boff! Crunch! Z-zonk! Touché! Flrrbbb!" As always, in the first part of the fight, the two have been overcome. Batman is buried in mattresses, and Robin is drugged. The Sandman's chosen fate for his vanquished rival? Batman is strapped onto a mattress-button-stitching machine, to be quilted to death!

Same Bat-time, same Bat-channel!

After the recap, the button stitcher promptly breaks open Batman's straps. The off switch is in easy reach. Robin is delivered to Catwoman, who places him in an electrified maze.

Batman finds them. It seems that Catwoman has been double-crossed by Sandman: "How else could I have found your lair?"

"You're so strong and forceful, Batman."

"And determined."

He asks for her help in releasing Robin and getting Sandman.

"And if I purr? So to speak."

"I'll testify that you cooperated. The rest is up to the court."

Batman goes into the maze and gets Robin out in no time. They rush "to the Batboat!" and to J. Pauline Spaghetti's island. Batman and Robin arrive and do battle. This time the fisticuffs are punctuated by this series of illustrative texts: "Z-zwap! Zowie! Whamm! Boff! Zlopp! Kapow! Sock! Kayo!" And the good guys win.

Back home, Aunt Harriet is discussing putting a maze on the front lawn. (Holy ironies!) Bruce Wayne describes the secret of getting through a maze, and his ward,

Dick Grayson, now understands how his rescue was accomplished. For now, peace reigns in Gotham City.

Notes

- Along with *The Many Loves of Dobie Gillis* and arguably *The Andy Griffith Show*, *Batman* is one of the few television shows to create a unique literary voice that is really its very own. No synopsis can really do it justice, since the genius of the show lay in the poetry of it and had nothing to do with the story.

- During the period of its creative height, *Batman* was presented in two-part episodes. A half hour on Wednesday night at 7:30 and the concluding half hour on Thursday at 7:30. Naturally, this caused problems for our BTVS formula, which was essentially designed to analyze individual half hours. Fortunately, we found that a simple statistical solution could be applied. Each episode was ranked separately, but then the two were averaged. Each element of the breakdown above is an average for the two episodes. This system has been applied to other two-part episodes, like Rhoda's wedding. With *Friends*, however, the two parts clearly stood on their own, and since they are seen as two separate parts in syndication, they were measured individually.

- There is a relatively high proportion of two-parters in the BTVS Top 100. After all, multipart episodes make up less than 2 percent of all sitcom episodes. It is our supposition, though it can't be proved, that this is because the stories that writers and producers believe merit the extra time and development to require two parts tend to be good ones.

- James Brolin is outstanding in his small part as a henchman.
- *Batman* was almost picked up by NBC after ABC canceled it. They were strongly considering it until they discovered that the set had already been destroyed. The cost of rebuilding it was enough to dissuade them.

16

from the "Fernwood Flasher" sequence

mary hartman, mary hartman

Episodes not titled
Episode number not available
Original series run: 1976–1978
Series total: 325 episodes

Credits

Open: Starring Louise Lasser, with Greg Mullavey, Mary Kay Place, Graham Jarvis, Dody Goodman, Debralee Scott, Victor Kilian, Philip Bruns, Claudia Lamb. Produced by Lew Gallo. Created by Gail Parent, Ann Marcus, Jerry Adelman, and Daniel Gregory Browne. Creative Supervision: Al Burton. Developed by Norman Lear. End: Directed by Joan Darling. Written by Ann Marcus, Jerry Adelman, and Daniel Gregory Browne. Executive Producer: Norman Lear.

Bruce Soloman as Sergeant Foley. Archie Hahn as Reporter Clemens. Jack R. Clinton as the Officer.

Episode Review

Mary is being interviewed by the reporter who is profiling the town in the wake of the unsolved Lombardi murders (a family of five people were slaughtered, along with a number of goats and chickens). Mary talks about a book she once bought about psychology, which was guaranteed to improve her emotional health. Did it? Yes, because it was while she was reading that book that she realized she needed glasses, and that made her feel much better. She also recalls the "hilarious story" of when she and Tom first spoke. She describes in great detail how he turned the water of the water fountain way up high while she was getting a drink, and it sprayed all up her nostrils.

Heather comes home from school. She is sullen and not hungry because she ate four boxes of M&M's. The reporter wants to ask Heather about the Lombardi case, but she

THE BIG TV SATISFACTION FORMULA	
SyndicoDurability	5
Comic Valence	8.9
Emotional Resonance	8.6
Writing, Story	9
Writing, Characters	8.8
Acting	8.8
Quintessence	9.6
Series Originality	9.7
Episode Originality	7.1
Historical Significance	8.9
Celebrity	7.6
Gimmickry	8.3
Theme Song	6.1
Kitsch	9.4
BTVS Ratio	**85.83**

says she has cramps, and Mary sends her to her room.

Loretta is practicing her country-music act, when her husband Charlie comes home. They coo to each other. She says, "I love you more'n a hundred million frozen Milky Ways." Then she sings a love song she wrote: "It Feels So Good When You Feel Me."

Tom and Mary are in their bedroom, and he says she looks cute sitting there cutting her toenails. Mary gets excited, but anything flirtatious at all makes Tom tense and unhappy. Just when they go to sleep, the phone rings. Grandpa Larkin has been caught by police for indecent exposure, for the second time in a week. The Hartmans gather at the police station. It seems that he crashed a luau for graduating nurses at the hospital. Everyone is yelling and bickering, but Mary tries to restore order by promising them a pancake breakfast.

Notes

- This show was a bold experiment, a satire of both soap operas and blue-collar America. Shot in the flat style of soaps, with totally deadpan acting, purposefully stodgy pacing, and no laugh track, it can take some getting used to. But line for line, it is as funny a show as the 1970s had to offer.
- Being a serial show, each episode includes reference to continuing story lines. The events mentioned in this episode—Lombardi's mass murder, Tom's sexual dysfunction, Loretta's country singing, and the "Fernwood Flasher" himself—were all played out over many episodes.

- After Louise Lasser quit the series, *Fernwood 2-Nite* was introduced as a summer replacement; in the fall, *Forever Fernwood* returned most of the *Mary Hartman, Mary Hartman* characters, with Mary Kay Place now the central figure. Place had won an Emmy Award in 1977 for her role as a supporting actress on the original show.
- This is one of two episodes in the BTVS Top 100 directed by Joan Darling. She also directed the famous "Chuckles Bites the Dust" episode of *Mary Tyler Moore*.

15
"The Giant Jackrabbit"
the beverly hillbillies

Episode 52
Original air date: January 8, 1964
Original series run: 1962–1971
Series total: 216 episodes

Credits

Open: Starring Buddy Ebsen, Irene Ryan, Donna Douglas, Max Baer. Created and Produced by Paul Henning. Written by Paul Henning and Mark Tuttle. Directed by Richard Whorf. End: Executive Producer: Al Simon. Millburn Drysdale . . . Raymond Bailey. Jane Hathaway . . . Nancy Kulp. Ravenswood . . . Arthur Gould Porter. Bill Tinsman . . . Peter Bourne. Janet Trego . . . Sharon Tate. Marian Billington . . . Kathy Kersh. Music: Perry Botkin. Theme played by Flatt & Scruggs. Song by Jerry Scoggins. Automobiles furnished by Chrysler Corporation. Animals furnished by Frank Inn.

Episode Review

Granny is complaining that they've got no vittles, thanks to all of Elly's critters! Jethro heads out to hunt down some food. At the bank, Miss Hathaway brings Mr. Drysdale the news that there is a kangaroo in his backyard. His wife is in hysterics. After thinking it through, he realizes that it is an elaborate practical joke sent by a friend in Australia. He has his man Ravenswood call the zoo.

The kangaroo, having broken out of its crate, has wandered into the Clampetts' backyard. Granny sees it and runs to find Jed. She says they don't need to go hunting because "There's a jackrabbit out back, that high!" Jed quietly takes away the XXX jug that was on the kitchen counter to flavor the stew.

"I tell you I ain't touched a drop!" But Jed tries to reason with her: "You and I have seen some good-size jacks in our time, but not five feet tall." She rushes off to find it and does, in the front yard. "Howdy, Mr. Jackrabbit," she says, "stay right there while I get someone to meet you."

Granny rushes into the house and through the curtains, but in the meantime Elly's chimpanzee has closed the pocket doors behind them. Granny konks her head and breaks her glasses. The chimp then puts the doors back, as Jed arrives. Now Granny is off balance, claiming she banged her head against the curtains, and Jed is positive she's been into "the corn squeezin's." He tries to mollify her, by pretending he can see lots of giant jackrabbits all over the front lawn, and he convinces her to go lie down.

Granny is setting the snare when the jackrabbit next arrives, and in one of television's most unbelievable scenes, they box! They trade lefts and rights until finally Granny runs for cover. As she later explains: "I had him cornered, but he fist-fought me!" Eventually Granny snares the jackrabbit and drags it into the kitchen . . . but the monkey unties it!

Now the kangaroo has returned of its own accord to its crate. Mr. Drysdale and Miss Hathaway are wondering why and suppose he must have been scared of something to prefer this crate to freedom. At that, we hear Granny yelling, "Have you seen any jackrabbit?" "No Granny," says Jane, standing next to the crate. "You won't find any jackrabbits in Beverly Hills!"

At that, Elly arrives and tells Granny and Jed that Jethro's been caught in Granny's snare. We see Jethro swinging upside down and the final credits roll without Granny ever getting her redemption. Jethro will forever think that she was just "in her jug."

Notes

- This episode packs a whole heap of comedy and whole mess of situation into one little ol' half hour. In addition to the Granny and the jackrabbit story, there is an elaborate parallel plot about Beverly Caterers, whom they call for food, thinking it is an individual named Beverly Caterers, the Widow Caterers who don't have a family of her own to feed.

- In a small in-joke of sorts, while Granny is puttering about her kitchen, she sings a song to the tune of the show's famous theme song. Her improvised lyrics: "Oh, I'm a going to cook up a rabbit stew; soon as Jethro shoots me one or two, then we're all going to eat. . . ."

- This episode may stand forever as the highest-rated half-hour situation comedy ever. When it first aired on January 8, 1964, it received a 44 rating. By comparison, the famous first appearance by the Beatles on *The Ed Sullivan Show* did a 44.6, and the first episode of *Roots* did a 40.7. Why did this episode rate so high? A number of factors went into creating this peak performance. First, it was an era of three networks, so there was less competition. Second, it was an extremely popular show throughout its run. Third, in January 1964, America was turning to escapist fare, still living in the shadow of the tragic assassination of President Kennedy.

- Sharon Tate appeared in numerous episodes of *The Beverly Hillbillies* as the bank secretary. She was also the very first "Billie Jo" on *Petticoat Junction*. She played that role in the unaired pilot for the series, but her part was recast after the produc-

ers learned that she appeared nude in *Playboy* magazine. She was married to film director Roman Polanski. In August 1969, at age twenty-six, she was murdered by the infamous group led by Charles Manson.

14
"Password"
the odd couple

Episode 62
Original air date: December 1, 1972
Original series run: 1970–1983
Series total: 114 episodes

Credits

Open: Starring Tony Randall. Starring Jack Klugman. Based on the play *The Odd Couple* by Neil Simon. Developed for Television by Garry Marshall and Jerry Belson. Produced by Jerry Davis. Written by Frank Buxton. Directed by Alex March. End: Executive Producer Garry Marshall. Executive Story Consultants, Mark Rothman, and Lowell Ganz. Co-starring Allen Ludden, Betty White, Elinor Donahue, Penny Marshall, and Ronda Copeland.

Episode Review

Oscar, taking advantage once again of the midlevel fame he seems to have as a sportswriter, has landed an invitation from Allen Ludden to come play on the game show *Password*. He gets to choose his partner and goes with Mitzi Ferguson. "Ditzy Mitzi Ferguson?" Felix is appalled that he has not been chosen. Luckily, Mitzi drops Oscar

THE BIG TV SATISFACTION FORMULA	
SyndicoDurability	9.1
Comic Valence	9.3
Emotional Resonance	8.9
Writing, Story	9.5
Writing, Characters	9.7
Acting	8.9
Quintessence	8.1
Series Originality	7.7
Episode Originality	9.1
Historical Significance	8.2
Celebrity	9.1
Gimmickry	9.6
Theme Song	8.7
Kitsch	8.8
BTVS Ratio	**85.92**

(because she thinks he's no good at the game), and Felix is the backup player.

So the boys take to the stage, where they play against game show regular Betty White and her partner, a woman named Millicent. As you may recall, the idea is to get your partner to name a certain word by using one-word clues associated with it. The teams take turns.

The first word is provided on screen to the audience. It's "gravy." Betty chooses to play and says, "Sauce," to which Millicent replies, "Mayonnaise." Oscar adds the word "meat," so Felix has the words meat and sauce to think about. His answer? "Lincoln." Oscar is baffled. Millicent gets it on the next clue. Aside, Felix explains to Oscar that Lincoln's affection for mayonnaise is well established.

The next word is "bird." Felix has what he think is the perfect clue: "Aristophanes." Oscar answers, "Greek," and Felix is frustrated with him. Millicent goes with "canary," and Betty gives the correct answer. Felix explains that everybody knows that

Aristophanes wrote a play called *The Birds*. Oscar call the clue "ridiculous."

By happenstance the next answer is "ridiculous." Oscar gives his clue "Aristophanes." Felix gets it: "Ridiculous." Then Felix manages to give a reasonable clue, "household," and Oscar gets "servant." However, Felix answers "lead" to Oscar's "graphite," and they lose the game. Felix argues that pencil lead is made of graphite and clay, and actually has to be dragged from the set. Allen Ludden apologizes to the home audience for this untidy spectacle.

Notes

- Writer-Producer Frank Buxton took on the role of the off-stage announcer.
- Jack Klugman and Tony Randall had both acted in the stage version of *The Odd Couple* before they made the TV series. Klugman took over for Walter Matthau, who originated the Oscar role on Broadway. Randall played Felix opposite Mickey Rooney in Las Vegas.
- *The Odd Couple* was never a big ratings success in its first run, but it had a long healthy life in syndication. Luckily for both Klugman and Randall, they had the foresight to get ownership of a portion of the production.
- Penny Marshall played a regular role on *The Odd Couple* as Myrna Turner, but when she wanted to leave the series for a part on the MTM production *Paul Sand in Friends and Lovers* they had her character get married to her boyfriend, played by her real-life husband at the time, Rob Reiner.

13

"Sammy's Visit"
all in the family

Episode 34
Original air date: February 19, 1972
Original series run: 1971–1979
Series total: 204 episodes

THE BIG TV SATISFACTION FORMULA	
SyndicoDurability	9.1
Comic Valence	8.4
Emotional Resonance	8.1
Writing, Story	8.9
Writing, Characters	9.3
Acting	9.4
Quintessence	9.4
Series Originality	9.2
Episode Originality	8.1
Historical Significance	8.7
Celebrity	9.9
Gimmickry	7.2
Theme Song	9
Kitsch	8.1
BTVS Ratio	**86.01**

Credits

Open: Starring Carroll O'Connor, Jean Stapleton. Co-starring Rob Reiner, Sally Struthers. Developed and Produced by Norman Lear. End: Directed by John Rich. Written by Bill Dana. Script Supervision: Norman Lear. Story Editors: Don Nicholls, Michael Ross & Bernie West. Sammy Davis, Jr. as himself. Mike Evans as Lionel. Allan Melvin as Barney Hefner. Isabel Sanford as Mrs. Jefferson. Fay DeWitt as Mrs. Haskell. Keri Shuttleton as Clarissa. Billy Halop as Mr. Munson. Based on "Till Death Us Do Part" Created by Johnny Speight. "*All in the Family* was recorded on tape before a live audience." A Bud Yorkin–Norman Lear–Tandem Production.

Episode Review

Archie returns home from moonlighting as a cab driver and has big news. Sammy Davis Jr. rode in his cab; what's more, he accidentally left his briefcase, so Archie has arranged for him to come to the house to pick it up. Arch warns Edith not to talk about Sammy's glass eye, and he suggests she go get some fried chicken. In the meantime Lionel arrives, and stays to get a gan-

der at the "Greatest Entertainer in the World."

Sammy arrives and everyone is excited, none more so than Edith: "I'm so excited, but then you can't imagine . . . because you never had to meet yourself!" Arch makes the introductions, and because of the way the group is standing, much to Archie's chagrin, Sammy thinks that Lionel is Gloria's husband. Archie is quick to correct him. The first of a series of outrageous acts by TV's original bigot.

Archie tells Sammy that he's a credit to his race; then, naturally, he is the one who slips up: "Now, Mr. Davis . . . you take cream and sugar in your eye?" Gloria and Mike keep trying to get Archie to stop with the racist comments. At one point, Sammy consciously helps himself to a taste of Archie's drink. Archie does a long take to indicate that he isn't ready to share a glass with a black man. Archie tells Sammy that the kids think he is prejudiced, "Can you believe it?" Archie asks: "Do you think I'm prejudiced?" Sammy answers him in a way that Archie understands to be confirmation that he's not. But Lionel, Gloria, and Mike understand.

Munson finally arrives with the briefcase—and a camera—for one more picture. Sammy says that's a great idea—1, 2, 3 . . . kiss. Sammy gives Archie a kiss on the cheek and freezes for a moment. It's one of the all-time classic moments in sitcom history. Sammy quickly exits.

In the tag scene, an envelope arrives from Sammy Davis. Again, Archie misses the irony and takes the inscription as a compliment. Sammy has signed it "To Archie Bunker, the whitest guy I know."

Notes

- No episode of the series more squarely and unflinchingly portrayed Archie's unbridled racism. Yet, as always, the writers and actors—Carroll O'Connor above all—managed to maintain Archie's humanity and even his vulnerability. It's an incredible balancing act, and part of the reason that the show was so successful and remains so fascinating. It takes outrageous characters to create comedy, but often those characters can quickly lose touch with reality, or become tiresome and one-dimensional. For the most part, Archie remained unrepentant. Eventually, he did slide somewhat into a softer, gentler bigot over the years. By the time he was changing baby Joey's diaper, the transformation was complete.
- *All in the Family* was the number-one-rated show for five straight season, a record that would later be matched by *The Cosby Show*. Two similar track records, but two very different approaches to dealing with realities of race in America.
- The show was based on a British television comedy entitled *Till Death Us Do Part*. After the success of *All in the Family*, there was a German series called *One Heart and One Soul*, which took a similar approach, with a racist bigot named Adolf taking the lead Archie role.
- In 1972, at the beginning of the show's third season, "Archie Bunker for President" became a phenomenon, as dozens of different items were sold in huge numbers. Later, when baby Joey was born, a "Joey Stivic" doll was marketed.

12

"How Smart Can You Get?"

car 54, where are you?

Episode 23
Original air date: February 25, 1962
Original series run: 1961–1963
Series total: 60 episodes

Credits

Open: Starring Joe E. Ross and Fred Gwynne. Written by Nat Hiken. Created and Directed by Nat Hiken. End: Starring Joe E. Ross . . . Toody. Fred Gwynne . . . Muldoon. Bobby Morse . . . Corrigan. Featuring Paul Reed . . . Captain Block. Beatrice Pons . . . Lucille. Produced by Nat Hiken.

Episode Review

Toody and Muldoon are on patrol. Toody jabbers away while Muldoon ignores him. Nonchalance, you see, is to Toody what makes for a really good ball player. Yogi Berra is very nonchalant, but nobody is as nonchalant as Mickey Mantle. He rambles on about who is nonchalant, who is not nonchalant and who is more nonchalant than whom. His endless ramble borders on the inane, but the taciturn Muldoon contentedly ignores it.

Meanwhile, the experts at headquarters are plotting. They've decided that Toody and Muldoon are ill-suited for each other, probably the most colossal mismatch in police history. Young recruits are assigned, and a brilliant Harvard graduate named Corrigan has been assigned to "college boy" Muldoon.

For now, the three of them will patrol together. Toody feels threatened by this new guy and his intelligence. Indeed, he is left out in the cold when Corrigan and Muldoon speak French, or agree to "hum something we all know: Tchaikovsky's Sixth."

Toody decides that the only way to keep up is an immediate self-improvement course, so he begins reading the encyclopedia. The next day, he tries to work his newfound knowledge into the conversation. While the other two talk about classical music and the conducting prowess of Leonard Bernstein, he keeps trying, unsuccessfully, to steer the conversation toward aardvarks. Muldoon finally asks him: "Gunther, what's this preoccupation with aardvarks?" Toody rants, "What's so great about Leonard Bernstein? Is he nocturnal? Does he have sharp claws? Does Leonard Bernstein subsist mainly on termites?"

The next day, Toody is exhausted by his studies, and, after trying to work in the fact that "tin is the principal export of Bolivia," he sees the writing on the wall and puts in a request to be split up with Muldoon.

It all looks bleak, but Muldoon's enthralling conversations have hurt his police work. He isn't patrolling, and wants his old pal back again. "Captain, would you get that guy off my back? All he does is talk, talk, talk."

Triple

At one point, Toody tries to define his cultural level. He says "I'm not a highbrow. I'm not a lowbrow. I'm a no-brow."

Notes

- This plot was a nod, no doubt, to actor Fred Gwynne's Harvard degree.
- Gwynne was a talented guitarist and cartoonist. At Harvard he drew memorable

cartoons for *The Harvard Lampoon* that were often visual puns of sorts. One showed two gigantic flies sitting in human postures, drinking coffee and reading newspapers, while dozens of tiny humans buzz around their heads, snack on leftover food, and struggle to escape from strips of flypaper (human paper?) He later, after his TV career, published children's books that he illustrated, which also relied on visual puns. One was titled *Look at the Mole on Daddy's Nose,* and showed a mole (animal) clinging to a man's face.

- According to some unreliable sources, there was actually a lost pilot to *Car 54, Where Are You?* that was so bad and so ludicrous, it almost doomed Nat Hiken's project, despite the reputation he had built with *The Phil Silvers Show.* The original story featured Fred Gwynne as Officer Francis Muldoon, the difference being that this Muldoon was a sort of Frankenstein monster, with bolts protruding from his neck and the whole works. Al Lewis played Officer Schnauser, a patrolman and Dracula-like vampire with a habit of turning into a bat. Joe E. Ross's Gunther Toody character was, like the others, a policeman, but also a Stone Age man who had been unfrozen from a fifty-thousand-year-old glacier. Obviously, ideas like these were far too absurd ever to make it on network television. Luckily, cooler heads prevailed and the characters became the simple human beings that made *Car 54, Where Are You?* such a wonderful show. For the moment, TV land was saved.

11

"Danny Meets Andy Griffith"

make room for daddy

Episode 85
Original series run: 1953–1964
Series total: 336 episodes originally aired, 195 shown in syndication

Credits

Open: Danny Thomas, Marjorie Lord, Rusty Hamer, Angela Cartwright. End: Produced and Directed by Sheldon Leonard. Written by Arthur Stander, Louis F. Edelman. Mr. Thomas's wardrobe by Botany 500, tailored by Daroff. Miss Lord's wardrobe by Ann Arnold. Special Guest Star: Andy Griffith. Featuring Ronny Howard, Frances Bavier, Will Wright, Frank Cady, Bill Baldwin, Rance Howard. A Marterto Production.

THE BIG TV SATISFACTION FORMULA	
SyndicoDurability	6.8
Comic Valence	9.2
Emotional Resonance	9.4
Writing, Story	8.6
Writing, Characters	9.5
Acting	9.2
Quintessence	6.2
Series Originality	5.9
Episode Originality	9.1
Historical Significance	9.8
Celebrity	9.1
Gimmickry	9.1
Theme Song	8.1
Kitsch	9.1
BTVS Ratio	**86.10**

Episode Review

Danny Williams drove through a stop sign just outside Mayberry. He went through because there was no crossroad. Andy explains that they had voted to put in a road, but so far, they had only raised enough money for the stop sign. Danny accuses Andy of setting up a trap for city folks, a mercenary ploy. He actually has a pretty good point, but he expresses his disdain for Andy and all these country bumpkins a little too strongly.

In his quest for justice, he demands to see the justice of the peace. While he rails at Andy, the sheriff reaches into his desk and replaces the sheriff sign with a justice of the peace sign, and announces that court is in session.

At this point Will Hoople, the town drunk, stumbles in, arrests himself, and locks himself up. Andy tells the whole story. He gets drunk every day, and it was so time-consuming for Andy to lock him every day, he finally "deputized him, so's he could arrest himself."

Danny finally gives in to his wife's pleadings and decides to pay the fine. Andy says that ordinarily the fine is $5 or $10; Danny whips out a huge wad of cash and peels off two fives. He then gives him another five, and another five, trying to rub it in that he doesn't care if Andy is robbing him. He's a big-time star, after all. Seeing that, Andy decides that this is a special case and announces his final decision: "One hundred dollars or ten days in jail."

Danny is steaming! Tyranny! Injustice! He gets in the jail cell. He demands his one phone call and calls the local newspaper, planning to expose this fraud. The other phone in the room rings: Andy answers: "*Mayberry Gazette*, editor speaking."

Later, Danny is talking to "Chet" the host of the TV talk show *Face to Face*, explaining that he has to cancel his appearance because he is staying in jail for ten days out of "the principle of the thing." He has sent the wife and kids ahead, but he had to stay. Chet suggests he could come shoot the interview from the jail cell, and Danny lights up at the idea! What a perfect way to show the world what a rotten guy this sheriff is.

But as the days pass, Danny gets a chance to see Andy in action. Opie's pet turtle is dead, stepped on by a lady. He wants the lady arrested, given a fair trial, and hanged. Andy takes Opie on his lap and gives him a classic warm and wonderful talk, planning a turtle funeral and talking about how hard it is to lose someone you love. Andy talks about how he lost Opie's ma, just like Opie lost his turtle. Opie asks: "Who stepped on Ma?" And Andy says, "Well, not exactly like you lost your turtle." Danny gets all sentimental listening to this. In another scenario, Andy solves the trouble of Henrietta Perkins, again impressing Danny with his kindness and humanity.

The day of the TV shoot arrives. Danny makes a long speech about tyranny and injustice, and then speaks of languishing in a cold, filthy cell . . . when Andy interrupts. "Now hold on just a durn minute!"

He hadn't intended to say anything, but when Danny said "filthy," why that was an insult to his aunt Lucy, who cleans those cells every day and does a fine job. After all,

Lucy wins the shirt-washing contest at the fair nearly every year!

The host then cross-examines Andy on the whole ticket and fine issue, and Andy explains how insulting and condescending Danny was. He also explains the $5 fine puts a pretty good pinch on a person in Mayberry, but the amount had to be more in order to make an impression on Mr. Williams. He speaks of city folk in a big hurry, missing out on all the good country in between the city they're leaving and the city they're going to.

Danny realizes that he was wrong and comes out of his cell to apologize to Andy. He offers his hand as the cameras roll.

Notes

- When Andy makes his very first appearance, he gets a big round of audience applause. He was already a popular stand-up raconteur and had appeared on television as such.
- This episode served as the pilot for *The Andy Griffith Show*. When Don Knotts saw it, he thought that maybe Andy should have a deputy and called Andy who, apparently, was open to suggestions.
- Frances Bavier, playing the same type that would become Aunt Bee, here plays Henrietta, the bilked widow.
- The town drunk was Will Hoople, played by Frank Cady, whose greatest TV fame was as Sam Drucker, the storekeeper frequented by both *Green Acres* and *Petticoat Junction*. The town drunk, once they went to series, was, of course, Otis Campbell, portrayed by Hal Smith.

10

"The Contest"
seinfeld

Episode 51
Original air date: November 18, 1992
Original series run: 1990–1998
Series total: 180 episodes

Credits

Open: Jerry Seinfeld, Julia Louis-Dreyfus, Michael Richards, and Jason Alexander as George. Executive Producer: Larry Charles. Supervising Producer: Tom Cherones. Executive Producer: Andrew Scheinman. Created by Larry David and Jerry Seinfeld. Written by Larry David. Directed by Tom Cherones. End: Executive Producer: Larry David. Executive Producers: George Shapiro & Howard West. Producer: Jerry Seinfeld. Producer: Si Mehlman. Program Consultants: Jon Hayman, Bob Shaw. Program Consultants: Bill Masters, Steve Skrovan. Estelle Harris as Estelle Costanza. Jane Leeves as Marla. Ilana Levine as Joyce. Rachel Sweet as Shelly. Andrea Parker as Nurse.

Episode Review

George, with no sense of self-respect, announces at the diner that he got caught by his mother. He stopped by the house, it was the middle of the day so no one was around, there was a *Glamour* magazine, one thing led to another. When she saw what she saw, she fell and threw her back out. She's now in the hospital in traction. "I go out for a quart of milk, I come back and find my son treating his body like it was an amusement park!"

George claims he is swearing off of "it," but the others are skeptical, which leads to the bet. Jerry: "I know I could hold out longer than you." George: "Care to make it interesting?" Elaine (taking higher odds, being a woman), Kramer, George, and Jerry all kick in to a winner-take-all pot to see who can remain "master of their domain" the longest.

Almost immediately, the men are challenged. Kramer spots a naked woman in the apartment across the street. He leaves while Jerry and George talk. Elaine arrives. Kramer returns, plunks his money on the table, and says, "I'm out."

Each of the others soon face temptation. While George visits his mother, who is in a semiprivate room, an attractive nurse gives the woman next to her a sponge bath. Elaine takes aerobics class right behind JFK, Jr. Jerry is dating Marla, a woman whom he and George call, accurately if demeaningly, "The Virgin." Jerry drives home after a lot of heavy petting. That night, only Kramer can sleep.

But all three make it through the night, grumpy, but with their dignity. However, Jerry is going across the street to tell the naked woman to pull her damn shades. Kramer begs him not to. Then, while Kramer gives a lascivious play-by-play of her movement around the apartment, Jerry starts singing "The Wheels on the Bus" along with a kids' TV show as a way of trying to distract himself.

Then there were two. Elaine pays up. Her fantasies about John-John led to her downfall. She's meeting him that night in front of Jerry's building. Also that night, Marla is about to let Jerry be her first when he foolishly tells her about the contest. Repulsed by this, she stomps out of the apartment. Jerry gives in and goes to his window to sit and watch the woman across the street. Elaine comes upstairs. JFK, Jr., didn't show up. But George arrives and says he sure did, he just drove off with Marla. Then the three of them go look at the naked woman across the way and see Kramer! He waves at them.

That night, everyone sleeps well at last. Jerry, alone. Elaine, alone. George, alone but hugging his pillow. Kramer, with the naked woman. Marla, no longer what she was, with an off-screen JFK, Jr.

Notes

• One of the new classics, it's the most touching episode of *Seinfeld*. It won the 1992–93 Emmy Award for Outstanding Writing in a Comedy Series (Single Episode) for Larry David.

- Prior to his eponymous series, Jerry Seinfeld's television exposure was limited to stand-up and a small role as a comedy writer on *Benson*.
- Julia Louis-Dreyfus is married to Brad Hall. They were both in the cast of *Saturday Night Live* from 1982–84; she continued through 1985.
- Louis-Dreyfus was also a regular on the short-lived 1988–89 sitcom *Day by Day*, about a yuppie couple who drop out of the rat race to run a day-care center.
- Actor Michael Richards and writer-creator Larry David were both in the ensemble cast of the sketch comedy show *Fridays*, which ran from 1980–82. Richards was part of the infamous *Fridays* sketch in which Andy Kaufman, live on national TV, pretended to just stop in the middle because he thought the sketch was no good.

9

"Edith's Accident"
all in the family

Episode 20
Original air date: November 6, 1971
Original series run: 1971–1979
Series total: 204 episodes

Credits

Open: Starring Carroll O'Connor, Jean Stapleton. Co-starring Rob Reiner, Sally Struthers. Developed and Produced by Norman Lear. End: Directed by John Rich. Teleplay by Michael Ross & Bernie West. Story by Tom &

Helen August. Script Supervisor: Norman Lear. Barnard Hughes as Father Majeski. Based on "Till Death Us Do Part" Created by Johnny Speight. "All in the Family was recorded on tape before a live audience." A Bud Yorkin–Norman Lear–Tandem Production.

Episode Review

Edith arrives home late and is evasive about what took so long. Archie is tenacious in getting the story out of her, and she finally admits that it's because he likes cling peaches. Edith, in her inimitable way, tries to tell the whole story, but keeps talking at length about the cling peaches in heavy syrup until Archie finally explodes and forbids her to say the word "cling peaches" again. Limited by this, she presses on, finally revealing that at the grocery store parking lot her cart got loose and hit a car, "and then this can of 'mmm mmm' in heavy syrup jumped out and made a big dent in the hood! It was a freak accident."

Archie is glad to hear no one was in the

THE BIG TV SATISFACTION FORMULA	
SyndicoDurability	9.1
Comic Valence	9.4
Emotional Resonance	8.6
Writing, Story	9.4
Writing, Characters	9.5
Acting	9.7
Quintessence	9.1
Series Originality	9.2
Episode Originality	7.2
Historical Significance	7
Celebrity	5.1
Gimmickry	6.5
Theme Song	9
Kitsch	6.3
BTVS Ratio	**86.45**

car, so it won't cost him anything, but it turns out that Edith left a note. He's flabbergasted. They discuss ethics, tricky garages, and cheating on your income tax. ("The finest people in the country do that. The government expects you to do that.") The owner of the car, John Majeski, calls on the phone from Smitty's Garage. He's on his way over to collect his "pound of fish."

Sure that he is going to cheat them, Arch calls "Smitty's Garage," posing as an insurance man, and finds out the repairs cost $197. How could a can of peaches cause all that damage? Edith suggests, "Maybe it was the heavy syrup." Archie is determined not to get taken. Maybe if they secretly tape the conversation? Gloria says that would be depriving him of his civil rights, but Archie knows better than that: "He ain't colored; he's Polish!"

Finally, John Majeski arrives—and he's a priest. He sits in Archie's chair. Archie tries to say no but can't quite bring himself to do it. Archie is taken aback, but is *still* sure that there is a scam happening. "This priest ain't kosher." He quizzes the Father about the 23rd Psalm, how does it go . . . in Latin? But Majeski passes every test, and finally tries to collect his $14. Fourteen? We thought it was $197? All of Archie's scheming and distrust is revealed, and Majeski explains that $14 was for the scratch, the rest was for a complete overhaul of the car. But given everything Archie has done and said, he doesn't even want the $14. He leaves, and Archie simmers unhappily. But then the priest returns and agrees to take the money.

Triple

In discussing Majeski, Archie disparages Polish people, as well as Italians and Jews. "Jews only change their last name, but they keep their first names so they'll know each other. Sol Nelson, Izzy Watson . . ." And Mike interjects to complete the triple: "Abe Lincoln." That's when Edith provides the classic quote: "I didn't know Abe Lincoln was Jewish."

Notes

- The long rambling tale of the cling peaches that begins this episode is one of Jean Stapleton's truly brilliant performances. She won three Emmy Awards for her role as Edith.
- The surprise arrival of a priest also occurred in *The Dick Van Dyke Show.* In the episode "A Word a Day" it seems that Richie has gotten in trouble for saying "bad words" at school. Rob and Laura finally track down the source to a classmate, and they are sure that his parents must be completely irresponsible—until the reverend and his wife arrive.
- In 1990 Jean Stapleton costarred with Whoopi Goldberg in a sitcom based on the movie *Bagdad Cafe.* It played that spring and returned in the fall, but didn't last beyond that season.
- During the development of *All in the Family,* one of the working titles for the show was *Justice for All,* and Archie's name would have been Archie Justice.

8

"That's My Boy??"
the dick van dyke show

Episode 64
Original air date: September 25, 1963
Original series run: 1961–1966
Series total: 158 episodes

THE BIG TV SATISFACTION FORMULA

SyndicoDurability	8.1
Comic Valence	8.7
Emotional Resonance	8.8
Writing, Story	9
Writing, Characters	9.1
Acting	9.2
Quintessence	8.1
Series Originality	6.7
Episode Originality	9.4
Historical Significance	9.4
Celebrity	7.9
Gimmickry	9.1
Theme Song	8.4
Kitsch	7.2
BTVS Ratio	**86.54**

Credits

Open: Starring Dick Van Dyke, Rose Marie, Morey Amsterdam, Larry Mathews, and Mary Tyler Moore End: Directed by John Rich. Written by Bill Persky and Sam Denoff. Produced and Created by Carl Reiner. Featuring Jerry Paris, Ann Morgan Guilbert, Amzie Strickland, Greg Morris, Mimi Dillard, and Featuring Richard Deacon as Mel Cooley. Executive Producer: Sheldon Leonard. In Association with Danny Thomas

Episode Review

At a dinner party everyone insists that Rob tell Mel the story of when they brought Richie home from the hospital. Another classic "flashback" episode begins.

We are in the hospital where Rob has fainted, but is recovering. He is solicitous in the extreme, keeping Laura from carrying anything as they gather everything to check out. The hospital is extremely busy, and the nurse keeps getting the Petries in room 203 confused with the Peterses in room 208.

Rob's growing doubts are fed by chance comments. This is where the subtle difference between a good sitcom and a great one is apparent. Rather than leaping to the conclusion in a plot turn *ex machina*, here the double entendres are artfully worked into plausible dialogue. Who does the baby look like? First he looked like Rob, then like Laura, but on the ride home he looked like Ralph Martoni, the fat, short, bald cabdriver. When they notice that the flowers they received as they were leaving the hospital are from "Dick and Betty Carter" and they realize that they don't know anyone by those names, for Rob, it's the last straw.

Rob doesn't want to upset Laura, so he instead confides in Jerry Helper. Jerry is skeptical, but he tries to help. They finally hit on taking another footprint, dyeing the baby's foot blue. Jerry's opinion that the footprints match only confirms Rob's suspicion, because they were given the wrong envelope, and are looking at Baby Boy Peters's paperwork.

Just as Rob is about to call the hospital to set things right, Mr. Peters calls because they discovered another package has been misdelivered. They have some dried figs intended for Laura. Rob stammers a bit, but he finally tells Mr. Peters that he believes their babies have been switched. Peters doesn't seem to believe it, but he promises to come over right away. He is going to bring the package by anyway.

Rob tries to break the news to Laura while they await the Peterses. "Honey, how much do you like that baby?" But she is hearing none of it, finding the whole idea preposterous. All of Rob's mounting evidence means nothing to her. Then the Peterses arrive.

When they step in the door, the live audience provided one of the longest laughs the show ever got, although almost all of it was edited out of the actual televised show. The Peterses are African Americans, played by actors Greg Morris and Mimi Dillard. Rob's take says it all. Why didn't Peters just tell him on the phone? "What, and miss the expression on your face?" he explains. Mrs. Peters also explains that she knows she shouldn't be up and about, but she just couldn't miss the fun.

In the coda, back in the present day, Rob muses that not everything worked out. Jimmy Peters goes to school with Richie, and Jimmy is a much better student. Maybe they did get the wrong one!

Notes

- Dealing with issues of race, even in such a light and politically correct way, made this a daring episode for the series when it was made in 1963. Even though the script was submitted to the NAACP for their approval, the episode came under fire from nervous sponsors and network brass be-

fore it was filmed. Executive producer Sheldon Leonard fought for it, challenging them to let the live audience decide if it was offensive in any way. The huge laugh at the moment of revelation allayed their concerns, and after it aired, the viewer mail response was uniformly positive. Leonard was a groundbreaking television producer in many ways, but he must be especially lauded for his history of representing diverse ethnicities in his shows. He was also the producer of *I, Spy* with Robert Culp and Bill Cosby, which represented the first starring role for a black man since the early days of television.

- "That's My Boy??" was one of Greg Morris's first television appearances. He had previously appeared only on an episode of *Dr. Kildare*. His most noteworthy role is that of Barney Collier, the mechanics and electronics expert of the IMF team on *Mission: Impossible*. In a clear case of art imitating life, when they remade the show *Mission: Impossible* during the 1988 writer's strike, the electronics wizard of the team was now Grant Collier, Barney Collier's son, and he was played by Greg Morris's son, Phil Morris.
- By the way, the entire script of this classic episode is available in the book *The Dick Van Dyke Show: Anatomy of a Classic* by Ginny Weissman and Coyne Steven Sanders. (New York: St. Martin's Press, 1983.)
- Mary Tyler Moore's biggest role before *The Dick Van Dyke Show* was as Sam, the sexy receptionist on *Richard Diamond, Private Detective*, a role in which only her legs

were ever seen on camera. She was also Happy Hotpoint, a dancing pixie in Hotpoint appliance commercials in the 1950s.

- When Dick Van Dyke started making his eponymous series, he left his role in Broadway's *Bye Bye Birdie*, which was taken over by Gene Rayburn.

"A Matter of Life and Death"

the honeymooners

Episode 5
Original air date: October 29, 1955
Original series run: 1955–1956
Series total: 39 episodes in the original syndication package

Credits

Open: Jackie Gleason, Art Carney, Audrey Meadows, and Joyce Randolph. End: Executive Producer: Jack Philbin. Producer: Jack Hurdle. Directed by Frank Satenstein. Writers: Marvin Marx, Walter Stone. Daytime Dresses by Pat Perkins. Entire Production Supervised by Jackie Gleason.

Episode Review

Alice took her mother's dog to the vet; coincidentally, Ralph had a checkup. Ralph reads the letter from the vet, thinking it is from his own doctor. It says he has a rare disease: arterial monochromia. His hair will fall out, his tongue will turn blue, and he has, at best, six months to live.

Ralph is shocked and dismayed, but he wants to protect Alice. He doesn't want her to know. He sits down to write his will. Ralph tells Ed he is going to leave him his bowling shoes. Norton is delighted. "I was just going to go out and buy a new pair of bowling shoes; this couldn't have happened at a better time!"

Ralph realizes he has nothing to leave Alice. Ed suggests he could sell his body to science: "If they pay by the pound, she'll be left a millionaire." Then Ed has a good idea, sell the story to a magazine. Ralph likes it, and starts brainstorming titles. Ed thinks his suggestion is too long, and he boils it down to this pithy headline: "In six months, blimp takes off!"

The magazine editor is dismissive, but his assistant sees possibilities. They like the "selfless" angle—he's just trying to make money for his wife. "We'll play it up big!" They warn him that he'd better not be lying, because that would be fraud, so he shows them his letter as proof. They love it. "When his tongue turns blue, we'll do a color spread!"

Alice sees the article and laughs and laughs, while he stares in horror at her callousness. Then Alice unravels the real story, and Ralph is granted a reprieve. He is going to live! Let's celebrate! He runs into the bedroom to get ready for a night out on the town. From off-stage, we hear a "realization" take noise. He reenters, now aware that he has committed fraud!

He faints, and Alice runs to the bedroom to get smelling salts. Norton enters, finds his buddy, and assumes that he is dead. In a truly classic performance, he manages to be all broken up over Ralph's demise, and to make a series of fat jokes: "By now, Ralphie is up at the pearly gates, and they're probably tearing down part of the fence to let him in."

Ralph is awake now and has to figure a way out. He talks Norton into posing as a doctor who has the only known cure for arterial monochromia. Dr. Norton (wearing a monocle, no less) comes along to the offices of *American Weekly*, where Ralph returns the check. However, the editor, Mr. Gersh, asks Dr. Norton a few questions and finds him out. Mr. Gersh still thinks only Norton is the fraud, "giving false hope to this sick man!" So Ralph is left with no option but to tell the real story. It turns out the editor agrees not to press charges if they can use the actual story. It will be even more popular than the first one.

Notes

- Toward the beginning of the episode, Ralph has a very funny line that doesn't get any laugh at all from the audience. He's talking about his doctor. "A very fine doctor. Did you hear what he did for Callahan the plumber? He kept him alive until his wife caught up with the insurance payments. A fine doctor." Perhaps it was too dark for that era's audience.

- Gleason claimed to have a photographic memory, and thus hardly rehearsed at all; however, the show is full of moments where cues are missed and ad libs added in. He had a tendency to improvise on stage, and everyone just had to follow him until he returned to book. Audrey Meadows was the cast member who always knew the lines, and she would sometimes "direct traffic," using subtle cues to point the boys in the right direction.

- *The Honeymooners* has attracted a loyal cult following over the years. There has been an active fan club, RALPH (the Royal Association for the Longevity and Preservation of *The Honeymooners*) and Donna McCrohan's 1978 book *The Honeymooners' Companion* is one of the best-selling television show books of all time.

- In 2000, for a series of short vignettes on TV Land, Art Carney reprised his Ed Norton role for the first time in more than twenty-five years. In them, he provided "Ed-Vice"—little tidbits to help viewers better enjoy television, and *The Honeymooners*.

6

"Reverend Jim: A Space Odyssey"

taxi

Episode 27
Original air date: September 25, 1979
Original series run: 1978–1983
Series total: 114 episodes

Credits

Open: Judd Hirsch Also Starring Jeff Conaway, Danny De Vito, Marilu Henner, Tony Danza, and Andy Kaufman as Latka Gravas. Created by James L. Brooks, Stan Daniels, David Davis, and Ed Weinberger. Produced by Glen Charles & Les Charles. Written by Glen Charles & Les Charles. Directed by James Burrows. End: Executive Producers James L. Brooks, Stan Daniels and Ed Weinberger. Special Guest Star Christopher Lloyd as Reverend Jim, with T. J. Castranova . . . Bartender. J. Alan Thomas . . . Jeff. Associate Producer: Richard Sakai. Executive Script Consultant: Barry Kemp. Story Editors: Ian Praiser, Howard Gewirtz. Program Consultant: Ken Estin. Taxis provided by Checker Motor Co. Executive Consultant: James L. Brooks. Executive in Charge of Production: John Charles Walters Productions: Ronald E. Frazier.

Episode Review

Tommy the bartender gets a rare bit of dialogue, the punch line even! Reverend Jim walks up and asks, "When are you going to clean those bathrooms?" Tommy replies, "You were in the kitchen." The gang asks Jim to join them at the table, remembering him from when he officiated at Latka's wedding.

He talks about his past, and his experimentation in the sixties. They get to talking about what he should do with himself, since he has no skills or experience. He suggests, "I've often thought I would make a good pharmacist," but they can see a cabdriver in him. They bring him back to the garage where the first test will be getting Louie to hire him. On that front, Jim takes matters into his own hands, slipping the dispatcher "a mild sedative." Moments later, a loosey-goosey Louie is singing old show tunes and hiring anybody who wants to work.

The next hurdle is the DMV, where he will have to pass the written test. The application asks some tough questions. "Ever experienced loss of consciousness, hallucinations, dizzy spells, convulsive disorders, fainting, or loss of memory?" Jim: "Hasn't everybody?" Bobby moves on: "Mental illness or narcotic addiction?" Jim: "That's a tough choice." But they make it through the application and are ready for the test. Jim: "I thought that was the test!"

The reverend sits down with his test, while his comrades stand nearby. Temptation is too much. He whispers the first question, looking for a little help: "What does a yellow light mean?" Bobby answers sotto voce: "Slow down." This sequence is one of the true classics in all of sitcom history, a truly sublime combination of character and performance. Jim takes Bobby literally and repeats the question more slowly. "What . . . does . . . a . . . yellow . . . light . . . mean?" Bobby answers again: "Slow down." Four times he asks, each time slower than the last.

Somehow, he passes. And at the garage Alex climbs in the back of his cab to take the very first ride. Jim throws it into gear and accidentally goes in reverse, smashing the cab through the wall of the garage.

Triple

When the gang considers the possibilities for their new friend Jim, they engage in a call-and-response triple led by Reiger:

ALEX: What kind of training could he possibly have?

THE REST: None.

ALEX: What kind of skill could he possibly have?

THE REST: None

ALEX: What kind of job could we possibly get him?

THE REST: Cabdriver.

Notes

• According to director James Burrows, he instructed the actors to just keep going with the yellow light scene. They knew it would be good, but nobody had any idea what magic would come from Christopher Lloyd's incredible combination of innocence, persistence, and exasperation as he played it out. You can see that Tony Danza and Marilu Henner are both trying very hard not to laugh themselves during the scene.

• In another episode, Reverend Jim reveals that "Ignatowski" was not his original surname. He was born into a well-to-do Massachusetts family named Caldwell. He took the new name under the mistaken impression that it was "star child" spelled backward.

• The jacket that Reverend Jim wore throughout the series had been found discarded in the bushes near Laurel Canyon in Los Angeles, a well-known hangout for real hippies.

5

"Good-bye, Farewell and Amen"

m*a*s*h

Episode 251
Original air date: February 28, 1983
Original series run: 1972–1983
Series total: 251 episodes

Credits

Open: Alan Alda, Mike Farrell, Harry Morgan, Loretta Swit, David Ogden Stiers, Jamie Farr, William Christopher. Guest Starring, Allan Arbus, G. W. Bailey, Rosalind Chao. Executive Producer:

Burt Metcalfe. Written by Alan Alda, Burt Metcalfe, John Rappaport, Dan Wilcox & Thad Mumford, Elias Davis & David Pollack, Karen Hall. Directed by Alan Alda. End: Producers: Thad Mumford, Dan Wilcox. Executive Story Consultant: Karen Hall. John Shearn . . . as the Chopper Pilot. Kellye Nakahara . . . as Nurse Kellye. Jeff Maxwell . . . as Igor. Lang Yun . . . as the Woman on the Bus. Jon Van Ness . . . as "Truman." Kevin Scannell . . . as "MacArthur." Arthur Song . . . Korean Man. Judy Farrell . . . Nurse Able. Jan Jorden . . . Nurse Baker. Enid Kent . . . Nurse Bigelow. Jun Kim . . . Woman with Shawl. Scott Lincoln . . . G.I. Herb L. Mitchell . . . 1st M.P. Blake Clark . . . 2nd M.P. David Orr . . . Soldier. Mark Casella . . . Jeep Driver. John Otrin . . . Ambulance Driver. Dennis Flood . . . Corpsman. Nurses: Shari Saba, Jo Ann Thompson, Brigitte Chandler, Gwen Farrell, Natasha Bauman, Jennifer Davis. Corpsmen: Roy Goldman, Dennis Troy, Bill Snider. Chinese Musicians: Laurence Soong, Byron Jeong, Jen-Chia Chang, Jim Lau, Frank Zi-Li Peng. Developed for Television by Larry Gelbart.

THE BIG TV SATISFACTION FORMULA	
SyndicoDurability	8.7
Comic Valence	9.2
Emotional Resonance	10
Writing, Story	9.8
Writing, Characters	9.8
Acting	9.6
Quintessence	8.1
Series Originality	8.8
Episode Originality	9.2
Historical Significance	9.9
Celebrity	5.5
Gimmickry	9.4
Theme Song	8.6
Kitsch	5
BTVS Ratio	**87.56**

Episode Review

A number of stories were interwoven throughout this two-and-a-half-hour epic. There are reports that peace talks seem to be nearing a conclusion, that the war may soon be over. Hawkeye is in therapy, incarcerated at the psychiatric hospital because he has apparently had a sort of breakdown. Throughout the episode, he argues with Dr. Sidney Freedman, the shrink, about his fitness to rejoin his comrades. He is pushed to recall an incident on a bus whose details he has repressed. Each time he tells the story to the doctor, new details emerge, until finally, cathartically, he tells the gruesome truth. (We won't say more than that, so that readers who haven't seen the episode can experience it themselves.)

Margaret and Charles's story concerns their plans on returning to the States. She is able to help him get an important post he covets, but he resents her for helping. Charles also meets five refugee musicians. He teaches them to play Mozart, and is deeply satisfied with the experience. He has finally opened up and formed a human bond through music with these foreign people whom he has been sewing back together.

Klinger is helping Sun Li look for family members who are lost. Their romance blossoms, and he proposes to her, giving her a wedding dress from his early days of cross-dressing. She cannot accept until she finds her family.

B. J. Hunnicut gets his discharge, and he's not waiting for the war to end. He's trying to get home in time for his daughter's second birthday. But it's not that easy. Potter still needs a surgeon, so B. J. has to find one for him. He does, and he manages to take off in a helicopter just as his travel orders have been rescinded. Potter actually gets that news in time, but he pretends he didn't hear for long enough to let B. J. get away.

An abandoned tank is sitting in the middle of the M*A*S*H encampment, making them a target for attacks, but they can't get the army to move it, for the usual bureaucratic reasons. When Pierce returns from the hospital to active duty, the first thing he does is get in the tank and drive it far from their encampment. As always, army protocol won't prevent him from doing the logical, courageous, and humane thing.

Father Mulcahy has lost his hearing from an explosion, but he is pretending that he hasn't because of his deeply felt responsibility to the orphanage.

The "new surgeon" returns. It's Hunnicutt. Another snafu has brought him back to active duty. They try to make him feel a little better by having a birthday party for a little Korean girl with the same birthday. (But not really, since there are no birth records. They just found a two-year-old and made it her day.)

Winchester's musicians get trucked away, playing Mozart as they go. The P.A. announcement of all the P.A. announcements is finally made: the truce is being signed. "The war is over." And, just then, joy and tragedy get slammed together as they so often do on M*A*S*H, and the wounded arrive by the busload.

Winchester is doing triage, and there is one of his musicians. The rest are dead. He is moved. He returns to his bunk and listens to his Mozart record. Then he smashes the record in anger. As he later says: "Music was once a refuge, and would now forever be a reminder."

Pierce is given an eight-year-old patient. Potter offers to switch, but Pierce is back from the brink: "No, I got it." At that, Sidney leaves; his work is done. The news of the cease-fire is broadcast. The guns go silent. Then the work of the O.R. quickly fills the silence.

Later they gather for what amounts to a farewell dinner. Potter suggests they each talk about their future plans. Klinger announces he's getting married to Sun Li. They have a wedding the next day (the first of two ceremonies they will have) presided over by Father Mulcahy. Houlihan catches the bouquet.

All that's left is for Pierce and B. J. to say good-bye, but that's not so easy for B. J. The two have been back and forth, with many misunderstandings about this leave-taking. But in the final moment as Pierce takes off in his helicopter, and B. J. rides off on his motorcycle, Pierce sees that his companion has spelled out "good-bye" in huge letters that he can see from the air.

Notes

- While in some ways, this movie-length episode was obviously atypical of the show, it was also true to everything that we had come to expect from M*A*S*H. There was humor, both light and darkly satirical; there was every human drama; and then there was drama in the true horrors of war. Though it may seem a bit unfair to compare this epic drama with the ordinary half-hour sitcoms, the nature of the BTVS ratio is such that it can provide a measure of objectivity to a seemingly incomparable episode.

- This episode first aired February 28, 1983. It earned a 60.3 rating with a 77 share. That represented 107 million viewers, the largest audience for a single program in TV history.
- *Maude, The Waltons, The Bob Newhart Show* and *M*A*S*H* all premiered in the same week in 1972 on CBS.
- Larry Gelbart, the original creator of the TV series (based on the Robert Altman film; which was in turn based on a doctor's book about his experiences in Korea) was a veteran comedy writer and playwright. He worked in radio and early television for such performers as Jack Paar, Bob Hope, and Art Carney. He wrote the play *A Funny Thing Happened on the Way to the Forum*.

4

"The Last Newhart"
newhart

Episode 184
Original air date: May 21, 1990
Original series run: 1982–1990
Series total: 184 episodes

Credits

Open: Starring Bob Newhart. Also Starring Mary Frann, Peter Scolari with Julia Duffy as Stephanie, and Tom Poston as George. Theme by Henry Mancini. Created by Barry Kemp. Co-Executive Producer: Bob Bendetson. Produced by Stephen C. Grossman. Developed by Sheldon Bull. Written by Mark Egan & Mark Solomon & Bob Bendetson. Directed by Dick Martin. End: Executive Producers: Mark Egan & Mark Solomon. Also Starring William Sanderson as Larry. Tony Papenfuss as Darryl #1. John Volstad as Darryl #2. Guest Starring Thomas Hill . . . Jim. William Lanteau . . . Chester. Kathy Kinney . . . Miss Goodard. David Pressman . . . Mr. Rusnick. Gedde Watanabe . . . Mr. Tagadachi. Sab Shimono . . . Sunatra. Shuko Akune . . . Sedaka. Frank Kopyc . . . Ed. Rodney Kageyama . . . Male Guest. Christie Mellor . . . Rhonda. Nada Despotovich . . . Zora. Lisa Kudrow . . . Sada. Co-starring Candy Hutson . . . Baby Stephanie. Executive Script Consultant: Brad Isaacs. Story Editor: Nell Scovell. Story Editors: Bill Fuller & Jim Pond.

Episode Review

A bizarre final chapter in the strange tale of Bob's life in Vermont, and an ending that immediately became a television legend.

Bob is giving a speech, and everyone

THE BIG TV SATISFACTION FORMULA	
SyndicoDurability	7.5
Comic Valence	9.1
Emotional Resonance	9
Writing, Story	9.5
Writing, Characters	9.2
Acting	8.7
Quintessence	9.2
Series Originality	7.5
Episode Originality	9.8
Historical Significance	9.8
Celebrity	8.1
Gimmickry	10
Theme Song	7
Kitsch	6.8
BTVS Ratio	**87.90**

mouths the words since he always gives the same speech. But all his pretty talk can't save the town, because Japanese investors have arrived to buy it all up and turn it into a golf course. Bob tries to lead the resistance, but no one will join him. After all, they're all going to get rich. It's capitalism at work, and that's the principle upon which America was built!

"Do you want to destroy America, Dick?" asks Chester.

"Not . . . not . . . if you're going to get, get, that upset," stutters Bob.

The episode becomes a grand leave-taking (fittingly), and Michael and Stephanie say an emotional farewell, including Michael's always-alluring alliteration. "Pray, may I nuzzle your napes that I might remember your scent?" There is also a strange parody of *Fiddler on the Roof* happening, but you have to see it to believe it.

Even George is taking the money and leaving. Bob and Joanna are surprised. They didn't know he owned any land, but he does: "I bought a few acres years ago, I was going to build Utley-land, an amusement park for handymen."

Time passes. Five years have gone by. Bob's inn is still in business, although surrounded by the golf course. The episode then veers into a weird and politically incorrect series of jokes about Japanese customs, accents, and names. The new maid is "Sedaka," the new handyman "Sunatra." (He attempts to commit hari-kari when he is turned down for a job with the golf corporation.) Joanna has embraced both Japanese traditions and golf, and is dressed in full geisha attire. Bob is a defeated man,

and he is finally ready to sell, but now it's too late. They have no interest.

Then, the old gang returns! Group by group, they all return. Apparently, they all planned a reunion when they left. Michael and Stephanie have a five-year-old who is the spitting image of Steph. Larry, Darryl, and Darryl are now married to three chatterboxes with Long Island accents. They blather on and on until finally Darryl and Darryl have stood all they could stand and they won't stand no more. After 183 episodes of total silence, they turn to their wives and yell: "Quiet!!" It doesn't take the live audience long to realize the momentous nature of this event.

The return of the natives is turning the inn into total chaos. Bob can't take it anymore. "I've got to get out of this madhouse," he yells. "You're all crazy." And as he steps out of the front door, in a wild slow-motion scene, he is struck on the head by an errant golf ball. He collapses in a heap and all goes dark.

Then comes the moment that made this show.

The light comes on in a strangely familiar bedroom. Bob says "Honey, wake up. You won't believe the dream I had."

A very sleepy Emily rouses herself, and we realize that *Newhart* was nothing but a long feverish nightmare in the mind of Dr. Bob Hartley. "Nothing made sense in this place. The maid was an heiress. Her husband spoke in alliteration."

Emily listens patiently and eventually tells him to go back to sleep. He does, but offers one last comment to his wife: "You really should wear more sweaters."

Notes

- Under the final credits we hear the theme song to *The Bob Newhart Show*, not the one from *Newhart*.
- Also under credits we see the backstage footage of that final shoot. Bob and cast are shown saying farewell to the audience and cutting a cake in celebration of the last episode. The MTM cat of the production slate, which was often used for various little jokes, delivers a nice echo in honor of this final episode. Instead of meowing, it yells: "Quiet!"
- Yes, Lisa Kudrow plays Darryl's wife, and she does a fine job as a screechy bimbo.
- This was the only episode to score a perfect 10 in the underappreciated Gimmickry category. Calling such a sublime twist a "gimmick" hardly seems fair. In any case, here are the other episodes from the BTVS Top 100 that scored high in this category.

Newhart, "The Last Newhart"	10
Sanford and Son, "Steinberg and Son"	9.9
The Patty Duke Show, "Perfect Hostess"	9.9
The Simpsons, "Krusty Gets Kancelled"	9.8
Murphy Brown, "TV or Not TV?"	9.8
The Dick Van Dyke Show, "It May Look Like a Walnut"	9.8
Night Court, "A Day in the Life"	9.8

3

"The Producer"
gilligan's island

Episode 72
Original air date: October 3, 1966
Original series run: 1964–1967
Series total: 98 episodes

Credits

Open: Starring Bob Denver, Alan Hale. Also starring Jim Backus as Thurston Howell III, Natalie Schaeffer, and also starring Tina Louise as Ginger, with Russell Johnson, Dawn Wells. Created and Produced by Sherwood Schwartz. Special Guest Star: Phil Silvers. Written by Gerald Gardner and Dee Caruso. Directed by Ida Lupino, George M. Cahan. End: Special Guest Star: Phil Silvers. Script Consultant: David P. Harmon. Music by Morton Stevens.

THE BIG TV SATISFACTION FORMULA	
SyndicoDurability	9.8
Comic Valence	9.6
Emotional Resonance	8.6
Writing, Story	9.4
Writing, Characters	8.9
Acting	9.2
Quintessence	9.1
Series Originality	8.9
Episode Originality	9.7
Historical Significance	8.1
Celebrity	9.3
Gimmickry	9.6
Theme Song	9.9
Kitsch	9.8
BTVS Ratio	**88.40**

Episode Review

A plane has been spotted. Perhaps this is going to be the episode they get rescued! Ginger is listening wishfully to the radio reports that tell that Harold Hecuba is circling the globe in his personal plane in search of new talent for his forthcoming musical extravaganza, tentatively entitled *Musical Extravaganza*.

The plane has gone down, and indeed it is Hecuba; he not only survives but arrives in the lagoon on an extravagant rescue craft. The Skipper and Gilligan meet him hopefully, but he is disdainful. "What are ya, some sort of Peace Corps dropouts?"

Harold Hecuba starts to give orders, and the Skipper protests, until "HH" points out that some of his "flunkies" are following behind him and if they want to be rescued, they had better play by his rules. The Howells are made into his servants.

Ginger, of course, sees her opportunity and takes it by serving as his waitress at dinner. Ginger does an earthy Italian peasant, then Marilyn Monroe—"I just wanted to show you what a versatile actress I am"—but she is cruelly rebuffed. "With that phony dialect, and that overacting! In a Harold Hecuba production! Ha!"

Ginger is crying, disconsolate. She won't go back to Hollywood; in fact, she is refusing to leave the island. As the Professor says: "I'm afraid this is serious. When Harold Hecuba laughed at her, she became emotionally disturbed and psychologically maladjusted." Gilligan adds: "Not only that, she's upset."

But Gilligan has a swell idea. To put on a musical to show off Ginger's talents for old "HH." They scramble through their library in search of a suitable text: *Four Masted Schooners I Have Known* (The Skipper's), *Integrated Calculus*, by Zimmerman (The Professor's), and *A Million Ways to Make a Million* (Mr. Howell). At last they come upon a copy of *Hamlet!* We could put it to music!

They rehearse at night, to hide their practice sessions from the demanding Hecuba. At dress rehearsal we finally see why Gilligan always wears the same shirt. A large number of clothes have been sewn together to make a nearly full-scale stage curtain for the island's outdoor theater.

The musical *Hamlet!* is a work of profound genius. As they perform it, Hecuba is awakened and watches, hidden in the bushes. They perform three musical numbers, each more brilliant than the last.

"Hamlet's Song" is performed by Gilligan as Hamlet, with Mr. Howell as Claudius and Lovey as Gertrude. It sets the oft-quoted "To be or not to be" soliloquy to music. "Ophelia's Song" is then performed by Ginger as Ophelia. She reprises the whole story of the play. Finally, the Skipper sings "Polonius's Song" to Mary Ann/Laertes. He echoes Shakespeare's words: "Neither a borrower nor a lender be" and "to thine own self be true."

The entire group comes on stage to sing this entire refrain, and at that HH comes out of the bushes . . . and takes over the production. Now it will be Harold Hecuba's *Hamlet*. After all, "up to now there's really been something rotten in Denmark!" After briefly directing them, Harold Hecuba takes over all the roles . . . "to show you how to do this thing right." He is Hamlet, then Ophelia, then Polonius, and then collapses.

The next morning, he is gone. He left without them, it turns out, so that he could take all the credit for the "greatest idea he's ever had"—a musical of *Hamlet*!

Triple

Jim Backus is one of the true professionals of comic acting, and he turns two great moments in the episode (aside from his fine contributions to the musical itself). One is a perfect "realization" take. He has been taking orders from Hecuba, and he starts serving drinks to the Skipper, the Professor, and Gilligan until they ask him why he is serving them. He looks up and realizes with horror that he has become accustomed to serving others!

Earlier he turns in a nifty triple with an assist from the Skipper. When he first meets Hecuba he is taken aback: "What nerve . . . What gall . . ." He is briefly interrupted by the Skipper: "Mr. Howell, he's going to get us off the island." And he continues without missing a beat . . . "What can I do for you?"

Notes

- This is an incredible episode that brings together a disparate group of talents to create a synergy that is larger than any of them. Yes, *Gilligan's Island* is a fine show. Ida Lupino a talented director. Phil Silvers an incomparable comic actor. William Shakespeare a fine playwright. And Bizet? The guy could write music. But put them all together? Wow. The songs are absolute dynamite. Frankly, if anyone had the guts to mount this pro-

duction on Broadway . . . Well, the Bard would be box office one more time.
- The tunes to the songs are taken uncredited from Bizet's famed French opera *Carmen*. Polonius's advice is to the tune of "The Toreador's Song"; Hamlet's song is "The Habanera."
- Maria Callas, the opera singer whose performance as Carmen is most legendary, sang her first opera in French (most of the canon is in Italian, of course) in 1958. That opera? The little-known work by Ambroise Thomas: *Hamlet*. Coincidence? Perhaps.
- This episode uses the "the Professor and Mary Ann" version of the theme song, as opposed to the "and the rest" version.
- After a Hollywood film-acting career, Ida Lupino turned in numerous wonderful guest-starring turns on television. She was Dr. Cassandra on *Batman*, spent two episodes flirting with Mr. French on *Family Affair*, and played a movie star lost in her past in a *Twilight Zone* episode called "16 MM Shrine." She also became a producer and director, counting among her television directing credits episodes of *The Ghost and Mrs. Muir* and *Alfred Hitchcock Presents*. George M. Cohan was the noted Broadway star, but George M. Cahan appears to be a real person, and not some sort of in joke about the "musical" nature of this episode.
- There are many fine theme songs, but none ranked higher than that of *Gilligan's Island*. Here are the top-ranking themes from among the BTVS Top 100 series.

Gilligan's Island	9.9
The Patty Duke Show	9.9

The Brady Bunch	9.9
The Beverly Hillbillies	9.8
Green Acres	9.7
The Flintstones	9.7
Mister Ed	9.7
The Addams Family	9.5
The Jeffersons	9.4

2

"Coast to Coast Big Mouth"

the dick van dyke show

Episode 128
Original air date: September 15, 1965
Original series run: 1961–1966
Series total: 158 episodes

Credits

Opening: Starring Dick Van Dyke, Rose Marie, Morey Amsterdam, Larry Mathews, and Mary Tyler Moore. End: Directed by Jerry Paris. Written by Bill Persky and Sam Denoff. Produced and Created by Carl Reiner. Featuring Richard Deacon as Mel Cooley, Ann Morgan Guilbert, Dick Curtis as Johnny Patrick, and Carl Reiner as Alan Brady. Executive Producer Sheldon Leonard. In Association with Danny Thomas.

Episode Review

Millie and Laura are in the studio audience of "Pay as You Go" when Millie is selected as the next contestant. Although she had just been griping that she would never get picked, she is now too nervous to go on. Johnny Patrick, the grinning high-energy

THE BIG TV SATISFACTION FORMULA	
SyndicoDurability	8.1
Comic Valence	9.6
Emotional Resonance	9.3
Writing, Story	9.4
Writing, Characters	9.6
Acting	9.6
Quintessence	8.6
Series Originality	6.7
Episode Originality	8.9
Historical Significance	7.1
Celebrity	8.2
Gimmickry	9
Theme Song	8.4
Kitsch	6.2
BTVS Ratio	**88.44**

emcee, and Millie talk Laura into going in her stead.

In Alan Brady's office, Alan, in a rare appearance, is holding court with his writers and Mel. Alan is constantly telling Mel to shut up, even when Mel picks up a phone and says "hello." They are getting ready to leave for a business lunch when Richie calls Rob to give him the message that Mommy is going to be on TV. The group at the office talk about what a tough interviewer Patrick is, and how he confuses people and gets them to say things they don't mean; Alan suggests they stay and see what he does to Laura.

As they watch, Laura is interviewed. Patrick finds out that her husband works for *The Alan Brady Show* and asks, among other tricky questions, "Is the show any funnier than it used to be?" But Laura manages to get through it all without saying anything embarrassing, lavishing praise on the show and on Alan Brady. Rob and the rest head out for lunch. Now, with no one from the office watching, Laura plays the game; afterward Patrick tricks her into revealing—on national TV!—the well-kept secret that Alan Brady wears a toupee and is, in fact, bald.

When Rob arrives home, Laura realizes he didn't see the whole show. She stutters her way through a retelling of what happened. It's a brilliant comic performance by Mary Tyler Moore, as her voice grows increasingly quivery, and she can't even find the words to describe the events and the prizes she has won, resorting to a mime of a rotisserie, and a sound effect to indicate a vacuum cleaner.

Rob can't believe it, and there follows a classic warm but funny, real but clever, Rob and Laura conversation. In it, among other things, Rob accidentally reveals to Laura that Alan Brady also had a nose job, so he realizes how easy it is to let something slip. The next day Rob goes to work to await his doom. He talks to Mel about the impending . . . whatever it will be. Sally arrives with the news that she saw Laura get on the elevator. "The elevator!" blurts Rob, and Sally answers, "Yeah, the elevator: You know, that little room in the lobby that goes up and down?" Rob realizes she's on her way to Alan, and he dashes off to intervene.

Alan is in his office with Mel, bemoaning the disaster, with all his toupees gathered around him at his desk. What follows is one of the most memorable scenes in the series. She tries to apologize and explain what happened to Alan, and she also tries to convince him that she has always thought that he looked better without a wig on. He mostly lambastes her for her big fat mouth. At one point, he asks Laura what he is supposed to do with all these toupees; she haltingly suggests, "There must be some needy bald people."

However, in a rare moment of humanity, Alan Brady decides to forgive Laura and Rob. It seems that the weight of keeping his secret had been burdening him for year, plus the publicity that was swirling around the revelation was great for Alan's career. And besides that, his wife and some other people had also been encouraging him to give up the toupees. Of course, just when everything seems settled, Laura blurts out the newly acquired information from Rob. "At least I didn't tell them about your nose!" Alan chases them out of the office waving his cane.

Notes

- Great shows have appealing characters, good writing, and compelling stories; but they also have great little moments. Small touches that give them true "rewatchability." There is just such a moment in this episode. It happens while the office gang is watching Laura on the game show. Alan Brady suddenly notices that Mel has been sitting and watching in *his* chair: "What are you doing in my chair?" Mel answers with genuine dumbfoundedness, "I don't know." It's an elegant and very funny piece of timing by the great character actor, Richard Deacon.

- Carl Reiner's acting—honed in the glory days with *Your Show of Shows*—has been overshadowed by his writing over the years, but he turned in many fine performances on *The Dick Van Dyke Show*. In addition to Alan Brady, he was also the artist Serge Carpetna who painted

Laura's nude portrait in the episode "October Eve" and he played a pretentious literati Yale Sampson in the episode "I'm No Henry Walden."

- Four different opening sequences are used on *The Dick Van Dyke Show*. In the first season a series of still photographs are used. In later seasons Rob comes home from work and either flips over the ottoman, walks around the ottoman smoothly, or walks around the ottoman but then catches his toe on the rug. The last is used in this particular episode.

1

"Chuckles Bites the Dust"

mary tyler moore

Episode 127
Original air date: October 25, 1975
Original series run: 1970–1977
Series total: 168 episodes

Credits

Open: Mary Tyler Moore. Created by James L. Brooks and Allan Burns. Written by David Lloyd. Directed by Joan Darling. End: Executive Producers: Allan Burns and James L. Brooks. Creative Consultant: David Lloyd. Executive Story Editor: Bob Ellison. Produced by Ed Weinberger and Stan Daniels. Co-starring Edward Asner as Lou Grant. Gavin MacLeod as Murray. Ted Knight as Ted Baxter, with Georgia Engel as Georgette Franklin, and Betty White as Sue Ann Nivens. Guest Star: John Harkins as Reverend Burns.

THE BIG TV SATISFACTION FORMULA	
SyndicoDurability	8.8
Comic Valence	9.7
Emotional Resonance	9.2
Writing, Story	9.2
Writing, Characters	9.3
Acting	9.8
Quintessence	7.8
Series Originality	6.8
Episode Originality	9.2
Historical Significance	8.5
Celebrity	6.5
Gimmickry	9.2
Theme Song	9.2
Kitsch	7.8
BTVS Ratio	**88.46**

Episode Review

Ted has been asked to be grand marshal of the circus parade, but Lou won't let him because it's undignified. Later, at Mary's apartment, Ted says that he is going to resign. He doesn't feel appreciated or respected. He's treated like a child! Mary defends Lou. She says it's not true, Lou does respect Ted and he knows that he's an adult. Then Ted pouts and whines, "Then why won't he let me go the circus!"

The day of the parade has arrived Chuckles the Clown has been chosen to take over for Ted. Lou comes into the newsroom in a haze of shock and consternation. He blurts, "Someone we all know is dead!" Then he says, "I won't tell you now; I don't want to upset you." But, of course, they demand to know, and the story comes out. Chuckles the Clown, the WJM children's show host, was killed by a rogue elephant at the parade. Chuckles was dressed as Peter Peanut, and the elephant tried to shell him.

Ted is on the air, and during the next break, Lou goes in and insists that Ted give the news of Chuckles's death and say something in the nature of a eulogy. Ted protests he hardly knew the man, but he does his best. Naturally, his announcement is a classic Ted Baxter composition. He somberly quotes Chuckles's wise words. "A little song, a little dance, a little seltzer down your pants."

Later Lou and Murray can't help themselves; they make jokes about the ridiculous nature of Chuckles's demise. Mary is appalled and chastises them. However, when the actual funeral arrives, Mary is overcome by giggles at the reverend's eulogy. It's an incredible piece of acting, as she fights herself, swallows the laughs, tries to compose herself. A truly classic scene.

Notes

- There it is, the single best sitcom episode ever created. It has it all, from a long beloved history in syndication down to a great gimmick. The writing was sublime; the acting even better. The episode balanced the talents of every cast member, and the material was deeply steeped in the characters that they had created for us every Saturday night. Lou Grant's breathless entrance with the news was a masterpiece of emotion and timing. Ted Baxter's eulogy was both idiotic and sincere. We've already canonized Mary's final scene.
- Chuckles is not seen in this episode at all, but he did appear in a handful of earlier episodes, played by Richard Schaal. He was later Dr. Sandler on the show *Trapper John, M.D.* He was also Valerie Harper's real-life husband for a time.

- John Harkins, who turns in a memorable performance presiding over the funeral, was a regular on a short-lived 1993 sitcom called *The Boys*. It was the story of a hip young writer who takes to hanging out and playing poker with the three cynical old men next door. Chris Meloni was the lead; the three men were played by Ned Beatty, John Harkins, and Richard Venture.
- In the 1996 book *Nick at Nite's Classic TV Companion*, we inadvertently gave directorial credit to Jay Sandrich, a frequent director of *Mary Tyler Moore* episodes. As noted correctly above, the director of this episode was Joan Darling.

the BTVS top 100

Here they are again, all in one place, for those wishing to take a look at the broad overview.

RANK	EPISODE	BTVS RATIO
1	*Mary Tyler Moore* "Chuckles Bites the Dust"	88.46
2	*The Dick Van Dyke Shaw,* "Coast to Coast Big Mouth"	88.44
3	*Gilligan's Island,* "The Producer"	88.40
4	*Newhart,* "The Last Newhart"	87.90
5	*M*A*S*H,* "Good-bye, Farewell and Amen"	87.56
6	*Taxi,* "Reverend Jim: A Space Odyssey"	87.01
7	*The Honeymooners,* "A Matter of Life and Death"	86.75
8	*The Dick Van Dyke Show,* "That's My Boy??"	86.54
9	*All in the Family,* "Edith's Accident"	86.45
10	*Seinfeld,* "The Contest"	86.40
11	*Make Room for Daddy,* "Danny Meets Andy Griffith"	86.10
12	*Car 54, Where Are You?,* "How Smart Can You Get?"	86.03
13	*All in the Family,* "Sammy's Visit"	86.01
14	*The Odd Couple,* "Password"	85.92

RANK	EPISODE	BTVS RATIO
15	*The Beverly Hillbillies*, "The Giant Jackrabbit"	85.90
16	*Mary Hartman, Mary Hartman*, from "Fernwood Flasher" sequence	85.83
17	*Batman*, "The Sandman Cometh . . ." and ". . . The Catwoman Goeth"	85.82
18	*McHale's Navy*, "PT 73, Where Are You?"	85.78
19	*Taxi*, "Latka the Playboy"	85.73
20	*The Jack Benny Program*, "The Income Tax Show"	85.71
21	*Ellen*, "The Puppy Episode"	85.48
22	*Mary Tyler Moore*, "The Lars Affair"	85.46
23	*The Phil Silvers Show*, "The Eating Contest"	85.38
24	*Cheers*, "I Do, Adieu"	85.12
25	*Leave It to Beaver*, "Captain Jack"	84.92
26	*I Love Lucy*, "Lucy Does a TV Commercial"	84.81
27	*Car 54, Where Are You?*, "Catch Me on the Paar Show"	84.57
28	*The Andy Griffith Show*, "Man in a Hurry"	84.49
29	*Batman*, "The Purr-Fect Crime" and "Better Luck Next Time"	84.46
30	*The Phil Silvers Show*, "Hillbilly Whiz"	84.32
31	*All in the Family*, "The Bonkers and the Swingers"	84.13
32	*The Honeymooners*, "The Golfer"	83.99
33	*Mary Tyler Moore*, "Ted Baxter's Famous Broadcasters' School"	83.82
34	*The Simpsons*, "The Crepes of Wrath"	83.81
35	*Bewitched*, "Divided, He Falls"	83.79
36	*The Many Loves of Dobie Gillis*, "Best Dressed Man"	83.76
37	*The Cosby Show*, "A Shirt Story"	83.68
38	*The Addams Family*, "Amnesia in the Addams Family"	83.61
39	*Murphy Brown*, "TV or Not TV?"	83.57

RANK	EPISODE	BTVS RATIO
40	*That Girl*, "This Little Piggy Had a Ball"	83.53
41	*The Donna Reed Show*, "The Foundling"	83.25
42	*The Patty Duke Show*, "Perfect Hostess"	83.19
43	*My Little Margie*, "Margie and the Shah"	83.15
44	*The Brady Bunch*, "Her Sister's Shadow"	82.87
45	*The Many Loves of Dobie Gillis*, "The Fist Fighter"	82.85
46	*Get Smart*, "When the Good Fellows Get Together"	82.84
47	*Cheers*, "Sam's Women"	82.82
48	*Gidget*, "Ego-a-go-go"	82.78
49	*Maude*, "Vivian's First Funeral"	82.58
50	*Laverne & Shirley*, "The Dating Game"	82.56
51	*The Odd Couple*, "Fat Farm"	82.18
52	*The Simpsons*, "Krusty Gets Kancelled"	82.10
53	*WKRP in Cincinnati*, "Turkeys Away"	81.84
54	*Sanford and Son*, "Steinberg and Son"	81.80
55	*Night Court*, "A Day in the Life"	81.72
56	*I Love Lucy*, "Job Switching"	81.71
57	*The Andy Griffith Show*, "Barney and the Choir"	81.64
58	*The Bob Newhart Show*, "Over the River and Through the Woods"	81.62
59	*Leave It to Beaver*, "Beaver the Magician"	81.44
60	*Seinfeld*, "The Soup Nazi"	81.18
61	*Bewitched*, "Illegal Separation"	81.14
62	*Mork & Mindy*, "Mork's Mixed Emotions"	80.90
63	*Seinfeld*, "Bubble Boy"	80.85
64	*Friends*, "The One After the Super Bowl, Part II"	80.84
65	*Green Acres*, "Never Trust a Little Old Lady"	80.78

RANK	EPISODE	BTVS RATIO
66	*The Bob Newhart Show,* "Caged Fury"	80.54
67	*The Wonder Years,* "Christmas"	80.52
68	*The Flintstones,* "Hot Lips Hannigan"	80.51
69	*The Monkees,* "Too Many Girls"	80.50
70	*The Dick Van Dyke Show,* "It May Look Like a Walnut"	80.14
71	*F Troop,* "That's Show Biz"	79.82
72	*Gomer Pyle, U.S.M.C.,* "Flower Power"	79.71
73	*The Beverly Hillbillies,* "Brewster's Baby"	79.56
74	*I Love Lucy,* "Lucy's Italian Movie"	79.45
75	*The Flying Nun,* "The Return of Father Lundigan"	79.25
76	*The Little Rascals,* "Mama's Little Pirates"	79.19
77	*Get Smart,* "The Groovy Guru"	79.15
78	*Barney Miller,* "Hash"	79.12
79	*The Abbott and Costello Show,* "In Society"	79.07
80	*The Munsters,* "Zombo"	79.06
81	*The Partridge Family,* "Soul Club"	79.01
82	*My Favorite Martian,* "Miss Jekyll and Hide"	78.94
83	*Green Acres,* "How to Succeed in Television Without Really Trying"	78.92
84	*Green Acres,* "The Case of the Hooterville Refund Fraud"	78.91
85	*Get a Life,* "Spewey and Me"	78.87
86	*Happy Days,* "Richie Fights Back"	78.76
87	*The George Burns and Grove Allen Show,* "Christmas Show, 1952"	78.64
88	*I Dream of Jeannie,* "The Greatest Entertainer in the World"	78.61
89	*The Andy Griffith Show,* "Opie and the Bully"	78.51
90	*Mister Ed,* "Ed the Beachcomber"	78.42
91	*Rhoda,* "Rhoda's Wedding"	78.17

RANK	EPISODE	BTVS RATIO
92	*Police Squad*, "Rendezvous at Big Gulch"	77.93
93	*The Adventures of Ozzie and Harriet*, "Tiger Dance"	77.51
94	*Welcome Back, Kotter*, "What Goes Up"	77.45
95	*Family Affair*, "Think Deep"	77.41
96	*Chico and the Man*, "Chico and the Van"	77.26
97	*The Jeffersons*, "What Makes Sammy Run?"	77.24
98	*Three's Company*, "Up in the Air"	77.13
99	*The Andy Griffith Show*, "Class Reunion"	77.01
100	*Hogan's Heroes*, "Casanova Klink"	76.93

where's
hazel?

THE HIGHEST RATED EPISODES OF SERIES THAT DIDN'T MAKE THE TOP 100

You say your all-time favorite series is not represented anywhere on the BTVS Top 100? We're certainly sorry to hear that, but perhaps it will be some solace to know how close they came. Here are the top-rated episodes from a selection of popular series.

OVERALL RANK	SERIES	EPISODE
126	*My Three Sons*	"Coincidence" Though it settled in to more standard family comedy adventures in its later years, in its black-and-white years this long-running show often tried unusual stories and plot devices. "Coincidence" is a prime example; it could well have been an episode of *The Twilight Zone*. Steve is fed up with the chaos of his house, but then, shortly after an encounter with a leprechaun-like gentleman (played by Billy Barty), he arrives at a parallel female version of his own household, meeting a woman and her three daughters: "Mike," "Bobbie," and "Kip."
134	*Roseanne*	"Roseanne and Dan Get High." Or do they? A classic under-the-influence episode.

OVERALL RANK	SERIES	EPISODE
197	*Diff'rent Strokes*	"Arnold's Hero." Arnold makes believes that he doesn't have long to live, in order to get the Champ to pay him a visit. Guest star: Muhammad Ali.
236	*Alice*	"Oh, George Burns." It seems that Vera has seen the film *Oh, God* many times, so when the actor George Burns stops by the diner, she believes that God has paid them a visit.
289	*The Joey Bishop Show*	"Double Time." Guest stars: Sheldon Leonard, Johnny Silver. An "evil twin" classic, as a prison inmate who looks like Joey takes his place to escape.
305	*What's Happening!!*	"My Three Tons." Rerun is asked to join a dance group. Why? Because of his impressive girth. Guest star: Wolfman Jack.
388	*Good Times*	"The Nude." Struggling artist J. J. receives a commission to do a portrait, but it will be done in the buff, and in the apartment!
405	*Our Miss Brooks*	"Mr. Casey." Mr. Casey's last will and testament is to be read, and everyone is invited. However, only Connie is aware that the late, lamented Mr. Casey was a feline.
409	*Nanny and the Professor*	"The Humanization of Herbert T. Peabody." An aged puppeteer gets a little of Nanny's "magic." Guest stars: Paul Winchell, Vince Van Patten, Dabney Coleman.
440	*Father Knows Best*	"A Medal for Margaret." Mom becomes aware that everyone else in the family has trophies, plaques, or honors.
495	*Please Don't Eat the Daisies*	"Say U.N.C.L.E." The twins—Tracy and Trevor—decide that their pop must be a secret agent. Guest stars: Robert Vaughn and David McCallum.

OVERALL RANK	SERIES	EPISODE
501	*It's About Time*	"Twentieth Century, Here We Come." This is the historic episode that brought the series from the ancient past back into the present, as Shad, Gronk, and the kids stow away on the spaceship.
661	*The Mothers-in-Law*	"How Not to Manage a Rock Group." Guest Star: Joe Besser (the very last replacement Stooge). Also the real rock group the Seeds, who portray a rock group called the Warts. The Hubbards and Buells invest in the group.
675	*Hazel*	"Cheerin' Up Mr. B." Hazel takes it upon herself to keep her boss from getting downhearted while his wife is away.
690	*The Courtship of Eddie's Father*	"Prince Charming." What's wrong with being the lead in the school play? Having to kiss a girl on the lips, that's what!
691	*The Adventures of Superman*	"Flight to the North." Another show that was more often drama than comedy; but when it was funny, it was very, very funny. Chuck Connors guest stars as a country bumpkin who just happens to be named Superman—Sylvester J. Superman. That's just the start of one of the loopiest and most improbable episodes ever made. Suffice it to say that Sylvester and his mule, Lilly Bell, end up carrying a lemon meringue pie into the Arctic reaches of North Alaska, while being tracked by an ex-con named Louie, who is after his pie.
771	*The Lucy Show*	"Lucy and Wayne Newton." A very young and chubby Wayne Newton guest stars as a farm kid who could be a big star—and Lucy's big discovery—except that he can sing only when surrounded by the farm animals he's used to. Wayne sings "Bessie the Heifer"—a serenade to his favorite cow.

OVERALL RANK	SERIES	EPISODE
799	*Yogi Bear*	"Bear Faced Disguise" The Ranger goes undercover as a polar bear in an effort to catch Yogi breaking park rules.
812	*Dragnet*	"The LSD Story." Though seldom intentionally humorous, Dragnet is best enjoyed today with an ironic viewpoint. Even using the standard BTVS rating system, created to measure comedic shows only, many episodes of this series score high. None higher than this episode, which is more popularly known as "Blue Boy" after its antagonist. Blue Boy's lunatic ravings and Joe Friday's square moralizing have made this episode one of TV Land's all-time most requested.
818	*The Ann Sothern Show / Private Secretary*	"The Lucy Story." The episode in which Lucille Ball guest stars, checking in to the Bartley House.

afterword

Hope you enjoyed the book. If you have any corrections or suggestions, we'd love to hear them. The best place to go is TVLand.com, where we do our best to answer your questions and take your requests!

—Tom Hill

Index

Doohan, James, 78
Dopan, Ann, 209
Dorfman, Sid, 162
double takes, 3, 13, 16
Doughman, Jim, 215
Douglas, Donna, 186, 292
Douglas, Michael, 62
Dow, Tony, 209, 272
Downey, Morton, 124
Downey, Morton, Jr., 5, 124
Downs, Hugh, 268, 269, 270
Doyle, David, 51
Doyle, Peggy, 238
Doyle-Murray, Brian, 166, 168, 202, 204
Dozier, William, 265, 289
Dr. Kildare, 69, 306
Dr. Quinn, 56
Dragnet, 42, 50, 74, 81, 330; haiku about, 108
dramas: lessons learned from, 9; and Satisfaction
    Formula, 134
Dreben, Stan, 182
Dreyfuss, Richard, 229, 230–31
Driscoll, Mark, 280
Duck Factory, 38
Duclon, David Warren, 224
Duell, William, 154
Duffy, Julia, 313
Dukane, Sy, 246
Duke, Patty, 61, 98, 125, 240
Dullaghan, John, 215
Dulo, Jane, 244
DuMont Network, 153, 260
Dusty's Trail, 38
Dylan, Bob, 189, 190

E!, 103
E/R, 104, 124
East Side/West Side, 104
Eastwood, Clint, 58, 62, 159
Ebsen, Buddy, 97, 125, 186, 292
Ed Sullivan Show, The, 40, 84, 294
Edelman, Herb, 65
Edelman, Louis F., 299
Eden, Barbara, 65, 160
editing: and top episodes, 140
Edwards, Douglas, 247
Edwards, Rick, 143
Eiler, Virginia, 142
Elbling, Peter, 204, 205
Electric Company, The, 61, 102
Elias, Alix, 215
Elinson, Jack, 212

Ellen, 276, 280–83, 323
Elliott, Bob, 167
Elliott, Chris, 166, 167
Ellison, Bob, 274, 320
Emergency, 80, 103
Emmy Awards, 61, 142, 279, 292, 302, 304
Emmy, The (O'Neil), 31
Emotional Resonance: and Satisfaction Formula, 131;
    and top episodes, 172, 238
Engel, Georgia, 155, 257, 258, 320
English, Diane, 246
Entertainment Tonight, 95
episodes: amnesia, 21–26, 249; and episode number,
    139; series-ending, 10; ten best genres of, 10; that
    didn't make top 100, 327–30; top 100, 11–12,
    128–326
ER, 104, 124
Ernest Goes to Camp, 74
Erwin, Lee, 182
Estin, Ken, 285, 309
Estrada, Erik, 106
Everett, Todd, 240
*Experimental Television, Test Films, Pilots and Trial Series,
    1925 through 1995* (Terrace), 31
Eyes on the Prize, 34

F Troop, 6, 22, 38, 105, 180, 189–90, 242, 325
Fabares, Shelley, 242, 244
Face the Nation, 124
Fairchild, Morgan, 246
Fairman, Michael, 220
falling down, 2
Fame, 68
Family, 46
Family Affair, 135, 148–49, 317, 326; haiku about,
    107
Farr, Gordan, 197, 211
Farr, Jamie, 310
Farr, Lynne, 197, 211
Farrell, Charles, 238, 240
Farrell, Gwen, 311
Farrell, Mike, 310
Farrell, Wes, 172
Fast Times, 71
Fat Albert and the Cosby Kids, 251
Fatal Instinct, 63
Father Knows Best, 167, 328
faux pas, 15–16
Fawcett, Farrah, 65
Faye, Herbie, 262
Faylen, Frank, 251
Fedderson, Don, 148

Fein, Bernard, 141, 262
Fein, Irving, 283
Feldman, Edward H., 141
Feldon, Barbara, 179, 233, 235
Feliciano, Jose, 147
Fellipi, Vittoria, 184
Fenneman, George, 123
Ferber, Mel, 224
Fernwood 2-Nite, 134, 205, 292
Ferris Bueller, 70
Ferris Bueller's Day Off, 70
Feydeau, Georges, 145
Field, Sally, 60, 182, 229
Fields, Sidney, 176
Filmways Presentation, 44
Finn, Herbert, 259
Finney, Sara V., 146
First You Cry, 47
Fischer, Corey, 218
Fish, 46
fish out of water formula, 16
Fitts, Rick, 166
Flagmond, Joyce, 263
Flebotte, David, 280
Fleming, Thom, 143
Flender, Harold, 14
Flicker, Theodore J., 178
Flintstones, The, 13, 53, 153, 185, 193–95, 223, 318, 325
Flipper, 21, 22, 35, 75
Florek, Dave, 166
flush, toilet, 5
Flying Nun, The, 182–84, 219, 242, 325
Flynn, Gertrude, 143
Flynn, Joe, 287, 288
Fogel, Jerry, 244
Foley, Dave, 6, 78
Fonda, Henry, 66, 71
Ford, Faith, 246
Ford, Gerald, 2
Ford, Glenn, 68
Ford, Harrison, 72
Ford, Paul, 262, 276
Forever Fernwood, 292
Forrest Gump, 58, 62
Fosse, Bob, 236
Foster, Jodie, 62
Foster, Phil, 225
Foster, Warren, 194
Fowler, Keith, 248
Fox, Frank, 238
Fox, Michael J., 59, 77
Foxx, Redd, 84, 217, 218–19

Franciscus, James, 52
Frank, Ben, 172
Franklin, Bonnie, 99
Franklin, Jeff, 225
Frann, Mary, 313
Fraser, Brendan, 73
Frasier, 6
Frawley, James, 192
Frawley, William, 84, 184, 214, 270
Frazier, Ronald E., 285, 309
Freddy's Nightmares, 71
Free Country, 262
Free to Be . . . You and Me, 119
Freeman, Kathleen, 141–42, 236
Freeman, Mickey, 262, 276
Fresh Prince of Bel Air, 16
Freund, Karl, 184, 214, 270
Frey, Leonard, 257, 258
Fridays, 303
Friends, 63, 64, 121, 200–2, 223, 290, 324
Fritzell, Jim, 142, 266
Frosty the Snowman, 62
Fry, Taylor, 166
Fugitive, The, 72
Full House, The, 192
Fuller, Bill, 313
fundraising marathons, 80
Funt, Allen, 110
Fury, Edward, 224
Futurama, 223
F.Y.I. (CBS news show), 247
FYI, 53, 247

Gabor, Eva, 44, 121, 168, 169, 199
Gabor, Zsa Zsa, 270
Gail, Max, 178
Gallo, Lew, 291
Galton, Ray, 218
Gammill, Tom, 207
Ganz, Lowell, 164, 225, 294
Gardenia, Vincent, 260
Gardner, Gerald, 192, 315
Garland, Judy, 58
Garr, Teri, 244, 246
Garrett, Betty, 225
Garrett, Leif, 225
Garrett, Lila, 255
Garson, Henry, 148
Garver, Kathy, 148
Gautier, Dick, 233, 234
Gaveltons, The, 91–92
Gaynes, George, 240

Hughes, John, 74
Hughleys, The, 63
Hullett, Gilbert, 181
Hunt, Helen, 62
Hunter, Blake, 220
Hurdle, Jack, 259, 307
Hurwitz, Alvin, 214
Huston, Anjelica, 72
Hytner, Steve, 208

I, Claudius, 4, 34
I Dream of Jeannie, 27, 65, 96, 160–62, 223, 241, 325;
    anagram for, 27; haiku about, 109
I Love Lucy: anagram for, 28; bedrooms on, 153; comic
    formulae in, 12, 17; and just the wrong thing, 17;
    and literary works that led to sitcoms, 120; and
    most popular shows in twenty-sixth century, 96;
    popularity of, 37; production of, 227; as relic, 266;
    Ricardo, Lucy, anagram for, 28; stunts on, 80;
    syndication of, 240; top episodes of, 128, 131, 132,
    135, 140, 184–86, 214–15, 219, 270- 72, 323,
    324, 325
I, Spy, 306
I'm Dickens—He's Fenster, 105, 227
Icelandic joke, 14
Idelson, Bill, 187, 224
Idelson, Ellen, 280
Idle, Eric, 56
inane comments, 13, 17
Ingels, Marty, 105
innovators of TV Land, 113–18
Insana, Tino, 154
inventions: ten best, 20
Irving, Charles, 142
Isaacs, Brad, 313
Isaacs, David, 231
Isler, Seth, 200
It's About Time, 329
It's Gary Shandling's Show, 84
Ives, Burl, 1, 62, 65

Jack Benny Program, The, 266, 283–85, 323
Jack Paar Show, The, 269, 270
Jackass?, 274
Jackie Gleason Show, The, 192
Jackson, Michael, 40
Jacobi, Lou, 218
Jacobs, Lawrence Hilton, 150
Jacobs, Ronald, 244
Jacoby, Coleman, 263
Jacquet, Jeffrey, 204
Jamal-Warner, Malcolm, 249

James, Bill, 130
James, Jerry, 162
James, Ralph, 204
Janis, Conrad, 204
Janowitz, Walter, 178
Jarvis, Graham, 291
Jean, Al, 221
Jefferson, George, 99
Jefferson, Herbert, Jr., 172
Jeffersons, The, 146–47, 161, 318, 326
Jennings, Peter, 77
Jensen, Sanford, 246
Jericho Mile, The, 47
Jerk, The, 63
Jetsons, The, 84, 95, 217
Jiffy Pop, 42
Jimmy Dean Show, The, 50
Jimmy Stewart Show, The, 284
Joey Bishop Show, The, 328
Johnson, Arte, 51
Johnson, Bruce, 187, 204
Johnson, Jim, 251
Johnson, Ray J., 111
Johnson, Russell, 315
Jolson, Al, 254
Jones, Anissa, 148
Jones, Carolyn, 248
Jones, David, 192
Jones, Davy, 56
Jones, Gordon, 176
Jones, O-Lan, 202
Jones, Shirley, 60, 172
Josefsberg, Milt, 225
Josie and the Pussycats, 152
Jostyn, Jay, 168
Julia, Raul, 72
Julia, haiku about, 108
Julian, Arthur, 189, 228
Jump, Gordon, 219
jumping to conclusions, 17
Junge, Alexa, 200
Junger, Gil, 280
Junger, Paul, 172
Jurist, Ed, 182
Just the Ten of Us, 45–46, 205
just the wrong thing formula, 17
Justice for All, 304

Kageyama, Rodney, 313
Kahn, Bernie, 255
Kairys, Valeri, 289
Kaiser, Tim, 207

McMahon, Ed, anagram for, 28
McMurray, Richard, 228
McNear, Howard, 86
Macnee, Patrick, 56
MacNeille, Tress, 255
McQueen, Steve, 103
McRaven, Dale, 172, 204
McRobb, Will, 135
Macy, Bill, 228, 229
Madden, Dave, 172
Madsen, R. E. "Tex," 181, 182
Mahoney, Jock, 265
Make Room for Daddy, 192, 276, 283, 299–301, 322
Malcolm in the Middle, 46
Malden, Karl, 62
Malins, Gregory S., 200
Maltin, Leonard, 182
Mamann-Greenberg, Suzy, 207
Man from U.N.C.L.E., The, 106
Mancini, Henry, 313
Mandel, David, 207
Mandel, Howie, 78
Manilow, Barry, 201
Mann, Jerry, 194
Mansell, Carol, 202
Mantle, Mickey, 263, 298
Many Loves of Dobie Gillis, The. See Dobie Gillis
Manza, Ralph, 147, 265
March, Alex, 294
Marcus, Ann, 291
Marie, Rose, 190, 305, 318
Marin, Paul, 143
Marinaro, Ed, 225, 227
Mark VIII, 45
Markus, John, 249–50
Marlens, Neal, 195, 280
Marr, Edward, 209
Marshall, E. G., 52
Marshall, Garry, 164, 204, 206, 224, 225, 294
Marshall, Joan, 283
Marshall, Penny, 63, 147, 225, 227, 294, 295
Marshall, Tony, 164, 204, 225
Martell, Donna, 238
Martin, Al, 171
Martin, Dean, 179
Martin, Dick, 64
Martin, Jeff, 221
Martin, Steve, 37, 74, 205
Martindale, Wink, 82
Marx Brothers, 11, 151
Marx, Groucho, 58, 123
Marx, Marvin, 307

Mary Hartman, Mary Hartman, 134, 291–92, 323
Mary Kay and Johnny, 153
Mary Tyler Moore: and actors who are directors, 63; anagram for, 27; development of, 279–80; directors of, 292, 321; hair crisis in, 112; inane comments in, 13; knockoffs of, 124; and Oscar Award winners, 61; as relic, 266; stunts on, 81; title of, 280; top episodes of, 217, 219, 229, 257–59, 278–80, 320–21, 322, 323
Masterpiece Theatre, 56
Masters, Bill, 202, 301
Mathers, Jerry, 209, 272
Matheson, Tim, 64, 66
Mathews, Larry, 190, 305, 318
Matthau, Walter, 74, 295
Maude, 228–29, 313, 324; Findlay, Maude, anagram for, 28
Mauldin, Nat, 215
Maxwell, Frank, 253
Mayberry, Russ, 238
Mayberry 101 (Brower), 32–33
Mayo, Whitman, 218
Mazursky, Paul, 192
Me and the Chimp, 38
Meadows, Audrey, 259, 307, 308
Meet the Press, 124
Mehlman, Peter, 202, 207
Mehlman, Si, 301
Meins, Gus, 181
Mekka, Eddie, 225
Melgar, Gabriel, 148
Mellor, Christie, 313
Melman, Jeff, 215
Melocchi, Vince, 208
Meloni, Chris, 321
Melrose Place, 64, 222
Melvin, Allan, 262, 276, 296
Melvin, Bob, 160
Menteer, Gary, 225
Meredith, Burgess, 134
Merrill, Larry, 158
Meshad, Janet, 211
Metcalfe, Burt, 311
Meyer, George, 221, 255, 257
Meyerson, Peter, 150
Meyler, Fintan, 242
Michaels, Lorne, 79; anagram for, 28
Michaud, Mike, 208
Midler, Bette, 221, 222, 223
Milan, Frank, 263
Milkis, Edward K., 164, 225
Miller, George, 73